The Story of Ireland

*A history of
an ancient family
and their country*

William Magan

E L E M E N T

Shaftesbury, Dorset • Boston, Massachusetts • Melbourne, Victoria

© Element Books Limited 2000
Text © William Magan, 1983, 2000

First published as *Umma-More* in 1983 by
Element Books Limited

This revised edition published in the USA
in 2000 by Element Books, Inc.
160 North Washington Street
Boston, MA 02114

Published in the UK in 2000 by
ELEMENT BOOKS LIMITED
Shaftesbury, Dorset SP7 8BP

Published in Australia in 2000 by
Element Books and distributed
by Penguin Australia Limited
487 Maroondah Highway, Ringwood,
Victoria 3134

Cover design by Slatter-Anderson
Designed and typeset by The Bridgewater Book Company
Printed and bound in Great Britain by Creative Print and Design, Ebbw Vale, Wales

British Library Cataloguing in Publication
data available

Library of Congress Cataloging in Publication
data available

ISBN 1 86204 729 4

CONTENTS

Acknowledgments

Preface

LIST OF ILLUSTRATIONS

A C K N O W L E D G E M E N T S

I CANNOT FIND WORDS to express my gratitude to my wife, Maxine, not only for her patient acceptance of my many hours of solitary scribbling, but also for her meticulous study of, and helpful commentary on, the text: many a beautiful phrase and profound observation have – very properly, I fear – felt the sear of the pruning knife.

My grateful thanks are due to an old and distinguished friend, the late Colonel Rodney Dennys, C.V.O., O.B.E., F.S.A., Somerset Herald, who, together with members of the staff at the College of Arms, were unfailingly helpful.

And I owe gratitude to the Chief Herald of Ireland for much research in his department on my behalf.

I must also record my debt both to the Public Record Office of Ireland, and to the Public Record Office in London, for their unstinting helpfulness.

I am grateful to John Murray (Publishers) Ltd for permission to quote a verse from the *Collected Poems of Sir John Betjeman.*

My thanks are due, too, to Nancy Christopherson for editing the text.

I would also like to thank my son George for his very generous support and assistance, and Mr Mark Bence-Jones and Mr Henry McDowell for invaluable information.

I would also like to thank the West Malling Branch of the Kent County Library for their very willing, generous and painstaking assistance.

For the early twentieth century photographs, I am indebted to the collection of my great uncle, the late Colonel Middleton Biddulph.

Anyone who writes an historical work cannot but be conscious of the debt he owes to those who have gone before, albeit with different objectives, and who have covered the same periods in their writings. Because I had no thought of publishing this book when I wrote it – it was intended as a private work for my own family only – I did not keep a bibliographical list of the authorities and works that I read or consulted. Rather, therefore, than attempt a detailed acknowledgement from memory, I hope it will suffice for me to record that I am very sensible of the debt I owe to the work and works of others.

W.M.T.MAGAN

PREFACE

THIS BOOK IS THE STORY of Ireland from the earliest times to the present day. That great newspaper, *The Manchester Guardian*, said of the first edition that it is:

Unputdownable ... No more impacted history of Ireland has come our way since Samuel Lewis's great Topographical Dictionary of Ireland *in 1837; or, for that matter, Lecky.*

This story of Ireland is illustrated by the story of the author's ancient Celtic Irish family which became one of the great Irish landowning families having, in earlier times, had the chieftainly equivalent of that status. It is a cadet branch of one of the major ancient Celtic Irish chiefdoms. Its history, therefore, in common with other such Irish families, stretches back into the mists of Irish legend.

The former leading Irish families retained their pre-eminence for some two thousand years. Their history was shaped by, and reflects, the often dramatic story of Ireland itself, and is directly relevant to the Irish situation today. This book, therefore, is as much about Ireland as it is about the family. The two are interwoven, and I have tried to portray them faithfully, 'warts and all'.

The correct pronunciation of the family name Magan is not obvious from its spelling. It is not pronounced like Fagan, but like the word 'began'.

And, as there are many different sorts of Irishmen, I think readers may wish to know where I stand. With our birth there was pinned to each one of us Irish a badge of faith and a badge of loyalty, and it is there that almost all of us continue to stand.

I was brought up in the depths of rural Ireland, but educated in England. Whilst my parents were Protestant and ardently loyalist, I think it is important to note that so old an Irish family as ours had strong and close Catholic associations. This has helped me towards an understanding of the religious dimension in Irish affairs.

I have had a problem when referring to mainland Britain and its inhabitants. I have solved it by a quite indiscriminate ringing of the changes on 'England', 'Britain', 'Great Britain', 'the English', 'the British' and so on.

The Irish are teased for their obsession with genealogy and history. But genealogy attracts widespread interest also in Britain and America today. People yearn to know more of their ancestral past. Perhaps it is that to learn something of the supposedly more stable life of our forebears might point the way to more secure conditions for ourselves.

And Gladstone, addressing a great Celtic gathering a century ago, the Welsh Eisteddfod, said this:

> *Rely upon it, a man who does not honour his forefathers, will do little to credit his country.*

An ordinary mortal can perhaps hardly be expected to have so lofty an aim. But if I could think that I had thrown a little more light upon the perplexing Irish dilemma, I would be satisfied.

W.M.T.MAGAN

BOOK ONE

The Ancient Past
of the Family in
its Irish Historical
Setting up to the
End of the
Elizabethan Era

CHAPTER 1

The Origins of the Magan Family

IT IS AUTHENTICALLY recorded in the Magan pedigree compiled by Sir Bernard Burke, Ulster King of Arms, in 1868, that the Magan family of Emoe – anciently Umma-More – Ballymore, County Westmeath, descends from 'Mac-Dermot-Roe dynast of Moylurg'.

Moylurg is a place. It is in the west of Ireland, in the County Roscommon, in the Province of Connaught. It is the far side, the west side, the Atlantic side, of that great Irish divide, the Shannon River. Mac-Dermot-Roe was a man. A dynast was a chief or sub-chief. In this case he was a descendant, and sub-chief, of MacDermot, Prince of Moylurg, who, in turn, was a descendant and sub-chief of the royal house of Connaught which anciently ruled that wild land beyond the Shannon; also of this clan of chiefs and rulers were the MacDermots, Princes of Coolavin. As rulers they called themselves kings and princes – Kings of Connaught and Princes of Moylurg and Coolavin. But a more faithful image of them is as tribal chiefs. They did not live in palaces, but more frequently in their encampments among their cattle and herds. But, in a sense, they were regal for all that.

Edward Gibbon, in *The Decline and Fall of the Roman Empire*, wrote of the European nobility:

The proudest families are content to lose, in the darkness of the Middle Ages, the tree of their pedigree, which, however deep and lofty, must ultimately rise from a plebeian root; and their historians must descend ten centuries below the Christian era, before they can ascertain any lineal succession by the evidence of surnames, of arms, and of authentic records.

Gibbon was writing about the Roman Empire, of which Ireland was never a part. What he says may have been true of that Empire, and of realms such as Britain which had belonged to it. For instance the earliest extant British peerage, the Barony of Kinsale, dates from no earlier than 1223. It was awarded for services in Ireland.

But Gibbon's statement was not in that sense at all true of the noble Celtic houses of Ireland. The Irish chiefs were certainly not content to lose the thread of their pedigrees only as far back as the Middle Ages. They were confident of their ancestry back to pre-Christian times. And it would never have entered their heads to suppose that they might have risen from plebeian stock. The hierarchical principles on which their society was based ensured that their chieftainly ancestry stretched back thousands of years.

And so it was with the Magans, with the family of MacDermot-Roe, and with the Princes of Moylurg and the Kings of Connaught from whom they sprang. The least of their claims was their descent from very ancient noble stock. And their mythology even pointed to celestial – to mysterious and mystical – far off origins stemming from the gods themselves.

The ruling house from which these families sprang was thus vested in the chiefs of the clan which was destined, at a much later date, to become the O'Conor family, of which the O'Conor Don has for many centuries been, and is to this day, the head.

For some two thousand years, this clan conglomerate of families asserted its fluctuating authority over substantial areas of Ireland. But thousands of years before they, or any other Celtic chiefs, set foot on the island, there were other peoples there who had settled in Ireland long before; people who are no less important to this unfolding tale than are the Celtic chiefs themselves; people, too, the blood of whose own chieftainly families became mingled with that of the Celtic rulers; people from whose nobility, therefore, families like these are also descended.

The Pre-Celtic Irish – The Real Irish

FIFTEEN THOUSAND YEARS AGO the whole of Ireland lay under a mile of ice. The last ice age, which had then lasted for seventy-five thousand years, was nearing its end. The ice was slowly melting. Four thousand years later, eleven thousand years ago, about 9000 BC, Ireland was at last free of ice.

To the north of Ireland, and also in the south polar region, much of the earth's surface water was still held as ice. Sea levels throughout the world were thus much lower than they now are. For another two or three thousand years, therefore, until the ice had melted sufficiently to replenish the seas, Ireland was joined to Scotland, and England was joined to Europe, by land bridges.

At first, after the melting of the ice, Ireland was an open tundra. Animals such as the giant elk found their way there. Fauna and flora spread from Europe across the land bridges. Bogs and forests developed with the increasingly milder climate. Some animals, snakes, toads and moles, for instance, failed to make it to Ireland before the seas rose, as the great icecaps melted, and the land bridges disappeared under water.

As the ice withdrew, plants and animals multiplied and took its place, and men followed them into the new areas for a more abundant living; and they themselves multiplied also.

The first trace of humans in Ireland is about 7000 BC, some two thousand years after the ice had gone. Their origins are unknown. It is supposed that they came from Europe via Scotland, but that is not certain. If that was their route, they may have come across the land bridges if they were still passable, or by their excellent boats, the coracles which have survived as useful vessels up to our own time.

Some, no doubt, came from, or came through, those areas of Europe which had not been engulfed by the ice. It would seem likely that it was the people who had been living nearest to the ice in Central Europe who were best placed to exploit the growing opportunities, and to spread northwards and westwards as ever wider areas became inhabitable.

Some may have come from as far as Africa and the Mediterranean, working their way either through Europe, or up the European Atlantic coast, but probably over many centuries. They were not farmers. They were hunters and food-gatherers. In particular it must be supposed that they were fishermen, as they had their living along the estuaries, rivers and lakes. They were not literate. Their history went unrecorded. Their languages are unknown, though shreds of them must survive in place names and within the Irish Gaelic tongue.

During the three thousand years following their first arrival, those early peoples, joined no doubt during all that time by others from the mainland, grew in numbers to populate the whole of Ireland. The evidence suggests that thereafter there were long periods of prosperity which in turn points to there having been effective government, and therefore effective leadership.

Ireland has, thus, from the time of the earliest arrivals, nine thousand years ago, been continuously inhabited, and it is of particular interest that very modern scientific research suggests that it is from that early pre-Celtic stock that there derive the most widespread genetic strains today.

The early Irish were an amalgam of diverse peoples who had drifted into Ireland during seven thousand years, and who had developed close enough affinities for it to be reasonable to regard them not merely as broadly an entity, but indeed as the Ancient Irish race, which the Celts are not. It is those Ancient Irish, whose descendants are still there, who are the rightful inhabitants of Ireland. The Celts are late-comers.

To talk of those early Irish ancestors of ours as Palaeolithic and Neolithic people – to talk of them as Stone-Age and Bronze-Age people – and to do so condescendingly, is to mislead ourselves with such stereotypes.

Our pre-Celtic Irish ancestors were not hirsute, ape-like, men, wielding large clubs and dragging their women around by the hair. They were clever people who survived by the use of their brains. They were not an isolated community. They were a remote fringe of the Indo-European comity of peoples. From an early date they were producing, on something like a factory scale, very fine, and much sought-after, stone axes, which they traded internationally.

Fresh skills no doubt kept coming in from the continent. By 4000 BC the early Irish were no longer confined to food-gathering along the waters' edges. They had conquered the uplands, and were farming all over Ireland. They had domestic animals. They were growing corn, a skill unlikely to have been of indigenous discovery. And they may be supposed to have been living in houses. The remains have been found of a rectangular timber house dated to nearly 4000 BC.

At that time they had no metal, but they were ingenious enough to fell enormous areas of forest with stone axes. They tilled the soil with wooden, stone and bone tools. They grew crops successfully. They raised and moved stones of over 50 tons in weight for their great stone edifices. They drove piles into lakes and made artificial islands. One of their achievements is a burial mound in Co. Meath. It is an enormous pile of thousands of tons of gravel, stone and earth. It is an acre in extent, and is forty-five feet high. A passage runs into the centre of it, with a cruciform burial chamber at its end. Its approximate dating is 2500–2000 BC. The Egyptians had long since built their great pyramids. Is there a connection? Why not?

To do all that they did implies excellent organisers and administrators, and some ingenious engineers, and an advanced pattern of decision making, work sharing, and organization of community life. That need not be surprising. Men had as much brains then as now. At comparable dates, much greater things were being achieved in the Middle East, nearer the heart of the Indo-European complex. Nor need we be surprised at the degree of inter-communication which we may suppose to have existed even with distant places. Before the Christian era, Africa had been circumnavigated by ships sailing from the Middle East. Before the Christian era, too, the Persians administered an empire that straddled thousands of miles of Africa and Asia, an impossible feat without very good communications and highly efficient administrative machinery. Communities like the early Irish, whom we may think of as primitive, must in fact have had complex and advanced social systems.

About 2000 BC, metallurgy began in Ireland, and the Irish became enormously successful makers of bronze, with an international trade. This is a seemingly curious development because tin, an ingredient of bronze, is not found in Ireland, and had to be imported, which is eloquent of the extent to which international trading was a part of the established way of life in Ireland even a thousand years before the Celts reached Western Europe. Nor were the foundries within Ireland particularly close to the copper mines. There must have been good internal communications. Pottery, of course, was made. There was native gold in Ireland, and the golden objects which have been found reveal the ancient pre-Celtic Irish as fine craftsmen as many centuries BC as they were to prove themselves excellent silversmiths in the eighteenth century AD. The work in gold has an affinity to similar early objects found in the eastern Mediterranean, which suggests a common influence, as perhaps also does the fact that the fishermen of the Greek Islands, like those of the Irish Aran Islands, are non-swimmers and wear woollen jerseys differentially patterned to show their port of origin in case of drowning. Wrought gold from Ireland at that time has been found in many parts of Europe, again underlining the extent to which trade was international in the second millennium BC.

A full, busy and thriving human community life was thus going on in Ireland for thousands of years before ever our Celtic ancestors landed on the island, and the descendants of those early people are still there. It was during their golden age that the Celts began to arrive. They brought new skills and a new metal, iron, which indeed was the source of the better weapons with which they made themselves masters of Ireland.

CHAPTER 3

The Celts

WHO WERE THE CELTS? Whence came they? And why did they come to Ireland? The answers to those questions are uncertain. Scholars disagree about dates and details. The Celts left no early written accounts of themselves. Classical writers of Greece and Rome give some record of them. Other information is largely from archeological discovery.

But some broadly acceptable statements can be made. The Celts almost certainly did not call themselves Celts. Nor is it likely that they were an ethnically homogeneous race. They were a group of tribes with a more or less common language, and a more or less common culture and social system. They were part of the westward movement of Aryan peoples which had begun possibly in Central Asia, perhaps some three thousand years BC. One of the tribes was known to the ancient Greeks as the Keltoi (Latin, Celtae).

As long as four thousand years ago, about 2000 BC, the Celtic tribes were identifiable as a broad cultural entity occupying Central Europe, immediately north of the Alps, from Austria to France. There were at that time three ethnographic layers in Europe. North of the Celtic area were the Teuton tribes. To the south of the Alps were the Latin peoples.

Perhaps about 1000 BC, or even earlier, and for reasons that are not known, but very likely for gain, there were expansionist Celtic movements. They were a warrior people. Some forced their way south-eastwards into Asia Minor. Some raided south of the Alps into Greece and Italy. Others moved further into Western Europe; some into Spain.

By perhaps 500 BC the Celts dominated parts of the Atlantic seaboard of Europe, whence some of them continued their westward movement across the seas to Britain and Ireland.

Although the legends point to a sequence of Celtic invasions of Ireland over a period of several centuries, it would almost certainly be wrong to suppose that Celtic incursions took the form of sudden onslaughts by great waves of invaders. The Celts are unlikely to have thought in such terms of conquest, and could hardly have had the necessary maritime and other resources. It is much more likely that during five centuries or so BC, relatively small parties of adventurous Celts made their way to Ireland, and there, probably by very slow degrees, and by dint of their strength of character and superior martial qualities, abilities and weapons, came to dominate the ancient Irish people.

There is probably a consensus of opinion that the warrior Celts set out initially to conquer Ireland. That may be so, but it seems no less likely that it was the existence of ancient trade links that first brought the Celts into contact with Ireland, and which may have resulted in Celtic mercantile settlements there which, in due course, led to a form of colonial domination of the Irish. Clausewitz might well have added to his famous statement that war is 'a continuation of political transactions', that it can also be a continuation of commercial transactions.

The pattern of those early events in Ireland may have resembled that of two thousand years later, when Western Europeans crossed more distant seas and colonized far parts of the world. That is to say, Celtic merchant adventurers may have led the way, and perhaps the footholds they established became the bridge-heads for relatively small numbers of warriors, superior in their training and weapons to the native people.

The parallel may go even further, because the legends hint at colonial rivalry in Ireland between different groups of Celts, just such as took place in the nine-teenth century between the different Western European colonial powers.

There may also be an additional resemblance to later events. Just as in the eighteenth century, a small number of English, led by hardly more than a thousand landowning settler families, totally dominated Ireland, so it seems possible that numerically the early Celtic element in Ireland was relatively small, perhaps a comparable number of dominant Celtic colonial masters who became the rulers of Ireland some two thousand years ago or more. That would not have been the whole Celtic population. It was a graded society. In addition to the overlords, there were those of lesser rank, dwindling to those who, like disbanded English soldiers at a much later date, melted into the ranks of the Ancient Irish peasantry.

And in one more respect the situation was similar. The Picts continued for centuries to resist integration into the Celtic nation. Distinctions between Picts and Celts lasted well into the Middle Ages.

Clio, the Muse of history, must smile wryly to see in the Irish Celtic, or Gaelic, revivalist movement an attempt to resuscitate the trappings of what to the real ancient Irish, the pre-Celtic Irish, must have been a form of alien colonial domination. Moreover, the truth probably is that there is very little left to revive or resuscitate, since the bulk of what remained of the true Celtic colonists was driven out of Ireland in the seventeenth century AD.

Legend and tradition have it that the latest, and ultimately dominant, Celtic incursions came from Spain. The earliest date suggested for their arrival in Ireland is about 300 BC, but some authorities prefer a later date. Those events are linked with the name Mil, or Milesius, a legendary Celtic warrior king from whom the chiefs who were the ancestors of the O'Conor clan, and therefore the ancestors of the Magan family, traditionally descend.

There are different versions of the Milesian story which vary in detail. Not all agree that Milesius himself came to Ireland. The O'Conor family legend has it that he had three sons, from one of whom, Heremon, descended the celebrated second century AD O'Conor ancestor, Con of the Hundred Battles. The proclivities of latter-day Irish caused one wit to wonder whether the sobriquet 'Con of the Hundred Battles' might not have been a mistake for Con of the Hundred Bottles.

Strict historical scholarship prefers at present to regard Milesius as a legendary figure rather than an historical person. That is a piece of scrupulousness with which we need not quarrel. But how much does it matter? To query the existence of Milesius, is perhaps comparable to querying the authorship of Shakespeare. Whether or not Shakespeare wrote it, it was written. Someone did it. Likewise, what is claimed for Milesius was done, more or less, by someone. Peoples with a Celtic language and Celtic culture did come from the continent of Europe, and did become dominant in Ireland in the centuries shortly BC, or at the latest about the beginning of the Christian era, and they succeeded in dominating both the Picts and the earlier Celtic settlers. They had some chieftainly leadership. In blood relationship from that leadership descended the subsequent Celtic ruling houses of Ireland. There can therefore hardly be much question that the ancient princely families of Ireland are the lineal descendants of the Celtic chief or chiefs who achieved domination in Ireland two or three centuries BC or a little later, whether or not one of them, perhaps the principal among them, had the name Milesius, or Mil of Spain.

An outline of the origin of our Celtic ancestors, therefore, could be this, but granted that the dates are uncertain. The Celts began drifting into Ireland perhaps as early as 500 BC. A couple of centuries or more later, a powerful Celtic dynasty was established whose lineal descendants are the O'Conor clan. That clan's base was Connaught. The names Conor and Connaught have the same derivation. Thereafter, for nearly two thousand years, the chiefs of that clan were Kings of Connaught, and for many centuries they were Kings of Ireland as well.

To get the feel of those Connaught ancestors of the family; to understand their heart and soul, their characteristics, and their motivations, it is necessary to have it firmly in our consciousness that their homeland was Connaught. And we need to be able to see in our mind's eye what Connaught is, what it is like, and why, being what it is, it is of such importance to an understanding of the family.

It seems reasonable to infer that in the days of Heremon, son of Milesius, Connaught was his own principality, and remained the land of his successors. In his time, two thousand years ago, the Atlantic cliffs of Connaught were the end of the known world. He who had reached that far stood on the brink of the unknown. The fearful, thundering ocean stretched out darkly before him to the edge of the world where the sun sank into the abyss. Beyond that was a spectral world peopled by mysterious beings and the souls of the dead. Some who lived along the coast were seafaring folk from amongst whom, even in very early times, no doubt a very few ventured far into the ocean either by chance or by design. But for the people in general the cliffs of Connaught were the end of the world.

The western half of Connaught, bordering upon the ocean is a wildly beautiful, but unproductive, land of mountains, bogs, lakes and rivers, often so shrouded in low curtains of cloud as to add to its desolation a special air of mystery. Even the rolling stony grasslands of the east of the province, bordering on the Shannon river, are much less hospitable than the lush pastures of Ireland's central plain. The Shannon river, with its chain of great lakes, is Connaught's eastern frontier, and effectively cuts it off from the rest of Ireland. It is a large river which in ancient times was most conveniently fordable at Athlone, and even then not passable when in flood, which could happen at any time of the year.

Thus isolated, inhospitable and even mysterious, Connaught moulded its people in its own rugged image. As those whose province and homeland Connaught was could go no further, it was not theirs to flee from danger. With their backs to the west; with the ocean behind them, they must forever face vigilantly eastward. At worst, the men of Connaught must stand and defend those wild lands against invasion. It is perhaps, therefore, not without interest that the Irish word for 'behind' means 'west', and the word for 'in front' means 'east'.

But because the lands of Connaught were comparatively infertile, and were in the most remote part of Ireland, they were not a great temptation to others. And because of the wild nature of the country, attacks upon it were hazardous, and therefore less likely to be undertaken. Contrariwise, those who lived in the harsh conditions of Connaught developed a corresponding hardihood, and were themselves constantly tempted to raid the softer and more luscious lands eastwards of the Shannon.

The early and legendary history of the ancestors of the O'Conors is entirely consistent with those conditions, which inspires confidence in the substance of the legends. Established at an early date as a ruling house in Connaught, they remained more or less inviolate for centuries in their wild country behind the barrier of the Shannon, little threatened by serious incursions or invasions, defying anyone who tried to subjugate them, and at times imposing their own will more widely over other principalities east of the Shannon.

Nearly two thousand years later, the English Lord Deputy and Chancellor of Ireland, Sir Oliver St John, in a report on Connaught, in the year 1614, to his sovereign in London, James I, wrote of that wild unchanging Atlantic hinterland:

Connaught, by ancient division amongst the Irish, was accounted the fifth part of the Island of Ireland, and was then, and still is, called Connaught, and continued the name and style of a kingdom in the posterity of Con of the Hundred Battles, one of three races descended from Mile-Spanaghe, or Mil of Spain, whom all the chronicles of Ireland agree to be the absolute conqueror of the whole island.

The ancient borders of Connaught were, towards the east and south, the river of Shannon; towards the west, the ocean. Of this Connaught, a portion possessed by the O'Briens was held within the government of Connaught until the beginning of your Majesty's reign. The residue of Connaught continued in the possession of the forenamed posterity of Con of the Hundred Battles, the ancestor of O'Conor Don.

At the first conquest, during the reigns of King Henry II and King John, the English had but little footing in Connaught, leaving no other remarkable monument of their conquest but the castles of Athlone at the east border of the province. Afterwards in the reign of Henry III the residue of Connaught that preserved themselves from the English continued in the hands of the ancient Irish lords, the chief of whom were the race of the O'Conors.

Until the beginning of the reign of Queen Elizabeth, the ordinary justice of the kingdom had little passage in Connaught. There was one sheriff whom the people little regarded.

For two thousand years, then, up to the time when Sir Oliver wrote his dispatch, the hardy Celtic chiefs of the O'Conor clan had, with fierce independence, continued to live out their almost changeless Connaught lives. Even Tudor sheriffs were given short shrift by them.

There were exceptional occasions when Connaught was temporarily and partly overrun, for instance successively by the Norman de Burghs, and the Geraldines, during the century following Strongbow's invasion, but it nevertheless remained the O'Conor homeland.

Those are the Celtic origins of the family; of the flesh as it is today, and of the blood that flows in its veins. But that is not all that has to be said about the early people from whom it springs. There can be no reasonable doubt that the early Celts who came to Ireland made marriage unions with the native peoples already settled there. Merchant adventurers and marauding warriors do not risk hampering their freedom of action and movement by carting a load of women about with them. Biology, and often politics, dictate that they make local matches. 'Conquering Kings' do not limit themselves to taking titles 'from the foes they captive make'. They commonly take the princesses of the ruling houses in marriage also, and in part to heal the breach between themselves and the conquered; and in Ireland no doubt to inherit the earth because there is reason to suppose that in the early Irish social order it was the females, the princesses, not the sons, who were the inheritors of their fathers' kingdoms. The Celtic conquerors must indeed have assimilated in at least some degree with the natives, or they could not have endured for two thousand years. Conquerors who segregate themselves are rejected before very long.

It must therefore be beyond serious doubt that those of us who descend from Irish Celtic conquering chieftains had also for our grandmothers of long ago the daughters of the early Irish, pre-Celtic Irish chieftains.

Just because Ireland was the outer limit of the Indo-European world; just because those very early, long pre-Celtic inhabitants who got that far could go no further; so there was nothing left to them but to strike their roots on those gaunt, gull-crowded Atlantic cliffs, and hold on there for evermore. And they are there still. Thus we have the very interesting consequence that old Irish families who can trace their ancestry back to the Celts, or to Celtic times, can also, without any great stretch of imagination, follow their origins back into the deep and very ancient roots of the Pictish layer below, and down to the very beginnings of human life in Ireland – and there are many such families in Ireland in all strata of society. And this is not just a freakish piece of anthropography. Just because it applies to, and is true for, so large a part of the people of Ireland, it is an important ethnic and cultural factor which is affecting Ireland to this day. Indeed, if we do not hoist in its significance, we cannot understand the Irish dilemma of our own times.

Gauguin, seeking to understand an ancient people – the South Sea Islanders – said with the deeply penetrating inner vision of an artist: 'In order to achieve something new, it is imperative to go back in time'.

Perhaps Ireland can achieve something new by going back in time and recognizing that the real Irish are the pre-Celtic Irish, and that their blood still runs strongly there today, dammed up as it has been for millennia by the Atlantic cliffs to the west, and by dominant Celtic and later overlords who came in from the east; and also by recognizing that the Picts were not just 'neolithic' and 'palaeolithic' primitives, but people who probably had a higher and more refined culture than had the nomadic Celts.

CHAPTER 4

The Character of the
Early O'Conor Kings

IF WE ARE PREPARED to take a chance with history,
we can invest with a little flesh and blood our very early O'Conor royal ancestors
– those who were living in the first century AD and the next two or three centuries.

Around the turn of the nineteenth/twentieth centuries, a work of scholarly
research into the origin of the O'Conor family was undertaken. Due reservations
were expressed about the Milesian legend and the very early history of the family's
Celtic origins. Nevertheless the scholars concerned were agreed that the pedigree
of the O'Conor family could be clearly traced to a first century AD monarch of
Connaught, Feredach the Just, who was given a date of about 75 AD and who was
claimed to descend from Heremon, son of Milesius. From Feredach onwards the
pedigree is continuous, although it was not till nearly a thousand years later,
when surnames began to be used, that the family assumed the name O'Conor.

'No family in Ireland,' says the preamble, quoting another authority, 'claims
greater antiquity, and no family in Europe, royal or noble, can trace its descent
through so many generations of legitimate ancestors.'

But scholarship today is sceptical about such early records because the Celts
are supposed at that time to have been illiterate, and not to have committed their
histories to writing, but to have passed them from one generation to another
orally. And furthermore, a few centuries later, when Christianity reached Ireland,
and the Celts became literate, they are known to have fudged the pedigrees of
their chiefs.

Their supposed illiteracy is believed to have been deliberate and due to their
belief that literacy inhibits memory. But there is surely reason to doubt that they
were illiterate. Their learned men were very learned. They performed prodigious
feats of memory. They memorized, and passed on accurately from generation to
generation, a comprehensive body of law and tradition, in addition to the histories
and mythology of the tribes, the genealogy of the chieftainly families, and a wealth
of literature, stories, songs and poems. Those men were not isolated from the
rest of the world. Surely they had enough scholarly inquisitiveness to learn to
read and write. Next to the chiefs, they were the most important people in the Celtic

hierarchy, and the most likely explanation of their reputation for illiterate scholarship is that knowledge bolstered their power, and they therefore discouraged literacy in others who would otherwise come to share their learning and their secrets.

It is therefore to be assumed that the Druidical caste did not commit their learning to writing, but that seems a weak case for supposing the tribal histories, and chieftainly genealogies, which they passed on orally, to be inaccurate. Any English schoolchild with a GCSE History pass can give a pretty good potted history of England during the past five hundred years, and rattle off the kings and queens of England from William the Conqueror onwards – nearly a thousand years – and without the assistance of the rhythmic and rhyming forms used by the ancient Celts to help them memorize all that they had to learn. Today, other people practise great feats of memory. In the Islamic world, for instance, there is many a *Hafiz* – a person who has committed the whole of the Koran to memory.

There is, then, surely, no difficulty in supposing that the learned men of early Celtic times, with their deliberately cultivated power of memory, and their explicit responsibility to preserve the genealogy of the chiefs, and the history of the tribes, may have had memories stretching back a thousand years, even though many of the stories had conventional embellishments to make them more interesting – embellishments that were well understood and discounted as necessary. The Biblical account of Jonah's involvement in the affairs of the city of Nineveh does not have to be doubted because we have reservations about the vivid and dramatic story of his encounter with the whale.

The fudging of the pedigrees may seem a more substantial reason for doubting the accuracy of early Irish chieftainly genealogy. The pedigrees of the chiefs were very important. The Celtic system of rulership was aristocratic. Certain families were hereditary ruling families. Eldest sons had no special rights of succession. But kings or chiefs could be elected only from within those families. No-one was admitted a member of that aristocracy, or was eligible for election to leadership, unless he could prove descent from a chief for at least four male generations back to his great-grandfather. Genealogy was, therefore, of the highest importance for purposes of continuity of government.

But, in early Christian times, the learned custodians of this genealogical knowledge cheated. The 'begats' of the Pentateuch, which are the dullest part of the Bible to most of us, were a veritable goldmine to the Druid class, and they yielded to the temptation to mine it, and to embellish the pedigrees, and the prestige, of the chiefs, by tracing their descent back to Adam and other Biblical figures, thus bringing the ancient Irish genealogies into disrepute. But it cannot be too difficult to filter out that sort of rather obvious adulteration, which need not therefore cause the wholesale condemnation of early Irish genealogy.

I therefore feel little reservation about using the early existing record of the O'Conor kings. It appears factual, and not legendary or mystical, like the Arthurian stories. It was accepted by scholars of a previous generation. It defies the imagination to suppose that anyone invented it. And, as it is a part of the O'Conor annals, I would have needed very strong grounds for ignoring it. Moreover, if we may use our intuitive faculties in making historical judgements, it can be said that it smacks of being in all probability well founded.

I have deliberately chosen the very earliest period of which we have something that looks like detailed factual history – the first few centuries AD, the period of illiteracy. It was a time when our O'Conor ancestors reached, and for several centuries held, a pinnacle of power and authority over large parts of Ireland such as they were not again destined to hold for nearly another thousand years.

The first recorded O'Conor king was, then, the first century AD monarch Federach. He was not only ruler of Connaught, but also King of all Ireland. For the next three hundred years his descendants succeeded him, sometimes as both Kings of Connaught and Kings of Ireland, ruling from Tara in Co. Meath. The Kings of Ireland never had absolute authority over the whole country. They were frequently challenged by the provincial monarchs. After the end of the fourth century AD any effective nationwide office of King of Ireland lapsed, and Ireland dissolved into a number of petty, and often warring, states under their own self-styled kings and princes. Because of the constant challenge to the authority of the rulers by rival chiefs, an endemic state of insecurity existed, and it is that which provided the clue to the kind of people who filled the chieftainly offices.

The period I have chosen covers 363 years, during which thirty Connaught monarchs reigned. The average length of each reign was twelve years. If we compare that with recent English history, we find that during a similar length of time, from Elizabeth I to George VI, there were sixteen reigns averaging twenty-four years. Life expectation for early Irish monarchs was, therefore, short by comparison. Their fate was this:

13 killed in battle.
2 assassinated.
1 deposed.
1 fled the country.
1 abdicated – and subsequently accidentally choked by a fishbone.
6 cause of death unknown.
5 died in their beds of natural causes.
1 struck by lightning – in the Alps.

The number killed in battle indicates the extent to which the Irish principalities fought each other. But more interesting is the fact that it puts it beyond doubt that the Kings themselves were brave men. They did not leave it to others to fight their battles. They personally led their followers and were not only ready to, but did indeed, die on the field. This was the essence of ancient Celtic tradition.

The Celts were first and foremost warriors. The kings were the leading warriors.

We may deplore the amount of internecine fighting between the tribes, but it did ensure that neither the people nor, in particular, their chiefs, became effete. It was an Irishman, Edmund Burke, who, many centuries later, was to say: 'He that wrestles with us strengthens our will, and sharpens our wits – our antagonist is our helper.'

That the warrior status of the Celtic Irish kings was of the utmost importance is exceptionally well illustrated by the fate of the one who abdicated and was choked by a fishbone. He was Cormac, son of Art. He reigned for about 40 years, AD 227–267. It was a fundamental rule of succession that princes could not be elected to, or succeed to, the throne unless physically perfect. After the death of his father, there was the not unusual rivalry for the succession. A rival succeeded in setting fire to Cormac's hair and beard, thus rendering him less than physically perfect and depriving him temporarily of his chance of the throne. Eventually he succeeded. He has come down to history as a magnificent man, a great ruler, a paragon among Irish kings. However, late in life he lost an eye, probably in battle, and even this much revered monarch was forced, on account of that defect, to abdicate.

Of the two assassinations, one was carried out by the monarch's deranged sister trying to secure the succession to the throne for her own son. That there should have been only one assassination, apart from that mad act, in a period of nearly four centuries, suggests a society in which close associates, vassal nobles, trusted comrades and personal retainers had a very high degree of loyalty to their chiefs. Indeed, this does no more than confirm the legendary loyalty of the people to their royal houses. It was traditional to protect, and to die for, their kings. The kings were the rallying point, the centre and the symbol of tribal unity, integrity and loyalty. To defend the royal house was to defend the tribe. A monarchical system had then, and has still, many merits. An elected president lacks the touch of magic.

But the fact that the Celtic system did not include primogeniture as the principal rule in the appointment of successors did nevertheless lead to much rivalry between claimants to chiefdoms particularly at the time of succession to a dead or deposed ruler. That five only, out of thirty, and possibly one or two more, whose cause of death is unknown, died in their beds, suggests that Irish kings had little more than a twenty per cent chance of surviving on the throne to the end of their natural lives.

The fact that nearly half the monarchs died in battle, does not imply that there was a fifty per cent likelihood that all males would meet violent deaths. The caste structure of the tribes was such that only the warrior caste fought in battle.

We are left then with an impression of the Connaught chiefs as brave men who were surrounded by reliable champions, and whose authority was challenged in major conflict by some other tribe, or rival claimant to their chiefdom, at least every dozen years or so; to say nothing of minor raids and skirmishes. If princes survived all the hazards of infancy, childhood, disease, famine and accident, and reached adult life, there was an eighty per cent chance that they would meet with misfortune due either to war or feud, rather than live out their lives secure on their thrones, or more realistically in their encampments, until the peaceful hand of natural death came upon them in their own beds.

The O'Conor clan ceased to be Kings of Ireland about the end of the fourth century AD and did not hold the office again until the twelfth and thirteenth centuries.

At the time of the rule of those thirty early monarchs, Christianity had not yet reached Ireland. But in the context of kingship it is necessary to say something of the beliefs that were current at that time, and which were not only relevant to the status of the monarchs, but also – looking to later times – very relevant to the place of the Magan family in Irish society.

Just as I have avoided stone-age and bronze-age stereotype images, so do I prefer to avoid reference to other religions as 'pagan', and other beliefs as 'superstition'. I accept that those words have conventional uses, and I shall not be too pedantic in eschewing them.

The mysteries in early Irish beliefs are in essence those which run generally through the religions and mythology of the Indo-European peoples, being akin to some that are even as distant as Hindu mythology, and they include the mysterious linking of the spiritual with the temporal world through exceptional births. And it was in those mythological, supernatural occurrences that the Irish kings had their origins, and the O'Conor clan was no exception.

The stories told over and over again round the fire – which itself had mystical associations – and some of which in effect contained the essence of the religious beliefs of the Irish tribes, and which were given the credence due to the tenets of a faith, involved mystical and supernatural origins for the families of the warrior chiefs, and invested them with an element of near divinity. Cormac, for instance, that magnificent O'Conor warrior king who had his beard singed, and later lost his eye in battle, had, according to the legends, a mysterious birth and a strange infancy suckled by a wolf and brought up with her cubs. Many other Irish mythological stories are no less familiar, in some other context, than is that one.

Even though in later centuries, when those old beliefs had been ousted by, or more often absorbed into, Irish Christianity, it is beyond possibility of reasonable doubt that ancient custom, even if its origins were more or less forgotten, nevertheless still continued in some degree to influence the attitudes of the Irish people to their gentry, and indeed the attitudes of the Irish gentry themselves towards everybody else. As late as the mid-nineteenth century, very ancient fairy-tales which had been part of the literary curriculum of the 'hedge-schools', which were themselves only then being superseded by the national schools – tales which have the same devices as, and similar plots to, ancient stories of the Orient and the Mediterranean – were still current in Irish folk-literature.

Thus, looking forward in time from those ancient days, to the life of the Magans and Irish landowners, we can understand that in the old Irish gentry we are not just seeing in the modern sense fortunate, well-heeled families of substance and property. In his own place and his own time a Magan, a MacDermot, or an O'Conor, was acknowledged to be a man in whose veins ran not only ancient royal blood, but blood mysteriously mingled in the long-ago mythological past with mystical elements. The chiefs were not just men. They were something more. There was a touch of divinity distinguishing them from ordinary mortals, and by which they, too, felt themselves to be set above and apart from the commonalty.

In their daily lives, the leadership role, and the warrior status, of the chiefs, was combined with that of large-scale graziers. Their lives were pastoral. They owned, and lived among, their large herds of small black Irish cattle, their flocks of long-haired sheep, and herds of horses.

But, although their life was rustic, they were not an uncultivated society. The constant need to move their herds from one grazing ground to another necessitated a semi-nomadic life which precluded the ancient Celtic Irish from leaving us a heritage of great buildings or works of visual art to compare with Greece or Rome. But they had an art form, then as now – eloquence. There surely can hardly have been another early civilization with so rich and strong an oral tradition. Poetry, story-telling, its own history, songs and dancing were its artistic heritage.

National characteristics – those things that stir the very soul of a people – are deep, durable and persistent. It is no matter, therefore, for wonder that the Irish authorities of today, having a high and instinctive regard to learning and eloquent narration, have provided a true haven for literary and artistic people who are welcome to live and work in Ireland, and there enjoy the fruits of their labour, gifts and skills, free from the inordinate rapacities of the tax-man elsewhere.

That pastoral life changed hardly at all in its essential character in centuries. To round off this impression, therefore, of early Celtic Irish chieftainly life, I have chosen an account recorded nearly a thousand years later of a particular occasion at the O'Conor court. It is contained in a contemporary thirteenth century document written by the King of Connaught's own historiographer. What he described was the induction into his reign of an O'Conor king. By the thirteenth century, the Druidical priests had given way to Christian bishops. As ordained by St Patrick, twelve bishops were present. Also by ancient ordinance there were present the twelve dynasts, or sub-chiefs, among whom was MacDermot, Prince of Moylurg, the king's marshal.

The number twelve has magical associations throughout Indo-European culture. From the annual twelve cycles of the moon derives the calendar of twelve months; then twelve signs of the Zodiac, twelve apostles, twelve pence in a shilling, twelve inches in a foot, and so on.

Each of the twelve sub-chiefs had a ceremonial duty associated with a useful office. One saw to the king's clothing and arms, and was master of his horse, and had the privilege of placing the royal rod of office in the king's hands. Three other sub-chiefs shared the duty of safeguarding the king's spoils 'whenever he camps to rest'. Another was appointed to guard his hostages. One was his chief treasurer and keeper 'of his precious stones'.

There was a chief of his household, a chief butler, a chief doorkeeper, and a physician – all of them dynasts. And, his realm being vulnerable not only from land attack, but also from the sea, two of the chiefs, O'Flaherty and O'Mallery, were appointed to command his fleet.

It is a very small vignette, but it illustrates in an intimate way how the separate sub-chiefs, each a lord in his own domain, were nevertheless closely and personally bound to each other in shared duties to the monarch. It was indeed a typical monarchic situation: a king surrounded by his nobles, and spiritually attended by his high priests.

The King had obligations to his nobles, and they to him. Some had the right to the perquisites of their offices. Others he rewarded in kind. For instance, 'twelve score milch cows, twelve score sheep, and twelve score cows' (presumably heifers) were to go annually each to O'Flannagan and others. For everyone, wealth was computed principally in cattle, sheep and horses. The tributary chiefs were bound to attend royal assemblies. 'There was not a king, or royal heir, or chieftain, or a hundred-cattle farmer, who was not specially bound to attend with his forces at the hostings – the mobilizations – of O'Conor. The free states of Connaught, Ui-Bruin of Brefney, Ui-Fiachrach of Moy, and the race of Muiredach, notwithstanding their freedom, are bound to attend with their forces at the hostings of O'Conor, and to assist him in all his troubles and difficulties.'

The backdrop to such assemblies would have been by no means unfamiliar to those accustomed to Irish fair days. There would have been a strong smell and noise of cattle. Many beasts in the vicinity of the assembly places. Nor would that have been all that would have served to obliterate the centuries and draw us close to our ancestors in a common heritage of shared experience.

Nature cast Ireland in an atmospherically mysterious mould, which strongly moved the very spirit of her people, no less then than now. The black stormy waters of winter lakes. The dark hills ever full of changing colour. The bog cotton moving in the wind, white against the red of the bog. The little blue waters in summer sunshine. The light of the ocean after rain in the western evening sky; and the spirit of melancholy descending with darkness across the land. Those are the things that make us Irish people timelessly one with each other, and with even the most ancient past.

CHAPTER 5

The Coming of Christianity

IF WE STAND UPON a high cliff and look down on the restless surface of the waters we can see, in the patterns of the waves, a record of the storms and lesser movements in the ocean. To reflect thus upon the stirrings of the sea, is to remind ourselves of their similarity to the course of history itself. Underlying the surface patterns of the ocean is the long slow swell rolling in from the deep – the aftermath of great and distant storms, and presaging those to come. They correspond to the rise and fall, and onward march, of momentous and inexorable historical events. Criss-crossing the long heave of that groundswell are patterns of smaller waves – all that remain of less violent and more local storms. They resemble the lesser occasions, turbulences and historical occurrences. And, as we continue to look, we see yet other movements, and at other angles, even to little scurries stirred by no more than a momentary breeze – the small happenings of our lives and times.

The small storms and scurries of the Celtic ascendancy remained a perennially unchanging part of life in Ireland even up to and beyond the time of which Sir Oliver St John was writing to James I in the seventeenth century, fifteen hundred years beyond the time of which I am now writing, and I need not weary anyone with a recital of them. But the great events of the groundswell of history are another matter, and are all important to the character of Ireland even to this day.

It was about the time that the early Celtic Connaught chiefs ceased to be Kings of Ireland, towards the end of the fourth century AD, that the first great wave since the coming of the Celts, several centuries earlier, rolled up on Ireland's shores, and washed strongly and quickly over the lives of all her people – the coming of Christianity. And with Christianity came literacy, and the beginnings of a written history of Ireland.

That influences travelled fast across great distances in early times is illustrated by the fact that the beginning of Ireland's conversion to Christianity took place within a century or so of its adoption as the official religion of the Roman Empire, of which Ireland was not a part. It is indeed remarkable that as conservative a people as the Irish were prepared voluntarily to change their religion, even though they retained many of their old beliefs as well – and do so to this day – and even though there was a good deal of resistance to the new creed during the first century or so of Irish Christianity. But the resistance seems to have been peaceable, and there are no early Irish Christian martyrs.

The reason why the Irish were prepared to accept Christianity may have been connected with the fact that the Irish were a pastoral, not an urban, people. They lived in the open in constant touch with nature. Mother earth was to them just that, a mother figure, a goddess. Their mythology was redolent of the mother role of nature. We have seen that the genealogy of the Christian scriptures probably made an immediate intellectual appeal to the learned Irish hierarchy. But the Irish as a whole, even those who would not claim to be learned, are anything but dull of mind. They are very highly and sensitively imaginative, and would readily have felt the call of another feature of Christianity. To the mass of the Irish people its principal emotional appeal has centred on the Virgin Mary. Surely Mary, as a focus for their reverence, appealed as much as, if not more than, other aspects of Christianity, because of their strong and ancient mythological veneration of mother earth. The Marian emphasis in the doctrine and rituals of the Church of Rome is a wise and sensitive response to the inclinations, needs and desires not only of women, but also of all whose lives are closely bound to the soil. Christianity came to Ireland and secured a foothold there at the very moment that the Romans left Britain for ever, in about 407 AD. The lights went out in Western Europe, and the Dark Ages stalked in behind the departing legions. And it was from that foothold in the monasteries on the farthest western edge of the vast Eurasian world that Irish monks bore back the cross of their new faith deep into Europe.

That may be a rather purple way of putting it. But the early Irish Christians deserve a bit of purple – even though it is not a matter about which the Irish themselves are given to being over modest. The Irish do not allow themselves to forget that theirs is 'the land of saints and scholars'. Christianity did not die out in Britain and North-West Europe, but a strong counter was needed to Anglo-Saxon paganism, and in providing that the Irish played a notable part. That is not just an Irish conceit. That colossus of scholarship, never given to praising the second-best, Samuel Johnson, wrote of that period, 'Ireland was the school of the west, the quiet habitation of sanctity and literature.'

Thus it was that Christianity came to Ireland, and that Ireland became for a time the chief centre of Christian learning, and the principal source of Christian propagation in Western Europe. Before the coming of Christianity, and because she was not a part of the Roman Empire, Ireland had lived in growing cultural isolation from the rest of Europe. Christianity reversed that trend. A tidal wave of Semitic religious and philosophical culture had rolled out from the epicentre of Eurasian civilization and had deeply inundated even its westernmost fringe. Religion now occupied the centre of the intellectual and cultural stage, and

Ireland thus became, albeit peripherally, a part of the great cultural and intellectual unity of the Christian world stretching from the Eastern Mediterranean to the Atlantic Ocean.

And so it came about that families like the O'Conor clan not only became intimately involved in Christian worship and the practice of Christian rites, and had perforce to modify their druidical inheritance in so doing, even in such great ceremonies as the induction, or coronation, of their monarchs, but also, at a later time, became directly implicated in the agonizing crises in which schisms within the Christian church were to play a large part.

And there was another development at the time that the Dark Ages closed over Europe that held ominous portents for the future of Ireland. The propagation of Christianity in Britain and Western Europe was not Ireland's only external mission or activity.

The weakening of the hold of the Romans on Britain in the last century or two of her occupation emboldened the Celtic Irish chiefs to make raids on the British coast. And, at the time of the departure of the Romans from Britain, the Irish established footholds in Wales and Scotland and founded royal dynasties in both countries. The Scots derive their name from the Irish 'Scotti' who settled there. Those Irish aggressions were early examples of an aspect of Ireland's relationship with Britain that was destined centuries later to result in the agonies she was due to suffer, and from which she is not yet free, namely the threat, or potential threat, that she posed to the British mainland.

CHAPTER 6

The Scourge of the Vikings

THROUGHOUT THE DARK AGES of early Christian times, the Connaught chiefs lived on as they had lived in the past. They remained rulers in Connaught, following their pastoral life among their people and their beasts. They did not live in towns and villages but continued their semi-nomadic lives between one grazing ground and another. Their sport, and a portion of their subsistence, was hunting in the forests, hawking, and fishing in the estuaries, rivers and lakes. Poetry, singing, dancing in the open, and games; the endless telling of old tales, and recitation of their history and fables round the fire; and the practice of home crafts in leather, linen, wool, clay, metal and wood; were perennial accompaniments to their life of herding and small-time arable farming.

But the great waves of history continued to roll at long intervals of time. The next to break, literally, upon the strands of Ireland four hundred years after the coming of Christianity, was the devastating onslaughts of the Vikings, the Norsemen and the Danes.

The Viking raids were not just an historical episode. Those who were alive when they began were to know no other condition of life for the remainder of their lives. And their children, and grandchildren, and generations even of the descendants of their great-grandchildren, were to live the whole of their lives under the Viking threat. Generation after generation of people were hardly to know that there could be any other way of life, any other sort of world, than one over which this dreadful menace hung perennially. This immensely long period of Viking aggression lasted for a duration of time about as long as from the reign of Queen Anne to the present day, nearly three centuries, from the late eighth century until the middle of the eleventh century.

During all that time, Europe, and in particular the islands of the North Atlantic in a huge arc from Ireland in the south-east, to Greenland in the north-west, was plagued by spasmodic raids from a stream of vigorous, aggressive people from Scandinavia. Their depredations resulted in an appalling loss of documents, records and works of art and craftsmanship. They wiped off the slate centuries of the recorded history of some of the communities in our islands.

The impetus of their raids took the Vikings not only as far as Spain in the west, but even further south into North Africa. They raided into the Mediterranean and attacked Italy. Although their only permanent foothold in Western Europe was in Northern France, their marauding took them across the whole continent, even to Constantinople.

An eastward thrust carried the Norsemen deep into Russia. There they appear to have settled and to have been absorbed into the local population. They were known by a name of Finnish origin as the Rus, from which the words Russia and Russian derive.

Ireland was subject to Viking activity throughout the whole of the period that they preyed upon Western Europe. As a seafaring people they concentrated their interest largely in the coastal areas and set up permanent settlements in Dublin, Waterford, Limerick, and elsewhere which became the first Irish towns of any size and consequence. But they also penetrated deep inland, particularly up the rivers, establishing themselves, for instance, in Lough Neagh by way of the River Bann, and in Lough Ree by way of the Shannon. They sacked the great monasteries and devastated their treasures and manuscripts. To contemplate the appalling losses resulting from their merciless savagery is indeed bitter.

The history of the Viking period in Ireland is very confused. Over so long a period, those who settled down became a resident part of the Irish population. They became converted to Christianity but, although they married Irish women, they were slow to integrate because of the isolated community life they led in the towns and ports they had created. Nor were they wholly taken up with plundering and raiding. From their ports, they carried on an extensive maritime trade. Some of their contacts with the Irish were therefore peaceable and mutually beneficial and fruitful, and it is claimed for them that they introduced silver to Ireland and craftsmanship in working that metal. During the Viking period internecine warfare among the Irish themselves continued unabated. At times they fought each other. At times they fought the Vikings. At times they fought each other in alliance with the Vikings.

With the consolidation of resistance against the Norsemen in Western Europe and England, the Viking strongholds at the ports of Dublin, and Annagassan in Louth, became the principal bases from which they mounted raids on the English mainland, and from which indeed they at one time ruled parts of Northumbria. Once more, as with the Irish raids on Britain at the end of Roman times:

Coming events cast their shadows before.

Here, again, was Ireland being used as a base to menace Britain. They suffered a notable defeat at the hands of King Brian Boru at the battle of Clontarf in 1014. The son of the first Prince of Moylurg led a sept in the battle. Brian and his son were both killed, and Ireland lapsed under weak leadership into a not unaccustomed anarchic state which enabled the Norse invaders to maintain their Danish coastal strongholds, in particular their Dublin kingdom, until they, in turn, after four centuries of occupation, were submerged by the next great wave to roll in from the ocean swell of history, this time even more destructively – the Normans.

The Coming of the Normans

THE NORMANS FAILED IN IRELAND. Or rather, they only partly succeeded. The upshot of their partial success was – since their subsequent strivings continued for centuries – another five hundred years of increased and more violent internal Irish conflict and turmoil. Connaught did not escape their assaults, but, as Sir Oliver St John reported to James I, they left, 'no other remarkable monument of their conquest but the castles of Athlone'. The O'Conor chiefs then restored, and continued, their own ancient Celtic rule.

It is tempting to think that it would have been better for Ireland had the Normans fully succeeded there, as they did in England, and united Ireland under their own rule as an associate state under the English Crown. Ireland might then have been saved the subsequent agony over centuries of piecemeal suppression by England. But England herself did not long remain united under the Normans. She was destined to suffer long periods of inter-baronial internecine strife. It must be even less likely that the restive, war-like and chauvinistic Irish would have long remained content to be held together in an artificial nationhood by foreign overlords. It must, therefore, surely be accepted that sooner or later the Norman attempt to conquer Ireland was destined to fail – or at any rate, to come to pieces.

The Normans did not invade Ireland of their own initiative. The initiative came from the Holy See in Rome. In the year 1155, eighty-nine years after the Norman conquest of England, Nicholas Brakespear, who, as Pope Adrian IV, was the only Englishman ever to sit in the papal chair, issued – or is said to have issued – a Papal Bull to King Henry II of England, the first Plantagenet king, inviting him to conquer Ireland on the grounds that the Irish were a 'rude and ignorant people', who had strayed too far from, or more properly had never been wholly assimilated into, the disciplines of the Church of Rome. There was also a markedly worldly condition attached to the Pope's blessing for Henry's Irish conquest. The papal coffers were to receive in future, as a perpetual royalty, a form of poll-tax on Henry II's Irish subjects.

Whether or not the Bull ever was issued is a matter of doubt. If it was, Henry II did nothing about it for more than another decade, by which time Adrian IV was dead.

A century earlier the Pope had inspired William the Conqueror to conquer England, and bring the Church in England more closely within the disciplines of Rome. Now, whatever the magniloquent political and religious language in which the project may have been, and may still be, dressed up, and whether or not it was put to Henry II in the form of a Papal Bull, the decision had been taken by the Papacy that it was Ireland's turn to be brought more closely into the Roman fold. Henry II was to be the tool; and ready and willing local 'party members', in the shape of Irish bishops were on the ground to welcome the take-over.

That Henry II failed to meet the wishes of Rome, argues strongly for the supposition that he regarded adventurings in Ireland as likely to be more dis-advantageous than beneficial to his own interests. Although he was King of England, he was a Frenchman. He was the son of the Count of Anjou, and sovereign by inheritance of large areas of France where much of his time, energies and resources were spent on vast projects of building and improvement. Notable among his many building achievements were the Castle of Chinon and the great Loire embankment, thirty miles long, which to this day holds back the flood waters of the river and protects large areas of the surrounding country. Ireland was not a tempting prize to him. Nor did Ireland pose any such threat to his dominions as to have required him to take action to eliminate it. To a prudent man, military involvement there would surely have seemed a potentially dangerous distraction from his English and continental commitments, ambitions and interests.

It is to be supposed, therefore, that had not the Irish proposition been put to him in such a manner as to make it appear exceptionally tempting and advantageous, Henry II would not have sanctioned the adventure.

That he was eventually persuaded to change his mind and fall in with the plans of the Papacy seems to have been due as much to the plausibility of one man as to anything else. At all events his decision arose directly and immediately out of a visit paid to him by that man.

On the head of an Irishman, Dermot MacMurrough, King of Leinster, rests the grave responsibility of having precipitated the Norman invasion of Ireland. He was the spark that fired the train that in the upshot was destined to lead to the long and almost continuous history of bitterness between England and the people of Ireland which he deliberately began.

He was almost certainly hand in glove with Church leaders in Ireland, but he was concerned primarily with his own personal interests and ambitions, and it was in furtherance of those ambitions that he invited the Normans to his assistance in Ireland. In doing so, he was in effect renewing the scourge of the Vikings, the Normans being the successors of Norsemen whose southward march had petered out in Northern France where, making an accommodation with the Franks, and adopting Christianity, they had settled in the territory called, after themselves, Normandy. They conquered England in 1066. But, like the Romans, did not continue into Ireland. It was not till a century later that these thrusting, ardent, ruthless people were called into Ireland by Dermot MacMurrough, to fight his own countrymen.

Dermot MacMurrough was an essentially masculine man, a warrior king, strong, bold, ambitious and aggressive. He was constantly involved in Ireland's internecine strife; endlessly at enmity with other chieftains. He was also a man of some culture. He supported the monasteries, promoted learning, and to him is attributed the responsibility for the production of one of Ireland's greatest mediaeval treasures, the Book of Leinster. In addition, therefore, to having close and influential ties with the Church, he may also have been, in the modern idiom of public relations, well able 'to protect himself'.

In the year 1166, exactly a hundred years after the Normans landed in England, Dermot, beaten to his knees by his adversaries in Ireland – notably by Roderic O'Conor, High King of Ireland – and deserted by his own followers, but with his unquenchable ambitions in no way abated, and his aggressiveness as fierce as ever, sailed to Bristol to seek foreign aid. He had nothing less in mind than the conquest of all Ireland, with himself enthroned as ruler. He first addressed himself to the Norman barons of South Wales. Learning from them that King Henry II was in France, he journeyed thither and presented himself.

Dermot was by this time a mature man in his late fifties. He was a man of great size, and we must suppose of strong personality and good address. Eloquence being the art form of the Irish, he was doubtless a man of skilful plausibility. At all events he won the support of the king, at least to restoring his rule over Leinster, and he returned to Bristol bearing letters patent in which Henry gave authority to any of his subjects, who might so wish, to aid Dermot. These letters were clearly intended for the Norman Welsh barons.

Why did Henry take the seemingly unnecessary step of agreeing to help Dermot? He almost certainly thought it to his advantage that some of his Norman Welsh subjects should have something to distract them from possible mischief at home. Although it was only a century since the Conquest, already the ancient royal blood of Welsh, English, and Norman monarchs mingled in their veins, and their pretensions and ambitions, spurred by their material poverty, posed something of a threat to him. But that cannot have been a compelling reason, or he would have acted earlier when first encouraged by the Pope to do so.

He may also have calculated that he would not be irrevocably committed to an Irish adventure if aid was limited initially to restoring Dermot to the kingdom of Leinster. But it seems unlikely that he would have had sufficient interest to give Dermot any encouragement had not the latter persuaded him that if, after regaining Leinster, he was given continued support, he could conquer the whole of Ireland, and would in that case rule as a vassal king, swearing fealty to Henry, paying him tribute, and securing the eventual succession to some other vassal of the King of England's choosing.

If that is how Henry saw the future in Ireland unfolding, he gravely miscalculated the situation. He ruled the whole of Western and Central France from Normandy to the Pyrenees. He ruled England, but the Normans, like the Romans, had not subdued Scotland. That would take more than another five hundred years. North Wales, too, had not been subdued. That would have to await Edward I, a century later.

With such a widespread kingdom with a great many internal problems, it was a lunatic decision for Henry to tackle Ireland while parts of mainland Britain remained independent of his rule. It was indeed a colossal and dangerous blunder into which he must have been blarneyed by MacMurrough. It spelt tragedy for Ireland, and a running sore for both Britain and Ireland, which is not yet at an end. It is to be wondered whether, if Henry II had been an Englishman, he would have made that mistake. The Roman Empire felt unable to take on Ireland. The subsequent pre-Norman rulers of Britain also held back from dangerous meddling there.

Back in Bristol, Dermot gave promises of land to those Welsh Normans who would venture to support him, and in particular offered the succession of his kingdom, and his beautiful daughter in marriage, to the impoverished Richard FitzGilbert de Clare, Earl of Pembroke, known as Strongbow, if he would gather a force for the expedition to Ireland.

With promises of future support, the restless Dermot MacMurrough did not wait for the Normans to mobilize, but, with a few early recruits, returned to Ireland, and in 1167 opened his campaign. He was captured and brought before the High King, Roderic O'Conor, who knew nothing of Dermot's understanding with Henry II. Dermot was forced to humble himself, and was pardoned on renouncing all further claim to the Kingdom of Leinster. In the following year, 1168, Roderic O'Conor held a great Assembly to celebrate his triumph. It was to be the last time, after more than a thousand years, that a Celtic High King of Ireland would preside over such a gathering.

May Day has a special significance in ancient and modern mythology, and ancient Irish mythology is no exception. The sons of Milesius were said to have landed in Ireland on May Day. It might therefore be seen as a judgement upon their Celtic successors that, on 1 May, 1169, the main body of Welsh Normans set foot on Irish soil. That the invasion was dressed up to look like a civilizing Christian mission – as were the marauding Crusaders – does not hide the fact that it was nothing more than naked, plundering, unprovoked aggression by foreigners against the people of Ireland. The Church, the French, the Welsh, and Dermot MacMurrough must bear the blame. The English were not there, but cannot be exonerated. Henry II came in the name of England, and it was not long before English settlers followed the Normans into Ireland to help themselves to stolen Irish lands. The consequence has been eight hundred years of strife, misery and bitterness; untold tens of thousands of innocent lives sacrificed. It is enough. Perhaps May Day should be made a day of atonement by some special gesture of common goodwill by the successors of all who were involved.

Had the Normans left Ireland alone, she might, though it may not be judged very likely, have been spared what she was destined to suffer centuries later at the hands of the English. During the Middle Ages, Western Europe was moving towards a linguistic division of the continent into independent nation-states, ruled by monarchies which had successfully united the warring baronies.

The Celtic rulers of Ireland had for more than a thousand years tended to be more monarchic than aristocratic, and had throughout that period been attracted to the concept of a dominant national king. There had thus been a series of kings and high kings of Ireland in name, even though they did not usually succeed in dominating and uniting the nation. But in the eleventh century, at the end of the Viking period, Ireland was for a time a virtually united monarchy.

The question must, therefore, be asked; might the Irish, with so much experience of kingship under their belt, and in line with the European trend, have succeeded in becoming a united nation-state, under a monarchy, in the coming few centuries, had they been left alone by Rome and the Normans, to evolve their own institutions?

If so, when the dire need came in the sixteenth century to safeguard the offshore islands of Britain and Ireland from the rapacious continental powers, the Kingdom of England and an independent Kingdom of Ireland might have allied themselves in a common need to safeguard their integrity. And that might have been the situation instead of the appalling disaster for Ireland that the Norman invasion of 1 May, 1169, made inevitable.

Nor do I think it valid to scoff at the supposition that the warring chiefs of Ireland might have been brought together in a united kingdom of Ireland. The greater part of Ireland, today, is an organic union of the nationalist Irish people in the twenty-six counties of the Republic of Ireland, proving that the native people of Ireland are capable of political union.

Scotland in the Middle Ages had succeeded in achieving a degree of centralized monarchy. Something similar might have been possible in Ireland. Continual hostility between Scotland and England may suggest that relations between Ireland and England might have been no better, but Ireland, unlike Scotland, did not have the aggravation of a common and disputed land frontier with England. While, therefore, relations between England and Ireland might not have been such as to prevent the future tribulations of Ireland, there would at least have been room for a possible accommodation between them. But the Norman invasion altogether destroyed that possibility. Thereafter, nothing short of total Irish submission to the Crown of England could give England the security that was to become her prime need.

The ensuing two years, 1169 and 1170, were thus destined not only to be among the most important in the history of Ireland, but also to prove fateful for Anglo-Irish relations. They were also to become alarming for Henry II. The Normans landed in sufficient strength to enable Dermot MacMurrough's Leinster territories to be restored. But in 1171 he himself died suddenly. Strongbow, now married to an Irish princess, Dermot's daughter, claimed the crown of Leinster for himself. Meanwhile, the greatest of all the Welsh Norman families, the Geraldines, who were prominently engaged in the Irish campaign, had made it clear enough that they had set their sights on nothing less than an independent Irish kingdom under their own rule.

Henry II, immediately realizing the threat to himself, and to England, of the possible emergence of a powerful independent Welsh Norman kingdom in Ireland, hastened there forthwith, re-asserted his authority over the Welsh barons, and proclaimed Ireland a part of his realm.

That was perhaps the most crucial moment in the history of Anglo-Irish affairs – the moment whereafter the principal underlying motive and cause of England's concern with Ireland was always to be the direct or indirect threat which Ireland posed to the security of Britain.

Henry II's claim to sovereignty over Ireland took the form of naming his ten year old youngest son – the future King John, of Magna Carta and the Wash – 'Lord of Ireland', a title used by English monarchs for another three hundred and fifty years, until Henry VIII proclaimed himself King of Ireland. The title chosen by Henry II, and the fact that he bestowed it on his ten year old youngest son, suggests that he looked upon Ireland as a peripheral vassal principality rather than as an integral part of the metropolitan realm.

But whatever the title, it did not reflect the reality. When the Normans landed in England in 1066, they were invading a kingdom, and were confronted by an English army. They defeated it. England was forced to capitulate. There was no Irish kingdom, or Irish army, in that sense. There were more than 150 different principalities in Ireland each with its own armed followers, to say nothing of the forces at the disposal of the old Viking and Danish coastal settlements. The High King Roderic O'Conor did muster a confederate army, representing a number of the chieftains, and numbering some thirty thousand men. The Welsh-Normans defeated him, but that nevertheless left the forces of many of the chiefs untouched. So long as they did not unite in a single force which could be brought to battle and defeated – a contingency rendered unlikely by their own internal quarrels – the terrain was in favour of the Irish acting piecemeal.

Ireland was still heavily forested, a condition greatly to the advantage of small forces of warriors engaging in guerrilla-type warfare. Norman progress in Ireland was thus slow. After a century, some three-quarters of the country was in their hands, but by that time the Norman barons themselves were becoming indistinguishable from Irish chieftains. They were no longer in any sense the agents of the English Crown. It was to be five hundred years after Strongbow's invasion before England finally brought the whole country under subjection.

One of the criticisms levelled continuously against Ireland has been that it never was a united country, a kingdom; and one of the aims of the Papacy in encouraging Henry II to invade was to unite Ireland under his rule, and to have therein a united and powerful Church strongly dependent on the will of Rome.

What saved Ireland from Norman domination, and what has enabled her national resurrection in the nineteenth and twentieth centuries was the very fact that she was disunited. The fact, too, that the bulk of the Irish remained a subject pastoral, peasant people, looked upon as outlandish, savage natives, not fit to be assimilated into the English way of life, resulted in the preservation of their Irish national characteristics up to our own times.

The psychological error made by Henry II when he approved of the assistance of the Welsh-Norman barons to King Dermot MacMurrough of Leinster is very directly relevant to the story of all the old leading Irish families whose blood inevitably became mingled with the strain of the Welsh Normans. Henry II clearly did not understand that there was a built-in and dangerous degree of affinity between the Welsh-Norman knights and barons and the Celtic chiefs which brought them naturally closer to each other culturally than they were to him as a Frenchman.

Before ever they sailed for Ireland the Welsh-Normans were already thoroughly infected with Celtic dynastic aristocratic traditions; traditions which in some degree were identical with those of Ireland as they had been brought to Wales by the Irish chiefs who had there set up their dynastic rule after the collapse of Roman rule in Britain.

Moreover, since the families of the Welsh-Norman barons had themselves been settled in Wales for as much as a century, they were by then third or fourth generation Welshmen. They spoke the Celtic tongue. Some of their mothers were Welsh, notably the beautiful Princess Nesta. She was of Celtic royal blood, daughter of Rhys Ap Tewdyr, Prince of South Wales. She had a chequered matrimonial career. When very young she was mistress of King Henry I, by whom she had two sons. She later had another lover, and was also married twice. Her first husband was a Norman, Gerald Fitz Otho, known as Gerald of Windsor. By him she became the mother of the Geraldine brothers of whom Maurice Fitzgerald was one of the principal leaders of the Irish invasion. He was founder of the great house of the Earls of Kildare, later to become the Dukes of Leinster. To raise and rouse the forces in Wales for the Irish adventure, the battle cry was, 'To arms! The Race of Nesta'.

In consequence of that background and those sentiments, and because the Norman ruling tradition was itself aristocratic, the Welsh-Normans took like ducks to water to the Irish monarchic tradition, and, in the years following the 1169 incursion, set themselves up in Ireland wherever they could as local rulers.

By degrees they became so powerful and turbulent, that England could not impose her will on them. They married Irishwomen, adopted the Irish language, and Irish customs, and not only became as Irish as the old Celtic rulers, but indeed so Irish that their very names are now known only in an Irish context. Fitzgerald, Fitzmaurice, Fitzsimmons, Burke (de Burgh), Dillon, Lacy (de Lacy), and many other such now wholly Irish names derive directly from the Welsh-Norman invasion of eight centuries ago.

England continued in the coming centuries to claim sovereignty over Ireland, but for the five hundred years following Strongbow's invasion she was never able to impose her authority over the whole island, and seldom over more of it than a small strip of the eastern coastal area north and south of Dublin, and stretching plus or minus twenty miles inland according to how her fortunes fluctuated. But even at her weakest moments, she continued to cling to that strip, known as the Pale, an area from which the Welsh-Normans had, at the time of their initial invasion, dislodged the earlier Danish settlers. But for five turbulent centuries the rest of Ireland was for the most part in the hands of local Celtic and Norman warring chiefs, kings and barons.

And so for those five centuries the Celtic kings and the Hibernicized Welsh-Normans, and some subsequent English settlers, the O'Conors, O'Briens, O'Neills, Fitzgeralds, Butlers, de Lacys, and others lived and ruled and continuously squabbled in Ireland to the constant discomfiture and embarrassment of the titular sovereignty of England. Nor were the English settlers who followed the Welsh-Normans into Ireland any more to be trusted by the English than the Welsh-Normans themselves. They, too, married the Irish, adopted Irish ways and the Irish language and became as Irish as the Irish.

The purpose of the project upon which the Papacy had unleashed these forces, the uniting of Ireland under the influence of the Church in Rome, had failed utterly.

The Irish Threat to England's Security

THE PASSAGE QUOTED EARLIER from Gibbon suggested that it was about 1000 AD that the use of surnames began – a little before the Norman Conquest. The Irish were among the earliest to adopt them. And when, in the year 971 AD, there died a Connaught King named Conor – a monarch of the Heremon Milesian descent – his son took the surname O'Conor, by which his descendants have ever since been known.

That the antiquity of the family is acknowledged, even in impeccable genealogical circles, is revealed by the fact that Conor himself is recorded in the pedigree material in the College of Arms as the 44th King of Connaught.

The 'O' with which his son prefixed the family surname means 'descendant – or grandson – of ... '.

King Conor's brother was known as the Prince of Moylurg, he whose son led a sept, a sub-tribe, of the O'Conor clan, in support of Brian Boru, against the Vikings at the battle of Clontarf in 1014. He had a wise and valiant descendant, Dermot, who died in 1165, four years before the Norman landing in Ireland. Dermot's son honoured his father by taking the surname MacDermot. The prefixes 'Mac' and 'Mag' mean 'son of ... '. Thus did the MacDermot sept – from which, in turn, the Magans descend – become a recognizable separate family almost at the moment of the Norman invasion.

Another four hundred years of internal turbulence were to elapse before the next great wave of history, following the Normans, was to break over Ireland – the scourge of the Tudor dynasty.

As the Tudor period lasted little more than the lifetime of a very aged person, something more than a century, it is possible to look upon it as a single piece. Indeed, a famous Irish lady, Katherine Fitzgerald, Countess of Desmond, is said to have bracketed the whole period of the dynasty. She died in 1604, a year after the death of Queen Elizabeth, the last of the Tudors. She is also recorded to have been 139 years of age, to have danced in pre-Tudor times with Richard III, and to have met her death through a fall from a cherry tree!

But before we look at the Tudor tapestry, we must set the scene. Hitherto, we have looked at Ireland from within. We must now look at her from without. We must look at her from England, through English eyes, and see how she appeared from the special and peculiar point of view of the Tudor English. We must also take account of other events that profoundly changed the world internationally and that were to seal the fate of Ireland, and, with her fate, that also of most of her ancient great families.

Taking us out of Ireland this chapter is an essential prelude to a statement of Tudor reactions to the new international situation. Its purpose is to explain the attitude of Tudor England to Ireland which is the key to all that was to happen to Ireland thereafter.

The year 1485 can be taken as the fulcrum date in this context. It is the beginning of the Tudor dynasty and brings us to the period of their history that the English know best.

The English have always scoffed at the interest of the Irish in their genealogy, and in their history. They wish the Irish did not have such long historical memories. There was justification for scoffing at the ancient Irish genealogy that got tacked onto the Old Testament 'begats'. English lack of sympathy with Irish attitudes to history is also understandable. It stems from the view the English have of their own history; and that is not unimportant in the context of English attitudes towards Ireland from the Tudor period onwards, particularly as the English have been wont to attribute Irish political obduracy at least in part to their perversely obsessive long-term interest in, and view of, their history.

The picture the English have in their mind's eye of their own history is altogether different from the Irish view of Irish history. In the mind's eye of the English, their history, English history, begins with the Norman Conquest, 1066. There then follows an almost totally blank period of five hundred years which they call 'the Middle Ages' about which they know little or nothing, and they are not sure whether or not it is the same thing as 'the Dark Ages'.

Although at school they learnt by heart the kings and queens from William the Conqueror onwards, they can tell you very little about any of them before the Tudor king, Henry VIII. Despite the fact that Shakespeare wrote plays about a number of them, they know nothing, for instance, about Richard II, Henry IV or Henry VI. But they have heard of King John and Magna Carta and the jewels lost in the Wash. They are not sure whether he was before or after William the Conqueror. They know Henry V won the Battle of Agincourt. Some of them even know the date, because it's easy, 1415. They have heard of the Battle of Crécy, but don't know the date; it's more difficult. Some of them know that William Rufus – they don't know who he was – had red hair and was shot with an arrow by-accident-on-purpose hunting in the forest. They know Richard III said, 'My kingdom for a horse.' They know about the Princes in the Tower, but don't know who they were or when they lived. And somewhere in the murk of the Middle Ages were Chaucer, and Caxton and printing.

But the real history of the English is the five hundred years from Henry VIII. They have a quite extensive mental picture of the Tudors, the Stuarts, and the eighteenth, nineteenth and twentieth centuries.

The English simply cannot understand that other peoples, including the Irish, see their history in terms of thousands of years. To the Persians, five hundred years ago is recent history. That was the time of Shah Abbas, contemporary of Queen Elizabeth I. The Persians see him as a recent monarch.

Before William the Conqueror, the English do not really look upon the inhabitants of England as English at all. They do not identify themselves with them; certainly not with the Ancient Britons who were primitive and painted themselves with woad. They had Druid priests in long white robes and mistletoe and did human sacrifices at Stonehenge – so they think. Rather Welshie sort of people; certainly not at all English, and not very nice.

King Arthur; yes, he was English, but historically out of time, before there were any real English. They don't know when he lived, but it was certainly before the Conqueror. They're not really quite certain that he did live. But he was English. That's certain, and he was the epitome of a decent, chivalrous, democratic Englishman; round table and all that. Alfred; he was English too, but also lived before the days of the real English. He was another democratic Englishman, ready to hobnob with old cottage women, and to take a scolding from them in good part; attractive veneer of English absent-minded muddler, burnt the cakes and that sort of thing.

The Venerable Bede means something. Pretty decent sort of monk. Lived somewhere up north; not really England. Canute, of course; they know inaccurately that he tried to stop the tide coming in. Some kind of foreigner. But, with the possible exceptions of Arthur and Alfred, there really were no English in their own view of history, before the Norman Conquest, and very little history between then and the Tudors.

But, curiously, they do take their history back two thousand years, not continuously, but in a bound, to something that is not English at all. The people with whom they do find a certain common identity are the Romans. They undoubtedly were a sort of Englishmen, and because of their occupation of Britain, the English really do regard themselves as the lineal successors of the Romans. And this partly explains the centuries-old English love affair with Italy. They feel an almost proprietary interest in ancient Rome, and it seems much more comprehensible, and much nearer in time, to the English, than, for instance, England in the twelfth century, which they can't visualize at all. The English call themselves Anglo-Saxons, but they have no idea what or who Angles or Saxons were or what they were like, and do not identify themselves with either of them. They were foreigners in English eyes. The English historical identity is with the Romans who really were, as they see it, typically English. When the Pope saw those slave boys from Britain in the market place, and made his kindly pun:

Not Angles but Angels, if only they were Christians.

it is with the civilized Pope that the English identify themselves, not with the unexpectedly well-washed little barbarian urchins from the savage island of cold and mists at the far north-western extremities of the Empire.

Contrast that English mental picture of their history with the Irish mental view of theirs, and we begin to understand why the Irish see things differently. The histories – the historical experiences – of the two peoples are different in kind.

The Irish were not overrun by the Romans. They were not conquered by the Angles and Saxons. They were not conquered by the Danes; nor by the Normans. They can look back and form an unbroken mental picture of themselves as exactly the same people for two thousand years and more. They do not look back *through* two thousand years. It is all one piece with the present. It is not so much that they have a long sense of history, as that they have little or no sense of history. There is no well-rehearsed ladder of kings up which an image of Irish history can progress. Ask an Irishman to recite the kings of Ireland, and he will say 'Brian Boru', and that will be the beginning and the end of it.

Irish history is in that sense much simpler than English history. The two thousand years from a few centuries BC to the Tudor period contain five distinct, well-known, and oft repeated historical episodes at curiously regular intervals of about four hundred years – the coming of the Celts, of Christianity, of the Danes, of the Normans, and then the Tudor suppression. The rest is, save to professional historians, the uninteresting trivia largely of local petty squabbling between rival chieftains.

Granted those five great landmarks, the past two thousand years is, to the Irish, a single historical period, all one slab of time, in which they see themselves as the same people, essentially unchanged. And indeed much has not changed, or has changed very little. Their mistake is to make the cut-off point at the early Celtic period of two thousand years ago. Really to understand their unchanging – or little changing – selves they should take the slab of time much further back. For a proper understanding of their history, of its deepest influences upon themselves, their historical perspective is not too long, but far too short.

In a sense, some of them do acknowledge the importance of their historical antiquity. Perhaps since the coming of the bicycle, and later the motor car, which caused the men to stay less in the home of an evening, the telling of the old tales round the fire has largely lapsed. But there are those who do cherish the ancient legends. They know they are not history. Equally they suppose them to have an historical foundation. They are historical literature, and all the more cherished for being literature. It is as though they know that history contains deeper meanings than can be extracted from it by a recitation of the proven facts. Who, to give such attitudes an English dimension, would swap Shakespeare's Richard II, Henry V or Henry VIII for the textbook accounts of the careers of those monarchs?

During the latter part of the two thousand year tableau which is Irish history – that is to say, during the last few hundred years, which seem to them like the day before yesterday – a series of very nasty things have happened to them, all at the hands of the English. That's the rub in Irish history, and it's still rubbing. It is the only part of their two thousand year historical set-piece that retains any real dynamic, any power to move and influence the people of Ireland to action. There is nothing else in their history that matters, nothing else that rubs, nothing else to be restored or corrected. The Gaelic ideal does not have that force. It is a delightful bit of national fun; that is all.

Indeed, the nineteenth century Gaelic revival was not really a truly Irish inspiration. It has all the hallmarks of Anglo-Irish romanticism. The real Irish, the cultural descendants of the most ancient Irish, do not think in those historical terms. To the true Irish heart there is nothing to revive, because nothing in the hearts of the people has changed, or needs to be revived, and the hearts of the people are all that matters, not external Gaelic or any other, trappings. Today is the same as two thousand years ago, a continuing, unchanging whole, except for grievous more recent injuries and wounds which still remain to be healed.

That is the essence of Irish historical sense and instinct. It is that that explains the different historical perspectives of the English and the Irish. It is also the reason why the Irish neglect their ancient monuments. They do not see them as ancient monuments, but as mere transitory excrescences upon the timeless face of Ireland. It is possible to get this sense of timelessness, of non-history, of all being at one with the past, elsewhere in the world. Stand in the Rift Valley in Kenya, and you are at one with the brontosauruses. There is no sense of an unfolding, onward march of history. You are at one with two hundred million years of time. The past and the present are at one with each other.

English historians and genealogists are as much affected by those different English and Irish historical perspectives as are the rest of their fellow countrymen. The national historical short-sightedness of the English is composed of almost ineradicable images formed very early in life when they learn their primary picture-book history. But some of their historians have tried to tell the English that they descend from a remarkable, ancient people who had an advanced social order long before the Normans, but they won't listen. They have an inbuilt, seemingly incurable, preference for a short historical perspective. Why are they so mesmerized by the ruthless, brutal, usurping, dogmatic albeit efficient and tyrannical William the Conqueror? And why are they prepared to listen only to fairy-tales about anything that happened before the Conquest? Whatever the answer to those questions, it is important that the English, if they want ever to understand the Irish, should comprehend the different Irish view of history, and why the Irish have it.

If 1485 was an important date in English history that was to prove fateful for Ireland, it fell also at a fulcrum period in the calendar of world history.

1485 was the year of the Battle of Bosworth Field. The Yorkists defeated. The Lancastrians victorious. Richard III slain. Henry VII, the first Tudor monarch, a strong and able ruler, ascended the throne of England. There were armed insurrections and more Yorkist plotting to come. But Bosworth Field was, nevertheless, the virtual end of the disastrous Wars of the Roses which, following the Hundred Years War, had sapped the strength of England and riven the fabric of state. England, under Henry VII, was at last a nation-state, and most sensitively conscious of the need to defend her new found integrity.

And England was changing in another most significant way. For four hundred years, ever since the Norman Conquest in 1066, England had not been the island kingdom of our present experience and understanding. She had been an off-shore part of a Western European power. Her rulers were Normans or of French origin. Throughout those four centuries a major concern had been their French possessions. The language of the court in England, and the official language of English administration, was French. The rulers of England looked not only inward, to England; certainly not westward to Ireland, but strongly eastwards to Europe, and particularly to France. There, in large part, was where their heart was. Indeed the French language has not even now entirely disappeared from our official vocabulary. Royal assent to Parliamentary bills is, for instance, announced in French. The Hundred Years War which began in 1337 was in part fought to uphold a claim by the English Crown to the throne of France.

But all that was changing. In the century of Bosworth Field, the fourteen hundreds, English began to supersede French as the official language of administration. The Hundred Years War was, in effect, the beginning of the end of a last desperate effort to retain the French possessions. Only half a century after the reign of Henry VII, the first Tudor king, England was to lose Calais, her last foothold on the continent of Europe, in the time of his grand-daughter, Queen 'Bloody' Mary.

England then, after four centuries, became what we have known her in our own time; what the English feel in their bones to be; what the English have gloried in ever since the Tudors set their seal upon it – their island monarchy, unique, exclusive, isolated by a moat of cleansing and protective tides from the contaminating and less favoured world without. Shakespeare put it in words to stir and quicken the hearts of English men and women bred in the Tudor tradition.

This scepter'd isle ... This seat of Mars ...
This other Eden ... This fortress built by Nature ...
against infection ... This precious stone set in the
silver sea ... which serves as a moat ... against
the envy of less happier lands.

That was a new-found, or re-found, condition wholly in keeping with England's island temperament. After four hundred years of warping foreign modes from

France, she was herself once again. That was an experience which was to repeat itself most strikingly on the occasion of Dunkirk in 1940. Faced with disaster, virtually disarmed, having suffered their worst military defeat for nearly a thousand years, and menaced by the most powerful forces the world had ever yet known, the reaction of the English was a sigh of genuine relief that they were now back in their own island and could go it alone, their efforts uncomplicated by foreign allies.

Throughout the five centuries that have elapsed since Bosworth Field, that exclusive insularity has been the prime characteristic of the way the English have felt about their island, and of their attitude towards those who live beyond its shores, even when they ruled an Empire covering a quarter of the world. And in Tudor times, the Irish were in no way regarded as fellow islanders. They were indeed much more foreign to the English than were the French. If, therefore, we are to understand the English view of the Irish, we must consider English attitudes in general to all other people to whom, as the English see it, the Almighty in his wisdom has denied the blessing of belonging to 'This scepter'd isle'; and Ireland, beyond the Pale, was definitely among those seen to have been denied that blessing.

Foreigners visiting England have always been made welcome, but they must put up with English ways. To be sure, there is patient tolerance of foreign eccentricities, but the English are not prepared to compromise their Englishness for anyone. If foreigners cannot speak English – too bad. The English are not going to start parlez-vous-ing just to suit them. To do so would cause guilty questioning in their hearts as to their continued worthiness to regard themselves as true-blue incorruptible English men and women. Again, the Bard had said it with incomparable and unmistakable clarity.

This above all, to thine own self be true.

The English are notable travellers. But while abroad, despite all the talk of when in Rome doing as the Romans do, they cocoon themselves in as English an aura of insularity as they can manage. They observe with interest, but involve themselves as little as possible. Beyond the barest limits of barest necessity, they avoid learning foreign languages. The handful of English who master foreign tongues and become expert in alien manners and customs are regarded with fairly awesome suspicion. A small number of dedicated Englishmen ran the Empire. They learnt the languages of the people they governed, understood their customs, and served them and the Crown to the limit of their ability. It was a satisfying life of service, but it was never home. Home was the dream of the future retirement cottage, and garden of English flowers.

A strong earthy vein in the English dimly senses art, music and intellectuality to be suspiciously un-English. Art and music are things foreigners are thought to do better. Though practised widely and enjoyed in England, it is suspected that they contain, with the possible exception of Church and martial music, at least a slight threat to the fibre of the nation. Intellectuality, the world of jargon, seemingly often of foreign origin, is sensed to be unhealthily un-English. But because of their patent awe of the incomprehensible, the English are apt, up to a point, to be bamboozled by spurious and pretentious intellectuality. But that said, the essential characteristic of the English is that they are people of robustly sound instincts. They are prepared to listen to anything, or anyone, and to do so with patience. They like a bit of fun – the more healthily earthy the better. But, at bottom, it is the integrity of their island home that is their first concern. They know, deep down, that the arts don't save you in war, nor, when it comes to a question of survival, do they grow the food to sustain your essential needs, or man the ships to keep your lifelines open. And despite their great literature, the English are suspicious of eloquence, and of too great a parade of cleverness. They prefer a limited vocabulary of straightforward phrases, adequate to the practical needs of life.

The Duke of Wellington, whose language was forthright enough for the bluntest Englishman, made a classic gesture of uncompromising commitment to the integrity of the British realm. His father was an amateur musician. But Wellington, his musical son, on becoming a soldier, burnt his own fiddle as a symbol of total dedication to his chosen profession of arms, and of dutiful service to the Crown, and, in doing so, gave his own customarily emphatic – even if exaggerated – English stamp to the essentially sound instincts of the English people for the proper ordering of priorities. The English will not fiddle while Rome burns. If a threat to the realm becomes serious, the fiddles will be put aside – if not burnt – and the citizens will arm themselves with their pitchforks, the only weapons customarily available to them at the outset of a conflict, for they greatly prefer peace to war.

It was in mid-Tudor England that that stamp of insular Englishmen, familiar to us today, or at any rate until the day before yesterday, became firmly established as typical of this people. England was free of continental dependence. Henry VIII had severed the Church from the dominance of Rome. Whatsoever was English would be ruled by the King of England, aided by his chosen advisers, and by none other. His authority he would not share with any external power, not even with the Head of the Church in Rome. Since mid-Tudor times it has never for a moment crossed the mind of members of the Church of England that God could be other than a Protestant Englishman. And since that time this island kingdom has been profoundly jealous of the safety of her shores, and of her absolute right to conduct her affairs as best she pleases. And she was defiantly concerned to protect those freedoms.

Come the three corners of the world in arms,
And we shall shock them; nought shall make us rue.

In what light then did this jealously insular people see the Irish and the island of Ireland itself?

The Irish they regarded quite simply as outlandish savages. Indeed, they looked upon them as worse than that. When we wish to attack our fellow human beings, we not infrequently justify ourselves by re-classifying them as wild animals. The English found no difficulty in genuinely regarding the Irish as such.

The whole of Ireland was Gaelic speaking. The English might understand some French, but Gaelic was incomprehensible gibberish, and clearly in no way resembled the language of a civilized people. Ireland had never come under the influence of Roman law. The Irish had an ancient legal system of their own which, to the English, appeared simply as lawlessness. True they were Christians, but their Christianity was seen to be shot through with ancient pagan superstition – even though the difference was more in kind than in degree to the vast pagan substructure of Christianity as a whole.

They did not live in decent settled communities, but semi-nomadically in primitive structures hardly better than temporary ramshackle animal shelters. They did indeed seem little higher in the order of things than the teeming animals among which they lived.

Their social customs, not least their wakes over the dead, were abhorrent. And their shaggy and wild appearance, together with their proclivity for fighting, confirmed in English eyes and minds the impression of a primitive and savage people.

A description exists of the visit of an Irish chief, Shaen O'Neill, paramount chief of Ulster, to London, to pay respects to Queen Elizabeth. His followers had long hair. Their clothes were saffron 'surplices' together with overmantles of the skins of wild animals. The people goggled at them as at those 'of China or America'. O'Neill chose to make his address in Irish, which sounded to the English like 'howling'.

The paradox that English settlers in Ireland rapidly became absorbed, integrated and Hibernicized to the point of being indistinguishable from the natives, inspired in England not curiosity as to the reasons, but fury that it should be so.

English officials who went to Ireland and became acquainted with the Irish at first hand, like their later descendant imperial administrators, studied the people and came to know them, and there are sympathetic and understanding contemporary English accounts of the virtues of the Irish and their customs. But the myopia of common and general English insularity knew no more of that than it was to know later of conditions in its far-flung imperial territories.

That is how the Irish appeared to the English in the time of the Tudors. But the Irish would be wrong to think that, even in that derogatory sense, they were in any way a subject of general interest to the English. There are some peoples, notable among them the Irish, whose character has a theatricality in its make-up which causes them to suppose themselves in a limelight with the world's eyes upon them. I cannot speak for the world. But I do know the English, and have no doubt that ordinary English people neither knew nor cared any more about the Irish in those days than they know or care today about their equally close neighbours, the Walloons in Belgium.

But if the Irish themselves seemed to the English mere savages, what importance did their country, Ireland, have for England?

Throughout most of her history Ireland had been of very little concern to Britain. The Romans in Britain had ignored her. Romans had of course visited Ireland, and traded with Ireland. Tacitus, the Roman historian, had written about Ireland. Ptolemy, the second century AD Egyptian astronomer, mathematician and geographer, included details of Ireland in his maps. But Ireland was of no serious political or military concern to the Romans. When the chaotic conditions following the Roman departure from Western Europe had subsided, England continued to ignore Ireland for another eight hundred years. But once the Normans had landed in Ireland, England could no longer overlook the threat that a powerful Norman kingdom in Ireland might pose to England's western flank. From then on England, at best, had uneasy feelings about Ireland, and looked constantly over her shoulder with suspicion at that rain-sodden land.

During the century and a half prior to Tudor times, England, distracted by her continental involvements, and then by the Wars of the Roses, found her already precarious hold on Ireland slipping. In particular the powerful Norman and English settlers were growing bolder and more menacing. A desperate attempt was made in the second half of the fourteenth century to bring them to heel. The notorious Statutes of Kilkenny imposed the direst penalties on any settlers who adopted Irish customs, the Irish language, or married Irish girls, thus becoming 'degenerate English'. But without the resources to enforce their will, the efforts of the English were bound to fail, as they did.

And in the fifteenth century the warning bell from Ireland sounded once again to caution England that thence could come dire threats to her safety and integrity. Richard Duke of York, a great-grandson of Edward III, from whom he was also descended on his mother's side, laid claim to the English throne. It was he, indeed, who started the Wars of the Roses, and he was father of both Edward IV and Richard III. Richard Duke of York did not think the Irish savages. He thought them a lovely people, and they responded by giving him their affection and support in return. Thus it was that he used Ireland as one of his bases for his assault on the English throne, and also as his refuge when in difficulty.

Richard Duke of York's gamble, and his life, ended at the Battle of Wakefield, in Yorkshire, which he lost on 30 December, 1460, to the Lancastrians, and in which he and one of his sons were killed. But that did not put an end to the Irish menace. By the time Henry VII came to the throne as the first Tudor monarch, Ireland's political status had become not far short of that of an independent kingdom, ruled by a great Irish Norman, one of the descendants of Princess Nesta.

Gerald, known as Garret More Fitzgerald, great Earl of Kildare, whose descendants were to become the Dukes of Leinster, is commonly accepted to have been the greatest Geraldine. Born in 1456, he succeeded his father in 1477, when twenty-one years of age. The English then tried to break his power. They failed, and two years later, in 1479, were forced to accept that he was in effect the virtual ruler of Ireland. He assumed the official title of Lord Deputy, in other words Viceroy, of Ireland.

Garret More Fitzgerald had, to an exceptional degree, the multicultural capacity which high-born Irishmen have for centuries had to assume. He was brought up both an Irish chieftain, wholly at home in Gaelic-speaking rural Ireland, and an English nobleman, no less at ease in English court circles – a sealed pattern for the future Anglo-Irish gentry. But he was more than that. He bestrode Western European society internationally. He was a Renaissance prince, and lived like one in his great fortress, Maynooth Castle, not far from his capital in Dublin.

His princely circumstances at Maynooth were no doubt qualified. Edmond Gosse's mother, having served as a governess in an Irish nobleman's house, described the conditions as 'a mixture of civility and savagery'. In that sense the great Earl of Kildare's living conditions could hardly have merited a different description.

But he was secure not only in his power, but also in his genealogical origins. His lineage could rival the best. That his ancestress Nesta was a princess was only one part of his descent. The Geraldines were a branch of the great Florentine Gerardini family whose origins stretched back to Troy, and the relationship had been maintained, and the kinship acknowledged, even up to the time of Garret More himself.

Here then, holding court in Dublin, too powerful for the English Crown to dislodge, was a man in his prime. Of great ability, great courage, great determination, he conducted himself and his affairs with the conscious authority of a prince. It is true that he did not command the support of all the other Irish chiefs and nobles, but he contrived judicious family marriage alliances with some of the most powerful Irish houses, and his position was unassailable. In him, once more, after three hundred years, we see a ruler somewhat equivalent to a High King of Ireland.

This in itself was enough to cause anxiety in Whitehall, but there was in it an element of great concern for Henry Tudor when, after the Lancastrian victory at Bosworth Field, he ascended the throne in 1485. Garret More, in the tradition of the erstwhile Irish supporters of Richard Duke of York, was a Yorkist. But he was only one of Henry's problems, one he did not dare to tackle until he had consolidated his hold on the English throne.

What happened next is of crucial importance in the long story of Anglo-Irish history. After the many centuries during which Ireland could be safely ignored by England as of no political or strategic importance, the threat posed by Strongbow and his Norman successors had seemed real enough to cause England at least to keep a vigilant watch on Ireland. But now, almost immediately after the Tudor victory at Bosworth Field, came the moment when that hypothetical threat became a reality – a reality which was to grow enormously for the Tudors in the degree of its menace during the succeeding century. Thereafter English attitudes to Ireland, English actions in relation to Ireland, for the next four and a half centuries, were to be overwhelmingly influenced by a single consideration – English national security, to which Ireland was seen to pose a constant threat.

When Henry VII came to the throne in 1485, no-one could foretell the future. The English throne was a precarious place. His predecessor, Richard III, had worn the crown for three years only. At the same time the boy king, Edward V, had, with his brother, disappeared into the Tower of London, and been murdered by someone. They were the Princes in the Tower. The father of those boys, Edward IV, had had a stormy beginning to his reign: and his predecessor Henry VI had been deposed twice, and was subsequently murdered. Henry VII was faced by rivals with as good a claim to the throne as his own, and Bosworth Field did not abate the Yorkist plotting. Who could say whether, and for how long, he could hold onto power? A man like Garret More Kildare was not quickly going to abandon his Yorkist allegiance in favour of a new and untried English sovereign. Kildare was a powerful man, and, in consequence, Yorkist eyes turned to Ireland once more as a safe base, and to the great Earl of Kildare as a likely ally. Thus it came about that in 1487, two years after Henry VII became King of England, there took place one of the most bizarre episodes in all English history.

In the early part of 1487 there arrived in Dublin from England a devious priest, bringing with him a good-looking, well-mannered, twelve year old boy, of seemingly good birth, who claimed to be the Earl of Warwick who had been incarcerated in the Tower by Richard III, and kept there by Henry VII, but whose story was that he had contrived to escape. If indeed he were the Earl of Warwick he would have been the nephew of, and next in succession to, both Edward IV and Richard III, and thus would have a more rightful claim to the throne than had Henry VII.

The boy's case must have been plausibly presented, because the Irish fell for it. Perhaps they were influenced by the fact that the Earl of Warwick's father, brother of Edward IV, the Duke of Clarence, notable for the alleged manner of his death (he was murdered in the Tower by drowning in a butt of Malmsey wine – an unauthenticated fragment of English history – was Dublin-born, thus giving the Irish a sort of proprietary interest in this little bit of Irish bloodstock.

Yorkist conspiracies were so convoluted that they are now difficult to unravel. But there can be little doubt that this particular plot was hatched by certain Yorkist noblemen acting together with Margaret, dowager Duchess of Burgundy, a former English princess, sister of Edward IV, and therefore aunt of the Earl of Warwick, and an inveterate enemy of the Lancastrians.

At all events, persuaded by the reaction to enquiries, both in England, and on the Continent, which were almost certainly addressed to the very sources whence the plot emanated, that there would be ample support for a Yorkist bid for the English throne, the great Earl of Kildare, Henry VII's Viceroy in Ireland, no less, took the amazing step of declaring this boy King of England. Thus, on Whit-Sunday 24 May, 1487, there took place in Christ Church Cathedral, Dublin, the most preposterous coronation in British history, when, with due pomp and ceremony, this boy impostor, Lambert Simnel, a baker's son, was, with the aid of a gilded circlet borrowed from the halo of a Virgin in a nearby church, crowned and declared Edward VI of England.

But that piece of near-musical hall farce was only the beginning. There was nothing farcical about the next act. It produced a moment of danger for England which was not soon to be forgotten.

The coronation of Lambert Simnel in Dublin placed the forces of the Irish at the disposal of the Yorkists. 'Edward VI' could not be left sitting in Dublin. He must be placed on the throne of England. That could be accomplished only by the defeat in battle of the forces of Henry VII. No time was to be lost. A week after the coronation, on 1 June 1487, a fleet set sail from Dublin bearing an Irish army of sorts, the core of which was, however, two thousand German mercenaries, recruited through the good offices of Margaret of Burgundy, who had also supplied money for the expedition.

The force landed on the coast of Lancashire and marched across to Yorkshire under command of one of the English plotters, the Earl of Lincoln, nephew of Edward IV, and heir presumptive of Richard III. They had expected much support from the disaffected counties of the north where Yorkist support was strong, but none was forthcoming. Englishmen were not prepared to throw in their lot with a mixed army of Irish and German invaders. But there could be no drawing back. There was now no alternative to marching on the capital.

So the Earl of Lincoln turned south and took his forces into Nottinghamshire.

There, on 16 June 1487, at Stoke, they encountered the English army that had come north to meet them, and to which volunteers had flocked in large numbers as they passed through the country.

In as bitter and bloody a battle as ever was fought in England, the Irish, after a three hour struggle, were defeated. The extent of the battle can be understood from the casualties. Four thousand Irish and German dead were left on the field, and there were very heavy English casualties. Moreover, that the English regarded the invasion as a major threat, is clear from the fact that Henry VII commanded his troops in person. The Earl of Lincoln and other notable Yorkists perished. And had the battle gone the other way, England would have been dancing to the tune of an Irishman, Garret More Fitzgerald.

Lambert Simnel was taken prisoner, pardoned, and humiliated with menial employment in the royal kitchens, where he immortalized his name a second time as innovator of the simnel cake.

It is my belief that the Battle of Stoke was to be the major influence on England's attitude to Ireland for another century. Whenever the question of Ireland was raised in the Tudor corridors of power, someone must have said, 'Let us never forget Stoke. Never give the Irish an inch. Don't let them raise their heads. They are too dangerous. We shall have another Stoke if we are not very careful.'

Thus crystallized the English concept of Ireland at that time as of a next-door island of literally howling, shaggy, dangerous, bellicose savages, little better than the wild animals in whose skins they were clad, or not much more than half-clad, who would be better exterminated lest, in combination with Britain's continental enemies, they should again seriously threaten the safety of the realm – 'This other Eden'. Here, at Stoke, in concrete actuality, was the emergence of the threat which Ireland, in the eyes of the English, was to pose to the realm for the next three hundred and fifty years, a secure base from which continental enemies could fall upon England from the rear. It was not a dream, not a nightmare born of obsessive, unwarranted and excessive anxiety. It was a fact. It had happened. And it had happened on that seemingly never-to-be-forgotten day, 16 June 1487, at Stoke in Nottinghamshire. And it had happened to an excessively dangerous degree. But, curiously, English historians do appear to neglect the importance, and even the significance, of the Battle of Stoke, and, indeed, even the fact that it ever took place. That is typical of English attitudes both to their own history, and to matters connected with Ireland.

And Stoke was not all. Henry VII was still not strong enough to deal with the Earl of Kildare, or to neutralize the Irish threat from that source. A new conspiracy arose. Four years after the Battle of Stoke, another nicely spoken, and well-dressed, boy, seventeen years of age, arrived in the south of Ireland. He was Perkin Warbeck, a boy of humble Flemish origin. From his deportment, the Irish assumed him to be a person of importance. They became convinced that he was one of the Princes in the Tower, Richard Duke of York, a Yorkist with impeccable claims to the throne of England, and they launched him on his campaign to claim the throne.

He returned to the continent and there received support from the meddling Margaret, Duchess of Burgundy, and also from the Holy Roman Empire. He was aided, too, by the Scottish court. But, this time, the great Earl of Kildare was wary, and Warbeck did not get the hoped-for weight of Irish support. But, that external powers and forces hostile to England thought Ireland a ripe base for their conspiracies against England is evident from the fact that Warbeck returned there twice during the following six years, seeking support. England had every reason to judge that Ireland posed a major threat to her integrity and her security.

Perkin Warbeck is a remarkable example of a singularly psychologically, or psychiatrically, aberrant person. He was a boy of no social standing employed in the silk trade. He knew himself to be an impostor. Everyone else knew him to be an impostor. Yet for years he not only pertinaciously pursued his totally unrealizable aim to make himself King of England, but also bamboozled some of the courts of Europe into giving him some support. The King of Scotland even gave him his own cousin in marriage. After reverses such as the later Irish refusals of support, what sort of irrepressible megalomania caused him to land in England, proclaim himself King Richard IV and, with totally inadequate forces, challenge the might of England with the inevitable consequence at the end of it all – a dangle at Tyburn? He was not struggling in some worthy cause. He did not sacrifice himself to put some wrong to right. It seems to have been none other than a sustained manic episode. John Ford, the seventeenth century lawyer and dramatist, wrote a play in 1634, 'The Chronicle History of Perkin Warbeck', in which he portrayed Warbeck as a dazzling figure who showed weaknesses at moments of crisis.

But in the world at large much greater things for both England and Ireland were afoot. At the very end of the thirteen hundreds, the fourteenth century, Western Europe was jerked out of a condition of effete dogmatism by some new, imaginative and unconventional thinkers, who sparked off an explosion of creative energy and change. In that respect the fifteenth and sixteenth centuries can be compared to our own experience of the nineteenth and twentieth centuries. Renaissance creative art and architecture are familiar to all, and survive on a breath-taking scale that we still cannot digest in a life-time. Leonardo da Vinci, whose life bridged the fifteenth and sixteenth centuries, epitomized the whole period in his personal range of abilities, gifts, skills and interests. There was nothing that did not excite his curiosity, and he foresaw centuries of development in science, engineering and medicine; aircraft, submarines, the steamship are a few examples. But it is ships, rather than Renaissance achievements as a whole that are important in the context of Ireland.

Thus, if the steamship did not come in Leonardo's, or in Renaissance, times, there was nevertheless a maritime invention, or development, in the fourteen hundreds, the fifteenth century, which was the most important of all Renaissance creations, and possibly the most fateful in the history of mankind. From it has flowed everything that has most affected the life of social man throughout the world during the past five centuries – the three-masted, or ocean-going, ship with its ingenious rigging and steering gear.

The Chinese had had three-masted junks at an earlier date, but they did not have the flexibility of sails, rigging and steering of these new European ships. Hitherto, in the Indo-European world, less sophisticated ships had been the general rule. They could not carry enough sail to drive large and well-decked ships. With such ships, isolated distant ocean journeys had been made, for instance by the ancient Greeks as far as the Azores and Iceland, but regular shipping and commerce was not possible beyond narrow and coastal water.

But now, for the first time, the new ocean-going ship, together with navigational aids that were simultaneously developed, gave man command of all the broad waters of the earth, even if journeys remained hazardous until the invention of the chronometer, in the eighteenth century, permitted the accurate plotting of position. With those new ships, world-wide trade began. Sea-power became dominant. The balance of world power, despite the menace of the Ottoman Turks, shifted dramatically from the Mediterranean and Middle East area – where it had been centred for millennia – to the Atlantic. The maritime nations of Western Europe, not the great land powers of old, became supreme. Sea-linked maritime empires began to be founded. Hitherto unknown lands, people, cultures, animals, foods and a host of other novelties were discovered by Europeans. Diverse ethnic and cultural influences began to change societies, sometimes catastrophically, sometimes beneficially. The almost empty continents of America and Australia were in due course to be peopled by European immigrants whose dynamism caused the resources of those great lands to add enormously to the momentum and the wealth of the emerging western material civilization that was to become the dominant force in the world.

Is it too much to claim that the ocean-going sailing ship was man's most momentous invention?

In the same decade in which Perkin Warbeck met his end at Tyburn, Christopher Columbus sailed the Atlantic Ocean and discovered the Caribbean Islands, in 1492, and opened the way to the Americas. The real importance of his exploit was not his momentous voyage, or his discovery of America. That had probably been accomplished centuries before. The Vinland Saga almost certainly describes a European landing in America. The recent intrepid voyage of the 'Brendan' in which my nephew, Arthur Magan, was a crew-member, almost certainly confirms the supposition that Irish navigators reached America a thousand years ago. The importance of Columbus's voyage was that, with the new ships, it was not just a freak journey, but one that could now be repeated over and over again. The oceans were mastered. Five years later, in 1497, Vasco Da Gama rounded the Cape of Good Hope and opened up the sea route to India; and in the same year John Cabot sailed from Bristol with his sons and discovered Nova Scotia, and in the following year made another voyage, this time to Labrador.

Those events were central to England's attitude to Ireland. The era of Western European maritime imperialism had begun. Sea-power immediately assumed an importance that it never had before. It became a paramount military preoccupation. An immediate consequence of ocean exploration was that Spain grew into a great, rich and menacing imperial power. And it was not long before England became acutely conscious of the threat, and of the relationship of Ireland to it.

From that time on, it was of the highest importance to the security of England that her western sea routes should be kept open. And to that end it was crucial that Ireland should neither fall into the hands of a hostile power, nor be allied to any such power, who could use her to stand athwart vital English lines of maritime communication.

The consequences for Ireland were to be her tragic fate in the coming centuries. A great wave in the groundswell of history was about to engulf her, and it would be more than three centuries before it began to wash back from her shores with the ending of the Napoleonic Wars – an historic wave that might never have been had not the Norman invasion of Ireland prevented all possibility of Ireland, like England, becoming a nation-state in the fifteenth century.

The Irish may nurse their grievances, and lament and keen. It is ever their wont to lament and keen. The English may forget. It is ever their custom to forget. And they may wish that the Irish would as often forget. But both attitudes are irrelevant. What was now about to happen was not England's fault, nor Ireland's fault. The dilemma in which the coming of the ocean-going sailing ships placed both countries was the cause. In the circumstances, what came to pass was absolutely inevitable. Nothing could have prevented it or altered its essentials. The details might have been different, but the overall consequences for Ireland of the new Western European maritime-dominated world would have been the same. Ireland's geographical position astride the western approaches to Europe, and her weakness by comparison with the greater European powers, put it beyond all doubt that one or other of them would seek to dominate her and to control those vital sea routes. And the power whose interests were most at stake, and the one most advantageously situated to achieve a dominant position in Ireland, was Tudor England.

CHAPTER 9

Tudor Reaction to the Irish Threat

WHEN HENRY VII DIED in 1509, his son and successor, Henry VIII, though only eighteen years of age, had, before long, to face the problems inherent in the new situation in Western Europe.

Henry VII had not succeeded in neutralizing the Geraldines in Ireland. Garret More, the great Earl of Kildare, was still alive, and lived for another four years, dying in 1513. Henry VIII then set about gaining the compliance of his son, Garret Oge – Gerald the Younger – to the English Crown. When conciliatory and peaceful political and administrative moves failed to achieve their purpose, Henry VIII reluctantly resorted to armed force. He imported heavy siege artillery into Ireland and reduced the great Geraldine stronghold of the Pale, Maynooth Castle.

By that time Garret Oge's son, known as 'Silken Thomas', 10th Earl of Kildare, had succeeded as head of the House of Geraldine. He was not at Maynooth during the siege, being away in Connaught seeking military assistance. One of his supporters was an O'Conor. Silken Thomas was later captured and, together with his five uncles, taken to England. All six men were lodged in The Tower of London, treated abominably, and cruelly executed in public a year later by being hanged, drawn and quartered. Thus was the House of Geraldine not just neutralized, but effectively liquidated, the heir to the earldom of Kildare being an eleven-year-old boy lying ill of smallpox at that time.

That was the first taste of suffering in store for the Irish nobility, the Irish chieftains, and the Irish people. Throughout the next three centuries, our sympathies cannot but be with the Irish in their agony. But that must not blind us to the dilemma of the English, among whom Cromwell alone, of the rulers of England, fought the Irish with relish.

The Tudors did not want to fight in Ireland. They did not want the distraction. They were much too preoccupied, first in the early part of Henry VIII's reign with their own European ambitions, and then with the dangers threatening them direct from Europe, and from Europe through Scotland. And they did not want the drain of Irish wars on their treasuries, which they could ill afford. But they could not neglect the danger which Ireland posed. Early in Henry VIII's reign there were plottings between both the French and the Spanish and the Irish.

By the time that the Geraldines had been suppressed, Henry VIII had two issues to settle in Ireland. He had by then divorced his first wife, Catherine of Aragon, with the resultant rift with the Papacy which had caused him to demand that the Church recognize him as its supreme head within his Realm. In addition, therefore, to the need to bring the baronies and chiefdoms of Ireland under his absolute political authority and allegiance, he had also to persuade the Church in Ireland to acknowledge his supremacy in place of the Pope.

He neither wished for, nor could afford, wars in Ireland. His policy once again was to use conciliatory means, which were surprisingly successful. The Irish nobility and chieftains showed a remarkable ready willingness to give him their allegiance on the generous terms he offered which, as had been the case in England, were well larded with substantial grants of land from dispossessed monasteries; and Henry VIII formally took upon himself the title of 'King of Ireland'. The bishops, too, were not unwilling to transfer their allegiance from the Pope to himself.

But those gains proved transitory. There was an inherent flaw in the internal politics of Ireland. Because the English Crown had never been strong enough to take Henry II's Norman invasion to its logical conclusion of incorporating Ireland fully within the Realm, and because, so long as England claimed suzerainty over Ireland, Ireland could not spontaneously evolve a central political authority of her own, the country had been condemned to an eternal state of internal strife with warlords great and small constantly manoeuvring against each other either to defend what they had, or to increase their power. Thus, although they may have been prepared to swear fealty to Henry VIII, their own internecine strife with each other was bound to continue unless England could by force of arms suppress the warlordism and hold down the country militarily in a state of peace. And the constant danger of the warlordism was either that the chiefs and barons would themselves seek help from England's continental enemies, and thus allow them a footing in Ireland, or that, as in the case of the Burgundians at the Battle of Stoke, continental powers would on their own account proffer assistance to the Irish.

The logic of this situation could only be that nothing short of conquest, and complete administrative control by England of all Ireland, could ensure that England's enemies would not get a foothold there.

The attempt to get the Church in Ireland to accept the supremacy of the English Crown also failed in the end. Henry VIII was succeeded in 1547 by his son by his third wife, Jane Seymour – Edward VI, a boy of ten years of age, who reigned for only six years. During his reign the reformation of the church took place, and the Book of Common Prayer in English became central to the liturgy in place of the Latin mass. But Irish was the language of Ireland, and the Irish were not prepared to accept the Book of Common Prayer in English, nor to give up the mass. They were not, therefore, prepared to accept the liturgy of the Reformed Church. Neither the Prayer Book nor the Bible was translated into Irish until some years later, but it was then too late; the Church in Ireland was firmly back in the arms of Rome and wedded loyally to the old liturgy. That was the moment, and the cause, of the calamitous religious division which has since proved such a formidable obstacle between the North and South of Ireland.

Following the failure of Henry VII's initiatives, the policy adopted by England and pursued for the next century and a half by the Tudor monarchs, the Stuarts, and by Cromwell, and including the Catholic queen 'Bloody' Mary, Catherine of Aragon's daughter, who succeeded Edward VI in 1553, was one that had been suggested by one of Henry VIII's representatives in Ireland, the Earl of Surrey. Essentially it was a policy of attrition which, from time to time involved limited military campaigns. The plan was that section by section the disloyal chiefs, noblemen, gentry, and people of Ireland were to be dispossessed of their lands, which were to be re-settled by loyal Englishmen.

It was in essence no different from the policy that had been followed since the arrival of the Normans. The aim was not, and never had been, to proselytize the Irish, and reform them on English lines, but to segregate them and hold them down under strong settlers, and keep them in the status of second-class citizens unworthy of sharing in the civilities of English-style life. But it was a policy that had never worked. All that had happened was that the bulk of the settlers had rapidly 'gone native'. But, pursued more and more vigorously in Tudor and later times, it was to become a very harsh policy. At its worst, it loosed on Ireland land-hungry, ruthless adventurers, who caused untold sufferings to the native people of Ireland. During the hundred and fifty years of its spasmodic implementation, thousands of Irish died.

The worst excesses were committed in Elizabeth's reign, in the last quarter of the sixteenth century. In some cases the Irish were hideously and cruelly slaughtered; men, women, children and infants; and many others were driven into forests to die of starvation. And not a few settlers succumbed to murderous assaults in retaliation by the Irish.

Did the English suffer qualms of conscience? Probably not, except for the few who knew the Irish intimately, and those on the spot who were horrified by the dreadful sights they witnessed. Ireland was, in the eyes of the ordinary Englishman, a remote, incomprehensible land of savages hardly better than the wild beasts of the soaking forests among which they dwelt. By some it was even considered meritorious to do away with an Irishman, comparable to the extermination of vermin. At best they were seen as sub-human. In an age when compassion was a rare indulgence, no pity was to be wasted on the fate of primitive savages. But compassionate accounts survive, written by civilized people who saw at first hand the consequences of English policies.

On what scale was this slaughter? It is not now possible to compute. There is reason enough for the emotional quality of some of the accounts of it, which, however, may well distort the real facts. But very large figures have come down to us. There is a record of no less than 30,000 people starved to death in a single period of six months in the province of Munster in 1582, in which province also more than half a million acres of land are said to have been taken from their owners and given to English settlers.

The wars, as conducted by General Mountjoy and a number of other English commanders, are said to have been literally wars of extermination. The devastations were not evenly spread, and people moved about so relatively little that to be witness to the excesses in a comparatively small area might lead an observer to suppose that the whole country was in like plight. The most rebellious parts of Ireland, Munster and Ulster, suffered most, as did those unfortunate enough to come under the most ruthless commanders.

If 100,000 people died, that is a dreadful tally, but, looked at factually, it would have been, in the result, decimation, not extermination. And it has to be remembered that this was in the nature of a terrible visitation upon the children unto the third and fourth generation for the sins of the fathers who had sought to overthrow the throne of England at Stoke. Also, to be fair, it must be said that much of what was done, was done by Irish Catholic soldiers in the service of English commanders. War is a horrible business, and remains no less so as practised by 'civilized' nations today.

Furthermore, the English policy in Ireland was one which did not find general disapproval in that age of European expansionism. It was the policy adopted in order to people the Americas with European stock, one in which the Irish themselves joined vigorously. The 'wicked' Red Indians were driven from their North American lands. South American settlers were paid so much a head for liquidated Patagonians. It was the policy that was to drive the Bushmen and the Hottentots from their homelands in South Africa; to dispossess the Aborigines of Australia, and so on around the world, even to our own times when the rare tribes of the Amazon basin are being sacrificed for forest clearance to create more cattle ranches for the descendants of European settlers.

Indeed, William Lecky, the nineteenth century writer of Irish history, goes so far as to say that one of the principal causes for the adoption of this policy in Ireland was that the spirit of oversea adventure that was abroad at that time made Ireland, so close to England, a particularly tempting hunting-ground for get-rich-quick piratical English gentlemen who could legitimately, or by an easy manipulation of the laws, lay hands on great tracts of fertile country in Ireland which would bring them to opulence in a very few years.

Lecky was writing at the end of the nineteenth century when England had not been under foreign threat for nearly a century. Had he been writing half a century later, after England had had to fight to the very limit for survival in two world wars, he would have been more conscious that Tudor and Stuart piracy in Ireland was not an end in itself, but simply one means that was to hand for securing the safety of the English Realm against the threat that Ireland constituted.

Given the least opportunity by the unfolding pages of history, Queen Elizabeth would doubtless have followed a different course. She was a traditionalist. She hated change. She worked immensely hard, but she worked to contrive, whenever possible, to do nothing. Action was dangerous. 'Prevaricate,' might have been her motto. She was history's greatest master of the art of indecision. She would have seen more good than harm, more safety than danger, in leaving the Irish chiefs alone to pursue their own kind of lives, had there not been the mighty third force – the threat of Spanish involvement with the Catholic Irish – which could not be ignored.

She also abhorred violence. She loathed war, and it meant expense she could not afford, because, in so far as she could, she paid for these things from her own resources, rather than tax her people to the point of setting them murmuring with discontent. Had she not often told her Council, 'No war, my Lords'? And had not her great and wily Secretary of State, Will Cecil, at the beginning of her reign, pronounced: 'A realm gains more by a year's peace than by ten years of war'?

Yet, save for Cromwell, Elizabeth's name is execrated in Ireland above all others for the excesses committed against the Irish during her reign. But the fact is that the mounting threat from Europe made it imperative to neutralize the danger of Ireland by whatsoever means. And if the gentlemen of England, following her father's policy, would do it piecemeal from their own resources, too many questions could hardly be asked about the means employed. And some of the most prominent gentlemen of England were there. Sir Walter Raleigh, for instance, carved out an Irish estate for himself, as did the poet Edmund Spenser, writer of the 'Faerie Queene'. And the threat to England, against which those measures seemed so necessary, was not illusory. The Armada did sail. It did reach the shores of Britain. And its purpose was no less than the conquest of the English Realm. It was a moment no less fraught with danger for the 'Sceptr'd Isle' than the Battle of Britain three hundred and fifty years later.

Nor was the Armada the end of it. 'No war, my Lords!' But it is nevertheless a crowning irony that it fell to the troops of Elizabeth the pacifist, Elizabeth the traditionalist, not merely to fight a series of wars in Ireland during the latter part of her reign, which reduced the country to near ruin, but indeed to win the most decisive battle in Irish history, the Battle of Kinsale, and thereby to put an end for ever to the two thousand year long period of dynastic aristocratic rule in Ireland, and to usher in, in its place, the era of British colonial administration. True it would be nearly another century before it could be consolidated, but that was the beginning.

Despite their Armada defeat, Spain did try again. This time by the back door. And they did land a force in Ireland. And on Christmas Eve, 1601, a British force joined battle with them and their Irish allies at Kinsale, on the south coast of Ireland, and decisively defeated them in half-an-hour. A little over a year later Elizabeth was dead. The Tudor period was at an end. The brilliant, if at times erratic, Tudors were no more.

That was how Ireland appeared to Tudor England, but now we must return across the water, and go back to the family, and see what Ireland really was like for them at the time of Elizabeth's death, the beginning of the seventeenth century, the beginning of the Stuart monarchs, the time when Sir Oliver St John wrote his report on Connaught.

We must take that well-worn route across the Irish Sea with its sights and sounds – and smells – so familiar to generations of Irish people. To get the full flavour, the journey must even now be by sea, not by air.

It is early morning after a rough night, and as we approach Dublin Bay we stand on deck watching the Hill of Howth loom nearer, while the clouds lie low on the Wicklow Mountains. The wind has dropped. The air is mild and soft. It is raining gently. And we know that we shall not have been five minutes ashore before, in contrast to the dismal drizzle of the grey morning, we shall have been treated to an excruciatingly droll piece of original epigrammatic eloquence, out of an absolutely straight, if stubbly, face, from under a battered hat, and a strong Dublin accent. And that first renewed encounter causes the heart of the exiled Irishman to sing, or sigh, with the Scottish bard: 'This is my own, my native land'; whether we be savages or no.

Old Irish Family
Life in the Early
Days of English
Colonization in
the First Half of
the Seventeenth
Century

Humphry Magan (c.1590) and his Wife Anne

IRELAND IS A TRADITIONALLY hospitable country. 'Come in, now. You're very welcome. Make yourself at home.' Those are familiar Irish greetings. And they are meant.

Come in, then, please; everyone, members of the family, friends and acquaintances, strangers; into our old Irish home, where there has always been a welcome for everybody, and share our hearth, our life, its ups and its downs, its good and its bad, during the coming four hundred years of this story. In particular, meet Humphry Magan, and his wife, Anne, and their children and grandchildren, and they will give you a glimpse of Irish life from within.

1588 was the year of the Armada. About then, Humphry Magan was born. He is the first bearer of the Magan name, descending from the old O'Conor and MacDermot Celtic Connaught clan, whose identity is firmly established, although the family had separated from the House of MacDermot-Roe a century earlier.

His family home was Emoe in the parish of Ballymore, a very small town in Co. Westmeath, Ireland. Emoe was anciently known as Umma-More, and I shall call it Umma-More. You will not find it a very comfortable place, but you will receive a full measure of all the warmth and hospitality it can offer.

Humphry Magan was a man of substance. Living in a rural, pastoral area of Ireland, that means that he owned large herds of those small black Irish cattle, flocks of the long-haired sheep, and herds of the Irish horses. He also had access to enough pasture for their grazing, as well as to additional land for corn growing.

I have put it in those terms rather than say that he was a landowner, because his life-style was that of an ancient Irish chieftain, rather than of an English-type landed gentleman.

He would also, by right of ancient custom, have had at his command a supply of labour adequate for his work, and to provide an armed force under his leadership to protect both his and their interests in time of need.

Apart from his lineage, we can deduce from marriage details that he was such a man of consequence. He married Anne, daughter of Sir Richard Owen of

Anglesey in Wales, a knight. That he could not have done had he not been of the same social status. Wealth was inseparable from knighthood.

The marriages of his children confirm that status. Of the three children whose records have survived, the eldest son, Richard Magan the Elder, who later succeeded his father at Umma-More, married Catherine, daughter of Oliver D'Alton of Westmeath. The D'Alton family was descended from Sir Walter D'Alton, a knight who joined Earl Strongbow in the invasion of Ireland, and whose only son, Philip D'Alton, acquired large possessions and built castles in Westmeath. The D'Altons, at the time of which I am writing, were still a local leading family, and lived at Mullaghmeehan, a mile north-east of Umma-More.

Humphry Magan's second child, Anne, married Henry White. He was also of Ballymore. And he, too, can be assumed to have been a landowner, for he was transplanted by Cromwell, a penalty particularly applicable to those who had lands of which they could be dispossessed. Furthermore, when Anne died, Henry White also married a D'Alton as his second wife, confirming that that was his social stratum.

The third child of Humphry and Anne Magan was Morgan Magan the Elder, later of Cloney, Co. Westmeath. It is from him that the Magans of today are descended, his elder brother Richard's line having died out.

There is thus evidence enough that Humphry Magan was a local magnate, and very likely of considerable substance. But, despite the turbulent times into which he was born, and the trials and tribulations that were to come, the family's greatest material prosperity was still in the future. During the following three centuries, they were to become increasingly large landowners in the Counties Westmeath, Longford, Roscommon, Meath, Kildare, Dublin, and possibly elsewhere. At the height of their fortunes they owned upwards of twenty thousand acres – perhaps nearer thirty thousand – the best grasslands in Ireland. It used to be said that they could drove their cattle on the hoof from Ballinasloe in Co. Galway to the Dublin market, more than a hundred miles distant, and stop them on their own land each night.

Humphry Magan's circumstances as a chieftainly Irishman, allied by significant marriages both to mainland Britain, through his wife, and to powerful Norman-Irish and Anglo-Irish families through his children, illustrates something of the enormously diverse influences that existed side by side, and in a variety of amalgams, in the upper strata of Irish life at the time. But the bedrock of Ireland remained the mass of the people, with whom the great lived cheek by jowl, since it was a rural, and not an urban, society, and with whom also they fostered their children, and who enormously influenced the cultural background of everyone great and mean. The people remained essentially the descendants of the ancient Picts who had continued to survive all the great waves of history that had rolled over them.

Within that social complex, Humphry Magan has to be seen as a person of natural, and wholly unselfconsciously aristocratic, character and cast of mind.

The assumptions underlying his place in society needed no intellectual justification. They were unquestioned. They were eternal. They stemmed not merely from the beginning of time, but from those mythological, mysterious and magical origins in the omnipotent spirit world. No other order of society, no other place in society, had ever been conceivable for a man so descended, ever since those far-off Celtic days, millennia ago, in Central Europe, and perhaps, even earlier, somewhere still further to the East.

The Celtic dynastic structure in Ireland can properly be termed an aristocratic system, and in that sense Humphry Magan was an aristocrat, a member of a closed oligarchy. To speak of such an aristocrat is to distinguish a particular kind of high-born person from the remainder of that society.

We may be prone to think of an aristocrat as a person of special grace, elegance, style, refinement and even magnificence. Humphry Magan may have had all, or some, or none, of such attributes. But that is not at all the essence of his case. Aristocracy in the sense in which the term is here used is concerned not with demeanour, manners or outward trappings, although those were not wholly divorced from it, but essentially with attitudes of mind about himself, both on the part of the individual aristocrat himself, and of the people in general.

The populace as a whole were born into a world of unquestioning acceptance of the inborn supremacy of an hereditary group of leading families to which they could never themselves aspire to belong. Only through birth could anyone enter the circle from which rulers could be elected.

For the aristocrat himself, to be a member of that high-born class was to come into the world predestined, from the first moment of comprehension, to enjoy the absolute and certain knowledge that it was part of the pre-ordained order of things that his birthright was an inalienable God-given and permanent superiority over the commonalty of the people, and nothing could ever erase that certainty of his status from his mind.

But he in no way resembled a Gainsborough-type eighteenth-century 'my lord', depicted in his deer park against the background of his Palladian mansion. The family was to come to that, but not till much later. That sort of man was frequently more plutocrat than aristocrat. He had begun to emerge in England shortly before Humphry Magan was born, but not yet in Ireland. Will Cecil, Queen Elizabeth's Secretary of State, had spotted the trend. To him is credited the remark that, 'gentility is nothing but ancient riches', adding under his breath, 'and they need not be very ancient'.

Indeed, in that sense, England had for centuries been more democratic than Ireland. Two hundred years earlier it was the case that, 'merchants became knights, and knights became merchants', but that was more a cheapening of knighthood than a raising of the status of merchants. That is not to denigrate the English aristocracy and certainly not in contrast to the Irish chiefs.

Although, from the sixteenth century onwards, English aristocrats may have been technically more plutocratic than aristocratic, their life-style was on a scale of magnificence much more aristocratic than that of the Irish chieftains. The difference between a technical aristocracy and a technical plutocracy is that aristocracy depends absolutely on lineage; plutocracy depends largely on wealth.

But ancient, or new, and unlike England, riches were not enough, indeed were wholly unavailing, in Ireland to admit you to the ranks of the aristocracy. Without adequate wealth for your security, and to enable you to fulfil your obligations, your successors inevitably melted into the ranks of the peasantry. But, given that you had wealth, then the essence of aristocracy in Ireland was lineage, not grandeur; an attitude of mind, not deportment, demeanour or possessions; and Humphry Magan, descended as he was, held the necessary passport to the ranks of that aristocracy.

How the Magans came to be in Westmeath we do not know, and need hardly conjecture – perhaps as a result of some successful marriage coup; perhaps part of some former O'Conor lands, going back centuries to the great days of Tara, which was not far away. At all events, living where he did, Humphry Magan's early life was spent just outside that small Anglicized territory of the Pale where the fluctuating fortunes of English rule had endured for four hundred years.

In the time of his Elizabethan boyhood, the country was greatly disturbed by the mounting Tudor efforts to impose their will on Ireland, and the consequential Irish resistance to the English onslaughts. At best it must have been a time of frequent, if not constant, anxiety for the family, even if it was mainly concerned to keep itself out of trouble. And whether by good fortune, or prudent conduct, or both, it did indeed succeed in safeguarding its interests. Otherwise, Humphry Magan could hardly have been so well endowed as he was.

After the Battle of Kinsale, in 1601, and the death of Queen Elizabeth, and although Ulster continued to hold out against the English, more peaceful times, both internationally, and internally in Ireland, inspired, in the reign of her successor, James I, a temporary moderation of English policy towards the Irish – except in Ulster. The middle years of Humphry Magan's life were, therefore, lived in comparatively tranquil times in his part of Ireland. But we must take note of what happened in Ulster, as it was destined thereafter to affect the whole of Irish history, and the fortunes of every Irish family, even to this day.

After the Battle of Kinsale, Ulster remained the most recalcitrantly Irish part of Ireland, and the English continued to exert such pressure there that six years later, in 1607, resistance collapsed. Nearly a hundred chieftains fled abroad, leaving their lands to be confiscated. That event has become known to history romantically as, 'The Flight of the Earls' – the two principal chieftains to flee being Hugh O'Neill, Earl of Tyrone, and Rory O'Donnell, Earl of Tyrconnell. That was the moment when one of the great waves in Irish history finally ebbed back and disappeared once more into the ocean of time. It was the very last moment of the two thousand years of Gaelic dynastic clan government in Ireland.

And England immediately began to consolidate the achievement.

Ulster was annexed to the Crown, and what has come to be known as 'Plantation' was at once put in hand. The confiscation was on a vast scale. Three and three-quarter million acres were annexed to the Crown.

Very large areas of what is now Ulster, and of some of the surrounding counties, were assigned either to English nobility and large landowners, or to what was in effect a London trading consortium – whose influence caused the old Irish port of Derry to be renamed Londonderry. The conditions on which those grants of land were given made it disadvantageous to those who received them to grant leases to Irish tenants. The result was a flood of mainly northern English Protestant, and Scottish Presbyterian, land-hungry immigrant tenants who settled in Northern Ireland during the following few decades. This was what came to be known as 'The Plantation'. The Scots were largely concentrated in the north-eastern counties; the English in central Ulster. They occupied the best lands in the province. The native Irish had to withdraw to the marginal hill and bog lands. And they are there to this day; and it is still a major grievance with them. The Irish question is not only one of history and long memories. It is also one of enduring fact and substance.

The Plantation was entirely consistent with the policy England had been pursuing for so long of trying to ensure the loyalty of Ireland by dispossessing the Irish, and re-settling the country with loyal subjects from across the water. But it had hitherto never been tried on such a scale. It is true that in the middle of the previous century, in the reign of Queen Mary, even though she was Roman Catholic, a major settlement had been attempted in two adjacent areas of central Ireland. In honour of Mary, and of her husband, Philip of Spain, those areas were named the Queen's County and the King's County, and their principal towns became Maryborough, and Philipstown. But there were differences not only in scale, but also in character, between that settlement and the Ulster Plantation.

The Marian settlement, like all others prior to the Plantation, although it might have resulted in the transfer to settlers of substantial areas of land, did not involve large numbers of people. The settlers were for the most part a limited number of gentry, or would-be gentry. They displaced the Irish chiefs. The peasantry and small tenantry might suffer, and sometimes did so apallingly, but were not themselves displaced by English of the same class.

The Ulster Plantation was different. A Protestant peasant, or small farmer, tenant class flocked in in large numbers from across the water, displacing the Irish tenantry and peasantry. The gentlemen settlers of former times, if they were to survive, had had to settle down and live among the Irish, and so had become absorbed and integrated. The Ulster Plantation created, and then filled, a vacuum in which few Irish were left in certain areas. There were not enough Irish with whom the settlers could integrate. This was the perfect solution from the English point of view. A settlement of a large number of British people who would never go native, and whose allegiance could therefore be relied upon indefinitely.

Paradoxically, unlike the English settlers, rapidly and consistently going native further south, the people of the Ulster Plantation were ethnically of the same stock as the Irish; a mixture of ancient Irish and later Celtic origin, many of whose forebears had in earlier times migrated from Ireland to Scotland and to the English border country. Nevertheless they were, and were destined to remain, culturally distinguished from the native Irish. Their Protestantism was destined to become the badge of their allegiance to the English Crown.

The Ulster Plantation occurred when Humphry Magan was a young man. Thereafter, the whole of Ireland enjoyed the enforced relative tranquillity that elsewhere in the country had followed the English victory at Kinsale. He thus grew to maturity at a time when, living as near to Dublin, the centre of English authority, as he did, and in conditions which were not discouraging to an Irish gentleman to come to terms with the new situation, a sensible man, which we may suppose him to have been, would not have found too much difficulty in accommodating himself to English rule, so long as it remained more or less benign, and left him in reasonable peace.

Given that those were his probable general circumstances, it is possible to reconstruct at least an outline of the man himself. He was a Roman Catholic. He was at least bilingual. His first language was Irish. He was also fluent in English. He was literate in both languages, and very likely also spoke and wrote Latin. Latin had been quite commonly known in Ireland in the sixteenth century, and by women as well as men. Humphry must also have known gallimaufry, a pidgin language which was a mixture of English and Irish. Possibly he also knew French.

His social position was such that he would not have been ill at ease in the viceregal court circles at the seat of government in Dublin. His manners and his Irish accent might have been somewhat provincial, but provincial manners and accents were at that time common enough even among the peerage of England. He was, therefore, in the aristocratic Irish tradition, a man of two cultures. His mother culture was old Irish; but he was no less at home in the Dublin version of English culture. From his time onwards, the gentry of Ireland were all nurtured in that twin culture, though the emphasis was soon to shift from dominance of Irish modes to dominance of English influences. Of a high-born type of person living simultaneously in more than one culture there are many contemporary parallels. Certainly until the recent revolution in Persia, men like the chiefs of my acquaintance of the Bakhtiari tribe lived for part of the year as tribesmen carrying on the nomadic life which had changed hardly at all in three thousand five hundred years or more. In their town houses in the lovely city of Isphahan, they had a life-style of an urban Persian gentleman. In their Teheran houses, they became modern cosmopolitan polished aristocrats. And from there they would jet to Zurich or Paris to have a tooth stopped, or for some more agreeable assignment. And much nearer home we have our own example. The Scottish clans have their Celtic origins in Ireland, and there is a similarity in the relationship that the chiefs of both countries developed with England.

Within my lifetime – and perhaps even to this day – there have been Scottish lairds who were bi-lingual in Gaelic and English, and wholly at home in their ancient clan relationships. They spoke two types of English – the Scottish vernacular with their shepherds and ghillies, and that of the educated upper-class English when sipping port in their London clubs. Their deportment could be indistinguishably English at the boardroom table in London, and no less Scottish at the board meeting in Aberdeen.

With somewhat rougher edges – edges were rougher everywhere – that, too, was the general pattern of the seventeenth century Irish chief's accommodation to the fact that he had to come to terms with England's presence and influence.

Humphry Magan's wife, Anne, would also have been multi-lingual. Welsh would have been her first language. Irish would therefore have caused her no difficulty. Her English would have been fluent. And, like Humphry, she very likely knew Latin and French, and was literate in all her languages. Her father, Sir Richard Owen, was probably a younger son of Sir Hugh Owen Bart., of Anglesey, by his second wife Lucy, daughter of Henry Percy, 8th Earl of Northumberland, through whom, therefore, we receive into our veins a dash of the blood of Hotspur, Harry, 2nd Earl of Percy, debonair and fiery soldier, hero of Shakespeare's play, Henry IV Part I. The name Percy has been used frequently in the family as a Christian name.

Part of the innocent fun of genealogy is the blood relationships or connections we discover with interesting, not to say notorious, historical people. If people can trace their forebears back far enough, and draw their pedigrees widely enough, they do not have to be of great and noble lineage to discover at least a few family members of more than passing interest. It has been said, for instance, that a quarter of the population of England should be able to trace its descent from Edward III!

Humphry Magan's wife, Anne, brought us also a dash of Welsh chieftainly blood. Her family, the Owens of Anglesey, were descended from the ancient Lord of Menai, founder of 'a noble tribe' of North Wales and Powys, from whom descended Roderic the Great, King of all Wales in the ninth century AD.

We have no portraits of Humphry and Anne. Sixteenth and early seventeenth century Irish portraits are rare. The Irish were not yet leading that kind of life, except some of the great Anglo-Irish nobility – Garet Oge, 9th Earl of Kildare, was painted in London by Hans Holbein. We can, nevertheless, draw some picture of Humphry and Anne in our minds. We know the kinds of clothes they wore.

At home in Umma-More, they would have worn Irish dress. It had changed very little in two thousand years, unlike English and Western European dress which had in the fourteenth century entered a phase of wildly, and extravagantly, changing fashion which has not yet burnt itself out even today.

We must not suppose that Irish dress of the early seventeenth century looked at all like that of a smart modern Irish pipe band. The ancient Irish did not wear a kilt. It was an eighteenth century modification of the lower half of the Scottish plaid. Nor did the Irish wear a sporran, or a plaid across the shoulder.

Traditionally, old Irish dress for males consisted of four principal garments. Two of them were of Eurasian origin from the heartlands of the Indo-European civilization and were brought to Ireland from the Mediterranean – from Spain – by the Celts. They were the dress of the Celtic aristocracy.

The other two garments were older Pictish dress. They had their very early origin in the forests of northern Europe, whence the Pictish people came to Ireland. They formed the dress of the lower orders in Celtic Ireland. But, by the time of Humphry and Anne, all four garments could be worn by anyone, great or mean.

The two Celtic garments were loose fitting, reflecting their origin in warmer climates. One was a long saffron linen shirt or tunic, and was the normal foundation garment for both men and women. It was a traditional ancient garment of two simple pieces of cloth sewn together with a hole for the head, and holes, or sleeves, for the arms. It corresponds to the Egyptian gallibeah of today – and is the ancestor of the modern 'T' shirt.

The other Celtic garment was the Irish mantle, a version of the simple Eurasian rectangular piece of cloth which formed the Roman toga, and the Indian dhoti and sari of today. The Irish mantle was essentially a blanket, heavy for winter, light-weight for summer, worn as a cape, and of a variety of distinguished colours, often with a border of a contrasting colour. Mantles were worn over all other dress, and were obligatory because it was unbecoming to appear in public without a long garment – and imprudent, no doubt, to risk being caught out at night without a blanket.

It is of some interest that the Scottish plaid originated, like the Irish mantle, in the Eurasian rectangular piece of cloth, but it was not brought to Scotland by the Celts. It was the old Irish version of the toga, pinched from the Roman frontier sentries.

The two traditionally Irish male garments were tight-fitting woollen trews and jackets, worn over the saffron shirt; clothing which had evolved for the cold northern European forest climate. Trews or trousers were worn by all northern 'barbarians' whom the Romans encountered.

Shoes, called 'brogues', were worn, sometimes elaborately cobbled, more often of simple rawhide. Hats were not usually worn, but a round feathered peakless cap was an occasional garment.

Knocking about, therefore, in his mainly outdoor life, Humphry would, according to season and occasion, have worn either a saffron linen tunic, belted at the waist, together with a mantle, and brogues on his feet, or a saffron shirt, trews and mantle, perhaps sometimes with the addition of a jacket. Occasionally he might have added the feathered cap.

There was a smart elaboration of the male garments for more formal occasions – 'visiting', for instance; the Irish did much visiting. The shirt would be tucked into the trews. The jacket might be coloured, embossed leather, waisted, with a short flared skirt, and fitted and buttoned to the neck, with a matching conical hat deriving from the ancient Irish egg-shaped battle-helmet – a very smart outfit.

The ladies' informal dress had similar origins. The foundation garment was a saffron linen tunic to the ankles; a jacket with an apron extension below the waist and overall a mantle, usually blue or brown for ordinary occasions. A cap of many folds of pressed linen was worn on the head, perhaps covered with a narrow-brimmed hat out of doors.

More formal evening wear for a lady consisted of beautiful, delicately coloured, simply cut long gowns, girdled and with long tassels. It was worn over a fitted saffron or white linen undergarment; linen folds on the head, covered with a small elegant coloured cap; round the neck a simple cross suspended from a plain black band; much country-made jewelry. The lady's hair 'plaited in a curious manner', as one contemporary English writer recorded, hung down over her back and shoulders.

The saffron garments were dyed from real saffron, the dye from an autumn-flowering crocus (*Crocus sativus*) – Arabic, *zafaran*; Irish, *croch*; Latin, *crocus*; Greek, *krokos*; the cultivators, at, for instance, Saffron Walden, were 'Crokers'. Its importance lay in the belief that it inhibited lice – a significant consideration in times of limited ablutions. Saffron is still grown in quantity in Kashmir, and much prized in India for its therapeutic properties in food.

When visiting Dublin, Humphry and Anne would have worn English dress, partly because Irish dress was illegal under an act of Henry VIII of 1539, and subsequent legislation, though no-one took much notice of that – not even O'Neill and his followers when they called on Queen Elizabeth in London – and partly because the cultural background in Dublin was English rather than Irish. It was the second city in the British Isles, with a population of fifty thousand inhabitants, and with a university and numerous bookshops, coffee-houses and other such meeting places, not unlike London.

Humphry would have been bearded, his moustache twirled and his beard brushed to a parting at his chin. His English dress in his early days would have been like that of Sir Walter Raleigh; later in life like a King Charles cavalier.

If Anne was lucky enough to be young enough to have escaped the lunatic and costly elaborations of Elizabethan fashions – farthingales, vast and complicated ruffs, wildly extravagant jewelled raiment; a physically hampering, and bankrupting nightmare – her clothes would have been in line with the less elaborate and much more comfortable fashions of the period of Queen Henrietta-Maria, Charles I's wife.

CHAPTER 11

Umma-More: the Magan Home

THE DWELLING HOUSE at Umma-More, in which Humphry and Anne Magan lived, is now no more, but it is not difficult to make an imaginary reconstruction of it.

The site is on a small elevation overlooking an area of low-lying boggy ground. It is an isolated place two miles from the small hamlet of Ballymore. The country round about would have been partly wooded, partly scrub grown up on formerly cleared woodland, and, for the rest, open, undulating magnificent grassland. An English traveller who passed through Ballymore in the seventeenth century described it as a beautiful countryside. He clearly much enjoyed his ride that day through Westmeath on his journey westwards.

There would have been no architectural grandeur about the house. We can forget eighteenth century country mansions, stately homes, country houses, or even gentlemen's residences. In rural Ireland there were at that time no gentlemen's domestic houses. In the state of perennial insecurity which had existed for centuries, unprotected gentlemen's houses were too vulnerable. Such houses were built only within the walled protection of Dublin, the few other seaports, and the even fewer small inland towns.

We can look in vain in Ireland for Tudor manor houses. A hundred years earlier, when the end of the Wars of the Roses had brought peace to England, one consequence was the marvellous outpouring of wealth, art and craftsmanship which covered England with glorious domestic Tudor houses. Between 1570 and 1620 more country houses were built in England than in any later period of fifty years. But there is only one Tudor mansion in Ireland, and it is attached to a castle, and even the house itself has some features of a fortress. And that state of affairs continued well into the second half of the seventeenth century.

Just as there are no Tudor houses in rural Ireland, so also, outside the protected towns, are there no Stuart houses. Even in the mid-seventeenth century, it was compulsory for any English settler who received a grant of land of more than a thousand acres to build a defended house and keep. No wholly unfortified gentlemen's residence was built in Ireland until that beautiful house, Beaulieu, in South Louth (1660–1666) one hundred and seventy-five years after Tudor building had started in England.

The general inability of the ruling authorities to give protection to their Irish subjects is dramatically illustrated by an event in Humphry Magan's lifetime, when, in 1631, Algerian pirates raided the south coast of Ireland and carried off more than a hundred people into slavery in Africa.

The home of Humphry and Anne Magan was of a kind that had evolved through long centuries of time and still retained many features that were very ancient.

There had been building in Ireland from early pre-historic times. Early man built stone tombs, megaliths, and sites of worship. Some of the existing ancient fortifications may also be pre-historic. There are, as I have mentioned, traces of a timber-constructed domestic dwelling as early as the fourth millennium BC.

In early Christian times extensive dry-stone building was mostly associated with places of worship, rather than domestic living, though windowless, chimneyless small stone beehive-like buildings were built as dwellings along the Atlantic cliffs. But they were not typical of Irish dwellings generally. Those who built them could wander no further, so had some reason to build with a view to permanence.

Elsewhere, throughout the plains of Ireland, our ancestors, the Celtic clans, moving frequently with their grazing herds, lived in encampments protected by earthworks. The dwellings within the earthworks were anything from quite substantial wooden buildings to rudimentary shelters – round huts for the most part, with poorly and loosely thatched roofs. Mobility being the essence of their existence, frequent erection and abandonment of temporary shelters was made necessary by the progress of the grazing herds from one area to another.

Mobility was also the key to both their defensive and their offensive military needs. They did not have to risk everything to defend a permanent stronghold. They could put a match to it, so to speak, move their flocks out of danger, and give battle at a place and time of their own choosing.

The coming of Christianity to Ireland brought a modification of the general principle of nomadic mobility. Great centres of Christian learning grew up. They could not move. They became fixed camps, in some cases enormous camps, of several thousand souls, mostly of small thatched timber round huts, with some larger central structures. They introduced a static element into social living, but, because they became prime targets – particularly during the Viking period – on account of their treasures, and the treasures of the chiefs and princes which they often housed, they, in turn, evolved a system of static defence.

Full protection could not be given to a large area of inflammable and otherwise vulnerable wooden buildings. To provide limited protection for treasures and for the precious manuscripts, stone churches began to be built together with the remarkable Irish round towers – first cousin to the belfry and the minaret – as the ultimate strong points.

Though over a thousand years old, more than a thousand round towers survive, the tallest ninety-five feet high. They were look-outs, belfries, and in the last resort highly ingenious fortresses. With thick outward-tapering walls at the base, windowless and doorless at ground-floor level, they were entered at the first floor by a ladder that could be drawn up into the tower, and were near impregnable, and with a clear all-round field of fire. They initiated the concept of fortress defence in mediaeval Ireland.

Then came a Norman innovation, new to the Celtic clans – personal land ownership. Had not the Normans compiled the Doomsday Book?

The Celtic Irish land system was of communal clan land, and common grazing rights. But there was nothing communal about Norman attitudes. When a Norman managed to seize a piece of Irish property, it became his outright possession. There was nothing semi-nomad about him. Like the Christian foundations, he was anchored to his parcel of land, and like them he had to stand and defend it. Like them, too, the Normans built strong stone defence points, but in their case European castles, not round towers.

Thereafter, the Celtic chieftains moved gradually towards some conformity with Norman and English landowning practices, while still retaining the essence of ancient Celtic conventional living – common grazing for the sept or extended family. The chieftainly families became estate-owners, but the chief and his people regarded and used the land as common land on which each had grazing and cultivating rights according to degree.

The chief had to see to the defences of the estate which he did by building himself as good a castle or fort as he could both afford and man, or as he judged necessary to his circumstances. And so, castles great and small came to be built in large numbers, particularly those small rectangular forts known as tower-houses. Ireland is dotted with their ruins. The dangers were real enough. The chief had need to be a man of resolution and of serious purpose. He was not play-acting in a deer park.

Those are the clues to what the Magan home at Umma-More was like, and they explain why I refrained from calling Humphry Magan a landowner, and referred instead to his 'access to' pastures for his flocks and herds, and to arable land for his corn. Even in his time, the old Irish were still living largely according to ancient Celtic law and custom relating to the use of land.

Although a man of property, with a fixed base at Umma-More to defend, he was still essentially a traditional Celtic chieftain with strong nomadic inclinations and needs. His life would therefore have remained semi-nomadic. His days would have been spent in the open air, and his nights often in encampments. He would have been much away from Umma-More, often hunting game, and even more often with his flocks, wherever they were grazing, particularly in summer. Not unusually, his wife – however magnificent her family background the other side of the Irish sea – and members of the family would have been with him.

His encampments would have been on the ancient Irish principle of temporary communal shelters made from light timber, brushwood and other handy natural materials. Life in those encampments involved for all a total and conspicuous lack of privacy.

At night the flocks would be herded round the encampment and lightly corralled, and the camp would be lulled to sleep by the sounds and smell of cattle – more soothing than might today be imagined. The smell of cattle has been sweet to the nostrils of man since the time of Abraham. Their cud-chewing and the muffled sounds of their slow movements at rest are balm to his ears. Man and his beasts have lain down to rest together for many more centuries than they have slept apart. There is between them an ancient and calming bond.

Umma-More itself, the Magan home, and the base for their grazier and hunter life, would have been much more like a camp than any sort of smart country house. It would have been a more or less protected ancient Celtic-style encampment of wooden buildings thatched with reeds, and meaner hovels, all clustered round the essential strongpoint, the stone tower-house fort. And attached to this complex of buildings would have been fortified, or well-protected, cattle enclosures, big enough for the protection of very large herds of beasts at night. There are today extensive cattle yard walls at Umma-More which may reflect that system. Humphry's home, therefore, was a mixture of nomad and Norman, a camp and a keep.

To this day, there is something of the nomad in the Irish. For many Irishmen a house is not so much a home as a shelter for the night. The men do not like being indoors. The open air still summons them. Even after the day's work, rather than be under a roof, they prefer to talk in the open air, usually leaning against a wall at a crossroads. The Irishman's heart does not at eventide warm to the cosy fireside life of the pretty English village of thatched cottages and houses clustered round the church and manor house, towards which the 'lowing herd winds slowly o'er the lea', and, 'the ploughman homeward plods his weary way'. Ireland does not have that sort of village life, which is an Anglo-Saxon development. The Irishman is off in the opposite direction, wending his way on a rusty bike to the nearest crossroads for a good talk in the open. One seventeenth century Irish scholar and observer noticed that the Irish were 'fond of news'. No doubt if you have no village life and gossip, and you lead a life of isolation, it is worth a bike ride to keep yourself abreast of whatever might affect your life and being.

CHAPTER 12

The Umma-More 'House'

WITHIN THE UMMA-MORE complex of buildings Humphry and Anne Magan and their family would have lived in the tower-house. But tower-houses could be very cramped. Furthermore, an Irishman was inherently more at home in a less substantial timber building with a flimsy roof of inadequate thatch through which some of the smoke leaked out in one direction, and most of the rain poured in in the other. Such were the structures that his ancestors had inhabited for two thousand years and perhaps much longer. It is therefore probable that Humphry and Anne Magan's dwelling would have consisted of the tower-house together with a poorly thatched timber annex; the tower-house remaining the fortress of last resort in the event of attack.

Norman castles were built for strength. They had few comforts, embellishments or amenities. Tower-houses, far from departing from that pattern of austerity, were primitive in the extreme in their appointments. The tower-house at Umma-More would have been a rectangular stone building with walls at the base three feet or more thick. Internal measurements, if it conformed to the prescribed fifteenth century pattern, would have been about thirteen by seventeen feet, the size of a small modern sitting room, and three, or more likely four, or even five, storeys high, with very narrow staircases. For security reasons the living accommodation would have been on the upper floors. The ground floor would have been windowless for protection. Such houses are in use in Southern Arabia to this day. The floors would have been of tamped earth, or perhaps stone.

Some tower-houses had fireplaces; others did not. Where there was no fireplace, there would have been a hearth in the middle of the top floor, the smoke, or some of it, going through a hole in the roof. There was no running water. Ablutionary and lavatorial arrangements would have been primitive in the extreme.

Even if the family slept in the tower-house, the main living room, or rooms, would have been in the wooden annex. That would have been more convenient for access to cooking arrangements and for administration, and it would probably have had a larger floor area, giving more room especially at mealtimes, when there might be a lot of people present. There would have been a hearth in the centre of the dining hall, the smoke, again, going out through a hole in the roof. It was in fact the Irish equivalent of the great hall in an English late mediaeval house.

There was a variety of possibilities, and some annexes would have had two stories. That was a common construction for timber houses in towns. But the total amount of living accommodation would not have been great. An English visitor to Dublin in the seventeenth century expressed admiration on seeing, on the outskirts of the city, the home of the Lord Chancellor of Ireland, which he described as 'an handsome large house of four rooms on a floor'. He does not say how many floors, but if it had three it would hardly have been a mansion. If that was regarded as splendour for one of the greatest in the land, we can judge that even high-born gentlemen would not have had a great amount of indoor living space.

Furnishings would have been sparse, rustic and local, without much, or indeed anything, in the way of luxurious appointments. There was also certainly a strong conservatism in such matters, impelling the Irish not to change their ancient customs.

There would have been some built-in wall cupboards in the tower-house. That was normal. There were rushes on the floors. Beds were flock, straw, rush or possibly feather mattresses. Sheets and blankets were used. Furniture in the tower-house, other than very small pieces, would have had to be built in the rooms, because larger pieces could not be got up the narrow stairs or through the small windows.

In the main hall of the annex there would have been a long table, possibly benches, and perhaps a chair or two, but bundles of rushes were commonly used for seating. They were springy and comfortable and had fewer fleas than straw.

It might be objected that to suggest such meagre furnishings at Umma-More is in contradiction of, for instance, the account of the appointments at the great castle of the Earls of Kildare at Maynooth when it was sacked by the soldiers of Henry VIII, a hundred years earlier, in 1535. 'Great and rich was the spoile,' says a contemporary account. There were tapestries, beds covered with cloth of gold, oriental carpets, valuable plate, and its contents were judged at the time to rival any of the richest houses in England. But the rest of Ireland cannot be judged by Maynooth castle or other great Irish castles of that time of whose contents inventories exist. They cannot be taken as the prototype in their furnishings for more humble tower-houses like Umma-More.

Moreover, Maynooth was totally impregnable to any indigenous force that could be brought against it in Ireland. It could not be, and was not, reduced until Henry VIII shipped heavy cannon to Ireland for the first time, to breach its walls. Its treasures had, therefore, up to that time been safe against any normal sort of Irish raid. A house like Umma-More was far from safe. Treasures there would have been an invitation to another predatory clansman, or an acquisitive English settler.

It was nevertheless a time of transition. Changes were taking place. With the coming of more peaceful times following the Battle of Kinsale, there seemed marginally less need for personal security; marginally less need to live in fortresses.

If Humphry and Anne were very up to date in their thinking, and if the area round Ballymore was reasonably quiet, and if their resources were sufficient, they might, later in life, have begun to make some of those improvements that Ireland was to see in the late seventeenth century.

Wings, built of stone, were added to tower-houses. They were more spacious and comfortable than the tower-houses, and better furnished. They were built as domestic dwelling places, not as forts. They had greater comforts – fireplaces and chimneys, and larger windows and wider staircases. They had no passages. Rooms led directly into each other, for the reason that privacy was of no importance. The tax man was soon after them, and taxed them according to the number of fireplaces. The south wing of another Magan home, Killyon Manor, Co. Meath, where my generation of the family spent so much of its time, is an example of just such an addition to a tower-house.

But, in the early seventeenth century, before the time had come for such improvements, there would, in addition to the tower-house and wooden annex at Umma-More, have been other buildings attached to the dwelling quarters; a dairy, wash-house, brew-house, malt-house, turf-house, pigeon-house, a forge, stables and kennels; stores for food and goods; also workshops of various sorts. Clothing, footwear, and other necessities were mostly made in the home. Hemp and flax were grown, spun, woven and dyed on the spot, as was wool from sheep.

The servants and retainers lived in windowless hutments that were hardly more than hovels, clustered round the tower-house for protection, the smoke pouring through holes in the roof. Beyond, but still within the encampment, were the cattle yards, grain stores and perhaps other outhouse structures.

Those of us brought up in Ireland half a century and more ago have no difficulty in imagining seventeenth century living conditions. We spent much time in the cottages of the country people. The floors were dried and hardened earth, with no coverings. Chickens, dogs, cats came and went as they pleased. But the floors were constantly swept, and although, as at Umma-More, there was no running water, and no sanitation, the cottages were not dirty, and they smelt only of the sweet smell of the smouldering turf fire.

By one of these small chances of history, a fragment of then trivial, but now interesting, information, was preserved for us when an English traveller in seventeenth century Ireland, writing of a call at an Irish priest's house, remarked that he and his party were kept waiting at the door 'until the room within was swept to receive us'.

Was there in Ireland, for whatsoever ancient reason, some special concern about the sweeping of floors which, together with the ever open half doors, and the delicious smell of burning turf, did keep the place clean and sweet? Fires had mythological significance. Perhaps some importance derived from the sweeping of the hearth.

When in camp, the Magans would have had bundles of ferns, or perhaps sometimes a board, for a table; they would have eaten their meals seated on bundles of reeds in the open air, in almost any weather; and they would have slept at night wrapped in their mantles lying on beds of reeds. The same Englishman who called on the priest also spent a night in a chief's summer camp. He said that the beds of green rushes were very comfortable. They were spread with sheets and soft white blankets, and the rushes were changed daily. The Irish said no-one ever caught cold if they slept on green rushes.

It was not unusual to spend nights out in even more primitive conditions. Then people would sleep wrapped in their mantles. An English observer who was in Ireland at the time of Humphry and Anne Magan said that both men and women, before wrapping themselves in their mantles, would soak them in water for greater warmth. The Scottish Highlanders did the same with their plaids. Under necessity of rough conditions, I myself had discovered, before ever coming upon this piece of information about the Irish and the Scots, that wet blankets are much warmer than no blankets. The primitive camp shelters being communal, everyone would have slept together in the one unpartitioned shelter. The same English traveller confirms that that is how it was in the chief's shelter where he spent the night. Privacy is not a universally coveted, or even understood, condition. It was unknown in England until Tudor times. There was no room for it until unfortified domestic dwellings became large enough to make it possible. There are many communities in the world today who would find the idea incomprehensible. To have a private bedroom at Umma-More would have been an unheard of novelty. Indeed, in a community so affected by superstition, to sleep in a room alone might have been a terrifying experience! Doubtless as many slept together as could be crammed into a sleeping chamber.

One habit among the poorer 'savage' Irish that was singled out by the English for special condemnation was what was known as sleeping naked. It was regarded by the English not only as savage, but also as immoral. The practice was that the whole family slept in one room – there was nowhere else to sleep – on the floor on some form or other of rush or straw mattresses.

Come bedtime, they all stripped naked, as did any strangers who were being put up for the night, and there commonly were strangers, travellers, pedlars, craftsmen and so on. All got into bed together. But the system was well regulated. The eldest daughter was at the far end by the wall, the other daughters in descending age down to the middle; then mother; then father; then the boys in ascending age. Finally the strangers, on the outer flank, furthest from the girls. Why naked? For the good practical reason that there was no point wearing out your clothes at night! Immoral? Of course it was not immoral. How could it be? It was just ancient custom, about which no one thought twice.

The practice certainly continued in Ireland up to the late nineteenth century, and probably into the twentieth century, and I expect was common until fairly recent times in other European rural communities. Indeed, I would bet my bottom dollar that it is practised somewhere in remote villages or valleys in Europe to this day.

The conditions in which Humphry Magan and Anne lived sound uncomfortable. But physical comfort is not particularly important as we all know who have found ourselves at times in circumstances no better than those at Umma-More. The conditions at Umma-More were not very significantly different from those in which British administrators lived in India, both at base, and in camp, particularly in remote districts. And, as I write, at noon of a week-end day in August, there must be many volunteer harvest workers in England sitting on bales of straw to eat their lunch. Tonight some of them will sleep on the floors of barns. In the morning they will get a wash under the yard pump, and will perform their devoirs where best they discreetly may. Discomfort will not be uppermost in their minds. It will probably not occur to them at all. A fully and physically occupied day; adequate diet; somewhere to lie down and sleep off both the day's work and the meal, are a not too bad foundation for living. And perhaps one of the most unexpected adjustments is how quickly we get used to not having a daily bath.

Not everyone of substance in Ireland lived like the rural gentry. In Dublin and the seaports a high material standard prevailed. There the houses of well-to-do merchants and professional gentlemen were more comfortable and better furnished. Town houses might be strongly built of stone, but many were of wood, as they were in London until the Great Fire in 1666. Dublin houses were the same pattern as London houses with the upper storeys overhanging the lower. The roofs were thatched. The seaport and town dwellers did not have to fortify their own homes. They lived within city walls.

The burghers were all trained to arms, and were themselves responsible for the defences. They must, nevertheless, have had more leisure than isolated country chieftains. Their wives too, were less engrossed in daily chores than the country ladies. The merchant gentlemen and their wives therefore had both more time and more cash, and better physical security within their city walls, than the country gentry. They were thus better placed to devote themselves to the cultivation of domestic elegancies. Moreover, their trade brought them into direct contact with foreign merchants, and provided them generally with knowledge and experience of high living standards in distant places; they were, for instance, no strangers to oriental carpets and the wares of Renaissance Italy.

Such were the living conditions of the leading citizens of Ireland, rural and urban, in the early seventeenth century.

CHAPTER 13

The Umma-More Estate

BALLYMORE, TWO MILES from Umma-More, along a muddy bridle track, has been described as the village with two ends and no middle. Seemingly, some ambitious improver at one time re-built it as though building a tunnel – from both ends – but ran out of money before the two parts could meet.

Long ago, Ballymore was named in Irish 'great town', but if ever it was great, it had ceased to be by the seventeenth century. A little to the north is a small lake, Lough Sewdy. In the seventeenth century a peninsula in the lake was fortified and used as a military strongpoint. East of the village is the hill of Mullaghcloe with splendid views as far as the Shannon river to the west. An abbey is said to have been founded at Ballymore about 700 AD. Nothing now remains of it. A later monastery was founded there in 1218, with separate quarters for monks and nuns. It was dissolved by Henry VIII. The D'Altons built a castle in about 1200. It was destroyed by their enemies not long afterwards. The De Lacys built another about 1309. Part of it has survived.

Ballymore district used to be renowned for its stalwart peasantry, and the people had a particular reputation for kindliness, generosity and hospitality to strangers; also as narrators and recounters of the gallant deeds of their fore-fathers. In the seventeenth century two fairs were held there annually. After the 1641 rebellion by the Irish against the English and Scottish settlers, which was said to have been planned not far away at the Abbey of Multyfarnham, a strong English garrison was stationed in the fortifications on the Lough Sewdy peninsula.

Situated on the central east-to-west route across the waistline of Ireland from Dublin to Galway on the west coast, Ballymore is almost exactly half-way between two towns of then military importance, Mullingar and Athlone, the fortified gateway across the Shannon to Connaught, and is about fifteen miles from each. The village itself very likely consisted at best of a few small timber houses, together with lesser shacks and hovels. Finally, and irresistibly, even if totally irrelevant, it is almost the exact geographical centre of Ireland.

There were therefore no centres of population within, for those days, a considerable distance, of Umma-More. Athlone and Mullingar were each a day's journey there and back, and even then were very small towns of not more than a couple of thousand people. There were indeed virtually no towns in Ireland other than the ports, and very few villages.

The Umma-More estate, therefore, was in the midst of a stretch of wild country flanked by two small towns thirty miles apart, and served only by a few appallingly rough bridle tracks. The roads of Ireland were much worse then than they had been centuries earlier when the old High Kings ruled, however loosely, from Tara. A central authority can exert itself through its dominions only if it has an adequate and rapid communications system. In those ancient days, as with Rome, all roads had led to Tara, and they were passable roads. The English had never been able to bring the whole country under central control, and had not therefore built up a centralized network of good communications. And so, in Humphry's time, that wild virtually roadless region was occupied solely, and very sparsely, by a few land-owning families, together with the lesser folk who were largely dependent upon them.

The appearance of the countryside was altogether different from today. It was for the most part either forest or wide-open rolling grassland, totally unenclosed, with no walls or fences. It had an air of desolation. Here and there were small castles and tower-houses, and mournful skeletons of ruined castles and ruined tower-houses, and the shells of former monasteries. There were otherwise, except in the very infrequent villages, no buildings that could be called houses, and there were none of those solidly built thatched white cottages which were not destined to be built for another half century, and which have ever since been the most familiar architectural feature of the Irish landscape.

Apart from the homes of the landowners, the only dwellings were those of the small farmers and peasantry, the merest more or less temporary windowless huts or hovels often built into hillsides. They could be built in a day or two. The sides were of mud and straw mixed, and the roofs were so inadequately covered with branches of leaves, reeds, bracken and sometimes straw, that for the most part no trouble was taken even to leave a hole for the smoke. It just leaked out of the roof everywhere, so that, as one traveller commented, the cabins often looked as though they were on fire.

The 'Blessed' Oliver Plunket, 'on the run', together with another bishop, when towards the end of the seventeenth century the Catholic clergy were suffering extreme persecution, wrote in a letter to Rome that the 'house' in which they were hiding was such that they could see the stars through the roof, and when it rained they got wet, 'refreshed' was the word that indomitable, long-suffering man used to make light of his miseries. He was himself an Irish aristocrat of long-since 'gone native' ancient Viking stock.

There was a very great deal of blindness in Ireland at that time. Some writers attribute it to the amount of smoke in the houses. Blind people often became minstrels.

The infrequency of the little cabins of the lesser folk, and their wretched tumble-down appearance, must have given the country a forlorn and poverty-stricken appearance, despite the great herds of small black cattle, long-haired sheep, and horses, which were to be seen grazing in the plains and on the hillsides.

It can reasonably be said that there is no Celtic Irish style of architecture, because, left to themselves, the Celtic Irish did not live in houses. In effect there was no architecture, and no need for it. The way of life that was natural to them was semi-nomadic, with its camp existence. They took to living in permanent dwellings only under the influence of external events. The upshot was the strictly functional architecture of the small fortress and the plain unembellished cottage.

There is reason to suppose that the lands available to Humphry Magan for grazing and cultivation may have stretched, though not continuously, through a distance of not less than six or eight miles from west to east, straddling Ballymore, with a similar straddle from north to south.

The set-up, therefore, was of Ballymore, a minute village on the highway – itself no more than a primitive bridle track – from Dublin to the west, providing elementary market facilities, and with, perhaps, a handful of artisans, and a rugged little basic store, possibly a little school, and perhaps a resident priest. There may have been a small chapel where the priest would have said mass, which he might also have done in the houses of the chiefs. The locality was probably spared the misfortune of a doctor who would have killed more with his well-meaning purges and bleedings than he would have cured.

Beyond and around the village, the forest and the open country were divided between a number of landowning families, holding the land according, in the main, to the old Celtic aristocratic custom of common land with grazing and cultivating rights for themselves and their retainers, rather than any formal title. Three of those families we have already encountered. The Magans, of ancient Celtic origin. The Whites, clearly of Old English settler origin 'gone native'. The D'Altons, a Welsh-Norman family, also long since 'gone native'.

The remainder of the widely distributed, very sparse population, apart from those resident at the chiefs' homes, were the dwellers in the miserable leaky cabins – the small farmers and independent peasants. A man's status as farmer or peasant made no difference to the standard of his dwelling. All lived in those dilapidated cabins.

At that time everyone, from the chiefs down, was Irish-speaking, and lived according to traditional Irish custom. Indeed, except for the later Anglo-Irish gentry, Irish continued to be orally the first language throughout Ireland until after 1847, that is, until after the Great Famine, and, incidentally, only 61 years before I was born. One Irish historian, writing of the seventeenth century, has said that probably no other people have been more steeped in tradition than the Irish, meaning all those, whatever their origin, who either were Irish or had 'gone native'.

Humphry Magan's traditional views on the use of land would have particularly affected his attitude to the small farmers and peasants. They were free men. That had a very important significance in Ireland. Ancient Ireland had practised slavery. Ownership of cattle, with grazing rights, was what gave you freedom. But in no society is anyone wholly free. All have obligations to the state, or to society.

In the old Celtic system, the free graziers owed allegiance to their chiefs. In effect, the small farmers and free peasants, and other owners of stock, artisans for instance, on the Umma-More estate, were Humphry Magan's tenants. That gave them the right to graze their beasts, and gave them access to some land for cultivation. They confirmed that right by some recompense to the chief. Their 'rent' may have been in kind, or in service, or both, or even in money, but money was very little used.

It has been traditional among the Irish to be good tenants. If they could possibly keep their obligations they did so, and were prepared to hand over not just any beast, but their best beast, to pay the rent. Ethics apart, they were shrewd enough to be concerned to live on good terms and at peace with their chiefs.

A man with a dozen beasts or so, horses and cattle, was reckoned a man of substance. For the many among those country people, life depended on no more than a few beasts, a few pigs, a few fowl, a very small amount of tillage, a 'garden' of cabbages, peas, beans and, from the latter part of the sixteenth century, that wonder crop the potato.

The potato was a truly marvellous food. It is usually claimed that it was introduced to Britain by Sir Walter Raleigh in 1585, round about the time of Humphry Magan's birth. But Mrs Beeton records that it was brought to Ireland by Sir John Hawkins twenty years earlier. However that may be, it grew well in light Irish soils, and its popularity spread rapidly. One man, with no other implement than a shovel – the Irish do not use spades – could, with no great expenditure of labour, produce enough potatoes to feed a family for nearly a year, and potatoes could be very simply stored in outdoor clamps, without any technical skills or aid. Indeed they could be stored for a considerable time just by leaving them in the ground.

Together with the traditional Irish dairy products, and cabbage, peas, beans, and a few eggs, the Irish family had in the potato a complete and wholesome diet. It may appear dull fare, but the Irish seemingly did not need a large or varied diet. Travellers noticed that they were small eaters. Is that still the case? They are a lean people. How often do you see a fat Irishman – some priests apart; and that is a compliment, and not insulting. Many a figure-conscious English lady has been horrified in Ireland to receive the compliment; 'you're gettin' very stout ma'am.' And how often do you meet a greedy Irishman? Thirsty ones? That's a different matter.

And so, part of the estates would have been occupied by such small graziers and cultivators, in effect Humphry Magan's subjects, but self-supporting in the necessities of life. Of the land not thus occupied, something less than ten per cent would have been cultivated from corn and other crops, but more than ninety per cent of the remainder of the estate that was not forest would have been grass-land, and the great herds of cattle, sheep and horses would have belonged to Humphry. I suppose that along with his cattle, there would have run the beasts of those dependents who worked directly for him, herdsmen and others. It is still common practice in Ireland to allow men who work for you to graze a beast or two of their own.

Humphry's wealth was his cattle. He would not, I believe, have looked upon his estate as a capital asset. It belonged, in the eyes of Celtic chiefs, not to them, but to the clan. What they owned was stock, and they needed only to assure themselves that enough land was available to them for grazing.

What made the Irish so rebellious in the sixteenth and seventeenth centuries was the English policy of emasculating them by dispossessing them of their common lands. To deprive a clan of its lands, was to remove at one blow the whole core of its existence. Land entered deep into the soul of the Irish, millennia ago. It is to this day the most emotive subject in Ireland.

Cattle in the country districts were everyone's investment. There was money in circulation, but people did not trust it. There was no mint in Ireland, and no standard coinage. Many different foreign coins were in circulation, some of them doubtful, others debased, and such coinage had no set value. At best it could be valued by weight. People did not want such money, and had very little need of it. The Umma-More estate would have been an almost wholly self-supporting and inter-dependent unit. Its additional requirements, some exotic things like salt, spices and tobacco, amounted to very little, and were catered for by itinerant pedlars. Very little else was needed beyond some long-lasting durables such as iron.

One English observer at that time found that the Irish valued leisure, and personal freedom from work, more than material gain. He was not being complimentary, he was accusing them of idleness. But there was also the fact that possessions beyond minimum requirements were a pointless liability in conditions of insecurity in which your home and your crops might at any moment be overrun and burnt. But your beasts could be moved on the hoof, and with luck you might get them away and save them before the raider got them.

No doubt partly for that reason, the acreage of arable land was kept low. But there were other factors. The land was difficult to plough. It had never been cleared and was full of rocks and old tree stumps and roots from the time it had been forest. There was also the climate. It is too wet, and the summer too short, in Ireland, for safe corn growing. Even nowadays, with powered machinery, it is only barely possible to save the harvest in very wet years.

Cattle and a little corn were not the sole products of the country. There was also some rural industry based largely on the family unit. The little bit of cultivated land adjoining the cabins allowed a patch or two for flax and hemp which were spun and woven in the dwellings, as was wool, and there was also home manufacture of shoes. The family clothes were made in the home, but over and above that there was a surplus organized by itinerant 'dealers' on a cottage industry basis. The dealers would supply additional raw materials that might be needed, and find a market for the surplus manufacture of the country people.

Although the conditions on the Umma-More estate may seem to have been primitive, and although much has been said about the evident poverty in Ireland, my belief is that the poverty-stricken appearance of the wretched cabins belied the reality. I doubt that, except perhaps on marginal bogland, and in mountain areas, there was much real poverty.

Ireland was fertile, productive and under-populated. The figures almost speak for themselves. The population was estimated at about a million inhabitants in the seventeenth century. The pasture was estimated at seven million acres, and the arable at half a million acres. In other words an average of seven acres of pasture and half an acre of arable, not to every family, but to every man, woman and child. That does not spell poverty even if the chiefs had the lion's share. Nor does the fact that in one year, in the mid-seventeenth century, Ireland was able to export a surplus of 40,000 live cattle, and 4,000 tons of meat and dairy produce, in spite of the difficulty of access to the ports because of the dreadful roads. Also, despite the relatively small amount of tillage, there was a net export of grain.

The miserable housing was not primarily due to, or a sign of, poverty. It reflected both insecurity and nomadism. Flimsy cabins were the time-honoured dwellings of a nomadic people. You could abandon them temporarily, or altogether, and move to some other pasture. Nothing was lost in doing so except the work of a day or two that it had taken to erect them. In time of danger you could flee from them, and their destruction would be no loss. Moreover, contemporary descriptions of the people themselves do not suggest a starving peasantry. The men impressed travellers as being strong and hardy, able to withstand cold with very little clothing, excellent runners and very courageous.

Despite, or perhaps because of, the comparative lack of seeming comforts and amenities in Irish life in those times, the Irish were observed to be very healthy. One seventeenth century English observer wrote: 'Deformed, decrepit, lunatic, or idiot people are very rarely, or never, found among them, which, being the defects of, or judgement on, luxury and debauchery, are commonly seen amongst our own and other refined people.'

There are, of course, accusations of rapacious landowners, grinding the faces of a down-trodden peasantry. But on two counts I doubt that that image fits Umma-More, or many other such estates.

Firstly, the old Irish sept or clan was an extended family, so constituted, and so moulded by time, that it had endured for centuries as an accepted hierarchical system. As we have seen, the Celtic monarchs of old did not get murdered by discontented people of their household, or their own retainers. I believe that, by and large, everyone accepted that they got a fair enough deal in the station in life to which they were born. That may not be a concept that would seem acceptable today but *autre temps, autre moeurs*. Moreover, the chiefs and their families lived much of their time intimately among their people, and at a standard hardly more comfortable than lesser folk. The extended family thus lived together as a necessarily harmonious unity.

Secondly, anyone who knows Irish life knows how easy-going it is. Too easy-going, many English people have thought. Too little discipline, not too much. Too much concern not to hurt anyone else's feelings, not too little concern. I believe that Umma-More would have been just such an extended family as that, where there was plenty of give and take; a very easy-going community with no harshness, and very little discipline, in whose relationships there was respect without servility, authority without severity, and frankness without friction. And because it was a time-honoured way of life, people uncritically and uncomplainingly accepted the disparity of their various stations in the community. It was a spiritually comfortable, if by our standards physically not very comfortable, way of life for all.

Life at Umma-More

THE UMMA-MORE ESTATE was a microcosm of a primitive principality with Umma-More its court, however rustic its atmosphere, however rude its appointments.

Next in importance to Humphry and Anne and their family would have been the bard. After the chiefs, bards were the most honoured and respected members of the community. He would have been a poet and learned man. He could recite old Irish poetry, sing old songs, and compose ballads for special occasions. He could declaim old legends and historical and mythological tales, tell stories and, above all, recite the genealogy of the family, illustrated with instances of valour, romance and renown.

An Englishman who visited Ireland in the seventeenth century recorded that: 'The people in general are great admirers of their pedigrees, and have got their genealogy so exactly learnt that though it would take two hours' work for them to repeat the names from whence they are descended lineally, yet will they not omit one word in half a dozen repetitions.' So, from listening to the bard, everyone had by heart much of the lore and custom of the land, its history, and the genealogy and history of their own family.

The same observer added that: 'Their greatest zeal is in keeping sacred some old sayings of their grandsires, and preserving some old relics of their grandmothers.' So, if we discover in ourselves a reluctance to part with 'old relics', we can lay the blame at the door of our Irish genes.

There would also have been a harpist, perhaps blind, like so many minstrels. The old Irish harp had brass strings. Some of the chiefs themselves learnt to play it. It is an instrument ever beloved of the Irish. There would also have been a piper; and someone might have been able to play the fiddle. It had evolved by the sixteenth century into its present form, and the Irish, being very interested in music, must have been concerned to have it and play it at an early date.

At its best, Irish fiddling is sweetly melodious, but all too often it is not at its best. More common is the pub or street-corner variety, and I pray I may not be condemned to be one for whom 'no minstrel raptures swell' if I appear unpatriotic in commenting that that sort of Irish 'fiddling' is very much an acquired taste. Foreigners should be warned that until they have acquired it they may find it an excruciating, teeth-rasping business that has little or nothing in common with 'playing the violin'. But it is the stuff that sets Irish feet flying in an Irish jig.

Irish dancing, like Scottish dancing, is one reason why Irish and Scottish deportment is so good. You can only do it well if you are naturally well poised, something learnt from an early age.

Although Ireland, like England in the nineteenth century, produced no great musicians – Sir Charles Villiers Stanford, if you like, and there's an Irish name for you, if ever I heard one! – visitors to Ireland in the sixteenth and seventeenth centuries found the Irish great lovers of music. From ancient times harpists and pipers had had a high place of honour in the Celtic hierarchy, not only for their artistry, but also for their bravery. They led the fighting men in battle, and stirred them to action with their martial music, and they were not uncommonly killed. 'The minstrel boy to the war' did indeed go, and it was all too often lamentably true that, 'the harp he loved ne'er spoke again.'

Irish music, like the beehive cells on the Atlantic cliffs, may not have changed much in nigh on two thousand years or even more, except that the words of songs have, in the Irish ballad-making tradition, kept prejudicially abreast of political events.

The music, if not great music, must surely have an honourable place in what might be called 'small music'. It was not composed for great choirs, orchestras, or swelling cathedral organs. It is the romantic folk music of scattered and isolated rustic communities, often performed extemporarily – and thus pre-dating and anticipating jazz – by very small numbers of people, more often than not soloists, with instruments limited in variety and quality. The harp is still the greatest of these, and now the rarest; then the fiddle, a variety of pipes and drums, and, of course, that lively, popular and, in Irish hands, truly rousing early nineteenth century addition, the 'melodie', as the Irish affectionately and graphically call the concertina.

The Irish female voice at its best is small, high, of flute-like purity, sweetly innocent and faintly melancholy – drops of crystal rain falling through Irish summer sunshine – or, less poetically, Kathleen ni Houlihan moaning over the sore feet she collected on 'the thorny road'. The male voice can also be soft and melodious, but is not always so. At its worst, the female voice, as vulgarly screeched in the streets, is, in common with the generality of male voices, of a penetratingly nasal quality hardly more felicitous than that other Irish ear-splitter, the sudden and forlorn braying of a lonely and dejected ass. Even that great singer, Count John MacCormack, who received a papal title, never altogether lost that nasal twang. Music, at all events, would have been an important part of evening life at Umma-More, and in the pastoral encampments.

The estate would have needed a number of herdsmen. As there were no fences, except very temporary ones round arable crops, the cattle, sheep and horses, had at all times to be herded, and to be brought into safe enclosures at night. Wolves were a menace to stock. They were common and were increasing in numbers in the early part of the seventeenth century. The estate staff would also have included ploughmen.

There would have been resident artisans, woodmen, some of them skilled in carpentry. The timber buildings would have been in need of constant maintenance and repair. There would have been a thatcher and a smith. Irish farming methods, and Irish craftsmen, were judged in those times to be in no way inferior to the English.

There were, of course, grooms or 'horse boys' as they were called, and a harness maker, skilled in all leather work. Tailors were itinerant, but no doubt some households had one resident.

If slavery was no longer practised, nevertheless the lowest orders of dependent workers at Umma-More had a status little better than serfdom. They were the menial element in the extended family of the chief, and were a part of what one writer has called 'the settled substratum of Irish society'. They received sustenance, clothing and a roof of sorts over their heads. Less tangibly, but no less important, they had the affection and trust of the family. Generation after generation of the family's children grew up in their warmth, devotion and confidence. They played an important part in the scheme of things. They had essential work to do and service to perform. It was a system that died hard. Even in our own twentieth century, unpaid, or virtually unpaid, servants, bred on the estate, have been not unknown in Ireland; and although, on both sides, the time-honoured differences of status were acknowledged, and the courtesies that depended therefrom were maintained, nevertheless such servitors were extraordinarily closely and confidentially knit into the family.

No-one would want to condone a system of serfdom, and no-one in his senses would seek to romanticize it, but there is probably a substratum in all societies which is scarcely able to fend for itself, and almost, perhaps actually, and even acutely, fearful of making the attempt, and who need a protected existence. Under the old Irish aristocratic system there was for such people a niche in which they could lead a sheltered life of wanted usefulness, for which, if the material recompense was small, they nevertheless received a measure, often an overflowing measure, of appreciative affection. Condemn the system if you like, and it was far from perfect, and not appropriate to modern conditions in the western world. But if we do condemn it, we must at the same time ask ourselves, whether, given the conditions of today, we do any better.

In a world which no-one has yet succeeded in making socially perfect, is a lonely person on the dole, with a 'scrounger' label round his neck, rejected, unwanted, unused, his self-respect draining away with the ticking of each idle minute, really in any better case, despite his higher state of material comfort; and is it all that comfortable, isolated perhaps at the top of a high-rise block of council-house flats? Are our sociologists too concerned with material egalitarianism; too little concerned with non-material causes that contribute to the inner quality of life?

The holy anchorites throughout history have been crying aloud, but crying in the wilderness, where men do not hear, that it is not material comforts or the material things of life that matter. The greatest satisfaction is to serve. Envy the active waiter, not the passive diner.

And are we not too prone to denigrate old-time customs and conventions for the very reason that we judge the past to have been necessarily inferior? Just because we are alive today is not sufficient reason to be arrogantly sure that we are wiser than our forefathers. The mere fact that we live in the present does not in itself necessarily invest our institutions with a superiority to those of the past, as we are often only too prone to suppose it does.

Some of the men at Umma-More would have been trained to arms. The Celtic caste system, like the Indian, had a warrior caste. It was a limited class which came next below the scholars, bards and wise men. Those roughly trained men constituted a small private garrison, as well as being part of the estate staff. And there might have been at Umma-More some of those mercenaries, common in the household of Irish chiefs, recruited as often as not from the Hebrides, known as Gallowgallases, descendants of Viking raiders against the Western Isles of Scotland. Umma-More had to be able to defend itself. There were no forces of law and order to do it for them. They would have had some firearms, but also bows and arrows, spears and pikes, daggers, dirks and broadswords. The Irish had a reputation for fighting lightly clad, indeed virtually naked, but chain mail was used, and Humphry might have had a few suits of it.

The women had their work. One farm function that was particularly their province was milking the cows, looking after the dairy, and producing the variety of dairy produce which formed such an important part of Irish diet. That constituted a great deal of work, as the proportion of cows in the herds was very large. Spinning, weaving, dyeing, making clothes, and embroidery, would have fallen also to the women. Then there was the house to keep, the food to prepare, and the children to look after. One seventeenth century observer of Ireland was of the opinion that Irishwomen were 'good nurses, but bad house-wives'. Those of us who spent our childhood in Ireland can endorse the observation with heartfelt gratitude. We received nothing but sensible, good-natured and humorous kindliness and consideration from the truly Irish women. We had a lovely time with them in our marvellously free Irish childhood. Yet there was nothing sloppy about their treatment of children. They did not condescend to us just because we were young. They may not have been good housewives, in the sense that they were not noticeably house-proud. As children we were allowed within reason to make free use of our homes. We respected our houses, but to all of us, young and not so young, they were more important as homes than as houses. In our own time nursing is a profession much sought after by Irish girls who make excellent nurses on account of their intelligence and their good-humoured good sense.

One custom prevalent in the seventeenth century which is by no means universal in Ireland now, was that everyone rose before dawn, and the day's work began with first light. They went to bed correspondingly early; about 9 p.m. being the usual bedtime. That routine was no doubt in part dictated by the very poor quality of such artificial light as they were able to produce for themselves.

The Irish were not regular about their meals, and their diet was considered monotonous. They were not in those days primarily bread eaters, though they did include an unappetizing form of bread in their diet. They ate meat boiled or roast, beef in the main, also mutton and pork. Dairy products were a very important part of their diet, and some vegetables of which cabbage was probably the most common, potatoes and some fruit.

Hunting, hawking, securing game by other means, and fishing, were favourite pastimes, and added deer, hares, rabbits, wildfowl, other game birds and a wide variety of fish, to the larder. Wolf-hunts, of necessity, and as a sport, would have been organized, and there would certainly have been Irish wolf-hounds at Umma-More. Indeed, there would have been many trained dogs with their own various duties in the field to perform.

A feature of Irish life that seems to have struck all visitors most forcibly was the hospitality, generosity and friendliness of all classes. They kept open house for everyone, and always gave to strangers of their best; and, however poor, would accept no recompense. There was a young English lady in the seventeenth century, wife of an English official, who left a contemporary account when she departed from Ireland to return to England, in which she recorded her great regret that she had to part from the friendly, warm-hearted, loquacious Irish, and of necessity to return to her much more reserved and monosyllabic fellow countrymen. Perhaps she was one who was dangerously on the fatal path to 'going native'.

The evening meal at Umma-More would have been the time of relaxation. The chief's wife presided, and she and the chief were at pains not to discuss their private and confidential affairs in the presence of lesser folk. The bard would have been there, and there would have been recitations, story-telling and music. And it was customary to dance round the fire. The fire, the central hearth, was near sacred, having mythological associations going far back in time, and in space, right across the Indo-European world.

Whiskey, as the Irish spell it, known to them in those times as *visce beatha*, literally water of life, *aqua-vitae*, more commonly *usquebaugh*, ancestor both of whisky and of the poteen of today – poteen because it was distilled in a 'little pot' – and also what was said to be very good beer, were liberally available.

On any night there would almost certainly have been some travellers, strangers or visitors, who would have been made particularly welcome. Other than infrequent inns, there was nowhere for travellers to stay, according to rank, save in local private homes, either the tower-house, the summer camp, or lower down the scale, the local cabin. All were most heartily welcome in one or other such dwelling.

There has survived a near contemporary, early eighteenth century, account, by a travelling English lady, of a gentleman's house in which she stayed. The house, she said, was no better than a large cabin. 'It belongs to a gentleman of £1,500 a year,' a rich man in those days. 'He spends most part of his time and fortune in that place. The situation is pretty, being just by the riverside, but the house is worse than I have represented. He keeps a man cook, and has given entertainment of twenty dishes of meat. The people of this country don't seem solicitous of having good dwellings, or more furniture than is absolutely necessary. Hardly so much. But they make it up in eating and drinking.' She no doubt meant in the abundance of their provision of food, rather than in the amount they themselves consumed.

'I have not', she went on, 'seen less than fourteen dishes of meat for dinner, and seven for supper, during my peregrination, and they not only treat us at their houses magnificently, but if we are to go to an inn they constantly provide us with a basket crammed with good things. No people can be more hospitable or obliging, and there is not only great abundance, but great order and neatness.'

At Umma-More, the women would have joined freely in the evening's entertainment. One visitor to Ireland said of the women that 'they are not so reserved as the English. Of nature they are kind and tractable. At meetings they offer themselves to be kissed with hand extended to embrace you.' 'Young ladies,' he went on, 'talk to you without restraint, and yet,' he added, 'cuckoldry is a thing unknown among the Irish.' A particular custom he mentioned was that if you had received a special invitation, you would be greeted at the door by the lady of the house, 'her female kinsmen about her all in a row; to leave any of them unkissed were an indignity.'

When Thackeray made a tour of Ireland two hundred years later, he wrote;

There are no more innocent girls in the world than the Irish girls. The women of our squeamish country are far more liable to err. One has but to walk through an English and Irish town, to see how much superior is the morality of the latter. That great terror-striker, the confessional, is before the Irish girl, and sooner or later her sins must be told there.

During his tour Thackeray visited an Irish Agricultural College which he thought more enlightened than anything to be found in England, and he was astonished to find girls working with the boys. He went to see the potatoes being harvested;

Among the potatoes, and the boys digging them, I observed a number of girls. Such a society of seventy young men would, in any other country in the world, be not a little dangerous, but Mr Campbell said that no instance of harm had ever occurred. The whole country bears testimony to this noble purity of morals. Is there any other in Europe which in this point can compare with it?

In the firelight of an Umma-More evening, there would above all have been talk. Magan males have strong rich voices. They have not let their vocal cords rust, and it is likely that the Umma-More evenings would have rung with the sound of Humphry Magan's voice. As the local leader, it would be surprising were he not also the leading talker. He would have been, not merely loquacious but indeed eloquent in the ancient Irish oral tradition which persists to this day, even though now in what is essentially a foreign vocabulary, English, for the Irish do not strictly speaking talk English. They use English words to speak a language which in some degree remains syntactically Irish.

That the Irish had retained their eloquence up to modern times was underlined when, half a century ago, a collation of vocabularies used in these islands revealed that illiterate Irish language speakers, in Kerry and other remote parts of Ireland, used a vocabulary twice as large as ordinarily educated English people, and ten times as large as some rural communities in England.

The Irish are not only at all levels of society eloquent, they are also more naturally histrionic than the English. There is nothing an Englishman dislikes more than to be called to the witness box. He is as monosyllabic and brief as he can be, and stays there as short a time as he must. An Irishman, on the other hand, looks upon it as a chance of a lifetime. He brushes his hair, straightens his tie, and hopes to hold the floor all day with a performance the court will not forget for a long time.

If Humphry Magan, and his bard, and others who sat at his table, had, as they very likely must have had, a vocabulary in excess of that of the supposedly illiterate Kerrymen, then they were excellently equipped for evenings of scintillating conversation, particularly as it also seems to have been customary not to be over-modest or too strictly confined by fact and reality; for, traditionally, the Ancient Irish were given to exaggeration and romancing. And it may be salutary to temper our admiration for the Irishman's reputation for eloquence down the ages, with the recollection that their patron saint himself, St Patrick, no less, was unimpressed by all that blarney. 'You lordly rhetoricians, powerful in discourse', he scathingly chided them.

And I sometimes wonder whether eloquence or loquaciousness may not in one respect be a dangerous liability to the Irish. I was at one time acquainted with the Arabs. Like the Irish they are exceptionally eloquent. They have a rich language with an enormous vocabulary. But it seemed to me that they were often in danger of exciting themselves by their own rhetoric to the point of adopting courses which might be less than prudent, and not in their own best interests. Do the Irish risk the same hazard?

There seems to be ample evidence that there was excessive drinking and gambling in Ireland in the seventeenth century. Backgammon and cards were the principal gambling media. But, clearly, not everyone was involved, any more than they might be now. The Magan family came through the appalling hazards of seventeenth century Ireland without suffering the shipwreck that was the fate of the great majority of Old Irish families. To have survived the storms of the seventeenth century with their estates intact, they can hardly have been other than prudent, cautious people not prone to injudicious activities of any kind, so I think we may suppose that they were not given to over-indulging themselves, however hospitably they may have treated their guests.

Sunday was the day of rest. It never can be a complete day of rest for men with herds to mind, and women with cows to milk, but it was as much so as it could be. There were not many recreations apart from the pursuit of game. But hurley, which can be loosely described as of the hockey family – but look out for yourself if you imagine it is hockey – was played by the men; and outdoor dancing, for both men and women, was a favourite pastime.

Life at Umma-More, with its tower-house, its cluster of lesser buildings, its retainers' huts, cattle yards and outbuildings, and on the scattered estate with its cabin-dwelling tenants, was a plain, sturdy, rustic existence, still clinging to the influence of ancient Celtic culture, and still little affected by even the English fashions of the Pale.

One writer on the period has said that he feels convinced that the Irish chiefs, with their aristocratic attitudes and cast of mind, must have lived a life of some magnificence. That, in a manner of speaking, is probably so. It was not the form of magnificence adopted later by the great English Whig lords of the eighteenth century, and then copied in Ireland. It was more in line with the magnificence of the near contemporary Shakespearean stage. It was low in props, but high in entertainment. Have an empty stage, and all attention is on the actor. The skill of the chiefs lay in their ability to act their parts. Their innately unselfconscious superiority invested them with a great natural air of distinction, reinforced by emphatic gestures, considerable eloquence, unashamed hyperbole, powers of instant decision, and in the last resort absolute personal courage. Their hospitality was as unselfconsciously, and unaffectedly, natural and genuine, as was their poise, and was also part of the grand manner of those born to occupy the centre of the stage and the limelight. The houses did not have a high standard of comfort, or many, indeed one might say, elegancies. The food may have been plain, if abundant, but hospitality was offered with a panache, liberality and urbanity worthy of a banquet.

The women, as we have seen, were not notable as housewives. The country people preferred leisure to material enrichment. The 'big houses' were sparsely furnished and had hardly more than the most rudimentary comforts. Yet the people, high and low, who seemed content to accept these, at best, fairly squalid conditions, were universally acknowledged, even by their enemies, to be warm-hearted, outgoing, friendly, notably courteous, and exceptionally hospitable. Could it be that the Irish were, and perhaps still are, more concerned with the inner quality of their life than with the material standard of living?

Another feature of their lives was that no-one was anonymous. Everybody knew everyone else. Everyone could, and did, feel that he or she had a known, accepted and respected personality. In today's suburban and urban life it is the fate of many to live in conditions in which even their nearest neighbours neither know nor care who they are. They live a life of crushing anonymity. Not so in those old Irish days. Even the greatest and the least knew each other well and on respectfully familiar terms. When the visiting 'quality' put up for the night, or came to stay for longer, they were well acquainted with the servants, and greeted them as the friends who, in their own station, they truly were:

'How are you, Mary?'

'Great ma'am, thank you; and how's yerself?'

'Great, thank you; and is your mother well, Mary?'

'Thanks be to God, never better ma'am; and how's His Honour?'

'Great, thank you, Mary. He'll be here shortly.'

'Isn't that great, now.'

'Great', is a word much used in Ireland. Despite the insecurity, the cattle raids, and what we would regard as the discomforts, I believe life was 'great' in the warmth of those community relationships, now so conspicuously absent from today's rows of two by two suburban-dwellers' villas.

And the chiefs appeared colourful not only in character and in speech, but also in their attire. I like to think of Humphry Magan on a high summer's day, perhaps on the hill of Mullaghcloe, with its wide and distant views, astride his horse, or perhaps on foot, a slim-shafted spear in his hand, his coloured light-weight mantle blowing gently about his spare figure, while he surveys his herds of beasts on the plains below – an arresting patrician figure of self-assured wiry and elegant alertness.

An Irish historian has remarked that a race meeting, or a fair, attended by men and women – particularly those that 'loved to be gallant' – in their many different coloured mantles, must have been a brilliant sight.

There, on some bright day, gathered with the people of the neighbourhood for some rural occasion, the many-coloured mantles a striking contrast to the rolling grasslands of Westmeath, we must leave Anne and Humphry Magan to enjoy their country life in the twilight days of ancient Celtic Ireland. By the end of their lives the aristocratic versions of Irish dress were disappearing. The modern world of English and European fashion was upon them. But blue mantles were universally worn by country people as late as the mid-nineteenth century and were not uncommon in the south-west of Ireland even in the early twentieth century. And distinctive Irish female costume continued to be worn by the country women until very recent times.

CHAPTER 15

The Wild Irish

THE LIFE LED BY Anne and Humphry Magan reflected the long evolution of distinctively Irish modes and manners that differed from those of England. Seen from the English mainland, Irish life was regarded as barbarous. But in stark contradiction of that view was the fact that English settlers in Ireland soon adopted Irish ways from preference. This is a dark, but important, corner of English-Irish misunderstanding into which it may be worthwhile to try to throw a little light.

For the past eight hundred years, since the time of Strongbow's invasion of Ireland, the English have disparaged the Irish. In part this has been customary propaganda, which began at the time of the Welsh-Norman attack. Whosoever you attack is your enemy. Honourable men only attack villains. You are yourself necessarily an honourable man. Ergo, the enemy is a villain. To confirm that fact in your own mind, and try to persuade others to agree with you, you loudly proclaim the enemy's villainies, supposed villainies, or those you invent for him. It is legitimate for us to engage in such propaganda. It is, of course, villainous for the enemy to do so.

But English disparagement of the Irish was not invented, and was not all propaganda. The English genuinely and honestly regarded the Irish as uncivilized. To this day 'the wild Irish' is a commonplace English cliché. But more than that, the English also, and again quite genuinely, regarded the defects of the Irish as irremediable. The Irish were not merely uncivilized, they were a lesser breed. And so we get the companion cliché, 'the mad Irish', who have been a constant butt for English humour, the customary role of minority communities and subject peoples.

There are numerous Englishmen who bear Irish names. They are the descendants of Irish immigrants to England. They are not noticeably different from, or inferior to, other English people. It seems therefore that we can forget the 'lesser breed' theory to explain the fact that the English found the Irish to be different from, and, as they believed, inferior to, themselves.

That the Irish were regarded by the English as uncivilized, begs the question: 'What is civilized?' We can concede without much elaboration that England, certainly from Tudor times onwards, was technically, and in the arts, ahead of Ireland. Ireland built a relatively small number of fine early ecclesiastical buildings, produced notable illuminated manuscripts, and preserved Christian learning for the West. But her achievements could not compare with the outpourings of England; the great number of magnificent cathedrals, churches and other buildings; the great painters, scholars, administrators, writers and musicians of the sixteenth and seventeenth centuries. It was partly a matter of geography. The nearer to the epicentre of the inspiration of Indo-European and Western civilization, the earlier its development. Thus the English saw the Irish as uncivilized. French Renaissance advances antedated the English, whom the French regarded as Philistine. The Italians had nothing to learn from the French. The ancient Greeks saw the Romans as vulgar imitators. The more easterly was apt to be a step ahead of the more westerly.

It was partly a matter of different modes of life. A nomadic, or even semi-nomadic, pastoral people, such as the Irish, was bound to lag technically behind more settled village and urban-dwelling communities. You cannot lug cathedrals and factories about on your migrations. So, inevitably, you fall behind, at any rate until the time when perhaps, who knows?, in the great rolling swell of history, the urban dwellers may be destined to suffer the fate of Sodom and Gomorrah, the cities of the plain.

It is easy enough to demonstrate that more technically and artistically advanced nations and communities are in that sense more civilized than others. Or is it? We do not have to go very far along the road of judging degrees of civilization by comparing technical advances before we come up with such a question as: 'Which is the more civilized, to kill your enemy with a bow and arrow, or with an atomic bomb?' We nevertheless can accept that, in the times we are considering, England's technical and artistic achievements were such as to justify her view that they were superior to those of the Irish.

But there is another area of comparison. That of modes, manners, social customs and conventions.

It so happens that the particular example of Irish savagery, villainy and lack of civilization on which the Normans picked as justification, or part justification, for Strongbow's invasion, was that Irish ideas of justice were so lax and primitive that in Ireland a murderer could buy himself off 'for a few head of cattle'. The murderer was not himself judicially murdered as in more civilized societies. That was an intolerable state of affairs, crying out to be put right.

The fact is that social development in England and Ireland had, over a very long period of time, come along different routes. England's laws, England's judicial system, England's social system, reflected Roman, Anglo-Saxon, Franco-Norman, and other influences, none of which had influenced Ireland whose laws were the ancient Celtic code, incorporating Pictish practice, and reflecting the different social and judicial view of murder that had evolved in old Irish society. Under the ancient 'savage' and 'uncivilized' laws of the Celtic Irish, which the English spent six hundred years trying to suppress, before they eventually succeeded, there was no death penalty, except in the last resort for treason. Indeed the philosophy of judicial revenge was entirely unknown in Ireland. There were no prisons, no law officers, no police. There was a comprehensive legal system, presided over by advisory judges, who were immensely learned and experienced. In accordance with their advice, the weight of public opinion was brought to bear in such a way as to enforce restitution in cattle, or in kind, to a point where a criminal's status in society, and therefore his honour, could be adversely affected. And as a means of dealing with crime in society it worked.

In the Celtic hierarchical society, your status was determined by the number of cattle you owned. Your honour depended on your status, and your honour was immensely important to you. Murder your neighbour, or offend the law in some other way; be judged guilty, and have it assessed by the people, on the advice of eminently learned and greatly respected judges, that you must make restitution of so many head of cattle and, in the result, your status and honour were liable to be adversely affected. That was punishment enough.

In short, your honour depended on your behaviour: and not only your own honour, but that of your family also. The family, rather than the individual, was the unit, and the family stood surety for its members. If one was impoverished and disgraced, all suffered in consequence. There was therefore a strong common interest in good individual behaviour. That concept would be wholly familiar to anyone who had served the Crown in the old Indian Army. The Indian Army, like the Celtic Irish, had no corps of military police. There was no need, because there was no crime in the Indian Army. Nothing was more important to an Indian soldier than his honour, the honour of his regiment, his family, his village, his tribe, his creed. He could never hold up his head again in his village if he did anything dishonourable. They were people who came from a technically and artistically unsophisticated society. A background of rural husbandry, and mud villages. They had built no Uffizi Palaces or Chartres cathedrals, or painted immortal pictures, or achieved great scientific and engineering inventions. But they have great refinement of feature, dignity of bearing, and impeccable good manners. An honourable life is important to them. Would Strongbow, Henry II and Pope Adrian VI have called them uncivilized?

If the hierarchical basis of such societies is destroyed, and egalitarian libertarianism substituted, those sanctions become inoperative, which is the sort of consideration that needs attention before sociologists start tinkering with established 'primitive' social systems.

There was, indeed, nothing 'savage' or particularly 'uncivilized' about the ancient Irish legal system. Every aspect of clan life which needed legal sanction or regulation had, from very ancient times, been covered by a body of formal law and custom of a very civilized kind. But they were laws and customs which in no way corresponded to Roman law. They reflected a social system, and manners and modes of thought, very different from those then current in England.

'Barbarous and bloodthirsty' were Cromwell's adjectives for the Irish. But how did the Irish view the English practices for dealing with malefactors, or even suspected malefactors? – methods which varied so very greatly from their own milder practices?

What did they think of a system whose punishment it was to place the suspect on the rack, disjoint him with unspeakable cruelty, leave him lying in excruciating pain all night in a cold and filthy rat-infested dungeon, drag him next morning bouncing in agony on a hurdle through the dirty and uneven street of London to Tyburn, there to hang him till he was more than half choked, cut him down before he was dead, then take a carving knife and, before his living eyes, emasculate him, and cut out his bowels – finally, butcher him and decorate a variety of flagpoles around London town with his remnants? The Irish must have found it hard to applaud that 'civilized' custom as an alternative to their own way of dealing with malefactors. It was to be another eight hundred years before the 'civilized' English were to adopt the 'barbarous' Irish custom of getting along without retributive judicial murder.

And how civilized did the Irish think the great and gifted Archbishop Loftus, an Englishman, a one-time chaplain to Queen Elizabeth, later Primate of all Ireland, and head of the Irish Anglican church, when he seized the Irish Roman Catholic Archbishop, and because backward Ireland was insufficiently technically advanced to own a rack on which he could be disjointed, he, the good Loftus, roasted his Catholic colleague's feet in hot metal boots; a mild roasting, maybe, compared with the wholesale roastings conducted a generation earlier by English bishops across the water, but sufficient nevertheless to give the poor man his early congé?

On the other hand, the – to the English – excessively crude Irish funerary customs were one manifestation of things which, in their eyes, underlined the uncivilized state of this barbarous people. Irish wakes and funerals they found an offence to the dead, and a disgrace to the living. The last great mystery, death, was to the English a moment to be treated with reverence, a moment for restrained and respectful mourning and contemplation. As treated by the Irish it was seen by the English to be grossly disfigured by prolonged and profane orgiastic junketing. But that was perhaps a myopically insular view of the matter.

In the early Mediterranean civilizations, death, the care of the dead, and the supposed life in the hereafter, were the very essence of their marvellous flowering cultures. Many of the earliest great architectural works of man were palaces not for the living but for the dead – in Egypt, Crete and Greece. Funerals were life's greatest ceremonies, and greatest expense. Priestly rackets, maybe, but universally accepted nevertheless as the centrally most important element in the culture of those times. There was no question of, 'funeral private, no flowers', ten minutes mumbling from a parson, and then a quick disposal. That the cult of the dead was also of great importance in Ireland in stone- and bronze-age times is made evident by the enormous number of ancient tumuli, very considerable works when we consider the handful of people who constructed them with hand tools – a cult that probably had Mediterranean origins. What is an Egyptian pyramid but the father and mother of a tumulus?

That ancient funerary culture has survived to this day in a debased form in Ireland, just for the very reasons of distant isolation – those far-flung, desolate Atlantic cliffs – that have caused so much else to survive there. Even when I was a boy an Irish funeral of anyone well-known locally, and most people seemed to be well-known locally, would, following the hearse and its black-plumed horses, and the carriages of black-creped mourners, be anything up to a mile long of dark-clothed, walking people, filling the width of the road. You stood still and raised your hat, and crossed yourself – it might be your turn next – as the coffin went past. The modern version is still a not insubstantial 'motor-cade', sometimes at walking pace, with a considerable pedestrian contingent of mourners.

But enough. I am not suggesting that the Irish could not be cruel, or that the English could not be crude. I am concerned only to make the point that the linguistically different Irish, were also in a great many other and important respects culturally different from the English. We are, in the deepest sense, all part of the Indo-European complex, with ancient similar roots to our cultures. But the long swells of history have washed so unevenly over us, and so often failed to reach the farthest Atlantic shore, that great cultural differences have also grown up. And, in their dealings with Ireland, the English have often been unable, or unwilling, or both, to acknowledge that the Irish could be different, without necessarily being worse. Of course the conqueror has to regard himself as superior, otherwise the justification for his being in the seat of power is more than half evaporated.

Nevertheless, barbarous or not in the sight of the English, we can safely accept that that old Irish life was a pretty good life for all those who had lived it for so long without knowing a better. But it was almost at an end. A terrible fate was about to befall it.

CHAPTER 16

Cromwell – and the
Sons of Humphry Magan

HUMPHRY AND ANNE MAGAN'S two surviving sons, Richard Magan the Elder, and Morgan Magan the Elder, each became the founder of a separate branch of the family; Richard Magan of the Roman Catholic branch, which died out in the male line in 1841; Morgan Magan of the Protestant branch to which the present Magan family belongs.

Our ancestor Morgan was known as Morgan Magan of Cloney, Co. Westmeath. We do not know his date of birth, nor, for that matter, the birth date of any Magan earlier than 1721. We can readily understand that, in conditions such as existed at Umma-More, so long as the oral bardic tradition continued and family details were remembered, little or nothing was likely to have been recorded and preserved in writing.

Morgan Magan the Elder spent his boyhood at Umma-More at a time of unusual tranquillity. But those peaceful days were not to last. When he was perhaps in his early youth, Ireland was plunged once again into her more customary state of turmoil. The tenaciously Irish people of Ulster had never accepted the Plantation, and the domination of the English, as irreversible. In 1641, they rose in rebellion. Settlers were murdered, or hounded from the land they had occupied. Some were the victims of appalling cruelty. Their houses and possessions were burnt, their cattle driven off. Ignited by the Ulstermen, the flames of rebellion spread to many parts of Ireland.

There are no accurate records of the extent to which the settlers suffered. It was the English settlers who endured most. But many Scots, too, suffered grievously. Wildly exaggerated accounts of casualties were circulated in England, in some cases for deliberate anti-Irish propaganda purposes. Nevertheless, however much some settlers suffered, the rebellion did not succeed in significantly reversing the Plantation. Many of the settlers survived, and their numerous descendants form the majority of the citizens of Ulster today.

But what mattered for the future was the impression of the Irish that gained currency in England in consequence of the reports, exaggerated or not, that were brought back across the water from Ireland. They were no longer seen merely as backward, lawless, barefoot, half-naked, shaggy savages, talking a gibberish language. Now they stood fully revealed as ruthless, bloodthirsty, murderous, brutal barbarians, who slaughtered innocent settlers by the thousand, burnt them out of house and home, pitilessly drowned them, and who would stop at nothing, and towards whom therefore there must be no more leniency. They must be totally crushed once and for all if England was ever to feel secure from the threat that Ireland posed, and if decent English Protestant citizens were ever to be safely able to people Ireland in place of the priest-ridden Catholic barbarian natives.

But that Draconian intention had perforce to be postponed for a few years yet. Within months of the outbreak of the Ulster rebellion, the Cromwellian Civil War in England began. No substantial reinforcements of troops could be spared to deal with the Irish rebels. Indeed, there were distinct threats during the Civil War that factions in Ireland who favoured Charles I, or at least preferred him to Cromwell, and claimed to be, in the main, under arms in his support, might contrive to send Irish troops to assist the Royalist cause. Here, again, in Cromwellian eyes, was Ireland posing a security threat to the English mainland.

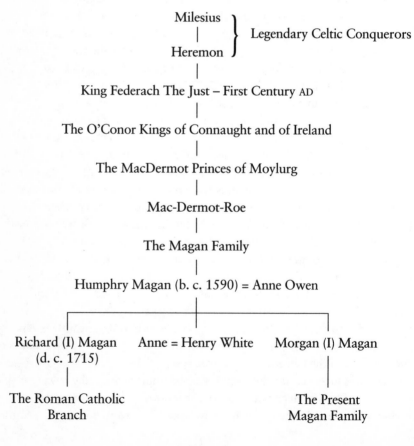

The English Civil War lasted seven years. It was a time of great confusion in Ireland. Catholics, Protestants, Presbyterians, Royalists, Puritans, Old Irish, and Continental powers, all had fish to fry; all pursued their own interests, sometimes by force of arms. The conflicting interests were such as almost to produce some sort of balance of forces, a stalemate condition.

It must nevertheless have been a time of acute anxiety and uncertainty for Irish landowners. They and their families, even the younger members, must have felt a constant and serious concern for themselves, their dependents, their properties, and indeed for the continued existence of society as they knew it. Thus, by force of such conditions, our ancestor Morgan Magan must, as an adolescent, have come to an early maturity of mind, and must have contributed to the successful efforts of the family to keep itself and its tenantry out of trouble, and to preserve its properties.

But the confused, uncertain and insecure state of Ireland during the years of the English Civil War, were as nothing to the remorseless certainty of the vengeance that was to fall upon the Irish once the Civil War was over and Cromwell was free to turn his attention to Ireland.

On a cold January morning in the year 1649, King Charles I, wearing two shirts to keep himself warm lest the people should mistake his shivering for fear, stepped from a window in the beautiful Inigo Jones Banqueting Hall in Whitehall onto the scaffold where, with unexampled bravery, and true aristocratic dignity, he suffered execution.

He nothing common did, or mean,
Upon that memorable scene.

It was a moment of dreadful foreboding for the Catholic gentlemen of Ireland. Charles I was, of course, himself a Protestant, but his leanings were high church. His wife was a Catholic. And his attitude to Catholicism was far more tolerant than the bigoted Protestantism of Cromwell's supporters, even though Cromwell was himself denominationally more broad-minded than they. The Protestant gentlemen of Ireland were in hardly better case than the Catholics, for many of them had openly preferred the Royalist cause to the Cromwellians.

There was no question that the Irish knew the fate that was in store for them once the Royalists had been defeated. Had the Royalists won, the English suppression of Ireland would have continued, but it might have taken a less ruthless, and more drawn out, course. But there was a compelling reason why a major English military invasion led by the terrible Cromwell himself was bound to follow his Civil War victory. He had to conquer Ireland and despoil her to pay his debts. Nothing could save Ireland unless her own disunited forces could defeat the battle-hardened, experienced English soldiers, led by well-tried commanders and directed by a military genius. There could be only one outcome.

There could in any case have been no question but that so great a political and military strategist as Cromwell would not have left unfinished the task begun by the Tudors a century and a half earlier of subjugating Ireland and securing England's strategic western flank. The Irish 1641 rebellion would in itself have been enough to impress upon him the urgency of that need. That was all a part of the inexorable movement of that great groundswell in the tide of history which impelled England to secure her defences against the Irish threat.

But lesser squalls were no less immediately impelling, and in particular Cromwell's debts to his supporters.

Cromwell had had inadequate funds to prosecute the Civil War. To raise the necessary wind, he had used Ireland as a promissory note. He had offered a third of all the best lands in Ireland to English supporters who would put up the money he needed. Ireland, the land of the Irish, he was treating like a lottery for mining concessions in an uninhabited wilderness. There were, of course, those in England prepared to back him and to finance him on those terms. The money that they put up was risk money, and those who subscribed it became known as the 'Adventurers'.

If Cromwell succeeded, the lands to be given to the Adventurers could come only by dispossession of the landowning gentlemen of Ireland; and those most likely to suffer would be Catholics who had preferred the Royalist cause.

Thus, the downfall and execution of the King invested with immediate reality the appalling Cromwellian threat which had been hanging over Ireland since the beginning of the Civil War. And, indeed, no sooner was the King dead, than Cromwell at once turned his attention to plans for his Irish expedition. Ireland was about to become a major battle-field.

No written record of the experiences of the family during the Cromwellian episode has survived. Perhaps they still relied upon the bard for oral preservation of the family's chronicles. The following account, therefore, of the predicament into which they were plunged by the Cromwellian invasion, and of their experiences, and of the anxieties of the times, is the best reconstruction I can make of what seems likely to have happened. But it can hardly be far off the reality.

Cromwell landed in Dublin in August, 1649, eight months after the death of Charles I. The pretext for his invasion was retribution for the 1641 rebellion, and restoration of the 'settlement'. On the very day that he set foot on Irish soil, laying claim as always, with a terrifying conviction in his firm belief in the claim, to be acting as the chosen instrument of God's will, he described the rightful inhabitants of the land as 'the barbarous and bloodthirsty Irish'. It was his clear intention to carry out the will of the English Parliament, and by implication the will of God, that Ireland be replanted with 'noble' English families 'of the Protestant religion'.

What would have been the effect at Umma-More of the news that Cromwell had landed? If Humphry Magan was still alive, he might have been sixty years of age or so. His two sons, Richard and Morgan, were men in their twenties and thirties, in the prime of life. His daughter Anne was married to their neighbour Henry White. During the Civil War, being Catholic gentlemen and landowners, and therefore acutely at risk in the event of a Cromwellian victory, they could hardly have failed to prefer a Royalist success. Whether or not they had chosen to declare any allegiance, or been forced by circumstances to do so, it must be quite certain that they were at all events not declared Cromwellians, and were therefore especially vulnerable to the Cromwellian depredations which now threatened. Indeed, they must have been fully conscious that they were faced with nothing less than a threat of swift annihilation. Nothing now stood between them and possible total disaster save their own resourcefulness, and the spin of the wheel of fortune.

If it was to turn out that their lands became forfeit, and their herds confiscated as part of Cromwell's debt to his supporters, then they would be faced with the stark alternatives of death, or banishment to a near-starvation peasant subsistence in the bogs and mountains of Connaught. And that was no mere nightmare. It was an immediate and actual and very real threat that now hung over them.

Numbing fear would not save them. Panic would be fatal. Nor was it a time for romantic, histrionic, heroic posturing. There could be no salvation other than in cool, deliberate, sapient and well-judged courage. It was Ireland's moment of greatest danger. The dancing, singing, story-telling and hawking must stop. In their place there would have been serious faces, and long, earnest and detailed conferrings.

There was immediate action to be taken, as well as detailed contingent planning. There would have been some wringing of the hands by the women; crossings of the breast; and invocations of the Blessed Virgin. But their work would have gone on without interruption, and without hysterics. Irish women are as well endowed with bold and courageous resignation, as are Irish men with unflinching active valour. Fighting drunk, may be part of the fair-day reputation of the Irish. But read the history of the Irish regiments for a different image of their martial qualities.

Every chief's household and estate being, of necessity for its own security, a self-contained quasi-military unit, the fighting men were at all times militia-minded. They customarily thought tactically, and were ready at a moment's notice to act tactically. In the most perilous situation ever yet known to them, they were now faced with two prime needs. First to provide themselves with the best possible information about Cromwell's military intentions, in order to enable them to take whatever timely action might be possible to safeguard themselves. Secondly, to keep the estate running while at the same time making the necessary plans to secure their people and their flocks should the estate itself fall victim to Cromwell's forces.

I once lived for a year, more than half a century ago, in an ancient mediaeval oriental city, separated from the capital by six hundred miles of mostly desert and wilderness. It was before the days of regular and general radio news broadcasting. The people were largely dependent on rumour for day to day information of what was afoot in their own country. It was an eerie and uncomfortable condition, and anyone with much at stake felt a strong need for more factual information. Those would have been the conditions at Ballymore. It is therefore inconceivable that the family would have left it to chance, and to rumour, to learn whatever might prove vital to them. Without doubt, a family of such seemingly prudent people would have taken the best possible positive steps open to them to obtain the information they needed. The slow filtering through of news and rumour to Ballymore could not be relied upon as an adequate source of information about Cromwell's movements. So important a matter could not be left to chance, or to anyone else. They must make their own arrangements to gather the necessary information. Some wholly reliable and responsible person would have had to undertake that task.

The leading Ballymore land-owner was Lord Netherville, a Catholic, and he may have done something to co-ordinate the local Catholic and anti-Puritan defensive arrangements. But I am going to suppose that the Magan family would not have been content to leave things in his hands, or have been too ready in that day and age to trust themselves to anyone else. People were engaged in every sort of double-dealing to protect themselves. Let us suppose, therefore, that the family decided to put themselves in the best possible position to look after themselves, and to see to their own interests, and the interests of those for whom they were responsible.

It seems likely that the Magans were one of the leading families of Ballymore. In that case they would have stood to lose much, and, for that reason, and because they might have been looked to by others for leadership, it is to be supposed possible that one of the Magan sons would have been entrusted with the intelligence-collecting task, both on behalf of the family, and to meet the needs of neighbours. The task would in all probability have fallen to the younger, our ancestor Morgan Magan, because it would have been logical for the elder, Richard, as his father's deputy, to remain, so to speak, at the command post at Umma-More.

If that was the arrangement, then, to the accompaniment of more breast crossing, lamentations, and invocations from the women, Morgan, and perhaps a couple of the best and most reliable men, would have set off, Morgan dressed like the men, in country clothes – saffron linen tunic, and a lightweight mantle – for Dublin. They would have been as unencumbered as possible; probably on foot. Horses could be conspicuous, as well as an encumbrance in some circumstances. The men, living as they did largely out of doors, were immensely hardy, and fleet of foot. It was no hardship to them, particularly in the month of August, to sleep in the open, or to seek the hospitality of a smoke-reeking cabin.

Their plan would have been to get near enough, and remain near enough, to Cromwell's forces, to give themselves whatever opportunities there might be to learn, if not their intentions, at least whatever might be known of their actual movements. When anything significant needed to be reported to Umma-More, one of the men, acting as runner, and able swiftly to cover great distances, would return there, and then rejoin Morgan according to pre-arranged rendezvous plans.

Meanwhile, at Umma-More, Humphry and Richard's first concern would have been the contingency planning for the evacuation of the estate. If it was overrun, disaster faced the family, but if the people and the flocks could first be got away, something might be salvaged from the wreckage. And let it here be said that these are not just vapid imaginings. During the next few weeks and months, the majority of old Irish families were destined to suffer total destruction in just such conditions as I am describing.

The outlook for the Magans, grimly making their plans, was bleak indeed. Ballymore was highly vulnerable. It was on the main route from Dublin to Athlone, the gateway across the River Shannon, to Galway, the important west coast port. That route was the waist-line of Ireland, and it would clearly be a tempting plan for any military strategist to secure it, cut Ireland in half, and deal with the two halves piecemeal. And, from what we can deduce of the nature of the Magan estate, it may be supposed to have straddled that route round about Ballymore.

Two things in particular would have been essential at Umma-More. First to arrange with other chiefs to the north and to the south for at least temporary grazing for the flocks if they had to be moved in either direction from Umma-More. At that time of year – the late summer – that would not have been an acute problem as grass would have been plentiful. Secondly, so to organize the estate that such moves could be carried out as swiftly as possible in case of need, and the estate evacuated.

If I have given the impression that the ordinary course of life at Umma-More had been suspended, indeed disrupted, then that would be the least that might be said of what had happened. It is not easy either to imagine or to describe what faced the people there. And what faced them faced people throughout Ireland. They were not steeling themselves against invasion. The enemy had already landed. A terrible, ruthless, merciless enemy, determined to shackle them as a nation, and rob them of their lands, and destroy their way of life. They waited in horror for what might be about to befall them. Meanwhile, everywhere, people were doing as the folk at Umma-More were doing – taking such probably largely ineffective steps as they could to secure some of the remnants of their lives. It might – probably would – all prove futile, but was better than doing nothing. The end of the world – their world – was upon them. The future was a dreadful, huge suspended question mark. What was it going to be like reduced, impoverished under the heel of that grim conqueror?

While arrangements for evacuation were being made at Umma-More, it must have been with at least qualified and temporary relief that those waiting anxiously there learnt from a messenger from Morgan that the English forces, with Cromwell himself in command, had marched northwards out of Dublin up the east coast. The messenger would have added that Morgan had also moved northwards on a parallel inland route to shadow the English army as best he might.

Thus, in due course, would they have learnt of the siege of Drogheda, and of its capitulation, and of the dreadful slaughter of men, women and children there; several thousand killed. Next would have come news that Cromwell had continued his northward march up the east coast and had captured Dundalk.

It would then have been with very great foreboding that a little later they would have received the intelligence that Cromwell, having sent part of his force further northwards into Ulster, had himself turned about and was now marching inland in a south-westerly direction. Indeed, the English appeared now to be moving almost directly in the direction of Ballymore. The stronghold at Trim was under siege, and it was being said that Cromwell himself was with his troops there.

Worse news was soon to follow. Indeed, doomsday must have seemed to be upon the family and all their neighbours. Trim had fallen. The English forces were approaching; moving further south-west. Skirmishing parties had already entered Westmeath. If the plan was indeed to cut Ireland in half, then Ballymore was now in imminent danger, being on the direct route from Trim to Athlone.

Then came confirmation that Cromwell was indeed marching into Westmeath at the head of his troops. Trim had been plundered and devastated with more slaughter. He had sent an ultimatum to the Earl of Westmeath to surrender to him his castle, Clonyn Castle, at Delvin, only ten miles north-east of Mullingar, or he would burn it to the ground, and tear it down stone by stone. The Earl sent Cromwell's emissary packing with a message to Cromwell, in modern parlance, to take a running jump at himself. Next day Cromwell had arrived at the head of his troops, but as he came over the brow of a hill and into view of Clonyn, he stopped and looked down in rage and disappointment upon the castle which was nothing but a smoking heap of ashes. The Earl of Westmeath had forestalled him and destroyed it rather than give the Puritans any opportunity to capture it.

There was no time now to lose at Umma-More. The contingent plans must be put into force immediately. The cattle and people, save for a skeleton staff of armed men, would now have to be moved. They would have to go southwards to comparatively safe grazing areas in the wild country in the vicinity of the great Bog of Allen. It was well for the Irish that they lived such hardy lives, and were so unused to luxury or comfort. Sheltering in temporary cabins on the fringes of the Bog of Allen would have been no unaccustomed hardship. Nevertheless, normal life had now ceased. This was war. The life of refugees.

Then the unexpected, indeed the incredible, a message that the Cromwellian skirmishers had come no further. Then that they had withdrawn. Then that Cromwell had returned with his forces to Dublin.

Then, greater relief. The storm was moving away; its mutterings getting more distant. Cromwell's plan was evidently not to attack westward through the heartland of Ireland, but to move south from Dublin down the east coast, and capture the ports facing England.

It is to be supposed that once Cromwell had moved south from Dublin, putting the Dublin and Wicklow mountains between his forces and the central plains of Ireland, that life and its essential routines would have been cautiously resumed at Umma-More. It was now autumn. Winter would soon set in. It would be likely to be spring of the following year before Cromwell's troops could finish their work in the south, and return north again.

But everyone at Umma-More would have remained acutely aware that the danger had not passed. Indeed, it had scarcely begun. What Cromwell had come to Ireland to do, had not yet started. All that he was currently engaged upon was destroying the capability of the Irish to resist the will of the English. Until that was done, the real work could not begin – that is to say the work of imposing the will of England upon the Irish.

Whatever that might prove to be, it could be nothing less than dispossession of the Irish of their lands on an enormous scale to meet Cromwell's obligation to the Adventurers and other creditors, and no-one could suppose that the rich grazing lands of Westmeath could be other than a particularly tempting prize to those acquisitive gentlemen.

Great anxiety must, therefore, have continued at Umma-More about the eventual upshot of the invasion. There could indeed, apart from the most intimate family affairs, such as births and deaths, have been no other significant subject of interest or concern during many months of 1649 and 1650, and particularly as Ballymore was not to be altogether spared the attention of Cromwellian troops.

But let us follow Cromwell's own movements, as those at Umma-More would have been following them as best they could.

Marching southwards he captured the ports of Wicklow and Wexford. Wexford was a military disgrace, which, together with the battle of Drogheda a few weeks earlier, greatly tarnished Cromwell's already harsh and ruthless reputation, and assured him a place for all time in the ranks of the world's bloody tyrants.

That the Irish had not touched their forelock to Cromwell, or offered him their allegiance on some terms or other, when he landed in Dublin, but instead had decided to fight him as and when they could, is great testimony to their courage – if any testimony is needed to the courage of the Irish. His reputation, and that of his more numerous and much better armed and equipped, and more experienced, troops, was well known to them. The odds were overwhelmingly against the Irish. But they fought. This is not the place to describe the campaign in detail, but Drogheda and Wexford have become a sufficiently important part of Irish folklore to merit a brief mention.

Drogheda was a bitterly fought battle. The Irish troops withdrew into the town and prepared for a long siege in which they hoped that Cromwell's troops, exposed to the elements outside the walls, would become decimated by shortage of food and by sickness.

The garrison reflected the topsy-turvy nature of Irish affairs. The Irish commander was a wooden-legged Englishman, a Catholic, a Royalist, named Sir Arthur Aston. His grandmother, the spirited old Lady Wilmot, he hounded out of the town at the beginning of the siege as a suspect subversive. And there were other unreliable factions in the town, reflecting the general inability of the discordant elements in Ireland to unite.

In siege warfare of the time, it was customary for a superior besieging force to call upon an inferior garrison to surrender, and to offer quarter. Failure to surrender carried the implication that no quarter was to be expected. Cromwell's much more seasoned troops outnumbered the garrison by nearly six to one. Moreover, despite the seeming impregnability of Drogheda, Cromwell, like Henry VIII's troops at Maynooth Castle a century earlier, had heavy siege artillery capable of breaching the walls.

On 10 September, 1649, Cromwell called upon Sir Arthur Aston to surrender. He refused. The battle began. This is not the place to describe it, but, after fierce fighting for the breaches which had been made by the heavy artillery, and after being repulsed by the Irish, Cromwell's troops eventually fought their way into the town.

There followed a day and a night of appalling and indiscriminate slaughter. Probably three thousand people or more were butchered. Cromwell could claim with considerable justification that that accorded with the accepted rules of siege-warfare, and that it would serve as a lesson that would cause other weak garrisons to surrender, and thus preclude further useless bloodshed elsewhere. But that is not the essence of the matter, which is that Cromwell, enraged by the stubborn defence of the 'barbarous' Irish, gave vent, in this fearful effusion of blood, to an uncontrollable fit of temper.

Wexford was worse. While parleying over terms of surrender was in progress, terms that included quarter of one sort or another offered by Cromwell for all, officers, soldiers and civilians, his troops broke into the town. A dreadful slaughter followed, which neither Cromwell nor any of his officers made any attempt to stop. It is estimated that, in addition to Irish soldiers, fifteen hundred civilians were killed, regardless of sex, which must have been the greater part of the population.

The English force that had been detached to deal with Ulster was successful. With the taking of Wexford, therefore, the whole of the east coast of Ireland was in Cromwell's hands by the onset of the winter of 1649–50. He then turned his attention to the south coast. Moving westwards from Wexford he captured Cork and other south coast ports. Thence he turned northwards, neutralized the Tipperary fortresses, and finally invested the great central citadel of Ireland at Kilkenny.

Fortunately for those at Umma-More, and their neighbours, even after those Cromwellian successes, enough strongholds were still holding out in the south of Ireland – Waterford, Clonmel, Limerick – to keep Cromwell's main forces occupied, and well away from the rolling grasslands of Westmeath, until pressure of events at home forced him to return to England. Thus Westmeath was at least spared the fighting and the immediate and personal revenge of Cromwell himself.

Nevertheless, as good a strategist as Cromwell could not be expected to neglect that important route across the waist of Ireland from Dublin to Athlone. It did thus come about that secondary columns of Cromwellian troops did operate in Westmeath during the winter of 1649–50. At first there was a good deal to distract them in the northern part of the county, well away from Ballymore, but later they turned their attention to the east-west route. The importance of Ballymore, exactly a day's march from the garrison town of Mullingar, and another day's march on to the vital frontier town of Athlone, did not escape their notice, and they set up a sizeable garrison there.

That winter of 1649–50 presents a confusing picture, with the Cromwellians pillaging the countryside in Westmeath, and bands of Irish soldiers often doing no less themselves. The English soldiers had to be circumspect about where they went. They did not talk the language. They were in the midst of a hostile and warlike people. Small parties would always be at risk. Only larger formations could move safely at any distance from the controlled routes. It was therefore possible for the Irish to make judicious use of the forest, the bogs, the marshes and hills, to keep well away from areas likely to be infested by Cromwellian troops.

The Magan family had to suffer an anxious and disturbed winter, but were sufficiently alert and adroit to safeguard the interests of themselves, their estate, and their retainers.

The war dragged on until the following year, 1651, but the aftermath was even more calamitous for Ireland than anything that had been feared, and far exceeded even the Ulster Plantation. Cromwell's edict was that Ireland was to be divided into three parts. First, from the whole of the south-east quarter of the country, comprising Dublin, the counties of Wicklow, Wexford, Kildare and Carlow, all Irish of all classes, every man, woman and child, were to be deported, and the whole area was to be re-settled with English settlers. It was truly monstrous treatment of a people in their own homeland.

Secondly, the whole of the remainder of Ireland, except for Connaught and County Clare to the far west of the River Shannon, was to be a mixed area of English and Irish, but within it the Irish were to be Anglicized and Protestantized. They must give up their distinctive Irish names and customs. Any who could not prove that they had actively assisted Cromwell's Commonwealth were liable to forfeiture of property, or even the death penalty. The penalty of death also hung over any who might be sentenced to transportation and who failed to evacuate their homes and land by the appointed date. Henceforth Ireland was to be a

Protestant country. The Roman Catholic faith was proscribed. The penalty for harbouring a priest was death.

Thirdly, those condemned to banishment were to be resettled on the unproductive marginal lands of Connaught. There the Irish were to be allowed to keep their Irish identity, and their Irish customs.

In the event, administrative and other difficulties made it impossible to put into effect in its entirety that vast project of scandalous injustices to a native people in their own country. For instance, whereas it had not been difficult to get lowland Celtic and Pictish Scots and Border English to settle in Ulster at the time of the Plantation, it proved impossible to persuade southern English peasantry to leave their English villages and take a chance in the wild, wet regions of Leinster.

Nevertheless, although the Irish peasantry were therefore for the most part not driven from their homes, the fate of the chiefs and landlords was very different. Probably more than half of all the rural ruling order of Old Irish gentry, including the long since Hibernicized and 'chieftainized' old Danish, Norman and English settlers, were largely stripped of their lands, their possessions and their power. The age-old leadership of Ireland was thus extensively and quite deliberately destroyed. It is supposed that not less than two-thirds of all the land in Ireland changed hands by confiscation and was for the most part transferred to Englishmen who did not even speak the language of the country.

And so it came about that, in the mid-seventeenth century, the people of Ireland suffered invasion from a ruthless conqueror who took from them – stole from them – two-thirds of all their lands, and handed them over to his foreign – for they were foreign – followers. Is it any wonder that Cromwell's name is execrated in Ireland above all others to this day?

The politico-religious aspects of the situation were complex in the extreme. Those landed gentry who had already become Protestant suffered a good deal less than the Catholics. The main towns and ports became almost totally Protestant strongholds, through the dispossession of the Catholics. A very strong middle and upper class of urban settler stock, comparable to the burgesses in English towns and cities, supplanted the urban Catholics and came to dominate the professional and commercial life of Ireland. They were educated, intelligent, enterprising and dynamic, and grew to be highly cultured. And because the towns of Ireland are small, and the countryside easily accessible to them, they did not lose touch with rural life and country pursuits.

The Native Irish in many towns were relegated to low-lying, or otherwise undesirable, areas which became little better than ghettos often known by some such name as Irishtown. When I was a boy the shops in the main street of Athlone were still mostly owned by Protestants. 'Irishtown' was a damp area of wretched houses low-lying along the Shannon river basin, and not infrequently flooded in winter. Even then, in the early twentieth century, that was largely believed to accord with God-given laws in such matters. Irishtown was good enough for the Catholic natives.

The confiscated lands went largely to four classes of Englishmen, and in some cases to Protestant Irish. First to Cromwell's parliamentary supporters, who were owed a debt for the backing they had given him. Secondly to the Adventurers who had put up the risk money for him, and whose pay-off was to be in Irish real estate. Thirdly, to officers of his army, in lieu of arrears of pay owing to them, and to contractors whose accounts had not been settled. Fourthly, to members of the rank and file of his army who had likewise remained unpaid.

Because of the hazard from which England had suffered through the centuries in trying to settle dependable Englishmen in Ireland, that settlers tended strongly to integrate with the Irish and become Hibernicized, it was a condition of Cromwell's settlement that marriage with Irish girls was forbidden. But, as with the grandiose plan of settlement itself, this regulation proved unworkable, particularly with the fourth class of settler, the military rank and file. They largely, and quickly, disappeared from, or melted into, the Irish scene. Some, finding themselves vulnerable on small parcels of land to revenge at the hands of the Irish, preferred to sell up to their officers who were happy to join additional property to their own land. Others married Irish girls and quickly integrated themselves, or their children did so, for the most part into the Catholic Irish peasant or small farmer community. It is on record that the Irish children of Cromwell's soldiers often could not speak English.

The first two classes of new Cromwellian Irish landowners, his parliamentary supporters and the risk-capitalists, probably became for the most part absentee landlords, letting their land on tenancy which led to gross abuses, and dreadful suffering for small-time tenenats, not least at the hands of low-class rapacious Irishmen. The the third class, the Cromwellian officers, probably, for the most part, took their new lands in hand and settled on them.

The Cromwellian episode had caused appalling and unforgettable suffering. Yet it was not to be the end of Ireland's miseries. The rape of Ireland was by no means over. But the time had come for another lull, to be followed a quarter of a century later by the final act that was to destroy the old Irish leadership for ever.

Meanwhile, we can gratefully take note of the fact that, by whatsoever chance, design or mercy of Providence, the Magans weathered the Cromwellian hurricane unscathed, or relatively so. They retained Umma-More, and we have no reason to suppose that the estate did not remain intact. It does seem remarkable that Umma-More escaped. Not only was the family Roman Catholic, but also there was at least some cause for the Cromwellians to judge the Magans guilty by association, if on no other grounds. It must be assumed that Morgan Magan and his brother Richard did not themselves play any active part in the fighting against Cromwell.

But it is to be supposed that their sister, Anne, and her husband, Henry White, were less prudent or less fortunate. The Whites seem to have been a more reckless, perhaps a more audacious, family than the Magans. Possibly Henry White was actively involved in the Royalist cause, or in the anti-Cromwellian campaign. He lost his properties at Ballymore, and was transported, no doubt to Connaught. It is to be hoped that he and Anne were spared the suffering of some of those unfortunate people whose transportation took place in the depth of winter, and that their lot may have been mitigated by the fact that Connaught was O'Conor and MacDermot country, where Magan kinsmen may have been able to give them succour. But, even if some such help was proffered, no family can have endured transportation without dreadful suffering.

Henry White had a second marriage. Did Anne perhaps die, as so many did, in consequence of whatever travail the transportation brought upon the White family? Whatever happened, it seems likely that in the end Henry White's Magan brothers-in-law succeeded in doing something to mitigate his misfortunes, and perhaps even to recover some of his lands for him, for he himself died not in Connaught but at Ballymore in 1690.

The colonization of Ireland had begun in 1601, with the English victory at Kinsale. From that time onwards England had her eyes firmly on directly ruling the whole of Ireland, albeit through a puppet government in Dublin. But it took nearly another century fully to achieve that end. Cromwell's *coup de main* went much further than any previous English blow towards the goal of total suppression of Irish opposition and of Irish pretensions to independence. But, nine years after his invasion of Ireland, he died, in 1658, with the task still not wholly done, and leaving Ireland to enjoy a lull before the next storm. Two years after Cromwell's death saw the restoration of the British monarchy. Charles II ascended the throne. He was to reign for twenty-five years, until 1685 – twenty-five years of relative tranquillity for Ireland.

1 Atlantic cliffs

2 A curragh

3 Irish country people, 1904

4 Connaught's eastern frontier – the Shannon River

5 Bringing home the peat (turf) in Connaught

6 Bringing home the milk in Connaught

7 *A Connaught cabin*

8 *"Stony seaboard,
far and foreign"*

BOOK THREE

The Family Survives the Dissolution of the Ancient Irish Chieftains in the Second Half of the Seventeenth Century

CHAPTER 17

The Last Respite of the Old Irish Aristocracy in the Reign of Charles II

DESPITE HIS PLAYBOY reputation, Charles II was an able man. No sovereign knew better than he the vulnerability of kings. His father, Charles I, had lost his head. His great-grandmother, Mary Queen of Scots, had lost hers. He was nevertheless daring enough, clever enough, and skilful enough, to exploit to the full, and to his own advantage, the revulsion of feeling against the arid and arrogant self-righteousness of Cromwell's dull, drab, puritanical dictatorship, and to do it without falling foul of the Puritans themselves, who remained a formidable body of people. As the antithesis to the Cromwell regime, Charles II's flamboyance, debauchery, frivolity, and general life style, appealed to the English instinct for not appearing to take things too seriously, to English humour, and to English enjoyment of at least mild ribaldry; it appealed to English humanity, and instinct for freedom of private thought and action, and to the English flair for joyous pageantry. He succeeded in the risky undertaking of raising a standing army for the first time in English history, and, with its support, of consolidating his own authority to the point where he became in fact the last sovereign of England to rule as an absolute monarch. Seeming tolerance and conciliation were the keys to his policy. That involved clemency towards the Puritans, while at the same time leaving the nobles and the upper gentry in peace to develop and enjoy their estates and wealth-producing enterprises.

In Ireland, his policy was to hold the coats between what was left of the Irish Catholic, and indeed old Protestant, landowning gentry, and the Cromwellians who had succeeded to their forfeited estates. His device was to effect a partial surrender of property by the Cromwellians in order to make a partial restoration to the former landlords. It pleased no-one, but was enough to keep Ireland relatively peaceful through his reign, particularly as it coincided with a period of exceptional prosperity in Ireland.

Tolerance of the Catholics in Ireland had to be tempered by a calculation of how much of it the Protestants would stand. There had, therefore, to be a measure of discrimination against the Catholics in order to satisfy the Protestants. Catholics were excluded from public office; possibly two-thirds of the land taken from them in Cromwell's time was not restored; but their faith was tolerated, and there was no additional hindrance to their prospering in their personal vocations of landowning, the professions, and commerce or trade. Perhaps it epitomizes the ambivalence of the policies that Charles II was constrained to follow that, on his deathbed, he was received into the Roman Catholic faith.

By the end of Charles II's reign in 1685, our ancestor, Morgan Magan the Elder of Cloney, was an ageing man. He had seen great changes in his lifetime, but the final and worst rigours of the Irish tragedy were yet to come. Some changes he experienced were for the better. For instance, the relative tranquillity of Charles II's reign brought with it a greater sense of security, together with the increased prosperity of the times, and enabled people to make improvements in their domestic housing. It was then that substantial stone-built wings were commonly added to tower-houses in place of the former wooden annexes. Furnishings and comforts, too, although still rustic, became more elaborate.

Changes took place in the system of land tenure which were to have disastrous psychological and economic consequences for the rural population, and which, since they involved settled ownership of the land in place of the old system of tribal common grazing lands, were also destined to bring to an end the semi-nomadic Irish life. People began to settle in one place, either as owners, tenants or hired labourers. And, where tenure seemed sound, they began to build themselves better houses.

Thus it was that in the second half of the seventeenth century there began to appear the substantial two or three roomed single-storey, white-washed, thick-walled stone cottages with good well-thatched roofs, which replaced the temporary, flimsy, porous, smoke-reeking cabins of old. The late seventeenth century type cottages have ever since been the principal rural habitations of the country people, even though all too many of the population still continued to live in wretched one-room hovels for the next two hundred years and more.

The new housing developments began to change the appearance of the countryside, and with them came other changes. Settled land tenure meant enclosure, and the great rolling grasslands began to disappear behind walls and fences. Much of the remaining forest, too, was cut by the Cromwellian settlers; a measure of their sense of insecurity. They took the timber as a cash crop, as an insurance against losing their lands should another rebellion occur. The forests of England had already been depleted, thus causing a ready market for any timber that could be had from Ireland. And so, in a very few years, in the second part of the seventeenth century, Ireland came to look very much as it does today, lacking only the future roads, railways, canals, and the great outcrop of Georgian and early nineteenth century houses that were to come, together with their landscaped demesnes.

Those were some of the changes that Morgan Magan the Elder witnessed in the years of his manhood and of his growing old. They were years of much sadness following the Cromwellian depredations, despite the good fortune of the family in having escaped the horrors of dispossession and transportation which so many of their friends, neighbours and kinsmen had had to endure.

We must suppose that life at Umma-More, and at Morgan's own house at Cloney, remained strongly under the influence of old Irish ways. Houses may have become more spacious and better appointed. Spoons and forks may have supplemented the knives and fingers of half a century earlier. Fireplaces with chimneys may have replaced the open central hearth and smoky rooms. Clothing may more often have corresponded to English fashion. Tenants and hired labour may have begun to replace the old extended family of graziers with their rights and obligations according to degree. But Irish was still the language of the home. Poteens continued to distil the water of life. The old stories were still told. There was music and dancing and singing. There were orgiastic wakes. There were ceremonies and offerings to ancient gods at holy wells and in thorn bushes. There was brushing of the hearth. Doors remained hospitably open to all comers, and nothing was stinted for their entertainment – including, let us hope, soft and innocent Irish kisses.

The Grandsons of Humphry Magan in the Reigns of James II and of William and Mary

THE LINE OF THE Magans of today, stemming from Humphry Magan and his younger son, Morgan Magan the Elder, was carried on by Morgan's younger son Morgan Magan the Younger whose older brother, Thomas Magan, had no children.

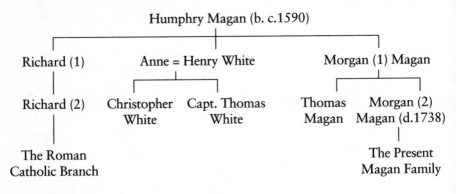

The story of the brothers Thomas and Morgan Magan the Younger illustrates the acute dilemma that faced surviving old Irish gentry families after the death of Charles II. The folly of his brother, and successor, James II, was about to engulf Ireland in disaster.

Also involved with the brothers Morgan and Thomas, in what was now about to happen, were their three first cousins. There was Richard Magan the Younger, living at Umma-More with his father Richard the Elder. And, living on their restored Ballymore property, were Christopher White and Captain Thomas White, sons of Humphry Magan's daughter Anne who, with her husband Henry White, had been transported by Cromwell, and had died.

The five first cousins, three Magans and two Whites, were men in the prime of life, probably spanning an age bracket from late teens to early thirties.

James II succeeded his brother Charles II in 1685. He was a Roman Catholic, a man of much energy, but of little judgement. He went bullheaded for the restoration of Catholicism in England. He even went so far as to commit the appalling folly of raising a Roman Catholic army in Ireland, and shipping part of it to England to support him, something immediately to arouse every 'scepter'd isle' Englishman's worst fears about the threat posed by Ireland to the Realm. That, and his other Irish policies, were to cost Ireland a century and more of such disruptive miseries that her recovery is not yet complete. It is ironic that James II, the Catholic, and Dermot MacMurrough, the Irishman, should rank as two of the prime instigators of Ireland's historic troubles.

After three years of James II's bunglings on the throne, the English leaders invited his Protestant elder daughter, Mary, and her Protestant husband, William of Orange, to intervene. They did. James II fled to France. His daughter and son-in-law ascended the English throne as joint monarchs, William III and Mary II, in 1688. They had no children and were in due course succeeded by Mary's younger sister, Anne.

In France, James II became no more than a tool in the hands of the powerful, ambitious, and seeming invincible, Louis XIV. In 1689, the year following his flight from England, James II was sent by Louis XIV to Ireland to rouse the Catholics, seize the land and, in effect, make it an outpost of Louis XIV's French empire, with James II as client sovereign.

England and Ireland were constitutionally two separate kingdoms with one king, and James II could still lay some claim to being King of Ireland.

He summoned a parliament in Dublin, re-established Catholic supremacy, took steps to dispossess 2,000 Protestants of their land, and brought the country under the control of his forces, except for a few bridgeheads which the Protestants continued to hold in the North. Most notable among them was the port of Derry (Londonderry) which survived a protracted siege which, together with the gallant ingenuity of thirteen apprentice boys, and the staunch leadership of a Protestant clergyman, George Walker, are the central theme of Ulster Protestant mythology.

Once more, therefore, after the comparative tranquillity, and prosperity, of Charles II's reign, Ireland was inevitably about to be thrown back into a state of civil strife.

But the issues involved a dimension much larger than the domestic fate of Ireland. These Irish manoeuvres were part of a great European contest that was raging at the time – the War of the Spanish Succession. The Spanish Empire was in decline. Louis XIV's ambition was to lay hands on it, and thus to dominate Western Europe. But he was opposed by an alliance of powers, the Grand Alliance, of which Britain was one.

Clearly, therefore, James II was not going to be left long unchallenged by the Grand Alliance as a French puppet in Ireland. That Louis XIV should have the resources of Ireland at his disposal, and Irish soil and Irish harbours as a base, would be disastrous not only for England but also for the other Grand Alliance powers. Protestant England, therefore, with support from her continental allies, was bound to take swift and strong action to try to remove James II and his forces from Ireland, and once more ward off the threat that Ireland posed to her strategic security.

In those circumstances, a Catholic family like the Magans was faced with an acute dilemma. On the one hand, it would be imprudent not to support James II so long as his ascendancy lasted; on the other, to do so would ensure their victimization – almost certainly their annihilation – in the likely event of his ultimate defeat by the forces of England and the Grand Alliance.

In other words, to play safe with the Catholic ascendancy in the short term was to invite almost certain destruction at the hands of the Protestants in the longer term. And the Magans must have been too experienced in Irish affairs to be in any doubt about the consequences of what, under William III, would be a Protestant victory. This time there would be no mercy from the Protestants. Cromwell had not done the job well enough. Despite his crushing defeat of the Irish Catholics, here they were once again; first a contingent of Irish troops on English soil to aid the Catholic James II, hell-bent on restoring Popery in England; and now their country and their resources placed at the disposal of England's Catholic continental enemies. The stench of Bloody Mary's burnings still reeked too strong in the nostrils of English Protestants for them to take any more chances. This time the Irish Catholics would be hard put to it to prevent themselves from being finally ground to dust. Nothing less than that would allow Protestant England to sleep easy.

As no contemporary family documents of that time have survived, we can only infer what the family did, but there is information which makes the outline clear enough. It must be supposed that there were urgent family conferences. The situation would have appeared to them no less hazardous than the Cromwellian one had been, but this time more complex. It would now be too dangerous to try, as a Roman Catholic family, to sit on the fence and remain neutral. They must take sides. But which side? To those living at any given time, even the near historical future is at best opaquely obscure, and in very disturbed and uncertain times, such as they often were in seventeenth century Ireland, the future may reveal no more of itself to frightened people than a terrifyingly impenetrable murk. Our ancestors of the seventeenth century did not have the benefit of the historical hindsight with which we can now view their situation. Ah! we say, they would have done better to have done this or that. But they were not to know. They had to consider the options that appeared to be open to them, and grope as best they could for the answers. But so uncertain must the future have seemed that they clearly judged decisive solutions to be out of the question. To chance all on the assumption that one side or the other would emerge victorious might, on the one hand, have been to play for high stakes. But, on the other, it was to risk a calamitous disaster. The dictates of prudence were that they keep the options at least as open as they could. The family therefore took what must have been the extremely difficult, if nevertheless imaginative and adroit, decision to divide their own ranks and take all the courses open to them. In the upshot – they must have calculated – something would almost certainly be lost but, providentially, not all. Much might be saved. Something might even be gained.

The central decision they made was to split the family and support both James II and William III. At all events, it can be inferred that that is how the two older Magan cousins, Richard Magan the Younger and Thomas Magan, acted; a decision endorsed by Richard's father Richard Magan the Elder. It can also be inferred that they agreed that whichever turned out to be on the winning side would not only give the other such protection as might be possible, but would also share the spoils with him. That pact held firm for the next century and a half.

That being the agreement, Richard the Younger and his father, Richard the Elder, adopted James II's Roman Catholic cause. Perhaps, as the senior branch of an old Roman Catholic family, that was judged to accord with propriety, and to be likely to be deemed fitting by their local Roman Catholic neighbours and rural retainers and supporters.

Thomas Magan, Richard the Younger's first cousin, and elder brother of our ancestor Morgan the Younger, took the other side, and supported William III and the Protestants. To save his face with local Roman Catholic opinion, the family would no doubt have been able to point to the fact that local interests generally could best be safeguarded if the Magans could remain strong and influential locally whichever side won. There have never been any indications that other Catholic families held it against Thomas that he supported William III. Indeed, on the contrary, there continued for the next century and a half to be close and fruitful associations between his successors and the Catholics. Moreover, changing one's religion was not a matter of great moment in those times.

The White family may have been less prudent, or more rash; less 'wise in their own generation', or more staunch in their religious adherence, than the Magans. We do not know what line the elder White cousin, Christopher, took, but the younger, Captain Thomas White, was forthright in his choice. The management by the Magan cousins, Richard the Younger and Thomas, of a hideously difficult situation in which, as an old Celtic dynastic family, they may have felt no strong loyalty either to James II or to William III, may have been skilfully adroit. Be that as it may, we cannot but admire the straightforward conduct of the fighting man, their cousin Captain Thomas White, who took up arms in what he must have considered a rightful cause. Presumably wholly at his own expense, he raised and equipped his own company of troops, and joined Colonel Arthur Dillon's Catholic regiment in James II's army. For him it was death or glory, or the next best thing; and, in the event, it was to be the next best thing. That he had the wherewithal to raise a small force, confirms that the White family, despite the Cromwellian transportation, had succeeded, during the reign of Charles II, in rehabilitating itself among the Ballymore landed gentry. Colonel Dillon's regiment was destined to become a part of the forces of France, and it remained a famous unit of the French army throughout the following century.

The fifth cousin was Thomas Magan's younger brother Morgan Magan the Younger, from whom we descend. He almost certainly continued to sit on the fence, and was probably able plausibly to do so because of his youth. It can reasonably be deduced that he was the youngest of the cousins, and that he may not have been more than about eighteen years of age at the beginning of the war that was about to take place, and which is known as the Jacobite, or Revolutionary, War.

Yet another cousin became involved in the fighting. I know him only as 'Young D'Alton' of Mullaghmeehan, a mile from Umma, where his father 'Old D'Alton' lived. I have omitted him from the family counsels. All that I know of him, which is very little, suggests that he was an imprudent young man, and I am surmising that the other cousins would have thought better than to share their highly compromising confidences with him. His grievous tale I shall recount in a moment.

The issues were more clear-cut than in previous Irish campaigns, and the course of the war was straightforward. In so far as it was fought to settle Irish issues, it was a straight fight for ascendancy between Roman Catholics and Protestants.

For the first year of the war the Roman Catholics were in control of most of Ireland. But the Protestants managed to hold onto their bridgeheads in the north through which forces from England were able to land, whereafter they overran the whole province of Ulster. In the summer of 1690, William III himself landed in Ulster, and marched southwards down the east coast, his objective being Dublin. Having taken Dundalk, he continued southwards, and came upon James II's Jacobite army encamped behind the River Boyne. Battle was joined on 1st July, 1690; the renowned Battle of the Boyne. Nearly 80,000 troops took part. William III's army of 40,000 contained a considerable number of Dutch, German and Danish soldiers. James II's force was a little smaller, and was stiffened by a French contingent.

The Battle of the Boyne was three battles in one. It was an English battle against Ireland – the last stand of the old Irish for their independence from England. It was secondly an English dynastic battle – the first bid of the Stuarts, in the person of James II, to regain the throne of England. Thirdly it was a continental European battle – part of the War of the Spanish Succession. In that war England, Holland and the Holy Roman Empire were the principal powers opposed to Louis XIV. It was that that resulted in the curious fact that in the Battle of the Boyne the Pope and William III were on the same side. That led the Pope, after the battle to express his satisfaction at William's Protestant victory over James II's Catholic forces. Once more, as in days of Henry II, the Papacy was involved in the suppression of Irish liberty.

As a military occasion, the battle was hardly a battle. Casualties were relatively light. James II's forces were out-manoeuvred, but not defeated, and withdrew, leaving the field to William III. James II fled to France, and thus ended any serious bid by him for restoration to the throne of England. But his army re-formed more or less intact, and carried on the war.

From the continental point of view the battle was unimportant. It solved nothing. Indeed, if the honours were calculated, it was more a victory for the loser than the winner. The fact that the Jacobite army, even without James II, remained intact, resulted in tying up in Ireland for the next eighteen months the 40,000 troops of England and the other Grand Alliance powers which might otherwise have opposed Louis XIV on the continent.

For the future of Ireland the Battle of the Boyne was of overwhelming importance. It left the Irish with no reasonable likelihood whatsoever that they could ultimately win a war against the forces of England, stiffened by the Grand Alliance. But the Irish army was nevertheless intact. It could still be a costly nuisance to England. And there was one extremely important objective for which it could continue to fight – an armistice or peace on good and lenient terms for Ireland. England might be persuaded to calculate that to continue the war to the finish would cost a great deal more in lives and treasure than she was willing to pay. So the Irish army abandoned most of the country and withdrew to the west and there, in accordance with ancient Irish instinct and tradition, with their backs to the Atlantic ocean, defied England to fight it out to the death.

The hour and the circumstances produced the man. Second only perhaps to Brian Boru, the victor of the famed Battle of Clontarf against the Norsemen in 1014, Patrick Sarsfield is Ireland's greatest military hero. He was a landowner of ancient origin whose family had gone to Ireland with Henry II in 1172, in the wake of the Norman invasion. He was a former officer of the English army, who had accompanied James II to France when he abdicated the English throne.

I must resist, as being outside the scope of this book, the temptation to recount the exploits of this colourful and competent commander. How, when the Irish were besieged in the city of Limerick, Sarsfield rode out at night with five hundred horsemen, evaded the English outposts, remained behind their lines all day, and on the following night intercepted their siege train in its bivouac on its way from Dublin, blew it and all its guns, gunpowder, ammunition and pontoons sky-high in a mighty explosion that shook the country for miles round, and returned safely with all his men to the Limerick defences. How, when the attack on Limerick came, he so galvanized everyone in the city to a citizen's defence that it must surely take its place as one of the epics of burgher courage and defiance. Men and women, wives and daughters, fought like tigers with every makeshift weapon they could lay hands upon, and the butchers rendered signal service with their carving knives. The German Brandenburghers of the Grand Alliance were not left long in their triumphant capture of the powder magazine. They and it were blown to smithereens by the Irish in one great explosion.

But we must here forego these stirring tales of heroism, save for one more, that of Sergeant Costume of Maxwell's Irish Dragoons. How, long before Macaulay ever wrote the epic of Horatius, he and a handful of desperately gallant Irishmen, in just such a feat of arms, laid down their lives to stem the Williamite advance at the Shannon crossing at Athlone. Who now remembers, when crossing the Athlone bridge, to mumble, 'God rest their souls'?

And who remembers the Irish poem, 'The Battle of Aughrim,' and the bathos of the words that tell of the no less gallant Englishman who seized the Athlone Shannon River crossings?

When, under shelter of the British cannon,
Their grenadiers in armour took the Shannon,
Led by brave Captain Sandys, who with fame,
Plunged to his middle in the rapid strame.

Both armies fought with great gallantry. But, reluctantly, I must leave their heroic deeds and get on.

That first English siege of Limerick took place in 1690. A year later, when besieged again, Sarsfield was prepared to lay down arms on extracting an honourable settlement from the English. The Treaty of Limerick was signed on 3 October, 1691. A few days later, substantial French reinforcements of men, arms and provisions for the Irish army arrived below Limerick in the Shannon estuary. The commander of the English and allied forces feared that this would cause the Irish to dishonour the treaty and fight on. Sarsfield remarked, and the remark should be remembered in the light of what is to come; 'We have pledged our honour and the honour of Ireland.'

The war was over but, once again, the Magan family had had to suffer the anxieties of war in Ireland. This time it must have come very close to them. The retreating Irish Jacobite forces did cross central Ireland and held out in a number of places against William III's army.

A battle took place at Ballymore, where a stand was made by an Irish force on that fortified peninsula in Lough Sewdy. General De Ginckle, the Dutch Commander-in-Chief of William III's troops, was himself in personal command. He later became the 1st Earl of Athlone, and died in Utrecht in 1703, where he had been born in 1630.

Ballymore could be considered the outer line of defence of the vital Athlone crossings of the Shannon, fifteen miles away to the west, and it was of importance to the Irish at least to delay the enemy there. They had done what they could to make their defences effective, but a small force of little over a thousand men, poorly armed, and with only two small cannon, was no match for the Williamite army with its artillery siege train. Besides, they had taken women and children into the fortified area to give them their protection.

The Irish garrison on Lough Sewdy was under the command of Lieutenant-Colonel Burke. A quarter of a mile away to the south-east was the old fourteenth century De Lacy castle held by an Irish sergeant and fifteen men.

De Ginckle opened on 7 June, 1691, with a cannonade on Colonel Burke's position, hoping to force his surrender, but the Irish stood firm.

De Ginckle thereupon sent a detachment to the old castle and called upon the sergeant to surrender. Although enormously outnumbered, the sergeant not only refused but let them have a volley for their pains, killing some of the English. When he was eventually forced to surrender, the Dutchman had him hanged for this spirited discharge of his duty; an outrageous way to treat a brave enemy.

On the morning of 8 June, De Ginckle bombarded Colonel Burke's garrison for several hours. He then lifted the fire and demanded the surrender of the fortress on pain of the same fate for Colonel Burke as the unfortunate sergeant if he did not comply within two hours. Burke replied that he was prepared to vacate the garrison only on terms that his force marched out drums beating, colours flying, and with bag and baggage intact. That was refused. The garrison, including the women and children, therefore held fast to endure the worst that De Ginckle could do to them.

De Ginckle then brought all his artillery and mortars to bear to pound the fortress out of existence. After suffering another four hours of bombardment, with absolutely no adequate means of reply or defence, the Irish were forced to hoist a signal of surrender. De Ginckle must have been a brutal man. He took no notice, but continued the bombardment for another seven hours. At eight o'clock that night the surrender of the garrison was accepted. Colonel Burke was not hanged. The Irish officers were imprisoned in Dublin. The men were incarcerated on Lambay Island off the east coast, north of Dublin, where many are said to have died of malnutrition and neglect.

I have no information of how closely this affray may have touched the family itself. Many of those in the fortress area of Lough Sewdy must have been Ballymore people, including all the women and children, nearly four hundred of them. Thus, if none of the Magan family themselves were in the garrison, there must have been many of their friends, acquaintances, and probably retainers among those who were.

The main provisions of the Treaty of Limerick were: that soldiers of the Irish army were given a number of options including transportation to France; that Roman Catholic members of the Limerick garrison, and other garrisons that surrendered, were promised a free pardon, and the restoration of their lands; that Roman Catholics were promised, 'such privileges in the exercise of their religion as they did enjoy in the reign of Charles II'. All that was asked of them was that they should sign an oath of allegiance to the Crown. No undertaking about their religious beliefs was to be required of them. Those provisions did not long remain in force. They were due shortly to be replaced by measures of quite exceptional severity. Nevertheless, the case of the Magan family was settled while the original terms remained valid. The family was thus fortunate that nothing worse befell it than did happen.

Richard Magan the Elder of Umma, father of Richard the Younger, was, presumably because he was the titular head of the Roman Catholic branch of the family, 'included in the articles of the Treaty of Limerick'. That means that he must either have been a member of one of the garrisons that surrendered and that he was pardoned, or that he was a sufficiently notable Catholic to be named as one to be permitted, after a caution, to continue to enjoy such privileges as had been his under Charles II.

If it is right to detect a certain prudence in the Magan family that had helped them to survive the vicissitudes of Irish history thus far, then it is likely that for that reason, and because he was elderly, Richard the Elder was not caught in one of the garrisons, and nor, we may suppose, was his son Richard the Younger, and that they had done no more and no less for the Jacobite cause than would have entitled them at least to be left in peace had James II been victorious. Being included in the articles of the Treaty of Limerick, therefore, meant in his case that he, so to speak, got off with a warning, and escaped with a whole skin and with his property intact; no doubt with the help of his nephew Thomas Magan the Williamite member of the family.

Captain Thomas White suffered the full penalty of the fighting men – exile to France. After the capitulation, the remnants of the Irish forces, 14,000 men, with their drums beating and standards flying, marched northwards out of Limerick and assembled on the north – the Clare – bank of the Shannon. Fully appreciative of this marvellous military material, King William offered to take them into the British forces. He wholly understood that these men were in no sense traitors or disloyal. They had been fighting for their lawful sovereign James II, King of Ireland. William was to them a usurper. But his sovereignty was now a *fait accompli*, and he was inviting them to acknowledge that fact. More than a thousand accepted. Another two thousand agreed to disband and return to their farmlands. Eleven thousand men, with Sarsfield at their head, placed themselves under the French flag and went into exile to continue their fight for James II. They earned themselves another romantic Irish name, 'The Wild Geese'.

Colonel Dillon's regiment chose to join the French forces, and thither, with it, went Captain Thomas White taking to France the Magan blood inherited from his mother Anne, daughter of Humphry Magan. Through his daughter he was destined to become ancestor to the Counts of Mons.

Two years later, Sarsfield became one of the glittering company to earn the exiled Jacobites' epitaph:

To my true king I offered free from stain,
Courage and faith, vain faith, and courage vain.

For him I languished in a foreign clime,
Grey-haired with sorrow in my manhood's prime;
Beheld each night my home in fevered sleep,
Each morning started from the dream to weep;
Till God, who saw me tried too sorely, gave
The resting-place I asked, an early grave.

He was killed at the moment of the French victory over the British and allied forces at the Battle of Landon in Belgium. His dying words were, 'Oh, that this were for Ireland.'

And here I must recount the dreadful story of the Magans' cousin 'Young D'Alton'. Like his other cousin, the gallant Captain Thomas White, he, too, joined the Catholic Jacobite army. But he deserted and enlisted in Athlone in the Protestant forces of the Lord President of Connaught. He turned Protestant and married the daughter of the Protestant Bishop of Elphin. Then he made a grave mistake. He returned to Ballymore.

It was one thing for the mature Thomas Magan, having no doubt ground-baited the countryside judiciously, to throw in his lot with William III, surely on a local and clandestine understanding that he would ameliorate the lot of the Catholics, while at the same time probably remaining a secret Catholic, and hearing mass surreptitiously, and quite another for Young D'Alton to desert to the enemy on the field of battle, and shamelessly and openly turn Protestant, and confirm and compound his traitorousness, and his apostasy, by marrying a Protestant prelate's daughter.

It was during a truce in the war that Young D'Alton decided to go and see some of his Ballymore Catholic friends. They received him with open arms, made him welcome, threw a party for him, and plied him with drink. They detained him beyond the time of the truce and then made him their prisoner. They then sent to his father, 'Old D'Alton', and asked what they should do with him. He sent back a reply, and it is not known whether it was meant literally, or as a figure of speech, asking why they had not already hanged the rascal, whereupon they promptly did so.

There are other examples of this curious theme of son-killing in Irish history.

One of the most notable is Strongbow who is said to have killed his own son, who was only a boy, and cut his body in two, for showing cowardice in battle.

Another famous case was that of John Lynch Fitzstephen, Mayor of Galway. In 1493, the son of a Spanish friend of his came to Galway as his guest. The Mayor's son, Walter Lynch, becoming jealous of the Spaniard's relationship with his sweetheart, murdered him.

The Mayor condemned his son to death. But no man could be found in Galway to hang him. The father thereupon strung him up himself. He felt that the example must be made because not only had his son committed murder, but he had also offended the tradition of Irish hospitality. After the hanging, Mayor Lynch returned home, and was never seen again.

And how did Thomas Magan, and his younger brother, our ancestor, Morgan Magan the Younger, fare in the Jacobite War? We know nothing of our ancestor Morgan's experiences, but we do know that he continued in his Roman Catholic faith for the next twenty years. He became known as Morgan Magan of Ballsallagh. He clearly found no difficulty in continuing to live in Westmeath as a Catholic landed gentleman.

The elder brother, Thomas Magan, must have been a man of exceptional parts. He can hardly have been other than a skilful, able, energetic and purposeful person. For any Roman Catholic to have survived the debacle of the Jacobite War with his prestige and property intact, was an achievement, but what Thomas Magan did went well beyond conserving his position and property.

Possibly, during the first year of the war, he remained as inactive as he could, while letting it be sufficiently known in the right places that he favoured the Williamite cause. After the Battle of the Boyne, he may have come forward with such additional offers of service to the Williamites as seemed prudent. Then, after the surrender of Athlone, the principal town in Westmeath, to King William's forces in 1691, he perhaps felt sufficiently secure to exploit his advantage to the full, and not only may have given all-out support to King William, but perhaps also turned Protestant himself.

After the Jacobite War, Thomas Magan can have lost few opportunities to promote his own interests and those of the family. We know that in 1695, 1697 and 1698 he was a Commissioner for raising supplies for William III in Westmeath. In 1697 he was also a Commissioner for raising money by way of a poll-tax. Presumably good pickings went with those offices. In those days you rewarded yourself as best you could out of any office of the Crown that you were able to secure for yourself.

Thomas Magan also purchased considerable forfeited landed property. Perhaps that is something we would rather overlook, but, without knowing the details, we cannot be too hard on our forebears for acting in ways that might now seem distasteful to us. We are entitled to assume that he acted in accordance with accepted practice of the times, rather than discreditably.

The estates he bought may have been forfeit willy-nilly, and he may even have been able to save their lands for some of his Catholic friends.

Some of the land he purchased had belonged to his cousins the D'Alton family. That may have been the only way to keep their lands within the family.

It would have been considered by all his old Irish neighbours of all classes to be far preferable for an ancient Irish family to take up any lands that had been irrevocably lost by other families for forfeiture, than that such property should fall into the hands of English settlers.

By 1705, fourteen years after the end of the Jacobite War, Thomas Magan had become the most powerful man in Westmeath, the High Sheriff of the county; the man responsible for administering the law and keeping the peace. He was then well placed to see that his Catholic relations and friends suffered the minimum of hardship or inconvenience. To have prospered so greatly himself, even at the expense of some others, must have proved a boon to many of the old native Catholic Irish whose interests he could help to safeguard in the harsh times that faced them.

He was known as Thomas Magan of Togherstown. Togherstown House is still standing, though altered in the nineteenth century. The parts of it that may go back to Thomas Magan's time are typical of a late seventeenth century post-tower house Irish gentleman's residence. It is a strong, unadorned, workman-like stone house; not very large, but with extensive stone outbuildings, and strong walled enclosures which must surely have been constructed for the protection of large herds of cattle. The house is three storeys high, the lower storey built into rising ground. Perhaps, in the ancient manner of the Irish of building their cabins into hillsides, Togherstown House may have had its origins in such an early hovel.

That Thomas Magan lived in such a house as Togherstown is another indication of the way the family had moved with the times. Their residences were now country houses. And, even though not very grand, or very large, and still somewhat rudely furnished, and strongly built for defence, nevertheless more nearly approaching the established English mode of the country homes of the rural gentry than was the Irish encampment life, and the tower-houses, of the beginning of the seventeenth century.

Thomas Magan's elevation to the post of High Sheriff in 1705 marks the culmination of a century during which the family had been transformed from ancient dynastic native Irish tribal leadership to high office in a colonial administration under the British Crown; a family story which precisely reflects the history of Ireland itself, where exactly a century had elapsed from the *coup de grâce* to ancient Celtic rule delivered at the Battle of Kinsale in 1601, to the consolidation of British Colonial rule following the Treaty of Limerick in 1691.

That was how fate treated one old Irish family. Their good fortune was exceptional. The majority of such families went to the wall. And that determined the fate of Ireland, and of her people. Limerick was the very last act of old Irish defiance. Well might Kathleen ni Houlihan weep for its downfall. Ere long she and her people would be too numb for tears.

We have now reached the threshold of the eighteenth century; historical times that are very familiar to us; times some of whose objects, if we are fortunate, are still in daily use in our homes. Glorious times, we are led to believe. But the glorious eighteenth century had a different fate in store for Ireland.

CHAPTER 19

Farewell the Chiefs

IRELAND, AT THE turn of the seventeenth/eighteenth centuries, was on the threshold of a remarkable period of eighty years of total peace. But it is not a time of joyous tranquillity that we are about to witness. It was the torpid passivity of a nation stunned into a deep sense of shock and misery.

There had been no need for the Irish to surrender at Limerick when they did, in 1691. They would have had to capitulate in the end. But had they kept the war going through the winter of 1691/92, William III's army would have suffered great losses from disease and privation. The Irish surrendered only because they had been able to negotiate lenient peace terms.

William III was a man of moderation. He would have been content to abide by the terms of the Treaty of Limerick. But his views were overridden by powerful Protestant cliques in both London and Dublin. The lenient provisions in the treaty were, therefore, soon ignored, indeed reversed. Lands were not restored to the Catholic gentlemen of Ireland. Instead, the old Irish gentry were finally and almost totally, stripped of their property and of such authority as had been left to them. In consequence, the way of life for everyone in rural Ireland suffered a cataclysmic change and decline.

The mere mention of the eighteenth century brings glowing pictures to the mind. And if we share the cultural background of the British Isles, we almost certainly carry with us a glamorous view of eighteenth century England as a time of exceptional magnificence and grand doings. The industrial revolution enriched the country. The globe was growing pink with British imperial possessions. The build-up was taking place for the nineteenth century image of a robust and genial John Bull who was destined to bestride the world. Englishmen were becoming larger than life. In the technical field, it was a time of unprecedented scientific, and engineering, advance and achievement. The energies and talents of the nation were liberated. There was a great outpouring of literature, music, art and architecture. It was the age of enlightenment, when men and women came boldly and gloriously out from under the lingering dark clouds of mediaeval superstition, and into the sunshine of freedom of thought and speech, but leaving not a few murky corners where obscurantist views and dark doings were still in order.

The seventeenth century had already been pointing the way to new conceptions. Life had been becoming more modern. More civilized modes had begun to prevail. Men had become more accustomed to settling their differences in the courts, rather than by resort to personal violence. Central power changed hands, if at all, and policies were modified, by political discussion and consultation instead of, as someone has said, by the dagger and the poison cup. Is England the only country in the world where, for the past three centuries, murder has been abandoned as a political weapon? Would that the question could be asked of Ireland.

Perhaps, above all, when we think of the eighteenth century, our minds turn to the ways in which the great English magnates visibly proclaimed the wealth, taste – not always impeccable – and glories of the age, in the magnificence of their life-style, the grandeur of their enormous new mansions, the range of their landscaped parks, and the vast power they wielded. And, taking a chance on disregarding the tenets of their faith, they laid up treasure as never before, and set an acquisitive example that in due course was to provide opportunities for moths and rust, and temptations for thieves, such as had hardly been known since the tombs of the Pharaohs – and a veritable Golconda for the sticky fingers of the tax man of later times.

The glorious eighteenth century was, indeed, not without its accompanying serious imperfections. Bribery, corruption and robbery were rife. Public executions of any importance resembled Derby Day. Enormous stands were erected for the benefit and comfort of the spectators, the most elegant of whom were arrayed in their Sunday best. The health hazards of that age were such that even the queen herself, Queen Anne, lost sixteen of her seventeen children in infancy, and the seventeenth died as a boy, and pre-deceased her. The Roman Catholics of England were cruelly persecuted. Rural poverty drove many of the agricultural population in the vales to work in the growing number of 'dark satanic mills'. Hogarth, Rowlandson and others depicted graphically, or described verbally, something of the squalor, the dirt, the cruelty, the drunkenness, gluttony, coarseness, and immorality.

But, for all that, there was a real smack of glory, at all events of historically short-term glory, about eighteenth-century England. The country was rapidly increasing its wealth, and even if its distribution was inevitably uneven, nevertheless, humble men, if not the very poor, had opportunities such as they had never had before to exploit their talents, enterprise, industry and ingenuity, and to rise rapidly, as many of them did, to positions of power, wealth and honour. Trevelyan says it was a free and easy society, not convention-bound, and he added, in a possibly rather over-romantic moment, that, 'perhaps no set of men and women since the world began enjoyed so many different sides of life, with so much zest, as the upper class of that period.'

When we turn to Ireland, it may seem that there, too, in imitation of what was happening in England, the eighteenth century was a splendid period of cultural flowering. Every visitor is still struck today by the elegant Georgian architecture, both urban and rural. And Ireland made her own original contribution in art and literature, furniture, silver- and glass-ware and interior decoration. She also scored some notable firsts. Was not Handel's *Messiah* first performed in Dublin? And did not the Shakespeare revival receive a special impetus from Garrick's first playing there of the part of Hamlet?

In the field of commerce and technical achievement, too, Ireland built the first inland waterway canal in the two kingdoms – for Ireland was then still constitutionally a separate kingdom. Another innovation was the founding of the Dublin Society which led the way in the voluntary promotion of industrial and agricultural experiment and advance. A young lady of fashion who knew both London and Dublin well in the early eighteenth century recorded that she found little difference in the level of civilized social life in the two cities. The population of Dublin had doubled in a century. It was still the second largest city of the realm, numbering a hundred thousand souls, and enjoying almost to the full the social and cultural amenities of the age.

But it would be misleading in the extreme to suppose from these, and other suggestive indications, that, as for England, this, too, for Ireland, was the dawning of a golden age, a moment of hope and promise, and of liberation, for all who might have the vision and the will to seize their opportunities. It was nothing of the kind. The manifestations of eighteenth century advance and enlightenment were in Ireland nothing but a superficial gloss upon the surface of a people in terrible distress. And the root cause of that distress was the deliberate destruction of the old ruling order of Irish landed gentry. If you have radical sympathies, you may not mourn the disappearance of what you might regard as a clique of aristocrats. But as you will now see, what occurred was not just the downfall of a patrician class. It was Samson and the temple. With the destruction of its pillars the whole fabric of society collapsed and has not to this day recovered.

We have seen that the old Celtic forms of society had proved very durable. They had been subject to the impact of new influences for centuries. Christianity had introduced the concept of large monastic communities, which had pointed the way to a settled life as an alternative to the semi-nomadism of the septs. The Vikings took the concept of permanent settlement even further with their walled towns and seaports. The Normans brought another variant of the settled life, the settled individual owning his own land. The chiefs and upper classes learnt to live in two cultures, the classical culture of western Europe, and their own ancient Celtic culture, and to deport themselves, when appropriate, like English gentlemen. The lesser folk, too, looked outwards even to the extent of some desire to learn Latin, the universal tongue of western education. Nevertheless, as we have seen at Umma-More, none of those influences had in the main prevailed over the old Irish pattern of semi-nomadic life that had continued to be lived more or less universally up to the time, in the latter part of the seventeenth century, when the lands were seized from the Irish and handed over to Protestant English settlers.

It was that Celtic attitude to land that had for two thousand years been the absolute core of Irish life. It remained the essential basis for such stability as there was throughout the community; the very essence of Irish ideas of justice, and the source of such health, contentment and well-being, and, perhaps above all, of such feeling of security, as every soul in Ireland might hope to enjoy. And the essence of that Celtic attitude to land was that by and large it should be treated as though it was common land. *De jure* – in law, a parcel of land might constitute the estate of a landowner. *De facto* – in point of fact, the landowner was still a tribal chief, and his estate was the common land of his tribe, clan, sept, extended family, whatever you like to call it. And by very ancient, and more or less inviolable, custom, everyone, according to his station and degree, save the serfs, who were guaranteed subsistence, had grazing and cultivating rights. And even the serfs were not so much unwilling slaves as the least capable members of the community whose small contribution was nevertheless valued and recompensed.

Within that system, all could live secure in the knowledge that everyone had a right to some share, normally at least enough for subsistence, of whatever was going. Of course there was some rough justice, and there were cattle raids, and inter-tribal forays. There were destructive climatic and other acts of God. But, given that no-one expected life to be without its hardships and its hazards, people did feel that the system assured everyone of as perpetual and secure a livelihood as Irish circumstances permitted.

And then, suddenly, that sense of security, indeed the whole basis of that security, was swept away. One morning, there was no more common land. Nowhere to graze your beasts. Nowhere for your patch of beans, cabbage and potatoes. Perhaps nowhere even to build your leaky hovel. It took half a century for the whole of Ireland to be enveloped in this fate, but it occurred mainly in two short bursts; the first following the Cromwellian campaign, the second after the Treaty of Limerick.

It was always, 'one morning' for someone, somewhere, when that day came. Every man, woman and child in Ireland, when that morning came, awoke to find himself or herself a potential beggar, totally deprived of the age-old right of access to land; and many were, quite literally, destined to be reduced to beggary.

The chiefs, in their capacity as *de jure* landowners, had been stripped of what were nominally their estates, lands which in reality were the *de facto* common lands of the people of the extended families of the estates. And those lands were given to English foreigners, or seized by them by force or fraud, and became their absolute property both *de jure* and *de facto*. No-one else had any longer any right of access to the land.

The fate that had now befallen the Irish was that less than one per cent of the population, the great majority of whom were English, Protestant, and not speaking the language of the country, Irish, now owned almost all the land, and wielded all the power, and had the whole of the people of Ireland at their mercy. Indeed, the situation looked even worse than that, because the bulk of the land was concentrated in even fewer hands, amounting to only one tenth of that one per cent. Fortunately, that tenth was the most enlightened stratum of these new English masters. But the stark fact that virtually every Irish peasant, and every Irishman who had been reduced to the ranks of the peasantry, now faced, was that unless an Englishman would take him on as a tenant, or as a hired labourer, he must beg or starve. The small amount of common land that survived into the eighteenth century was soon enclosed by the big and powerful graziers.

This may seem an over-dramatic way of putting what happened, and it may be that it is; it depends on how you like to express such an appalling experience for any nation, but I leave that to your judgement when you have read on, and have seen what did happen. Furthermore, knowing English history, if you do, you may say that enclosure of common land had already been going on for centuries in England, where much of the land was already privately owned. That is true, but in England things had been different. Land enclosure had begun in a small way centuries before. The process had been very gradual.

Then, in the late Middle Ages, England was so depopulated by the Black Death – bubonic plague – that for a time there was more land than there were people to occupy it, so enclosure hurt no-one. Then, again, the English could hardly have forgotten that, in early Tudor times, when the population began to increase once more, and there was once again a relative scarcity of land, further enclosure was deeply resented by the rural people and led to riot and insurrection, and to that consequent menace of the landless unemployed, the 'sturdy beggars' who roamed the country. Enclosure had to be curbed by law, so that much common land remained in England even up to the latter part of the nineteenth century.

Indeed, it can reasonably be argued that enclosure had reduced life in rural England to a lower level than that enjoyed on the old Irish extended family estates. It had caused poverty and beggary to become endemic in England, whereas in Ireland they occurred only in the old days as the spasmodic result of acts of God, or man. In England, even in the eighteenth century, landowners employed no more permanent labour than they could help. The villages were full of people who had no permanent employment. All they could hope for was casual work at very low rates of pay during busy seasons. No wonder the English regarded 'the poor' as a part of God's ordering of society. I truly believe that for most people in rural England in the eighteenth century life was much worse than it had been on the common lands of Ireland a century earlier, before the coming of Cromwell.

It was this huge pool of half-starved manual labour that fuelled the employment needs of English factories in the Industrial Revolution.

What was so shocking in Ireland was the suddenness, and the callousness, with which people were totally deprived overnight of their common right of access to land. It was the old case, at any rate seen from as far away as Whitehall, of it didn't matter what you did to those savages, they deserved no more consideration than the wild beasts of their forests. Nor did it matter if they starved. The less of them the better.

From that day to this, land has remained at the centre of every Irishman's heart. Up to that time it was taken for granted. Since then it has been a dream, often an obsessive dream, beyond the realization of many. If the land of Ireland was today to be parcelled out equally, there would be enough for 20 acres for every rural family. If that proposition was to be put to the vote, it would be overwhelmingly endorsed. The Irish are not materialists. They would willingly accept a lower standard of material life in exchange for a bit of land of their own for evermore. Land is their love.

But to be fair to the seventeenth century English, it is difficult to see how the Irish tragedy could have been avoided. Granted that the English had concluded that the security of their realm demanded no less than the destruction of the Irish Roman Catholic leadership, it could hardly have been contrived that the English who supplanted them could carry on the old clan system based on common access to land. If England's solution to her Irish problem was to settle the country with reliable English settlers – and no other solution had, since the time of Henry VIII, a century and a half earlier, seemed to offer England the strategic security which was to remain her paramount need for more than another century – then it could be achieved only by transferring the land absolutely to the new English owners.

At all events, it was thus that England finally succeeded in her determination to emasculate the Irish and to settle the country with reliable, that is to say loyal to England, Protestant English settlers.

A few simple figures bring home the scale and nature of the change that took place in the landowning rulers of Ireland. I have divided into three categories the families who, according to the 1904 edition of Burke's *Landed Gentry of Ireland*, made up the landed gentry of Ireland at the end of the nineteenth century. I have omitted the peerage, whose members would not have significantly altered the ratios which this analysis reveals. The landed gentry of Ireland at the end of the nineteenth century numbered, in round figures, 1200 families. Divided into three categories, their numbers were:

Pre-Norman old Celtic stock, 86 families.
Post-Norman, but pre-Tudor stock, 76 families.
Sixteenth century onwards settlers, about 1030 families.

Between the beginning of the eighteenth century and the end of the nineteenth century, some of the first two categories, who are the old Irish chiefs, would have died out. Otherwise there would not have been substantial changes in those figures during those two centuries. The figures for those two categories of Old Irish stock amount to 13 per cent of the total. That was all that was left of the former ruling aristocracy. The remainder of the landowning families, the third category, were now English Protestant settler stock who are shown in Burke's *Landed Gentry* to have acquired their Irish estates, for the most part, in the seventeenth century.

The figure that history customarily quotes for the amount of land which the Old Irish were dispossessed in the seventeenth century is about 80 per cent. Some authorities prefer a figure exceeding 90 per cent. My analysis, therefore, supports the belief that not less than four-fifths, and perhaps significantly more, of the old Irish leadership was driven from its lands, leaving an enormous leadership vacuum.

The harsh brutality of what had happened was to some extent mitigated by the fact that it occurred in two waves, nearly half a century apart, enabling some of the settlers to accommodate themselves to local conditions before others arrived. But it was no more than a mitigation of the dreadful wounding that Ireland had to endure.

An Englishman, Vincent Gookin, wrote, at the time of the Cromwellian dispossessions and transportations, a pamphlet condemning not only the hideous cruelty of driving people from their homes and into penury in Connaught, but also the unwisdom of destroying the fabric of Irish life: 'The unsettling of a nation', he wrote, 'is easy work; the settling is not.' Too true. The consequences of the unsettling continue to this day. The English knew full well what they were doing in destroying the Irish leadership and the Irish hierarchical system. They prized their own system too much not to know its value. And Shakespeare had stated it with emphatic authority:

> *How could communities,*
> *But by degree, stand in authentic places?*
> *Take but degree away, untune that string,*
> *And, hark, what discord follows! Each thing meets*
> *in mere oppugnancy.*

And Dr Samuel Johnson, more than a century later, said: 'To punish the Irish by confiscation and other penalties, as rebels, was a monstrous injustice.'

That, then, was the very end of the old Irish aristocracy. With its passing there went, too, the old observances of chieftainly life. The bards and pipers were heard no more. Much family history that had been handed down orally for centuries and never recorded in writing must have been lost in the very short time that it took for the oral tradition of repeating family annals and genealogy to come to an end, a compelling reason not to disregard such genealogical tradition as may still be current in Irish families. The Magan family is an example. We know the identity of no member of the Magan branch of the O'Conor-MacDermot clan earlier than Humphry Magan. But, around his fireside, the bards no doubt reeled off his ancestry for fifty generations back, and into the mists of O'Conor legend, but no-one was concerned to write it down. The oral tradition was sacrosanct, and marvellous Irish memories, it seemed to those living, would never forget, or have reason to forget. But they were wrong. It was all to be swept away in an historical twinkling of an eye.

An Irish poet of that time bewailed the passing of all that was joyous and gracious in old Irish life – the singing, the dancing, the music, the ancient learning and story-telling, and its replacement by what he regarded as the boorish ostentation of upstart, purse-proud English oppressors of the poor. That did less than justice to the best of the new rulers of Ireland. They were one element in that amalgam that W. B. Yeats was to call, 'one of the great stocks of Europe'.

At all events, whether or not we share the old poet's distaste of the new English settlers – and we shall soon have a chance to meet them – eighteenth century Ireland was in their hands. We must now, therefore, in a fresh chapter, turn our attention to the state, or the plight, of Ireland under that new regime, and we must also draw a picture of the new rulers themselves. But before we do so, let us spare a last passing valedictory thought for the old dispossessed Irish chiefs for whom, if there was to be no other memorial, it can at least be said, without any fear of contradiction, that they had served their people with an exemplary degree of personal courage for thousands of years. What became of them?

Many went into exile. But they did not go alone. Whatever their shortcomings, there is ample evidence that they did have the warm and genuine affection of their peoples. It is not therefore surprising that enormous numbers of lesser folk – some of them the cream of Irish brains, ability, courage, husbandry, craftsmanship and skill, which was greatly to enrich the wider world, as it had done Western Europe in the sixth century – who were not prepared to stay behind and either beg, starve or seek employment from English Protestants, accompanied their chiefs into exile in foreign lands. Tens of thousands of Irishmen died under arms in the service of France alone during the eighteenth century, many of them fighting against England, and by no means all the exiles went to France.

Some of the old aristocracy remained in Ireland to eke out a bare subsistence on marginal land in Connaught and the far west. It has even been suggested that the striking poise, dignity and courtesy often to be found among the cottage folk, particularly in the far west, is at least in part due to the impeccable manners bequeathed to them at their mother's knee as an inheritance from the dispossessed chieftainly forebears from whom some of them descend. Some of course perished on the dread transportation route to Connaught. Some married peasant girls and melted into the ranks of the peasantry. Some, all too optimistically, took no decision save to remain inactive in Ireland hopeful that a divine dispensation of Providence would restore at least part of their estates to them, as had happened in the reign of Charles II. At last, disappointed, destitute, too proud to accept menial employment, particularly from the despised English usurper upstarts, as they regarded them, who had supplanted them and now occupied their lands, they took to the woods, and joined those lesser folk, who, like themselves, were faced with the choice of starvation or highway robbery.

Of course, they could not survive, and, when caught, were summarily hanged. Of course, too, and perhaps emulating Charles I, father of their Roman Catholic king, James II, to whom they had given their allegiance, they died bravely. And, like him, they 'nothing common did or mean', but, again in his image, made short and dignified speeches from the scaffold, which were remembered and became a part of Irish folklore.

And they gave a word to the English language. 'Tory' is the Anglicized form of the Irish word meaning a robber. Those fugitive highwaymen were in particular known as tories, and the word became colloquially attached generally to supporters of James II and the Stuart cause in the late seventeenth and early eighteenth centuries, and thus passed into the English political vocabulary.

And so, farewell to the old Irish chiefs. Farewell to true aristocracy in Ireland. Farewell to the nation's leaders. And now let us look at the state of a leaderless country. Let us see what happens when a nation is 'unsettled'.

BOOK FOUR

The Colonial Suppression of Ireland in the Eighteenth Century; and the Accommodation of the Family to the New Protestant Settler Ascendancy

CHAPTER 20

The Unsettling of a Nation –
the first half of the eighteenth century

BEFORE WE CAN rejoin the family in the intimacies of the life that faced them in the post-Treaty of Limerick era in early eighteenth century Ireland, we must first set the scene with which they now had to try to come to terms; and we must meet the new English settler masters of Ireland, and judge what sort of people they were.

In the wake of the London and Dublin Protestant lobbies' success in overcoming William III's desire to honour the provisional terms of the Treaty of Limerick, upon which the Irish had surrendered, there followed a terrible series of enactments and legislation against the Roman Catholics of Ireland known, notoriously, as the Penal Laws, or the Penal Code, which were to remain in force for nearly a hundred years, and some of them for longer. Catholics were not the only sufferers. Extensive disabilities were also heaped upon dissenting Protestants – Presbyterians and others. But it is with the fate of the indigenous Irish Catholics that we are here primarily concerned, since they were the real and original people of Ireland.

The unilateral abrogation by the English of the terms of the Treaty of Limerick, and the introduction of the Penal Laws, were nothing short of acts of gross bad faith. Patrick Sarsfield had pledged his honour. Why did the English not abide by theirs? Fear was the overriding immediate reason – Protestant fears in both Ireland and England. The Battle of Stoke may have been but dimly remembered. But in rural areas of Ireland, where Protestants were in a tiny minority, the great Rebellion of 1641 was far from forgotten. Recollections of the brutal murder of English settlers, the burning of their homes, and the destruction of their goods and property, were in the forefront of every settler's mind, together with the fact that they had just experienced a moment of the greatest peril at the hands of James II, and the Catholics, during the short time that he ruled in Ireland before the Battle of the Boyne. They were acutely aware that they were in the midst of a potentially, and often actually, and actively, hostile population, to them foreigners, talking a foreign tongue, on whose stolen lands they were trying to consolidate their hold.

In the measures they took to safeguard themselves and their new-won properties, they did not lack support from their Protestant English brothers across the water. They, the Protestants of England, for their part, were only too well aware that the Stuart cause, and Catholic ambitions, were far from dead. And they were to be proved right. There was to be at least limited civil war in Britain during the coming half century, particularly in 1715 and 1745, when the Stuarts, supported by foreign powers, tried to regain the throne of England, and the Catholics strove for the ascendancy. And English Protestants were highly sensitive to the possibility that the Irish Catholics might once more, as in the past, give aid and abetment to their enemies. Indeed they were not capable of seeing the Irish Catholics in any light other than as the enemies of England, and they habitually referred to them as such. And there were indeed real threats of French expeditions to Ireland in the first half of the eighteenth century.

The Protestants, both in Dublin and in London, resolved therefore, to destroy Roman Catholicism in Ireland if they could; and to the extent that they could not, to reduce Irish Roman Catholics to a state of such total impotence that they could never again rise above a status hardly better than that of ignorant, ragged, poverty-stricken serfdom. And to that end the Penal Laws were enacted. It was not mainly their Catholicism that was the object of hostility, although that, in view of the Stuart threat, was seen to be dangerous enough. The object of their hostility was the native Irish people themselves, identifiable as such by their Catholic badge.

There is something so abstract and distant about a recitation of the Penal Laws as to make it difficult to record them in such a way as to bring home the full force of the human misery that they entailed and engendered. To read a catalogue of them is comparable to learning that the Yangtse Kiang has burst its banks and a million people are homeless. It is a calamity too distant and on too great a scale to touch the heartstrings. Nevertheless, at least some account of them is unavoidable if we are to see how the Magan family coped with and survived their consequences.

The overriding principle that justice was to be denied to the Catholics was embodied in the law forbidding them the right to sit in the Irish parliament – a monstrous prohibition in an overwhelmingly Catholic country. The governing of Ireland was thereby to be wholly in the hands of a small Protestant minority.

Worse was to come. After 1727 Catholics were deprived of the vote. They could not, therefore, even elect Protestants of their choice. Catholics could hold no public office under the Crown, not even the most insignificant. They could not be members of the armed forces. They could not be members of, nor practise, any learned profession, save medicine. No Catholic could be a teacher, or keep a school. Then what on earth, we may ask, was there left for educated Catholics to do?

The answer is that there were to be no educated Catholics. Catholics were debarred from receiving any education either in Ireland or abroad. It was a deliberate policy to ensure that no Catholic should ever again rise above a state of ignorant impotence. After 1733 Catholics were allowed to attend a particular and special type of school which was set up for the express purpose of securing that the pupils should adopt the Protestant faith. In other words the educational alternatives for Catholics were, either to be brought up in total ignorance, or to be taught at the cost of subversion of their faith. A price was placed on the heads of clandestine Catholic teachers.

The laws which were most damaging to the fabric of Irish life, which were the most short-sighted, and which were destined to have the most harmful long-term effects on Ireland's political and social future, were the laws affecting landed property. They were designed to ensure that all land should pass into the hands of Protestants, and that the overwhelming Catholic majority should never again rise above the status of tenants or peasant labourers. Right of access to, or ownership of, property is the most stabilizing influence in society. As Wilfred Scawen Blunt wrote:

> *Nor has the world a better thing*
> *Though one should search it round,*
> *Than thus to live one's own sole King*
> *Upon one's own sole ground.*

Nothing is more likely to cause a person to think and act responsibly than a stake in a piece of immovable real estate.

To dispossess the great majority of all such rights, and to divide society into a small class of haves, and great mass of have-nots, as was the case in eighteenth century Ireland, is inevitably to invite an upsurge of revolutionary politics of envy. To ensure that those divisions are further distinguished by differences of creed, is to invite a perpetual state of religious discord which was underlined by a law forbidding Protestants to marry Catholics.

The greater part of the land having already been taken from the Catholics and given to Protestants, additional legislation was enacted further to limit Catholic land ownership. For instance; the few Catholics who still owned land might not bequeath it to their eldest sons, except in cases where the eldest son turned Protestant. Otherwise the land must be divided between all the children, the hope being that some of them would turn, or be forced by circumstances to turn, Protestant. If an eldest son turned Protestant, his father became little better than his tenant. The father could no longer sell, or lease, any of his property, or give or bequeath any of it to his other children or to anyone else. Catholics could not buy or inherit property, or receive it as a gift, from Protestants. That was to prevent friendly Protestants either from helping their Catholic neighbours, or doing a deal with them. Catholics could not hold annuities or mortgages on land.

Any Protestant had the right to force forfeiture to himself of any land discovered to have been surreptitiously bought by a Catholic.

Most cruel of all, a Catholic could not be the guardian of minor children A dying Catholic landowner had therefore the additional anguish of knowing that his children would be removed by the courts from the custody of his wife to be brought up as Protestants by some nominated Protestant guardians, and it needs no great stretch of imagination to suppose what would have become of the property.

Without taking this catalogue of disabilities further, it can be seen that it was the purpose of these laws to degrade Catholics to the lowest dispossessed levels of society. It can also be readily understood that they opened up a vast field of abuses to petty spies and disaffected members of families whereby, by laying cases in the Protestant courts where Catholic defendants could expect no redress, they could enrich themselves at the expense of their neighbours or their relatives.

Catholics were allowed to engage in commerce, but only on payment of special taxes, and they were excluded from living or trading in some of the main ports and cities, notably Limerick and Galway. Vexatious and restrictive conditions were attached to Catholic enterprises, such as that a Catholic might not employ more than two apprentices, thus hampering the enterprising. Catholic bishops might not reside in, or visit, Ireland. Priests might perform only restricted duties, and then only on licence. No priests could be trained in Ireland or abroad. Catholics must pay tithes to the Protestant Church of Ireland. And I suppose I must include the well-known law that no Catholic might own a horse valued at more than £5. Any Protestant had an absolute right to demand from a Catholic the immediate surrender of his horse, however good, on payment of that sum.

But oppression was not limited to the Penal Laws. Not only were the Catholics individually reduced to impotence in so far as it was possible, but Ireland itself was also rendered as near commercially bankrupt as could be, and robbed of such substance as she might thereafter have left.

The chief source of Irish earnings had been the export of meat to England. In the latter part of the seventeenth century, legislation was enacted to prohibit that trade, thus threatening to destroy Ireland's principal export at a blow. Alternative continental markets were found, but a more secure future seemed to offer if the pastures were turned over to sheep. Wool of excellent quality was produced and a remarkable and flourishing wool trade was developed. But in 1699 crushing legislation was enacted which destroyed the Irish wool trade.

Ireland was promised in its place some encouragement for her linen trade, but what she got was an imposition of heavy duties on sailcloth imports into England, and a total prohibition of exports of certain linens to the British colonies.

Ireland has excellent natural harbours. Her central position in the post-Renaissance world of ascendant sea power gave her natural entrepôt advantages in the increasing cycle of trade both with the New World, and with the growing colonial possessions of Britain and other European countries. Although the Irish are skilful with small inshore boats, they are not notably a sea-going people. Indeed, they largely neglected the abundant fish in their coastal waters, looking upon fish as hardly fit for human consumption, appropriate only for the part-penitential fare of a fast day. Nevertheless, they might one way or another have learnt to exploit their natural maritime and mercantile advantages had not England forbidden the use of Irish harbours, or the employment of Irish shipping, in all that growing international trade.

In addition to those disablements, she had to bear the full expense of a Protestant army garrisoned in Ireland, and she continued to pay those troops even when they were drawn upon to serve in England in the Jacobite wars.

The most lucrative appointments in Ireland went to, and all the chief offices were filled by, Englishmen. And scandalous 'pensions' – enormous pensions – were paid from the Irish exchequer to persons who had not only rendered no service to Ireland, but had never set foot on Irish soil, or indeed rendered any but infamous service to anyone; royal favourites, discarded royal mistresses, and royal bastards – among them Charles II's natural son by Nell Gwynn, the Duke of St Albans, who had an Irish pension of £800, a very large sum in those days.

The Protestant church, too, with, of course, notable, pious, and Christian, exceptions, conspicuously failed in the person of some of its priests in its good Samaritan duty to render aid to this poor prostrate wounded country; and joined instead in the stripping and robbing. There was shameful abuse of church livings. One English bishop held an Irish diocese for twenty years without ever setting foot in it, and put his benefices up for sale. Another spent a total of eighteen months out of twelve years in his diocese. Another gave all the livings of value to his brothers and relatives. The collection of tithes was not infrequently farmed out to the worst sort of brutal low-class Irish rent collector; and tithes were payable only on the small arable holdings of poor Catholic tenants, and not on the great grass pasture ranches of the large Protestant landowners.

To ignore the disabilities suffered by dissenting Protestants would be to give an unbalanced picture of Irish eighteenth century conditions. The large Presbyterian population, particularly in Ulster, being technically dissenters, and outside the law, were, for instance, in 1709 expelled from public service, and debarred thenceforth from holding public office. That measure alone is sufficient to indicate the degree of oppressive Anglican Protestant measures against them.

The situation, then, in Ireland, at the beginning of the eighteenth century was this. England, ultimately for purposes of her own strategic safety, held Ireland prostrate and allowed her no chance to develop an independent existence of any commercial or other strength. The new Protestant landlord class insisted on widespread disabling legislation to keep the Irish Catholics in a state of perpetual submission and weakness. Virtually the whole native population of Ireland was reduced to a near starving condition as miserable serfs to, or insecure tenants of, the new Protestant landlords, and condemned to perpetual ignorance and deprivation of all means towards civilized self-improvement. The large Presbyterian population was treated as a community of second-class subjects, loaded with restrictive disabilities, and deprived of the right to participate at any level in government.

But if a country is deliberately impoverished, then everyone is liable to suffer, and, in the first half of the eighteenth century, the consequences for the Irish generally, even for many Protestants, were little short of disastrous.

The first consequence of those harsh policies was the loss to Ireland of many more of her best citizens, not only Catholic, but Protestant and Presbyterian as well. Ireland, denied opportunities to prosper, denied her share in the chances offered by the Industrial Revolution, and growing world trade, and with fierce discriminatory laws against the majority of her people, was no place for able and enterprising citizens. There they could only rot and waste their God-given gifts and talents. They went abroad in enormous numbers, and not only Roman Catholics. Even though the number who emigrated from other denominations was much smaller, it has nevertheless been estimated that not less than a quarter of a million Presbyterians went to America during a period of less than a century, and were destined to play a much larger part there than emigrant Irish Catholics in the coming American War of Independence against Britain. Indeed, few Catholics went to North America in the eighteenth century. It was at that time a Protestant British colony. Many of the most able Protestants also left Ireland for ever.

Since their religion was suppressed, and education forbidden, mass, often by connivance of Protestant landlords, was said by the Catholics under the hedges, on stone altars in the fields and among the furze bushes, and in tumble-down barns and outhouses; and so-called 'hedge schools' grew up in similar conditions. It had been noticed by seventeenth century visitors to Ireland that the Irish were avid for learning. Nevertheless, it cannot seem other than extraordinary that the ragged, barefoot, half-starved children of the eighteenth century Irish peasantry, sat, if not literally under Ireland's dripping hedges, at best in wretched farm structures, fervently learning Latin to equip themselves for eventual emigration, and escape to, and employment in, Europe, and away from their dreadful lot at home.

And so it was that many of the best of the Irish flocked out of Ireland and went anywhere and everywhere in the world where their talents and abilities might be wanted, appreciated and, above all, fully used; and they peppered the world with a huge abundance of illustrious Irish names.

There was nothing altogether new about that. Ireland had never been able to offer sufficient scope for all her talent. As early as the end of the Roman Empire in Britain, Ireland had provided leadership across the water by founding dynasties in Scotland and Wales. Two centuries later, Irish divines had played an important role in Britain, and deep into Western Europe, giving leadership to the reviving western Christian world. We would be wrong to look upon those seventh century Irishmen simply as gentle, holy, itinerant monks. Inside those habits were resolute men of strong purpose, much courage, great enterprise and marked ability. A brief glance at a few entries in the Irish Roll of Honour in the eighteenth century is therefore less a matter for amazement than for a little acclamation.

The Irish are great soldiers. Many emigrants joined foreign armies; 'Fighters in every clime; in every cause but their own,' and, to England's great loss, not infrequently in the ranks of her enemies. At least one Irishman became a Marshal of France. Two became Russian Field Marshals. Several became Spanish Generals; one a Spanish Admiral. And there was the colourful Ambrosio O'Higgins, only one of many great Irish names in South America. As soldier and administrator, he rose to be Governor of Chile, Viceroy of Peru, and the King of Spain's principal representative in South America. But it was not only in military uniform that Irishmen succeeded. One became a French Archbishop. The physicians to the kings of France and Spain were both Irishmen. The Irish excelled in diplomacy, several representing European countries as their ambassadors. And Irish immigrant families have given the United States of America fifteen of her Presidents.

Thus it was that the Penal Laws and other restrictive legislation caused Ireland an enormous loss of leadership material, talent and ability in the eighteenth century. In particular the numerically greatest part of the population, the Catholics, were left leaderless. The Roman Catholic gentry had all but disappeared. The Roman Catholic bishops who might have helped to fill the vacuum could not lawfully reside in Ireland. Such leadership as there was, therefore, devolved largely upon the persecuted priests. They were the only Catholics with any semblance of a role, even locally, involving some corporate and co-ordinating authority. But, in a well-ordered society, it is undesirable, and not in the best interests of the community, that the role of the priesthood should extend beyond the pastoral field. They are not brought up or trained to secular leadership. And in eighteenth century Ireland they were progressively drawn from the peasantry whose habits, inclinations and prejudices they shared. They were ignorant and poor, destitute save for what they were given by, or could extract from, the peasantry. Their courage, their zeal, and their celibate morality were never impugned, but they were in no position to provide a respected leadership, particularly in a community long used to an elitist aristocratic tradition.

There was a stratification of Irish life into five main classes. The most important, and the one to which the Magans belonged, the resident landed gentry, will need a chapter to themselves. The other four were the absentee landlords, the merchant and professional classes, the small mainly Protestant farmers, and the Catholic peasantry.

Of all the scourges that Ireland suffered in the eighteenth century, the absentee landlords have attracted the greatest odium. Many of them were already men of substance in England. They had no need to live on their Irish estates, and certainly no wish to live among the hostile, barbarous Irish. They had often obtained large tracts of land as a recompense for some service rendered, or in discharge of some debt owed to them by the English government. They regarded it simply as an investment on which an income could be raised by letting it out to tenancy. Nor were they concerned in many cases, to squeeze the last penny out of it. They were prepared to let it go at a quite reasonable rent to a secure tenant.

But that was only the beginning, and the beginning of an industry, a racket. The tenant-in-chief would then sub-let to lower tenants, who came to be called 'middle-men'. The tenancies might then be sub-let again. Some land was saddled with four or five layers of middlemen, each needing a cut on the rent, before finally at the bottom of the pile the land was parcelled out in penny packets at exorbitant rents to the half-starved Catholic peasants, whose only access it now was to land, and who were usually too poor to own any farm implement beyond a shovel, and who, with nothing beyond nominal security of tenure, and with no redress in the Protestant courts, had always hanging over them the threat of eviction, which happened only too often – for instance if the land was taken from them, under whatsoever trumped-up pretext, by a large grazier who wished to extend his pasture – and who were then thrown back on those dread alternatives of beggary or starvation. For them the wonders of the age of enlightenment offered no palpable social advance over, but indeed far worse conditions than, the primitive tribalism of the ancient Irish sept, privileged aristocratic hierarchy and all.

Nor were the absentee landlords themselves always so ignorantly benevolent as that may suggest. One absentee peer of the realm with huge estates in the North of Ireland, imposed, when the leases fell in, enormous fines on his tenants which they were quite unable to pay. He then let the land over their heads to two or three rich Belfast merchants. The entire population of a vast district were driven from their homes, forfeiting all such improvements as they had made to their holdings in the expectation of renewed leases, albeit at higher rents.

Another trick, when leases fell in, was not to offer them directly to sitting tenants, but to put them up for offer through advertisement. The sitting tenant then had no recourse but himself to offer the highest rent at which the holding would be marginally viable in order to give himself the maximum protection he could afford against being out-bid and evicted. Can anyone wonder that land is an emotive subject in Ireland?

Although the mercantile life of Ireland was severely hampered by trade restrictions, it was not something that could be entirely destroyed. Without some trade, and services, such as banking, the country would have been totally destitute. The English had vested interests in Ireland that they were not prepared altogether to jeopardize or destroy. Besides, as happens to this day, merchants find means to evade embargoes and sanctions, by the use of legal and quasi-legal expedients, and, as happened on an undoubtedly large scale, from the remote bays, coves, ports, harbours and estuaries of Ireland, illegal devices and contrivances, including smuggling by great and small alike.

It is notable that only a few thousand residents of Ireland were registered in the eighteenth century as converts from Catholicism to Protestantism, but of those a large number were lawyers, whose conversion as often as not was thought to have been a merely nominal matter of convenience. The whole of the legal system, judges, professional lawyers and jurymen was in the hands of Protestants. Indeed, Roman Catholics were virtually denied the protection of the law. The Lord Chancellor and the Lord Chief Justice laid it down from the bench, 'that the law does not suppose any such person to exist as an Irish Roman Catholic.' There was therefore a most urgent need for seemingly recanting Roman Catholics to work within the legal system to afford Catholics whatsoever protection they might.

Commercial and professional life did, therefore, go on, even though much less vigorously than would have been the case had it not been for the Penal restrictions. And, although the advantages were always heavily weighed in favour of Protestants, some Catholics did succeed not only in enriching themselves, but indeed in becoming wealthy.

The smaller Protestant farmers, the men of fifty acres up to a few hundred, of whom there were some thousands, earned themselves a bad reputation in the eighteenth century which, though undoubtedly richly deserved, is now hard to credit. Anyone who has known that type of yeoman Irishman during the past half-century, whatever his creed, and there are thousands of them of all denominations in Ireland, knows him and his wife and family to be essentially hard-working, shrewd and thrifty people, with a very real countryman's understanding of what they are doing.

But the mainly Protestant newcomers of the early eighteenth century have left a picture of themselves as flashy, extravagant and querulous. Many of the 'middlemen' were of this class. They have been described as having combined the pretensions of gentlemen with the manners and deportment of boors.

They rack-rented their properties to miserable tenants whom they treated worse than slaves, while they themselves lived in idleness, hunting mangy half-starved packs of hounds, going from race meeting to race meeting in their laced coats, gambling recklessly, drinking more than they could afford or hold, and not infrequently becoming embroiled in disgraceful public quarrelling and fighting. They altogether lacked those sound and solid middle-class virtues which were then in England, and are today also in Ireland, so large a part of the core of the political, economic and social fabric of the country.

Then there were the peasantry. Left to themselves in the old tribal days, they were a hardy people, content, and truly content, with very little in the way of material things. In the late seventeenth and early eighteenth centuries they would still have been content with that. But contradictory conditions prevailed. The semi-nomadic life was at an end. The fortunate owned a few acres as peasant proprietors with enough to give a subsistence existence, and with rights on a bit of red bog to give an assured supply of fuel. They enclosed the land with walls or fences, and perhaps built one of those substantial, well-thatched, thick-walled cottages, and even possibly some comparable outbuildings to shelter the animals.

The next most fortunate were tenants of good landlords, with secure tenancies, who similarly could settle down, and, in reasonable confidence, build permanently upon, and otherwise improve, their holdings. Thus Ireland became dotted with strong white cottages, and small fields enclosed with fences, more often than not of whitethorn, very beautiful in the spring. In other places the boundaries were no less beautiful loose dry-stone walls. Elsewhere were built the enormous banks that the Irishman and his horses have ever since jumped with huge zest.

But much the greater number were far less fortunate. Their tenancies were either insecure, or rack-rented to a point below subsistence, or insufficiently productive to feed a family for twelve months in the year, leaving at least two hungry months in the summer between the end of one potato harvest and the beginning of the next, when armies of people habitually took to the roads and begged, or stole, or both. An able member of the Irish parliament, who was later promoted to be Governor of Carolina, Arthur Dobbs, surveyed the economic state of Ireland during the first part of the eighteenth century. He estimated that there were some 34,000 people reduced to begging the whole year round – roughly 1,000 per county – and the figure rose to 100,000 for the whole country for up to three or four months during the summer.

Those conditions and the debilitating consequences of the Penal Laws so inhibited enterprise that the economy of Ireland was at best at a standstill in the first part of the eighteenth century. And an ominous new factor was beginning to appear. The very poor of Ireland were becoming enormously dependent on the potato. But now and again partial failures of the crop were already occurring, with consequent partial famine conditions in the early part of the eighteenth century, foreshadowing the dreadful calamity of a century later. Indeed there was a major famine in 1740–41. Contemporary figures put the death toll at about four hundred thousand – twenty per cent of the population which, if the figure is accurate, is as high a proportion of the nation as perished in the great nineteenth century famine.

The Penal Laws had other and more subtly damaging consequences for the fabric of Irish life. If the authorities harass the people with intolerable laws, there will be no loyalty to the government. More probably there will be active disloyalty. Furthermore, there will be disrespect for the law, and habits of law-breaking will become the rule. The whole Catholic community of Ireland was forced into just that condition. There could be no remission from their miseries save in breaking, evading or avoiding the enormous mass of discriminatory legislation that was so oppressive and destructive that Dr Johnson, when condemning British policies in conversation with an Irish Protestant clergyman who, like many other Irish Protestants, viewed the plight of the Catholics with compassion, said; 'They would have been better off dead.'

And law-breaking was not confined to the laity. Only by breaking the law, only by evasion, subterfuge and disguise, could the Catholic bishops visit their flocks, and then only at great danger to themselves. And not only were the priests hand in glove with the mass of the people, but, for their own safety, had often to be most closely associated with the worst criminals, robbers, smugglers and the like, who had developed the most effective and efficient means of law evasion. As the people could feel no commitment to the government, their church became the focus for their loyalty; and its leaders, at least at the level of the local priests, despite their fortitude in the face of constant danger and persecution, were inevitably sometimes men who, as one writer has put it, were at least apt to look 'with very insufficient abhorrence upon crimes which, as religious teachers, it was their first duty unsparingly to denounce'; men, too, who, because of their own poverty, were not above falling upon the poor 'armed with the terrors of damnation', to demand their full quota of offerings. Those were indeed unhealthy proclivities to have forced upon any community or nation.

To what extent can England be said to have been justified in following the policies that she adopted towards Ireland at that period of her history? In general, for more than two centuries, from the time of Bosworth Field onwards, Protestant England had been under threat, and under intermittent attack, from her powerful Catholic continental neighbours. In particular, she was, at the time the Penal Laws were introduced, under threat from the Catholic Stuart claimants to the throne, and from Louis XIV of France, whose ambition was no less than to make himself master of Europe, and who could boast forty years of military success. So great were the dangers that the battle honours whereby the Duke of Marlborough broke the power of France still ring like music in English ears – Ramillies, Blenheim, Oudenard, Malplaquet. And the Irish had shown themselves only too ready to ally themselves with England's foes.

Seen, therefore, in the light of England's defence interests, there can be only one answer to the question. England could not be other than justified in her own eyes in pursuing policies in Ireland calculated to ensure her own strategic integrity. Moreover, in a very important sense, the policy worked. For the first time in two thousand years Ireland was to have internal peace. For the eighty years that followed the Treaty of Limerick there was absolute tranquillity from any sort of rebellious activity in Ireland, and for more than two hundred years, such rebellious activity as occurred from time to time was, save for the 1798 rebellion, for the most part on a much smaller scale than the perennial internal strife of former times.

But might England not have been more humane, and less brutally severe? Perhaps it is now pointless to say more than that those policies were in line with the customs of the time. Legislation against Catholics in England was scarcely less harsh, and in some respects more so, than that applied in Ireland, or than legislation in continental Catholic countries directed against Protestants. Indeed the Irish Penal Laws were more or less modelled on the French legislation against the Huguenots, and were almost mild by comparison with the deeds of the Catholic Spanish Inquisition of the late seventeenth century.

That Ireland was thus raped, oppressed and held in bondage in the sixteenth, seventeenth and eighteenth centuries, was directly due to the shift of the epicentre of world influence from Eurasia and the Middle and Near East to the Atlantic, which enormously increased Ireland's politico-geographic importance. Her relative situation changed from that of a largely forgotten, neglected and unimportant distant shore on the outer fringe of the civilized world, to a crucial position almost at the hub of it. Ireland, a small country, relatively backward, and internally divided, was unable to hold her own against the much more powerful European Atlantic nations. Moreover, the Western powers themselves could not ignore the enormous importance of her situation, and certainly could not trust each other to do so. She was therefore condemned to the role of a pawn. And she was not to be given the chance, during the next two centuries, to fit herself for the part of a principal, albeit a small one, in European, let alone world, affairs.

We can study the storms and squalls of history as we may. We can condemn Cromwell, and burn him in effigy if that makes us feel better. We can relieve our feelings, if those are our feelings, with Swiftian outpourings of odium, vituperation, abuse, contumely, reprobation, denunciation, objurgation, vilification, damnation, and a dozen other kinds of good round abuse, upon the head of the English government for its abrogation of the Treaty of Limerick, and the hideous cruelty of the Penal Laws. But, when all is said and done, and no matter what the details of history might have been, the coming of maritime imperialism rendered inevitable in some form or other the fate that Ireland suffered between the sixteenth and eighteenth centuries. Her geographical position was so important that she was bound to be subordinated to the will of one or other of the great powers. And the possible alternatives to England as her master might have been even worse.

If the Spaniards had won the battle of Kinsale, it might have been the Inquisition, and there might have been no more native Irishmen left in the world today than there are original native inhabitants of South and Central America and the Caribbean Islands.

If James II had defeated William III, the Irish would have had a pig-headed English monarch whom they would have liked little, and they and he would have had to dance to the tune of Louis XIV, with the possible consequences for themselves comparable to the fate of the Huguenots. The least assertion of any spirit of independence would have brought down on their heads a repetition of the appalling persecution suffered by the Protestants of France.

And if, a century later, the French money and French support, that aided the

1798 Irish rebellion, had achieved their aim, Ireland would have had Napoleon for master. The citizens of Moscow know what that would have meant.

Ireland was inescapably caught in this web of international power politics. Nothing could have saved her from the dominance of one or other of the powers. The cause of Ireland's fateful history during the sixteenth to the eighteenth centuries was not race, religion, or culture, but something altogether irremediable; her geographical position in the age of the ocean-going ship. She was inevitably doomed to become the client, willing or unwilling, of some greater power, so long as the nations of Western Europe were at odds with one another.

The Gintry

IN THE NEXT CHAPTER we shall return to the Magans and the consequences for them of these great changes that were being wrought in their Irish homeland. But, before we do so, we must, on two counts, meet the new masters of Ireland.

In the first place, the Magan family was now about to join them, and to adopt their ways; indeed become a part of them. Secondly, at that period of history, when landownership was a pre-condition of power, it was this group of English settler families, together with the few old leading Irish families that had survived, which came to hold virtually all the power that anyone in Ireland was allowed by Whitehall to hold. It is therefore necessary to make their acquaintance, and see what sort of people they were.

I have advisedly called the settlers the new 'masters' of Ireland. I have used the word 'leaders' for the old chiefs. 'Masters' the newcomers were, and rulers, but never leaders in the sense that the chiefs were. Leaders, with a few exceptions to prove the rule, they could never become.

Culturally they in no way resembled the people they supplanted. They were quite unlike the Celtic chiefs. Their mould was that of a squirarchy of England.

In Ireland, as a class, they acquired a number of labels. 'The Protestant Ascendancy.' 'The Anglo-Irish.' More particularly, 'The Landed Gentry of Ireland.' But to the people of Ireland they became 'The Gintry', and that is the title that best suits them. It is more than just the Irish pronunciation of the word 'gentry'. It is descriptive of the fact that they came to mould themselves sufficiently to the local scene to be accorded by the generality of the people a respectful place in Irish life. They came also to regard themselves not only as Irish, but as 'The Irish'. The rest, to them, were 'the natives'. But, although they rooted strongly and flourished exceedingly in the soil of Ireland, they were never other than an exotic species. They remained essentially British, though no longer English. They did not, indeed could not, like earlier settlers 'go native', or become largely Hibernicized.

They were no longer, as were the much earlier settlers, a minority of scattered expatriate landed gentry surrounded by a majority of old Irish landowners whose daughters they might marry and into whose social life they might merge, and whose customs they would therefore adopt. The situation was now reversed. The minority of old Irish landed families that remained, their daughters included, had now of necessity to integrate themselves into the great majority of newcomers, and embrace their English customs, in order to survive within the new ruling order of society.

But while the new settlers were to become in due course essentially, indeed almost fanatically, British, seeing their Irish homeland as a permanent part of the Imperial realm, they did not long remain typically English. They became different enough for it to have been said of them that in Ireland they were British, but in England they were Irish. They developed a dual personality, one part British, one part quasi-Irish.

It took time, generations, for them to acquire those partly Irish characteristics that enabled them to fit easily and comfortably into the Irish scene. But, that they came to be accepted by the Irish under the indulgently respectful title of 'The Gintry', betokens not only that the rural people of Ireland, accustomed as they were by ancient tradition and habit to an hierarchical social system, still continued to feel the need of a chieftainly class of some sort, but also that the newcomers, when they had settled down, proved themselves worthy of the regard accorded to them by the real Irish.

The founders of the Irish 'Gintry' families, whether they were officers of the English army, or British officials, serving in Ireland, or however else they came to acquire their lands, were drawn mainly from the ranks of the rural gentlemen of England; largely no doubt from the less well-off among younger sons and distant cousins. They took their chance of settling in Ireland either because they were serving there already, and poised to receive grants of land, or even seize it by force, or because it was their only chance of becoming estate owners and landed gentlemen in their own right, and on a scale that would have seemed out of the question for most of them in England, giving them a status, and a seeming opportunity to acquire wealth, that would at that time have been highly prized, when landownership was the principal source of power, influence and social position.

And, indeed, for the descendants of those who took the chance, the century and a half following the mid-eighteenth century was, despite some periods of turbulence, destined to be one of the longest, most agreeable, and highly privileged, if nevertheless tough and rugged, holidays that any community of a thousand families has ever enjoyed since the world began.

As officers of the army, or officials, who had been prepared to undertake oversea service, and to exile themselves in Ireland, the settlers were a part of that explosively energetic element in British society that was at that time creating the Empire. Nor could they have done what they did without the ready co-operation and acquiescence of their wives. They were of the same stock as the men; country girls, daughters of landowners, well able for an outdoor, rural life; self-possessed, down to earth women. Had they been less hardy and less capable, they would not have gone to Ireland, or would not have long remained there.

The settlers that Ireland received were indeed some of the cream of the most robust men and women to be found among the lesser country gentry of England. Husbands and wives must in every case have together made the positive decision to brave the seeming dangers – the 1641 rebellion was not easily forgotten – and accept the discomforts and isolation of life in Ireland, a foreign land, speaking a foreign tongue. They were perhaps a shade romantic, and may indeed have needed to be sustained by a romantic view of themselves as courageous, long-suffering, hardy pioneers, doing what they did , in part at all events, from a spirit of loyalty to the English Protestant cause, which needed their presence in Ireland as a sure defence against encircling, menacing and powerful Papist foes.

And they were destined never to lose their hardihood. Life in Ireland continued for them, as for the old Irish chiefs, to be mainly an open-air affair, farming, hunting, shooting, fishing, boating, riding, walking, climbing, with the girls scarcely less adept than the men. A lurking need for vigilance against possibly latent native Irish hostility endowed them also with a touch of the mark of frontiersmen.

Those characteristics, together with the burning loyalty to the Crown which was later to distinguish them, and their romanticism, predestined them to become, and to remain for a long period of time, a magnificent recruiting ground for the officer ranks of the armed forces of Britain. Soldiers tend to be romantic; an image of themselves as dashing dragon-slayers, and damsel-rescuers, helps to lure them to the colours.

And some of the cultural baggage they took with them to Ireland consisted of the social and philosophical customs and tenets of England of their period. And, although those attitudes were destined in time to be blurred a little by the more easy-going ways of Ireland, they never thereafter altered in their essentials, and the new Irish gentry and their descendants continued down the years to be guided in the main by their English code of ethics.

Writing some two centuries later, George Santayana said that:

> *What governs the Englishman is his inner atmosphere, the weather in his soul. Never is it a precise reason, or purpose, or outer fact which determines him; it is always the atmosphere of his inner man.*

The atmosphere of the inner man of the seventeenth century settler gentry derived from the place that they occupied in the English social system.

The Irish system was a *caste* system; layered castes of chiefs, learned men, warriors, musicians and so on, determined mainly by birth. The English system, by contrast, was a *class* system in which the principal division was between two main classes, the 'gentle', and the 'base' or 'simple', determined largely by the extent of a person's landed property. To be a 'gentle' man was to be a member of the elite who ruled the land. The term 'gentle' in that sense, did not mean 'mild'. It derived from the Roman usage of the word 'gens', to denote a surname, which was applied only to Roman patrician families, to proclaim and preserve the fact of their noble lineage.

An examination of Burke's *Landed Gentry of Ireland* (1904 edition) reveals that almost all the land-owning families who acquired estates during the periods of Protestant settlement of Ireland had their origin in the ranks of the elite gentry of England.

The essence of the English system was acceptance of a cast-iron belief in a divine ordering of the universe. God was in his heaven. Below him were tiers of angels. Below them was mankind, in ordered ranks of precedence. Below man were the higher and then the lower animals and so on down the scale through supposedly mindless creatures of the lowest order, to plants and inert elements, fire, air, water, earth.

In this scheme of things, the King was at the top, by divine appointment and right; then the nobles, the knights, esquires, and gentlemen. To be 'Tom Smith, Gent.', was to be somebody – a member of the very small body of the elite.

Only a tiny minority qualified to be regarded as 'gentle', and ownership of land was a prerequisite of that distinction. But that did not mean that the commonalty were of no account, though there was considerable distinction of rank between the top and the bottom of their stratum.

Merchants generally belonged to the commonalty, which included citizens and burgesses of cities and towns; very substantial people, some of them holding city offices, and eligible to sit in Parliament. Their equivalent in rural areas were yeomen, often independent – but smaller – landowners normally farming not less than a hundred acres; again men of substance, eminent locally, and regarded as a very important element in English life, but themselves making no claim to join the ranks of the gentry.

That was the structure of society in which the new Irish settler community had been brought up in England, and in which they firmly believed, and whose ethics they brought to Ireland with them, and which from then on was to condition the attitudes to social rank of the new rulers of Ireland. When considering those new Irish landed gentlemen, therefore, we are once more, as with the Celtic chiefs, dealing with a class that was for the most part innately elitist.

Like the old Irish chiefs, too, they regarded their position in society not merely, or even mainly, as one of privilege. The core of the status of gentility was an active philosophy of obligation. The lives of the English gentry were dominated by an ideal which was summed up in the word 'virtue'.

Virtue in that sense did not mean only goodness. It meant the totality of an honourable life and honourable conduct. Goodness, certainly, but courage, generosity, industry, justice, moral excellence, uprightness, absence of vice, and all other aspects of nobility and rectitude.

It was not just an abstract ethic. It was an active code of conduct which was of practical importance. The healthy state of the nation depended in large measure upon the virtuous actions and generosity of the well-to-do. There were no social services, and little or nothing in the way of public local authorities. Until late Tudor times, the poor and the unemployed were largely treated as criminals. The only concern of relief measures was to forestall disorders which might result from excessive deprivation and discontent.

Service, therefore, was the essence of virtue, and to serve the state the highest virtue. To be open-handed, to provide employment, to give relief to the poor, to perform public works and to set a good example; those things were important, no less than liberality in your hospitality generally. And such actions were of particular importance in the degree to which they contributed to public tranquillity, and thus to law and order and internal security, at a time when there was no police force, and only a rudimentary standing army.

But those virtues you could practise only if you had the wherewithal, which in rural areas, in those times, meant land and wealth. Thus, what the Irish saw as purse-proud in the English, the English saw as the essential, indeed the only, means to a virtuous life, in conditions in England in which jobs, and sustenance for the people and the peasants, no longer depended on access to common land, because there was not enough of it to go round, but on the ability and willingness of the landowners to provide them. Wealth, plutocracy, was the essential prerequisite of a virtuous life in the sense in which a seventeenth century English gentleman understood virtue. It was the essence of riches that they were to be put to good purpose. English gentlemen of that time would have very well understood and approved Francis Bacon's aphorisms that: 'Riches are for spending,' and: 'Money is like muck (manure), not good except to be spread.'

Thus, whether or not the rural people of Ireland ever understood it, once they had lost their common lands, a despised and well-to-do, 'purse-proud' English usurper was all the more likely, on account of his wealth, to be a reasonably virtuous landlord, and, as a wealthy patron, their best hope of salvation.

And so it was that, whereas they acquired their estates in Ireland in large measure to better themselves materially, the settlers were nevertheless people imbued from their earliest years with a strong sense of service, duty and obligation, and who had had some pretty decent ideas dinned into their ears from earliest youth on the subject of living respectably, responsibly and honourably, and with a due sense of obligation to their Sovereign, their country and their fellow-men. And was Thomas Magan acknowledging his acceptance of their code, on behalf of himself and his kinsmen, when, at the time the Magan armorial bearings were confirmed, in 1705, he adopted the motto for the family, 'Virtute et Probitate'? The Coolavin motto is 'Honore et Virtute' and the coat of arms is similar to the Magan coat of arms. The MacDermot Roe motto is 'Honor et Virtus'.

But that abstract account of the underlying principles that guided the lives and conduct of the English settler landed gentry needs qualification because it conflicts with the way the English think about themselves, and certainly with the way they express themselves. Stated like that it is seemingly too dogmatic, too precise and too self-conscious, indeed almost too serious, an ethic. Here is Santayana again.

To say that the Englishman's inner atmosphere was simply a sense of well-being would be too gross. On the other hand, to say that it was the vision of any ideal, or allegiance to any principle, would be making it far too articulate and abstract. When he is compelled to condense it into words, it may precipitate some over-simple theory; but its puerile language does it injustice. It fights under its trivial fluttering opinions like a smoking battleship under its flags and signals; you must consider not what they are, but why they have been hoisted and will not be lowered.

Those words written by George Santayana in the twentieth century can be applied to the eighteenth century English settlers because they were not unlike the English of today. They had left the mediaeval era behind, and were living in the modern world. It had been in Elizabethan times that there began the embryonic growth of the modern-type society that we now have. There were a number of conspicuous instruments of change.

Protestantism, confirmed by Elizabeth as the state religion, with its rejection, once and for all, of clerical authoritarianism, and with its Lutheran abandonment of absolution, at one and the same time released great energies by freeing men's consciences, and engendered a greater sense of responsibility for their own actions, thus 'concentrating their minds wonderfully'.

Then, both the dangers and the opportunities implicit in the new age of ocean exploration, commerce and adventure, required the cultivation of habits of deep and careful thinking, and called forth new forces and methods to meet new demands and new problems.

Then there was Elizabeth's novel reliance on corporate and intellectual policy-formulating and decision-making by a lay secretariat-type administration free from the doctrinal and dogmatic clutter of mediaeval clerical attitudes, and the abandonment of French and Latin for official business, and the general use of English instead. Her officials thought in English, and they thought on paper. They made rough drafts in English, scratched them out, hacked them about until they made as good sense as could be managed, just as we do today. England was beginning to build up a corps of largely introverted, and therefore highly dedicated, officials practising that form of practical professionalism in the discharge of public business which the succeeding centuries have taken as their model throughout much of the world.

And there was a curious, almost mechanical factor of great importance – the improvement in handwriting. Again, it was through the influence of Elizabeth that the difficult 'Secretary' script was largely abandoned, and the 'Italic' script, the basis of our modern handwriting, substituted. In the seventeenth century it was much better written than it now is. Its chief merits were that it could be written quickly and easily and was easy to read. It greatly facilitated the despatch of government and other business, and the spread of education. Look, for instance, at Oliver Cromwell's handwriting. It might have been written yesterday. It did not even have the long 's' of later times. It was much better than nineteenth century handwriting which was ruined by the innovation of the steel pen.

Thus it was that, in the company of late seventeenth century settlers in Ireland, we would have felt in pretty comfortably familiar circumstances. My grandfather knew their grandchildren. We are as near as that to them. The education that they received at an assortment of grammar schools, high schools, and other educational establishments, was scarcely different from the education he received, and not greatly different from the remnants of the classical ladders in schools today. The idiom of their ordinary speech was a little different. But we would have had little social difficulty, though some of us might have been struggling intellectually, in joining Dr Johnson and his friends for a chat at the Mitre, or partaking in the talk round Mrs Thrale's tea-table.

And none of us who has lived in an officers' mess, sat at any boardroom table, or been involved in any corporate professional policy-making, can have any difficulty in feeling at one with Nelson and his captains as they held meetings and talked shop round his cabin table for hours on end. They were eighteenth century men precisely of our own kidney. Their relaxed, un-theatrical, democratic and considerate form of discussion and decision-making would have been wholly familiar to us. Those were just the type and class of Englishmen who became the Irish 'Gintry'.

Some of the descendants of those English settlers were, when I was a boy in Ireland, still living lives that had changed little since the eighteenth century. I myself, therefore, have no difficulty in conjuring up a flesh-and-blood image of the late seventeenth century newcomers to Ireland. That delightful, sensitive and observant travel writer, the late H. V. Morton, visited, and wrote a book about, Ireland in 1930. Let me quote him:

> We go to Christie's and we pay enormous sums of money for chairs made by Chippendale, Hepplewhite, and Sheraton. We go to Sotheby's and pay enormous sums of money for calf-bound books of the eighteenth century, and for sporting prints of the same period which show the hunt in full cry, the mail-coaches racing on the Great North Road, the bustle outside inns as the horses were changed, and all the other scenes of that red-faced hearty age. In Ireland this time has not passed away. In Ireland the candles of the eighteenth century are not burnt out.

So, when we are considering the early generations of the Irish Protestant

Ascendancy, we are dealing with people like enough to ourselves, and certainly to our grandfathers, to be quite comprehensible to us.

Nevertheless, we may find difficulty in reconciling the lives that those people led with an abstract view of their ethic of virtue. The English upper classes would never have claimed that efforts to be reasonably virtuous amounted to the same thing as saintliness. On the contrary, they would have regarded excesses of piety as rather unhealthy. Perhaps I may take Nelson again as an example.

His life was certainly not blameless. His lapses indeed went far beyond what was generally regarded as tolerable even in the eighteenth century, and were distressing to other people, not least to his brother officers, his captains, his band of brothers, who tried tactfully to persuade him to stay on the rails. But, despite such flagrant lapses, it can surely with reason be said that this greatest of all sailors, this leader whom every man would follow to the death, this warrior of unflinching courage, this wholly dedicated servant of his country, his king, and his people, this deeply religious man, was none the less a man of virtue. That not only his brother officers, the 'officer class', saw him as a man of virtue is strikingly confirmed by a letter he received from the lower deck.

When he finally gave up the Mediterranean command where he had served so long, and had so greatly distinguished himself by destroying the French fleet, he received the following letter from some humble men whose very existence history would otherwise have altogether forgotten:

My Lord, it is with extreme grief that we find you are about to leave us. We have been long with you in every Engagement your Lordship has been in, both by Sea and Land; and most humbly beg of your Lordship to permit us to go to England as your Boat's crew, in any Ship or Vessel, or in any way that may seem most pleasing to your Lordship. My Lord, pardon the rude style of seamen, who are but little acquainted with writing, and believe us to be, my Lord, your most humble and obedient servants -
BARGE'S CREW OF THE FOURDROYANT.

To be a man of virtue, rather than a wholly virtuous man, must have been the common and general aspiration of those who strove to abide by that code. Shakespeare's lines, using 'gentle' in the sense in which I have used it in this chapter, make the point:

His life was gentle, and the elements
So mix'd in him that Nature might stand up
And say to all the world, 'This was a man'.

'The elements so mix'd' is the point. Shakespeare was not claiming that Brutus was a blameless man. He had, after all, just murdered Caesar! But he was a man in whom the elements were mixed. A fully rounded man, and 'the noblest Roman of them all', and thus necessarily a man of virtue.

Whether or not the new 'Gintry' of Ireland are judged to have lived up to those notions of a reasonably virtuous life, the notions themselves very emphatically formed a part of the cultural inheritance that they took with them to Ireland, and by which they believed themselves to be guided.

Those, then, were the new masters of Ireland.

The Family in the First Half
of the Eighteenth Century

THE SITUATION OF the Magan family in the first half of the eighteenth century, when the Penal Laws came into force, was perilous. They retained most of the characteristics of an old Celtic landed Catholic family – one of only very few such families to have survived the Cromwellian and Williamite settlements. And possessing, as they did, a considerable amount of prime land, they must have been a tempting target for land-hungry, acquisitive English settlers who now had ready-to-hand the oppressive Penal Laws wherewith to force their will upon the Catholics.

The Magans owned at the beginning of the eighteenth century at least three estates in Westmeath, each in the possession of one of the grandsons of Humphry Magan.

The senior branch of the family, Richard the Younger, and his aged father, remained Catholic and still held their old estate at Umma-More. Richard had made an old-fashioned dynastic chieftainly marriage, to Margaret, daughter of Francis Ryan, the O'Mulryan, also called Lord of Owney, whose wife was a daughter of the head of all the O'Conors, the O'Conor Don, thus continuing the close association between the Magans and the ancient Connaught house whence they had sprung, and underlining their Celtic Catholic orthodoxy.

The descendants of Richard and Margaret Magan were to remain staunchly Catholic until the senior branch of the family died out in Ireland in the male line nearly a hundred and fifty years later.

The junior branch of the family were Richard's first cousins, Thomas, who had supported William III, the only Protestant in the family, and who had no children, and his younger brother Morgan the Younger, our ancestor, who remained a Catholic. Each had his own separate estate. Morgan was at Balsallagh where he had begun to raise his large family.

Although Thomas had made himself rich and powerful, his position was far from invulnerable, particularly as it fell to him to shelter and protect his Catholic cousin, and his Catholic brother, and their estates and families.

Despite his wealth, and the fact that he had become High Sheriff of Westmeath in 1705, he continued to live at Togherstown in the austere and still fairly primitive conditions of the late seventeenth century. There was no gracious eighteenth century living for him; no beautiful William and Mary, or Queen Anne mansion; no out-of-place Palladian palace exiled from the slopes of the Apennines and shivering on the edge of an Irish bog. Togherstown remained the plain and rugged late seventeenth century house that the back of it is to this day. And Thomas himself did not survive much longer. He died in 1710. Being childless, he left his brother, our ancestor Morgan the Younger, his principal heir. But he also left lands and mortgages to his Roman Catholic cousin, Richard Magan the Younger of Umma-More.

That may seem extraordinary. 1710 was the time of the full flush of the Penal Laws. It was illegal for Catholics to acquire property or mortgages, and illegal for Protestants to sell, give, or bequeath them to Catholics. The incident, therefore, seems to underline and illustrate three things. That the Magans had deliberately taken both sides in the Jacobite War, and had agreed on equal shares whichever side won; that, despite the perilous times for Catholics, the Magans were locally so powerful that they could afford to flout the law and do as they liked, though no doubt they kept their weather eye very much open, and acted with studied circumspection – I get the impression that the family was at its best and most

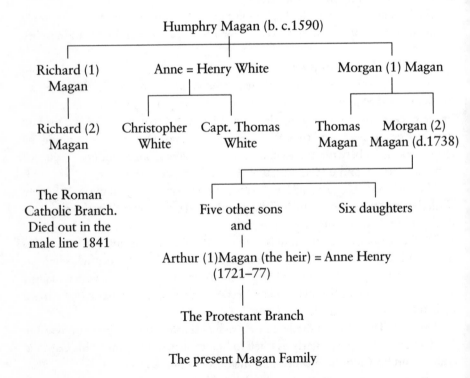

prudent in times of difficulty, such as it faced in the seventeenth and eighteenth centuries. Thirdly, that, as with the grandiose Cromwellian plans for depopulating the province of Leinster, and Anglicizing and Protestantizing most of the rest of Ireland, the Penal Laws were on such a scale as to be only partially workable. Indeed, apart from local powerful families themselves, and, from time to time, more or less marauding bodies of government troops, the law-enforcement agencies amounted to very little.

There, having fulfilled his obligations to his Catholic cousins, we must leave Thomas Magan. We should remember him not only as someone who saved his family from extinction at a time when it was the determined policy of England to destroy such houses as ours, but also as one who, in the face of all odds, even raised us above the heads of the conquerors themselves.

We may, of course, prefer to adopt a high moral stance and say that it would have been more honourable for the family to have allowed itself, and no doubt many other less powerful Catholics whom it protected, to be liquidated. But who is to judge, and on what criteria? Recently a French nobleman was asked whether he was not very fearful of the consequences to himself of the possibility of a Communist government in France. 'Of course not,' he replied. 'Under the Ancient Regime my family were ruling aristocrats. Under the Republic we have seen to it that we have held high offices of state. Under a Communist government, I shall be a Commissar!' The romantic may scorn it. The practical may applaud it.

Thomas in his will described Morgan the Younger as his 'only brother'. Remarkably, and despite the Penal Laws, Morgan had remained a Catholic up to the year of Thomas's death, 1710. But it was clear that that could not continue. The future of the family's interests could be protected only if the head of one of the two branches was a Protestant.

At that time the Stuarts were still strongly claiming their right to the English throne. They had many supporters. It was the decade of Marlborough's great battles against the French. The 1715 armed rebellion of James II's alleged son, the Old Pretender, and the 1745 rebellion of his son, the Young Pretender, Bonnie Prince Charlie, were yet to come. There must have been not a few people who still believed it possible that a Catholic dynasty might be restored. The policy the family adopted at the time of the Jacobite War therefore still held good. They continued to keep a foot in each camp, with one branch of the family Catholic and the other Protestant. But, more important still, in the short term, the Protestant branch, having become very large and powerful landowners, could exert enormous influence over a wide area in helping to mitigate the Penal Laws for Catholics generally.

So, in the year 1710, Morgan Magan the Younger 'read his recantation, and took the Oath of Supremacy'. In other words, renounced the Catholic faith and turned Protestant. We do not know whether he did so before or after Thomas's death, but it is likely to have been a quick conversion while Thomas was on his deathbed, because, once dead, the inheritance for his Catholic brother Morgan would have been in jeopardy.

The Act of Supremacy is revealing of England's concern with her security, and of her determination to preserve her independence from all external powers. It defined royal supremacy as 'the sovereignty over all persons, ecclesiastical and temporal *so as no other foreign power shall have authority over them.*' – My italics.

Morgan did not, we must suppose, experience a 'Road to Damascus'. He did not have a blinding flash of holy inspiration that caused him to change his faith. His adoption of the Protestant creed had nothing to do with religious zeal or conviction, and was no more, and no less, than a sapient act of temporal self-preservation on his own account, and on that of his family, and of the Catholic community at large. He remained a Catholic at heart.

After the death of his brother Thomas, Morgan moved from his home at Balsallagh to Togherstown, where he, too, continued to live in the rustic style of the late seventeenth century. The house had therefore become the principal residence of the Protestant branch of the family, but no eighteenth century-type additions or alterations were made to it. Morgan out-lived his brother by twenty-eight years, and died on 3 August 1738. He and his wife, Elizabeth, had twelve children.

When a few years ago my eldest son George visited Togherstown, the owner, Mr James Sloan, played him a record of Irish folk tunes including one called 'Murtagh McCann', and alternatively, 'Welsh Morgan', which is said to have been composed for 'Morgan Magan of Togherstown who died in 1738'. The nickname 'Welsh Morgan', may have been a reference to his grandmother, and possibly his mother who may also have been Welsh.

When Morgan and Elizabeth moved to Togherstown they already had six children, three boys and three girls, all, we may suppose, baptized Catholics. The remaining six children, another three boys and three girls born at Togherstown were necessarily baptized Protesants.

With so many in the family, there must, together with the servants, have been a pretty fair scrum in the not over-large house, and there had to be room also for the frequent guests and travellers who would have stayed there. But, although that was country-house living of a sort, it was only a step or two removed from the old life at Umma-More. No-one was yet much concerned about privacy or over-crowding, and the enormous walled cattle yards close to the house ensured that the sounds and smells of beasts remained in their senses as of old.

But we have, nevertheless, now come to a new generation of the family, and things were never going to be the same again. There can be no question of the very important influence that that generation – the children of Morgan Magan the Younger and his wife Elizabeth – were to have upon the family.

It was they who weaned it from its old Celtic Catholic character, and made it into what it then became, a part of the Protestant Settler Ascendancy, essentially loyalist, monarchist, imperialist and Protestant. Their father and his brother Thomas had had hard and anxious lives trying to preserve themselves and others from the debacle of the aftermath of the Jacobite War. Nostalgically, too, the older generation must have regretted the passing of the old Irish life, and the disappearance no doubt of many friends. Despite the Penal Laws, and despite their recantations, they doubtless remained Catholic at heart. It would be very surprising if mass had not been regularly said secretly at Togherstown, well into the eighteenth century, to the brothers Thomas and Morgan, and to the family and their retainers.

But the young are forward-looking and adventurous, and ready, indeed eager, to drop what they regard as outmoded conventions. To them the English settlers were not foreign usurpers. They had been there and known to them all their short lives. To them they were not newcomers. They had become a part of the landscape, and were just simply their neighbours. And their children were their friends, and indistinguishable from themselves. And, because of their English connections, the settlers had exciting innovations, and the latest fashions from across the water; none of your old Irish stuff. And they were the pace-setters. They ruled the roost. To be anybody you had to belong to them, and you had to be acceptable in their class-structured life with its multitude of signs and pass-words which immediately revealed whether or not you were 'one of us'. Though you spoke Irish, your first language had now become English. Your old Irish chieftainly aristocratic blood no longer counted for anything; indeed for less than nothing. It was best forgotten. In Protestant settler eyes, you belonged, if you were known as a Celt, to an inferior race. And a Celtic chief was at best a figure of fun, a slightly absurd anachronism.

A few there were, but very few, who persisted in those old ways, even for generations to come. Down-at-heel, Irish-speaking, old relics of former landed chieftaincies. Living out a shabby existence in a tumble-down ancient keep. Eccentric objects of curiosity, maybe, and of some local reverence. But, shorn of wealth and land, they no longer cut any ice in the realms of power, prestige and privilege, or in the ranks of go-ahead smart and acceptable society. No; the old Irish life was now a dead-end. The way ahead was as a part of the Ascendancy. It was not an apostasy for that generation of the family, and for the old Irish gentry at large, to merge with the Ascendancy. It just was the world into which they were born and in which they grew up.

But it was not only the old Irish who were changing. The settlers themselves were changing too. As the landed class amounted to only a little more than a thousand families, with a few thousand smaller farming families, they were a widely scattered and tiny minority in a total population by then in the region of two million. They brought their English ways and attitudes with them. Their language was English. English was talked at table. But culture is a two-way traffic. The settlers were greatly outnumbered by the Irish peasantry and retainers on their estates. If they wanted their relationship with them to be agreeable, they had to modify their attitudes and come to terms with Irish ways. And they needed to cultivate the friendship of Irish gentry families like ours who could advise them and show them the ropes and do something to smooth their path.

The transition for their children to an Irish characteristic of sorts was automatic. They learnt to speak Irish in the cradle from their Irish nurses. And, like all of us brought up in Ireland, much of their time as children was spent in the warm-hearted kindliness of the cottage folk. And so, in that generation, or thereabouts, were born 'The Gintry'. Time and tide and evolution had thrown up a new species, which will occupy the remainder of these pages. Of course the prototype had existed for a very long time in a few old settler families which had resisted taking the easy line of going native, but now it was to become general for the upper class.

The marriages of the Magan children of that generation strikingly reveal the transitional state of the Irish landed gentry in the first half of the eighteenth century.

All six daughters of Morgan Magan the Younger married. It would have been unthinkable for any of them to have married other than landed gentry, which they duly did.

Two of the three girls who had been baptized Protestants, Frances and Jane, married into Protestant settler families. The third girl who had been baptized Protestant, Ann, made a marriage which involved a cross-section of most of the confusions of those difficult times. Her bridegroom was a Catholic. To marry him was illegal under the Penal Code. He was her cousin. His name was John Fetherstonhaugh. His mother had been a Catholic Magan – Mary Magan, daughter of Richard Magan the Younger of Umma-More.

The Fetherstonhaughs were a Cromwellian English settler family, but with a quirk. They were Catholic, not Protestant, and were royalist refugees from Cromwell's England. John Fetherstonhaugh's grandfather, Cuthbert Fetherstonhaugh, came of a Northumberland family. He had fled to Ireland in 1651 after his own father, Sir Timothy Fetherstonhaugh, together with the Earl of Derby and others had been executed following the defeat of the Royalists at Worcester.

The three Magan girls who were baptized Catholic all married Protestants. All three marriages were therefore technically illegal under the Penal Code.

Sarah married John Mears of Mears Court, Westmeath, descendant of an English army officer settler of 1641.

Elizabeth married James Daly of Castle Daly, Westmeath, an ancient Irish Catholic family which, under the dispensation of Charles II, received patents for their lands as 'Innocent Papists', but during the reign of Queen Anne conformed as Protestants. Castle Daly, their home, was a new name given to a place whose real Irish name was Kilcleagh. Pretentious affixes or suffixes to family names such as 'Castle' Daly and Mears 'Court' – castle this and castle that, were a commonplace conceit also prevalent in England, e.g. Castle Howard. It was part of the English plutocracy's effort to turn itself into an aristocracy, and was aped in Ireland.

The marriage of Susannah, the third girl who was baptised Catholic, gave the family a further twist away from the days of the old Celtic chiefs and into the new world of the Protestant Ascendancy overlords. She linked the family to the new peerage and baronetage, such as it was, and it was not much to be proud of, but was an up-and-coming force. She married firstly a Protestant baronet, Sir Arthur Shaen. This introduced the family to important Irish contacts. Sir Arthur Shaen's mother was Lady Frances Fitzgerald, daughter of the 16th Earl of Cork, commonly known as the Great Earl of Cork. The Earls of Kildare and Cork were two of the most powerful magnates in Ireland at that time.

Despite the name, I suppose Sir Arthur Shaen's family to have been settlers. There is a romantic story attached to this marriage. Sir Arthur and his groom, benighted by a storm on Christmas Eve, were given shelter at Togherstown, and he fell in love with Susannah. There was no son of the marriage, and the title died out. But there were three daughters, one of whom, Frances, married John Bingham, a Sligo landowner. Their grandson was created Baron Clanmorris in 1800.

After Sir Arthur Shaen's death, Susannah married again; this time a Galway landowner, Robert Dillon of Clonbrock. By him she had a son through whom she became the grandmother of Robert Dillon, 1st Lord Clonbrock. That peerage became extinct in 1926.

Sir Arthur Shaen, was the 2nd Baronet. The title of Baronet is associated with Ireland. There had in the past been a rank of hereditary knights, Knights Banneret, entitled to bring their vassals into battle under their banner. The rank had largely lapsed by the sixteenth century but James I revived it in the form of Baronet, early in the seventeenth century, partly to raise money, and partly to keep Ulster quiet after the Plantation. Anyone who was a gentleman by birth, not in trade, possessing property of the value of £1,000, prepared to undertake to keep thirty men under arms in Ulster at eighteen pence a day each, could claim the rank, and can do so, in theory, to this day, as the Act creating this order of chivalry has not been repealed.

Queen Elizabeth had kept the numbers of peers and knights down to a low level, and there were no baronets in her reign. But within thirty years of her death her successor, James I, and his son Charles I, had more than trebled the number of peers, to say nothing of creating showers of baronets, and had thus correspondingly cheapened the orders of chivalry. But if James I and Charles I debased the peerage in England, it was nothing to what happened in Ireland. Who then were these new Irish grandees some of whom contained Magan blood?

The bulk of Irish peerages were eighteenth century creations; landowners who controlled most of the parliamentary boroughs and manipulated the seats in Parliament for reward, the chief prize being a peerage or a step up in rank in the peerage. Lecky, the historian of eighteenth century Ireland, says:

The dignity of the peerage was habitually made the reward of corruption. The lavish distribution of peerages proved the cheapest and most efficacious means of governing Parliament. The sale of peerages had become the ordinary recourse of the government. The taint of corruption had sunk deeply into the great borough owners. The peerage was systematically degraded; the majority of Irish titles are historically connected with memories, not of honour, but of shame.

In one session alone of the Irish parliament in the eighteenth century, the Viceroy was able to secure the support he needed only by recommending eight commoners for peerages, thirteen peers for a step up in rank in the peerage, five appointments to the Privy Council, and seventeen people for civil pensions, in addition to other favours. And even that he considered a modest hand-out, as a lot of other grumbling people were left unsatisfied. To this day the dispensation of peerages and honours has not ceased at times to be disgraceful. It is a matter in which the English should have hearkened to their Bard.

O! that estates, degrees and offices,
Were not derived corruptly …

But such taints have nevertheless not much diminished the regard in which the British and Irish peerage has generally been held, or the fascination that it has long aroused, due in no small part to its own sense of responsibility and obligation.

The House of Lords, whatever the best forgotten origin of not a few of its members' titles, is a civilized and civilizing place, and it, and its members individually, set a usually high standard to the nation, not only in decorum, but also in the conduct of public business. Many of those who have entered its doors would, with considerable justification, have been black-balled if the noble gentlemen already there had had any say in the matter. The fact that they have little or no say, and that the creations have at times even been in the hands of rogues, has, in the event, been on the whole a boon. The House has, over the years, been enriched by all sorts, who have, when they have got there, commonly adapted themselves to the dignified conventions of both its members and the place.

If there are to be further modifications in the nature of the peerage, and in its constitutional place in our society, it is to be hoped that the nation will find ways of making them without altogether losing the great contribution that can still be made by this unique, useful and highly colourful British institution. No orders of nobility in other countries have anything like the same cachet. Leave us our Lords! They are part of the fun.

The story of the sons of Morgan the Younger and Elizabeth is a sad one, and once more reminds us vividly of the health hazards of the eighteenth century.

When Morgan died, he was succeeded by his eldest son, Thomas, who died on 30 May, 1750, leaving no children.

The two next brothers, Herbert and William, had both died before Thomas, leaving no children.

The fourth brother, Edward, then succeeded, but he too died childless and unmarried, on 28 November, 1745.

The fifth son, Morgan, was killed in a riding accident.

The sixth, and youngest son, Arthur the Elder, succeeded to Togherstown and the considerable estates of the Protestant branch of the family. He was born in 1721, and married on 20 July, 1754, aged thirty-three years, a few months before he succeeded his brother Edward.

Marriages in those days were largely arranged. Property considerations played a large part. But they were not the only consideration. Due regard was at the same time paid to the affections of young couples. Their happiness and compatibility were considered with care. No-one wanted to see domestic disunion or disharmony in marriages.

That general concept of marriage endured in Ireland among the country people certainly until very recently. The Irish do not believe in romantic marriage, and their marriages are very stable. They have a saying that it is unlucky to marry for love. Like so many old wives' sayings it is probably founded on observed fact. And those attitudes were not confined to Ireland. They were shared by enlightened England. Queen Elizabeth was incensed by romantic alliances among the maids of honour and gentlemen of her court. Her attitude was in part determined by the knowledge that such matches often proved unstable. Will Cecil said, 'Infatuation matches begin with happiness and end in strife.' Dr Johnson said, 'Sir. Marriages would in general be as happy, and often more so, if they were all made by the Lord Chancellor.'

Whether or not it was by design, the arranging of the marriages of the Magan girls did have the effect of greatly easing the threatening conditions in which the family had been living. For its own safety, this Celtic Irish family, heavily tainted, as it must have appeared, with Popery, had to become – or at any rate had to contrive to appear to be – unequivocally Protestant, however Catholic some, particularly the older members, might have remained secretly and at heart. So it was that five of the six daughters of Morgan Magan the Younger, a man who had been born a Catholic Celtic chieftain, married Protestants; and five of the marriages were with settler families.

But if the marriages of the girls did much to take the family well and truly into the ranks of the Protestant Ascendancy in one generation, they were nothing to the astounding marriage of their surviving brother Arthur, which gave the family altogether another dimension.

His marriage was light-years away from the old-style Celtic dynastic marriages, such as that of his Catholic cousin, Richard the Younger of Umma-More to a granddaughter of the O'Conor Don. It was indeed altogether outside the ranks of the landed gentry, and into those of the classless urban *nouveau riche*, and moreover, into a family only just emerged from the obscurity of the despised Ulster Presbyterian Plantation stock, but a family that, in today's idiom, had made a killing.

It is to be supposed that there was a genuine enough bond of affection between Arthur and his bride. But, for all that, it is hardly possible that either side failed to calculate carefully the mutual advantages to both families in this unaccustomed kind of match.

Arthur Magan's bride was Anne, daughter of Hugh Henry of Straffan, County Kildare. He was a rich banker, merchant and Member of the Irish Parliament. Hugh Henry's father had been a Presbyterian minister from Carrickfergus in Ulster, who settled in Dublin. It is therefore reasonable to suppose that the family were Ulster Plantation settlers. Rugged old aristocratic Celtic Catholic countryman, Humphry Magan, would have turned in his grave to think of his great-grandson marrying the granddaughter of a Presbyterian townee minister from Ulster, even though her father had turned Protestant, which he must have done to be eligible to sit in Parliament. He occupied successively two Ulster constituencies.

Hugh Henry's wife, the new Mrs Magan's mother, was Anne Leeson. Her brother was Joseph Leeson, Privy Councillor (Irish) M.P. (Irish), who inherited a brewing fortune. He obtained a peerage, as Baron Russborough, in 1756. He then did some smart steps up the promotion ladder. Viscount Russborough 1760. Earl of Milltown 1763. The title is now extinct. An extant portrait of him shows a spare, strong, sharp, intelligent fighter of a man; tough, angular, wiry. It might not be prudent to take him on in a boxing ring or at the poker table. The system of granting peerages may have been scandalous, but peerages were much prized. They may often have been shamefully got, but they were not easily come-by. There was tough and stubborn in-fighting for them among the contestants. They did not go to softies.

That Lord Milltown secured for himself not one peerage, but three in a row in eight years was no mean feat. That his heirs died out was a deplorable loss of a line of audacious, mettlesome, spirited, purposeful, resolute, and staunch genes!

He built perhaps one of the grandest houses in Ireland – Russborough, County Wicklow. A great collector, he filled it with treasures. Russborough was recently the scene of one of the greatest art thefts ever. The stolen paintings, valued at eight million pounds, were recovered by the Irish police. Hugh Henry, Anne Magan's father, is said also to have owned an important collection of pictures. Lord Milltown's town house in Dublin is now the Kildare Street and University Club in St Stephen's Green where No. 77 was the Magan town house.

But the political ramifications of the Henry family went even wider, because the new Mrs Magan's brother, too, was a Member of Parliament and was married to a girl whose father also obtained an Irish earldom – Earl of Moira 1762; now extinct.

So Arthur Magan had, on the one hand, married the kind of person the family would not have dreamed of marrying a century earlier. The Henrys were not only not landed gentry. They were not gentry at all. They were the commonalty; merchant-class Presbyterian; hard-headed, capable, gritty Northerners.

On the other hand, in the changed world of the Protestant Ascendancy, and the Industrial Revolution, he can be seen to have married into the class that was now gathering power and wealth – and peerages. They were the up-and-coming plutocracy, and, judging by the houses they built, immensely rich, and by no means lacking in taste, creativity and artistic appreciation. They were the eighteenth century in all its glory, and in all its ruthless acquisitiveness as well. They were exciting people with whom to be connected by marriage, if you were prepared to snap out of your old moth-eaten aristocratic world and move with the times; something the Magans showed themselves prepared to do. They seem not to have been too much bound by convention.

This very unconventional marriage for a man born the son of one who had started life as an aristocratic, semi-nomadic, Catholic tribal Celtic chief, was shrewd and timely. The family's precarious situation as members of the despised and downtrodden Irish race, suspected of being under-cover Catholics prepared to harbour priests, and to hear mass, and concerned to mitigate the Penal Laws for other Catholics and therefore vulnerable to charges before a merciless Protestant court, must, despite their local influence, have been a cause of constant underlying anxiety. To make a match with the daughter of a rich Dublin Protestant settler magnate and Member of Parliament, sister of another M.P., niece of another very wealthy M.P. and Privy Councillor, who was aiming for the peerage, was obviously to provide the family with an immensely powerful protective shield at the very heart of government.

And it is to be supposed that there was also a very handsome dowry – a change from the bride-price of cattle and sheep of former times. Anne's father was already dead, so she no doubt had a good inheritance. Indeed, there is every reason to believe that she was very rich.

And what did the Henry family get out of it? To secure their social status, they needed to become landowners and country gentry. As barely lapsed Presbyterians, it may not have been easy to sell themselves among the toffee-nosed English settlers. What they presumably got, therefore, was that particularly desirable landed gentry status for one member of their family as the wife of an old-established family of landed gentry of considerable estate and position in the County Westmeath. Anne's brother, Joseph Henry, was himself at a later date to make the grade by becoming High Sheriff of County Kildare. He also built a notable Palladian house in the latter part of the eighteenth century, Lodge Park, Straffan, County Kildare.

I think there was one more thing the Magans got out of this marriage. Some fresh blood with a good deal of bustle in it.

And so it was that, in that one generation, the marriages of the children of Morgan Magan the Younger and his wife Elizabeth lifted the family out of its two thousand year old Celtic chieftainly mould, and placed it firmly in the ranks of the ruling Protestant settler Ascendancy.

It may seem from all these rather satisfactory marriages among the landed gentry, and from the material successes of the Henry family, as though Ireland had, after all, a rather splendid social life, was reasonably prosperous, and was not half such a bad place in the first part of the eighteenth century as has been made out, despite the Penal Laws.

But that was not so. Living conditions, even for the gentry, continued to be very primitive. There was very little building of grand eighteenth century houses. Of what later might have been catalogued as the country houses of Ireland, only very few, mostly old castles, and tiddled up tower-houses, had been built by the beginning of the eighteenth century. A small number of mansions were built during the first half of the eighteenth century. Not far short of half the country houses in Ireland were built in the second half of the eighteenth century, and as many more in the first half of the nineteenth century. It was in 1732, right in the middle of the period we have now been considering, that the encounter took place with the well-to-do hospitable country gentleman, in his pretty place by the river, living with his male cook in a house that was little more than a tumble-down, old-style leaky Irish cabin.

As to the state of the country as a whole, whereas there were some who prospered, and some areas where there was less distress than others, conditions in general, and for the majority, were such that it was the time when enormous numbers of Catholics, large numbers of dissenting Protestants, and not a few Anglican Protestants, bundled up what little was left to them and emigrated, to return to Ireland no more. Emigration has ever since been a sickening and heart-rending sore in the souls of the Irish.

Things may not have been too bad for those living around Ballymore and Togherstown. Westmeath is a fertile area. As it is mainly grassland it never had other than a relatively small population, as it takes only a few people to herd beasts. There was not therefore much pressure on the available sustenance. The Magans, because of strong Irish conservative inclinations to cling to old habits and ways of life, and because of their under-cover Catholic leanings, and because they were living among the same country people with whom they had lived for centuries, and with whom they must, in the old Irish tradition, have had close foster relationships, probably carried on life with their family retainers, and the people on their estates, much as before, and no doubt, from their position of power and influence, encouraged their neighbours to do the same. The management of their estates would have retained something of the principles of common land usage.

There was also in those times another factor that beneficially affected the relationship at least between good and prosperous landlords and their tenants, retainers, staff and work people. There were two curiously different and paradoxical veins running through society, at least in England, and it is to be supposed that they had their echo in Ireland, particularly among the settlers who would have brought with them as much of their English atmosphere as they could transplant.

Times were, on the one hand, dreadfully harsh. It was the time of cock-fighting, bear-baiting, and much gratuitously hideous cruelty to animals just for the enjoyment of cruelty. It was the time also of the stocks, the pillory, public whipping and ducking, man-traps, transportation, and public hanging for a host of trivial offences. There were more than two hundred capital crimes, even in England.

At the same time, and on the other hand, because life for most was rural, and everyone knew everyone else, there was extensive familiarity between great and lowly. A commentary by a German visitor to England, which was published in Dublin later in the eighteenth century, describes this relationship as he saw it, and it is perhaps not unreasonable to suppose that at any rate the best of settler landowners in Ireland tried from the beginning to cultivate some such association with the Irish peasantry. They certainly succeeded in doing so when in later generations they had become a part of the Irish landscape. The German traveller commented:

> *That perfect equality which nature hath at all times established among men, presents itself but too forcibly to the minds of these haughty islanders, and neither dignity nor wealth are capable of effacing it. The proudest Englishman will converse familiarly with the meanest of his countrymen. It is not surprising to see two persons engaged in conversation, between whom there is the greatest disparity.*

That foreign observation is indeed echoed by G. M. Trevelyan in a passage dealing with the upper echelons of English society in the eighteenth century. It is his view that the social aristocracy, 'included not only the great nobles, but the squires, the wealthier clergy, and the cultivated middle class who consorted with them on familiar terms.'

While, therefore, the Penal Laws were making Ireland an intolerable place for the many, there were some respects in which both relationships and conditions were improving as the middle of the eighteenth century was reached.

CHAPTER 23

Religion

CHANGES OF FAITH IN the early eighteenth century may prompt the question whether members of the family were lacking in loyalty to their churches. Religious confusion within the family may also suggest that discord could hardly have been avoided. Thomas Magan turned Protestant while the rest of the family remained Catholic. Many years later his brother, Morgan the Younger, also turned Protestant, six of his twelve children being baptized into that faith, the other six having already been baptized Catholic. The six daughters made marriages which in some cases involved spouses of the opposite religion; and their brother Arthur married into a family with strong Presbyterian associations.

A less religiously loyal, or more religiously discordant, family would be hard to imagine; but, for all that, there probably was little heart-burning, and no discord. During the centuries following the Reformation, religious attitudes were different from today, even though there were elements in the religious differences of those times which remain fundamental to current problems.

Henry VIII's quarrel with the Pope was not about religion. He lived and died a Catholic, practising Catholic observances. But his was a non-papal Catholicism. His quarrel with the Pope concerned authority, not religious doctrine. His stand in the matter had somewhat complex British compromise characteristics, because, in the limited and strictly theological field, he recognized the Pope's prelatical pre-eminence as supposed lineal successor to St Peter, and Vicar of Christ. But he insisted that in England all authority must vest in the Crown. Therefore the Sovereign, not the Pope, must be the governing head of the English branch of the Catholic church.

Heresy against Roman Catholic doctrine had however been making itself heard in Europe, particularly in Germany. Martin Luther was Henry VIII's exact contemporary. Six years older than Henry, he died a year before him. His concern, unlike Henry's, *was* with doctrine, not with authority. To root out what he denounced as corrupt practice in the Catholic church was his aim. The heretical and schismatic infection which he engendered spread strongly in England at the moment of Henry VIII's quarrel with the Pope and opened the way for the Protestant schism after Henry's death.

In those times religion had a central place in the lives of everyone in England. It ranged from crude superstition to high theological scholarship, but whatever its form it was a matter of the highest personal importance to all. Hence, for two hundred and fifty years, throughout the sixteenth, seventeenth, and first half of the eighteenth centuries, the upheaval in the church which had begun with the breakaway from Rome, remained uppermost in men's minds and interests until the defeat of the Young Pretender, Charles Stuart, at the Battle of Culloden, in 1746, removed the threat of a Roman Catholic revival of temporal power in England.

But religion never came to a head as a political issue. The nearest England came to religious civil war was the two forlorn Stuart risings of 1715 and 1745, and they were more dynastic than religious. In the sixteenth century, the Bishops, while they still had a measure of temporal power, hounded heretics and burnt them. The Catholic Queen, Bloody Mary, while on the throne, pursued a cruel, bloodthirsty vendetta against Protestants. In the half century of the Jacobite claim to the throne, up to the mid-eighteenth century, English Catholics were cruelly persecuted. But those were aberrations that marred more typically English attitudes. When civil war did come to England, it was about power and authority, not about religion. Charles I, like Cromwell, was a Protestant, not a Catholic. It is not in the nature of the English to be religious zealots.

In that great religious debate, which lasted two and a half hundred years, it was Queen Elizabeth who voiced the true heart of England, in a few telling phrases that soar above all petty controversy. And it was that that made it possible for families like the Magans to tread the tortuous religious path of those times without internal strife and friction.

From her we learn how England coped in its stolid, empirical English way with those two and a half centuries of highly emotive and perplexing religious change; and from her we get an insight into English ways of dealing with problems. We see that English 'muddling through' is in fact English resourcefulness. During centuries of pastoral life the English, with a climate that changes hourly, had learnt flexibility. 'Planning' was not the answer to most of their problems. You could not plan very precisely when you did not know whether in six hours time it would be wet or fine. Planning is an off-shoot of Middle Eastern dogmatism which has been washing strongly over the West for the past millennium and a half in theological and, more recently, in lay and intellectual concepts; and it suits us little.

Elizabeth was concerned to make plain to others what was crystal clear to herself; and she was so in tune with the spirit and character of the people that, like Churchill, when his time came, she was greatly emboldened because she was, and she knew that she was, voicing the heartfelt views of the great, sound, and normally mute, mass of her subjects. It was to their souls that she spoke, not to

their minds. She cut right through the intellectual. And so she cleared the wa
for countless families like the Magans to handle those matters with good sens
and without controversy.

By the time she came to the throne, the Catholic and Protestant churches ha
become distinguished from each other by fundamental differences of belief in th
origins of spiritual authority, and by liturgical differences in their forms of worshir
Elizabeth dealt with that problem in a simple scathing sentence. 'There is onl
one faith,' she said. 'The rest is dispute about trifles.' On the lower plane c
individual priests, persecuted, and hanged as spies, and of the severe Protestan
reaction to the Marian Catholic excesses, it was anything but a matter of trifles
but on the higher national political plane her words lifted the issue right abov
all churches. And she kept priests at arm's length from herself. There were neve
any among her close advisers or friends.

She was fully aware that it was impossible to segregate religious from
political issues. Bigots at home of both main religious parties, and her enemies
both at home and abroad, were far too busy trying to exploit religion fo
political ends. But she was not going to be provoked by such activities into course
which would be to the detriment of, and alien to, the sentiments of her subjects
whatever their beliefs.

She well understood that a very large number of her English subjects, includin
great and powerful people, remained Catholic, in the sense that in religiou
matters they continued in their hearts to regard the Pope as their spiritual head
But she knew her people, and trusted them in all other aspects of thei
lives to remain loyal and patriotic English men and women. To injure then
were inhumanity. To alienate them were folly. 'Let it not be said that our Refor
mation tendeth to cruelty,' were her words. But for all that, it takes courage tc
be trusting – enormous courage, and a very clear head, in the dangerou
circumstances of those times.

And none of her subjects knew better than she the terrors of cruelty. She wa
in the highest degree intelligent. She had been brought up, for the most part, no
at court and among courtiers, but banished to country houses, her chief companion
commoners. She even knew what it was to be in want, with not enough money
for adequate clothing. Above all, she knew the terrors of the abuse of power. She
had been a prisoner in the Tower of London. She had lain awake at night
awaiting the sentence of execution. She had asked with dread implication whethe
Lady Jane Grey's scaffold was still standing. Those were horrors she was no
going to inflict on her loyal subjects because bigoted priests and others migh
dub their beliefs heretical.

She hated bigotry. She believed in freedom of conscience. As monarch, sh
was head of the church. The country had therefore to have an acknowledgec
national church of which she could be the formal head. That church was th
Church of England.

There was a great spirit of independence in England. The land was flexing its muscles on the eve of the greatest show of imperial power the world had ever seen. Protestantism was in tune with that spirit. A national church, owing allegiance to a Pope in Rome, was altogether out of sorts with it. England was in no mood to acknowledge any foreign master in any sphere of her national life. Therefore everyone must accept the formality that the Protestant Church, acknowledging the Sovereign as its head, was the church of the realm.

That settled, Elizabeth did not care what her subjects thought in private. But they were not to get arguing and brawling about it. Fisticuffs on religious issues she would not have. Heresy she did not mind, so long as people kept it to themselves. Disorder she would not tolerate. Listen again to her marvellously sensible words:

We never had any intent that our subjects should be troubled or molested by examination or inquisition in any matter of their faith or ceremonies, as long as they shall in their outward conversation show themselves quiet.

But she had a political role to play and, for political reasons, as was to be the case later, in the time of Charles II, there had to be a show of discrimination against Catholics, lest powerful Protestant elements, upon whom she had mainly to rely, be grossly offended, and indeed alarmed. But to have measures on the Statute Book was one thing; to enforce them rigorously was another. Here again is her authentic voice, speaking from the heart of England, which is often more to be trusted than its head:

I have in my time pardoned many rebels, winked at many treasons, or altogether slipped them over with silence.

Thus, in England, despite the volcanic dimensions of the religious eruption that occurred in the sixteenth and seventeenth centuries, political polarization on religious grounds was avoided and, by and large, it remained a matter of individual conscience. Elizabeth was only too well aware that not everyone could find it honestly in their hearts to believe what they were told to believe. To try to force them to do so must inevitably lead to Torquemada. English bishops had in the past shown themselves no less ready than Torquemada to go to the most bestial and brutal lengths to suppress what they considered heresies. Elizabeth would have none of that. Bishops would get short shrift from her. The land was ruled by her – by princes – not by bishops. She broke the temporal power of the bishops by ignoring them. Never since has any English Protestant layman felt any cause to fear a bishop.

Although they were greatly more turbulent religious times than we now live in, and although personal faith played a much larger part in people's lives then than now, the religious barriers were, curiously, much less rigid. Religious loyalty, as we know it today, did not exist. The question mark that hung over your faith was in essence political – whether or not it might suggest sentiments of national disloyalty.

For reasons of expediency, therefore, and more particularly in England, people changed from one church to another at will, and back again if necessary. No-one thought the worse of that. Some members of a family might be Catholic, others Protestant. Catholics and Protestants inter-married. To most people the difference between Catholicism and Protestantism did not, as one writer has said, seem any greater than between high church and low church today.

The religions of the English monarchs in the sixteenth and seventeenth centuries are revealing in this context.

	Henry VIII	Catholic
His son	Edward VI	Protestant
Edward's sister	Mary	Catholic
Her sister	Elizabeth	Protestant
	James I	Protestant
His son	Charles I	Protestant: wife Catholic
His son	Charles II	Protestant, turned Catholic on his death bed
His brother	James II	Catholic: wife Protestant
James II's daughter	Mary II	Protestant: husband William III Protestant

Thus it was that, at the social level of the Magan family, changes of faith at the time of Thomas and Morgan Magan the Younger, at the turn of the seventeenth/ eighteenth centuries, would have been no great matter for surprise, and would have had no religious stigma attached to them. The political stigma in Ireland was mitigated by the practical advantage to everyone over a wide area that lay in the existence of a Catholic-sympathizing powerful Protestant family.

But, after the middle of the eighteenth century – after the Stuart Catholic threat to the throne had been removed by the victory of Culloden; approximately the time when Arthur Magan the Elder came into his inheritance from his father, Morgan the Younger – discrimination against Catholics in England dwindled to a point where religion ceased to be a factor of any importance in English politics. The need, thereafter, to change one's faith for reasons of expediency also vanished, and people became more enduring in their attachment to one church or another. And in conformity with that new pattern, the two branches of the Magan family settled down to being one solidly Catholic and the other solidly Protestant, though they maintained a very close relationship with each other, and the Protestant branch continued to give the Catholic branch its protection for so long as the Penal Laws were in force.

CHAPTER 24

The Family in the Second Half of the Eighteenth Century

EVENTS WITHIN THE family in the second half of the eighteenth century underlined and confirmed the changes that had been taking place in its character. By the time that Arthur Magan the Elder came to marry his rich bride, Anne Henry, in 1754, only the very old could any longer remember the days of the Irish-speaking chiefs and the common grazing lands.

It was sixty-three years since the Treaty of Limerick. Virtually no-one had personal recollections of it. Arthur's father, and his uncle, Thomas Magan, were both many years dead, taking with them their bitter recollections of the Jacobite War and its terrible consequences for Ireland, their homeland, and its people. Hardly anyone then living knew any world other than that ruled over by the English-speaking Protestant settler Ascendancy; a peaceful Ireland, too, in which no-one any longer remembered the inter-tribal strife, the cattle raids, and the burning of homesteads.

Arthur and Anne Magan moved from Togherstown. From a certain Sir John Leicester Bart., they bought Clonearl, near Philipstown (now Daingean), on the border of the King's County (now Offaly) and Westmeath. It was very likely at that time a tiddled up tower-house, and more commodious than Togherstown. Clonearl was to remain the principal family home and residence for the next century.

Arthur and Anne lost no time in starting a family. The first two children were born within exactly two years of their marriage. But it was a small family for those times – five children only, two girls and three boys.

Arthur became High Sheriff of Westmeath in 1759, thus maintaining the family's local power base. We may suppose that he and Anne were largely, and fully, occupied with their estates, family matters, their social life and the affairs of the county. He died in Dublin on 14 September, 1777, aged fifty-six. Anne outlived him by nearly sixteen years, and died in England.

Death remained ever present. Miserably, the two girls of the family died young and unmarried. Edward, the eldest son, also died young, in 1779, two years after his father's death. He was only twenty-four, and left no children. Rich the family may have been, but they had a dreadful lot to put up with from the old man with the scythe.

Of the two surviving children, the elder, a son named Arthur after his father, born on 26 July 1756, succeeded to the estates, aged twenty-three, on the death of his brother Edward. Baptized a Protestant, Arthur the Younger underlined the, by then, wholly Protestant complexion of this branch of the family by marrying the daughter, and co-heiress with her sister, of a rich land-owning Protestant clergyman. Even though fraternal support for the Catholic branch continued, it is nevertheless certain that secret mass was heard no more by the Protestant branch. Morning prayers and grace at meals were now in order.

It was on 13 May, 1783, that Arthur, aged twenty-seven, married Hannah Georgina Tilson, of Eagle Hill, Co. Kildare. She was twenty-one, six years his junior, having been born in 1762. It was a marriage that took the family another step away from their rural, Celtic grazier background. The Tilsons were a settler landed family but with strong professional links. Hannah Georgina's father was the Very Reverend Dean Tilson, product of Lincoln's Inn, and M.A. of Cambridge University. His father had held the important post of Clerk to the Irish House of Commons, and his grandfather had been Henry Tilson D.D., Bishop of Elphin.

Dean Tilson was about fifty years of age when his daughter, Hannah Georgina was born. It is supposed that the children of older parents often show an especially high degree of intelligence. Certainly Hannah Georgina appears to have impressed herself on people. Her name was still ringing down the family a hundred and fifty years later.

She was not only her father's heir, but was also heir to her mother who had been Anne Bushe, whose father, William Bushe of Dangan, Co. Kilkenny, was the descendant of a settler soldier who had received a grant of land in 1670. Hannah Georgina's only sister married their first cousin, Charles Coote, who became the first Lord Castlecoote – one of the disgraceful politically jobbed up peerages, now extinct.

The Protestant Church, the peerage, deans, bishops, parliamentary functionaries, gaiters, coronets and ermine – a far cry from those old communal encampments, of not so long ago, where all, great and lowly, had lain down together on their bundles of green rushes, in their smoke-laden, leaky shelter, to be lulled to sleep by the gentle sounds of their beasts.

Hannah Georgina Magan's inheritance of Bushe family property in Kilkenny from her mother, and of Eagle Hill, Kildare, and other Tilson property, from her father, made her a substantial heiress. Of those estates nothing now remains. At Eagle Hill the gateposts still stand forlorn, but not a stone of the house is to be seen. There is no sign even of the foundations.

But Hannah Georgina Magan did nevertheless leave a substantial monument to herself. She endowed, or provided considerable endowments for, the Protestant church at Crinken, just north of Bray, Co. Dublin where there is a Magan burial vault.

The fifth and last child of Arthur Magan the Elder, was Hugh Henry Magan, and he, together with his mother, was to give the family yet another twist into he loyalist camp. There is in Bath Abbey what one member of the family once described as: 'a dingy little tablet rather high up,' inscribed:

Anne, widow of Arthur Magan, died April 9th 1793. Also to the memory of Hugh Henry Magan, Major-General of His Majesty's Service. Died 2nd June 1805. Both interred at Walcote burying ground.

And so, by becoming a Major-General in His Majesty's forces, Hugh Henry, youngest son of Arthur Magan the Elder, and grandson of an Irish-speaking grazier Catholic chieftain, had set the seal upon the late eighteenth century status of this family as dedicated loyal subjects of their Sovereign in London. Every generation thereafter was destined to give officers to the armed forces of the Crown.

Born in 1760, Hugh Henry Magan must have received his commission about the time that his father died, in 1777.

His mother no doubt remained on as chatelaine at Clonearl until her son Arthur the Younger married Hannah Georgina in 1783. Thereafter, all that was left to her in Westmeath was the life of a rural dowager. But she was not a rural person. She had been brought up in a rich home where her family were among the leaders in the all powerful political world of Dublin, the second city of the realm, where social and cultural life were almost on a par with London. It is therefore to be supposed that she decided to make a home in England for her only remaining child, her bachelor army son – for Hugh Henry never married. In England, life and living standards were culturally a century ahead of rural Ireland, and much more comfortable than the alternative that faced her in the Irish bogs.

Hugh Henry is said to have served in the West Indies, but he could hardly have been there long and survived the appalling incidence of disease. His service may therefore have been spent for the most part in England. He had grown used to the agreeable life of 'an officer and a gentleman' in the British army, a life in which hardihood, and readiness for hard campaigning, went hand in hand with elegant living in exquisite, cultivated and distinguished company. That he held high rank means that he was in manners and deportment indistinguishable from an English gentleman at those times. England, with its now mellowing Tudor manor houses, and its growing crop of eighteenth century mansions, had, in its elegancies and civilities, much to offer him that had hardly yet begun to exist in rural Ireland.

What more likely, then, than that the bachelor major-general should have decided to settle in England among the brother-officers and friends with whom he had shared his service and his working life, rather than return to try to take up the now ageing threads of his origins among the greater discomforts and uncertainties of Ireland. He and his mother could well afford to pick and choose an agreeable gentlemanly English establishment for themselves. No longer would life be lived against a background of the all pervading smell of cattle, and the endless sound of the soft chewing of the cud. Now it would be the glittering chandeliers of an English country house.

And so it came about that this son of a recently old Celtic Catholic family found, together with his mother, a last resting place in a quiet and peaceful English Protestant churchyard, and that they are commemorated, in however dingy a corner, in one of England's great abbeys, far from the waving bogcotton and the light in the western sky between the dark hills.

Back at home in Ireland, General Hugh Henry Magan's surviving older brother Arthur the Younger, settled down to raise his family and run his estates. He was destined to live only fifty-two years, dying in 1808. His life, therefore, almost exactly spanned the second half of the eighteenth century. It was the half-century when the Protestant Ascendancy reached the zenith of its influence. Arthur's marriage to a rich Protestant parson's daughter, and the careers of his children no less than that of his major-general brother, make it plain that the Protestant branch of the family had by then passed completely into the ranks of the Ascendancy and were thus able to enjoy the prestigious fruits of its pre-eminence. It maintained its links with the remnants of the Catholic gentry, but, by the latter half of the eighteenth century, that had become a perfectly respectable thing for Protestants to do. The Catholic gentry were by the end of the century seen more as being gentry than as being Catholic, and were acknowledged to be among the most loyal subjects of the Crown.

The children of Arthur the Younger and Hannah Georgina epitomized the pattern of Irish ascendancy life at the turn of the eighteenth/nineteenth centuries. There were twelve of them, six girls, and six boys, and some more who died in infancy.

The three eldest girls died unmarried. The fourth, Louisa, married a foreign nobleman, Baron von Reitzenstein, a colonel in the Hanoverian Life Guards. The fifth, Emily, married George Medlicott, of a settler family originally from the village of Medelicote in Shropshire. That their daughter, Louisa Medlicott, did not die until 1906, two years before my own birth, brings the eighteenth century near to us. Louisa's own marriage to John Prendergast Vereker was to result in due course in a trickle of ancient Magan Celtic grazier blood mingling with that which had flowed in the veins of the paragon, Sir Philip Sidney. The sixth daughter, Henrietta, made a conventional country gentry marriage to John Hawkesworth, whose settler ancestor had received a grant of land in the Queen's County for service as an officer in the forces of King William III.

The six sons illustrated almost the whole gamut of Protestant Ascendancy life of their time. The eldest died in infancy. The second succeeded to the, by then, magnificent family inheritance of wealth and property. The third became an officer of the Royal Navy; and the fourth an officer of the British army. The fifth, my great-grandfather, summoned up an echo of the past by marrying the Catholic daughter of an old Irish house, and raising an enormous family. The sixth and last son went to the furthest lengths in the opposite direction. He became an Anglican clergyman and died unmarried.

The eldest survivor of those boys, the heir, William Henry Magan the Elder, was born in 1790, thus bringing us to the very end of the eighteenth century.

I have focussed attention on the eighteenth century marriages of our forebears because they, more than any other feature of the social life of the time, illustrate the character, and more particularly the changing character, of the family.

An analysis of marriages throughout the Protestant Ascendancy generally would probably show them to have been sound, durable and stable. Many were with close neighbours among land-owning families. That had partly to do with the consolidation of holdings of property, but also stemmed from bad communications. Social life was largely confined to association with neighbours. Roads, although they improved enormously in the eighteenth century, and were better in Ireland than in England, were often still little more than rutted bridle paths. Ten miles out and ten miles back was a day's journey.

That had another important consequence for marriages. The families lived very similar lives. One house and one family was much like another. Young people shared a common background, and a largely common society of friends. They belonged to the same class and, by the end of the century, in nearly all cases, to the same church. Thus, the adjustments to be made on marriage hardly extended beyond the necessity to reconcile a male with a female. And even that adjustment was not great because the nature of the country was such that the isolated homes in their rural settings, and the primitive communications, caused boys and girls to have much in common. All could, and indeed needed to be able to, ride and walk, climb and manage a boat; and girls no doubt often joined the boys in the pursuit of game and fish essential for the larder. They were outdoor girls.

Moreover, the Protestant Ascendancy was at all times conscious of the latent threat to itself from civil strife and rebellion. It therefore kept itself hardy, and its children were deliberately unpampered by their parents. It has been said that mothers of the Protestant Ascendancy bestowed more affection on their dogs and horses than on their children. That was a factor favouring happy marriage because often in marriage young people must have given each other a degree of affection beyond anything they had known from their parents. And the men worked at home on their estates. Thus the running of the home and the estate was a partnership in which husband and wife worked together, and the tasks of one complemented and enriched those of the other.

A girl from the ranks of Irish gentry of those times would be no stranger to me. She would differ little from the Irish girls of my time. She would not have been an Irish-speaking Celt. She spoke, no doubt, a little kitchen Irish to the country people on the estate whose first language was still Irish, though by that time English was commonly known throughout much of Ireland. I know just how

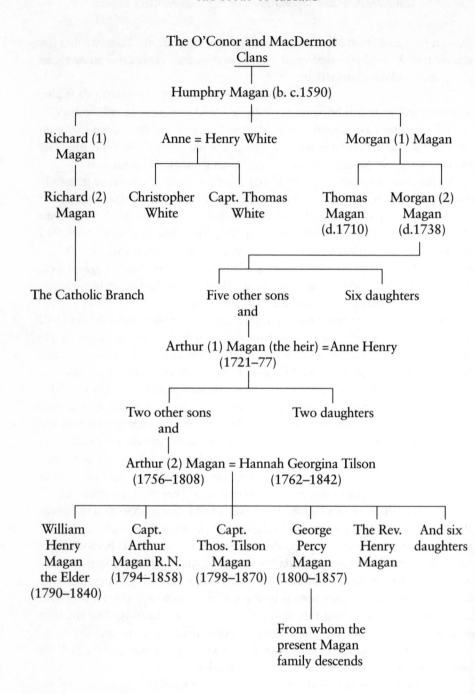

The O'Conor and MacDermot
Clans

Humphry Magan (b. c.1590)

Richard (1)
Magan

Anne = Henry White

Morgan (1) Magan

Richard (2)
Magan

Christopher
White

Capt. Thomas
White

Thomas
Magan
(d.1710)

Morgan (2)
Magan
(d.1738)

The Catholic Branch

Five other sons
and

Six daughters

Arthur (1) Magan (the heir) = Anne Henry
(1721–77)

Two other sons
and

Two daughters

Arthur (2) Magan = Hannah Georgina Tilson
(1756–1808)   (1762–1842)

William
Henry
Magan
the Elder
(1790–1840)

Capt.
Arthur
Magan R.N.
(1794–1858)

Capt.
Thos. Tilson
Magan
(1798–1870)

George
Percy
Magan
(1800–1857)

The Rev.
Henry
Magan

And six
daughters

From whom the
present Magan
family descends

she spoke. I can hear her voice. Her language was educated English. But she spoke it softly with that faint touch of an Irish accent, familiar in the Protestant Ascendancy – and music in the ears of an old exile.

I have been asked how it was that such a substantial land-owning family as ours, so influential and prominent in one of the wealthiest agricultural areas of Ireland, and so relatively close to the capital, Dublin, failed to become ennobled in the eighteenth century when money and influence could secure peerages for those with enough determination.

It is probably significant that the family kept away from central government politics where such pickings were to be had. An Arthur Magan sat in the Irish Parliament from 1761–1768 for an Ulster seat. He was replaced as having been 'unduly elected.' He may have been Arthur Magan the Elder, and was perhaps a placeman for his wife's political relations.

Beyond that, the family was not politically active. They have left behind them an impression of caution and prudence. The aura of Celtic, Catholic taint hung about them well into the eighteenth century. They had a great deal to lose on their own account, and cheek by jowl with them in Westmeath were their Catholic cousins, always at risk and, by association, a hazard to the Protestant branch of the family. The family policy was doubtless quietly to consolidate and increase their influence at local level. So they steered well clear of political life in Dublin.

Despite their wealth, and despite the example set by their cousins in the Henry family, they refrained from doing in the second half of the eighteenth century what so many families did, and what they certainly had the means to do, that is to say to build themselves a large neo-classical mansion. They made do with the discomforts of some less notable – and less noticeable – older building. Like Brer Fox they lay low and said 'nuffin'. Of eighteenth century honour, Lecky wrote, 'the highest honour of which an Irish family can boast is that it passed through political life untitled and unstained.' So, at least, our eighteenth century Magan forebears had the honour to remain untitled.

They appear also to have remained unstained. They were a stable family, living decently, while patiently and adroitly accommodating themselves to the new conditions of Ireland, and succeeding in transmuting themselves from the old Celtic aristocracy into a situation giving them a firm hold on what had become, by the latter part of the eighteenth century, a new elite. The family's position therein was securely based on extensive ownership of land. No tales of scandal have come down to us. There were no divorces – divorce was, of course, almost out of the question legally – and there were no annulments of marriage, or broken homes.

CHAPTER 25

Ireland Towards the Close of the Eighteenth Century

IF THE FAMILY HAD changed its character in the eighteenth century, it had done no more than reflect the changing Ireland of which it was a part. The Protestant landed gentry now ruled the land. But although they were overwhelmingly of English settler stock, their families had by the latter part of the eighteenth century been in Ireland for a century or more. Ireland had become their homeland. For several generations they had been born there. In England some of them could deport themselves so as to be hardly distinguishable from the English gentry. But in Ireland they had no doubt that they were Irish. The blue mountains, the dark waters, the red bogs, the ocean light in the western sky; the soft accents, the leisured pace, the frequent rain, the endless talk, the green of the grass and the rushes – those were the background to their lives. Those were the influences that had from birth sunk deep into the hearts and souls, and which did indeed make them Irish, if a very different sort of Irish from the natives; Irish who were, at the same time, fiercely British. That they ruled Ireland was important. But, at least as interesting, if not more important, is the fact that they gave Ireland what was in effect a new aristocracy.

To be a Protestant in Ireland was to be, and to feel yourself undoubtedly to be, a superior person; indeed, greatly superior to the great mass of native Catholics, who did not exist in the eyes of the law, and who were mostly impoverished, ignorant and unskilled, because forbidden to acquire knowledge or skills, and who spoke a despised, and supposedly inferior, native tongue. And, indeed, the Catholics were for the most part in fact inferior. I do not refer to their capacity or ability. I do not know how that is to be judged. That it took nine hundred years of frequent attempts to conquer them, from the coming of the Vikings until they were finally subdued in 1691, may suggest what their true capacity perhaps is. But if you set out to disable a people by the total suppression of all means whereby they might exist above the lowest level of peasantry, and maintain that suppression for a century or more, then you will create at least a temporarily disabled people inevitably inferior to the favoured section of the community who command, and exclusively enjoy, all the facilities for self-betterment. That is what

the Protestants, and the Whitehall government, did set out to do, and they succeeded in doing it. They were sufficiently fearful of Irish potential to damage
England, to be concerned to destroy it.

So, by the late eighteenth century, Ireland had resumed the thousands of years
old social complex in which attitudes of mind played so large a part in determining
your place in society. To be a Protestant was to be, and to feel yourself to be, and
to see it as your absolute birthright to be, a member of a superior caste. That
attitude of mind was an ineradicable part of you from your cradle. To be a
Catholic was to feel yourself inevitably to be the opposite. You had experienced
the fact that you were born inferior, and it was clearly your destiny, and that of
your children, to remain so.

And to be a member of one of the thousand ruling and land-owning families
of Protestant gentry, was to believe yourself to have been born above all the other
Protestants, as well as greatly superior to the Catholic natives. That belief contained
the essential ingredients of the aristocratic cast of mind. Your birth alone gave
you an unassailable social position. You had been born superior. Nothing could
deprive you of that, and no-one of lesser birth could acquire that magic status.
God was a Protestant. Not just a Protestant, but a Protestant gentleman.
The angels apart, you were next to God. Yours was a God-given superior status
conferred at birth, and denied to everyone not born into your class, and you
believed that absolutely. And, as we have seen in the Magan family marriages, by
and large the landed gentry married only the landed gentry.

Thus there developed a closed aristocratic class by breeding and birth. Either
you were, or were not, by birth, 'in the book.' It was not a plutocracy. Many
Irish landed gentry families were far from rich. Not a few were pretty down-at-
heel aristocrats, who, unlike the more pragmatic and sensible English, could
not see themselves as other than innately superior to successful self-made
merchants and burghers of the middle classes into whose families they therefore
despised to marry.

Curious though it may seem, the mass of Catholic Irish very readily fell in
with these assumptions of superiority on the part of the Protestant gentry. Indeed
they even encouraged, and perhaps in part initiated, that attitude. An aristocratic
tradition was native to Ireland. The Irish understood it; liked it; felt comfortable
in it. They also like a show of style and some glamour in their lives. They prefer,
too, to attach themselves to personalities rather than to causes. They missed their
chiefs. They missed the interest, excitement, reflected status, and relative security,
of attachment to a leading local family. It was, therefore, not more than a few
generations before the once despised purse-proud, boorish, English land-grabbers,
had become the 'gintry' and the 'quality', and were addressed respectfully as 'yer
Honour', and their Protestant parsons as 'yer Riverence'.

On their estates the landlords were not infrequently hardly less feckless than
the most feckless of the natives themselves. They were flamboyant, reckless, hardy,

and yet easygoing. They took the lead in every kind of outdoor sport. They had learnt from, and come to agree with, the native Irish that courtesy has a value greater than punctuality or other such meticulous precisions in the conduct of life. They were scrupulously careful not to violate local customs or to give offence against local beliefs and usages. In line with ancient Irish custom they were lavish – indeed extravagantly so – in their hospitality in the hall, and the doors of their kitchens were always open to their lesser tenants and others with some claim to their generosity. When I was a boy no tramp was ever turned away from the kitchen. Money they might be denied on the pretext that they would drink it. But they were always given food.

The settler gentry had, too, by the eighteenth century, established for themselves a magisterial authority locally, and could give their full support and protection to all within their domain. And association between all classes was regulated by a perfect familiarity tempered on the one hand by a due respect for rank, and on the other by a full and tacit acknowledgement of the dignity of the individual.

Writing 150 years later, Stephen Gwynn said that, brought up as he was, through his boyhood years, in rural Donegal, twenty-five miles from the nearest railway station:

The best thing I learned in those years was to be as easily at home in an Irish cottage as in the houses of my own class. For in Ireland we recognised class as a matter of course; and, as a result, well-bred people, in cottage or 'big house,' were never 'class conscious'.

In a sense that is misleading. Class-conscious, or caste-conscious, is just what people were. But they were not class-antagonistic. They knew nothing of the Hegelian dialectic or Marxist historical materialism. Differences of class were accepted without embarrassment or resentment as a natural part of a structured, layered society, the only form of society they had known for two thousand years, and perhaps a great deal longer.

In their role as the focus for local authority, the eighteenth century gentry, almost in imitation, as it might seem, of the old Irish chiefs, also placed themselves in a martial sense at the head of their able-bodied tenants and retainers who willingly followed them in their efforts to police the land, keep the peace, and prevent insurgency.

The settler gentry, living on their properties, were more often than not too lenient with their tenants. They let their lands at rates that were too low. That invited the curse of the middleman and multiple sub-letting. Some authorities have claimed that the system was not all bad; that in moderation it made for efficiency, because the final tenant, with at least a realistically high rent, must necessarily be efficient to make a living. The most run-down estates were said to be those on which the landowner acted as his own agent, and let the land at low rents to chosen tenants who were not allowed to sub-let. They could make a sufficient living without much effort, and the land went to pot.

It speaks volumes both for the eighteenth century mass of the sorely tried Catholic Irish, and for the favoured gentry at local level on their estates, that between them they arrived as often as they did at a fruitful compromise and accommodation.

Something of the extended family conditions grew up again between the gentry and both their employees in their houses and on the home farms, and their tenants on their estates, and there was thus once more great mutual affection, confidence and respect between these, in so many ways, very disparate conditions of people.

We hear much of evictions, exploitation, oppression, and so on, on the one hand, and of smouldering ancient resentments on the other, and those things existed. But despite the real and great disadvantages under which the Catholics laboured, as often as not Protestants and Catholics came to live together in mutual respect and amity.

How, it may be asked, could such conditions have developed in the eighteenth century when the Penal Code remained in full force against the Catholics? The question can be answered by analogy. If in war you give the troops on opposing sides half a chance, they will stop shooting and, within half-an-hour, will be fraternizing, playing cards together and exchanging rations. Human beings at close quarters may often react differently to each other from the way they might react when regarding one another from a distance as political, ethnic, religious or other kinds of abstractions.

Even at the level of government, changing attitudes were discernible. In the 1760s, the first Catholics were recruited into the armed forces of the Crown – one thousand two hundred marines. From then on, the prohibition against Catholics serving in the army was quietly allowed to lapse, and from that time to this day, hundreds of thousands of Catholic Irishmen have served the Crown with total dedication. The Germans in the second world war made a point of recruiting 'quisling' traitorous forces from among the prisoners they captured. Most nations produced their quota of disaffected men to fill the ranks of those disloyal units. The Irish must have seemed a very fruitful field from which to recruit such a force. But I believe it is a fact that not a single Catholic southern Irishman from among those captured from the many thousands serving in the British forces came forward to join the quislings.

That the Catholic Church hierarchy were responding to the better atmosphere is illustrated by the fact that, in 1767, prayers for the King and the Royal Family were offered up in Catholic churches for the first time since the Rebellion of 1641.

By the 1770s there was widespread Protestant and, even in Ulster, Presbyterian, connivance at the open practice of the Catholic religion. Chapels – or mass-houses – were being built, and bishops, priests, monks, and Catholic schoolmasters, lived and practised openly without molestation.

Lecky says that at that time the English government was anxious to maintain a complete Protestant ascendancy in the Irish Parliament, but nevertheless had every wish 'to govern wisely, mildly and justly, and they were activated by no spirit of malevolence.' Viceroys were instructed, 'to show a sincere desire for the well-being of Ireland.'

Widespread evasion of the Penal Code was creeping in. Officials turned a blind eye. And Protestants were actively helping their Catholic neighbours and friends in such evasions.

In 1782 the Provost of the Protestant University of Dublin, Trinity College, admitted publicly – although it was illegal – that he connived at the entry of Catholics into the University. Nor need they have any fear for their religion. 'They need not,' he said, 'attend the Divinity professor. They may have their own.' And he went on:

The present laws are disgraceful. They prohibit Roman Catholics from receiving any education at all. They should be abolished. Roman Catholics should receive the best education at public expense.

In the same year, 1782, a meeting attended by a number of the most prominent Protestant political figures in Ireland, passed a resolution stating:

We hold the right of private judgement in religion to be equally sacred in others as in ourselves. As men, as Irishmen, as Christians, as Protestants, we rejoice in the relaxation of the penal laws against our Roman Catholic fellow subjects.

But they had, nevertheless, no intention of yielding up any of their land or any of their political power to the Catholics.

In the late 1770s, and early 1780s, legislation was passed giving relief from some of the Penal Laws against the Catholics, as well as relief from enactments against Presbyterians and other dissenters. But those reliefs stopped short of giving Catholics or dissenters the vote, or the right to sit in Parliament.

It was the defeat of Bonnie Prince Charlie, the Young Pretender, at Culloden, almost half way through the eighteenth century – 1746 – that had led to those more lenient attitudes towards the Catholics in the second part of the century. So long as the Catholic Stuart threat to the English throne had lasted, bolstered by powerful foreign interests who saw the Irish as potential allies, the English clamps on Ireland remained rigid. After 1746, it was sensed that that grip could safely be progressively relaxed.

But a new Irish problem was emerging for Whitehall. The settler Ascendancy was flexing its muscles in a strong show of independence on its own account. Although the two houses of the Irish Parliament in Dublin, the Lords and the Commons, were wholly in the hands of the Protestant landowners, they could pass no laws that were not sanctioned by England. Irked by this continuing close Whitehall control of every detail of Irish legislation, the Protestant settler leadership of Ireland became restive for greater freedom in the management of Irish affairs; and the example and the opportunity were at hand – the American War of Independence (1775–1783).

In order to protect Ireland against raids by the French, who had allied themselves with the American colonists who were in revolt, the Irish Protestant landowners mustered a very efficient armed Protestant volunteer force of a nucleus of the small farmers of the Ulster Plantation. It rose to a strength of thirty thousand men under arms – some authorities put the figure as high as a hundred thousand – and became in effect the private army of the Protestant Ascendancy.

Taking their cue from the successes of the American colonists, and using the volunteers as a lever, and conscious of the fact that England and Ireland were not united, but were two separate kingdoms under the one crown, the Irish landlord Parliament succeeded, in 1782, in obtaining a measure of independence from the English government who were not prepared to risk a confrontation with the volunteers.

But it was a much qualified and circumscribed independence, as the Viceroy and Chief Secretary continued to be appointed from London, and were able, at the behest of ministers at Westminster, to manipulate virtually all the legislation in the Irish Parliament. A member of a settler family was to sum up the position a few years later in a prophetic outburst of oratory in the Irish House of Commons:

We may pride ourselves that we are a great kingdom, but the fact is that we are scarely known beyond the boundaries of our own shores. Who out of Ireland ever hears of Ireland? What name have we among the nations of the earth? Who fears us? Who respects us? Where are our ambassadors? What treaties do we enter into? With what nation did we make peace or declare war? Are we not a mere cipher in all these, and are not these what give a nation consequence and fame? All these are sacrificed to the connection with England. A suburb to England, we are sunk in her shade. True we are an independent kingdom; we have an imperial crown distinct from Eng-land; but it is a metaphysical distinction. Who governs us? English ministers, or rather the deputies of English ministers, mere subalterns in office.

It is asked why, after all the acquisitions of 1782, there should be discontent? This country has been governed worse since then than ever it was before; and why? Because it has been the object of English ministers ever since to countervail what we obtained at that period, and substitute a surreptitious and clandestine influence for the open power which the English Legislature were then obliged to relinquish. The people of this island are growing more enlightened every day, and will soon know and feel their power. Near four million people in a most defensible country ought, perhaps, to be courted, but ought certainly not to be insulted with the petty pilferings, jobbing, corrupting tricks of every deputy of a deputy of an English Minister that is sent over here. Where, or when, or how, is all this to end? Is the Minister of England himself sure he sees the end? Can he be sure that this system, which has been forming for the coercion of Ireland, may not ultimately cause the dissolution of the Empire?

That from a member of a settler family illustrates the extent to which the settlers had come to regard themselves as essentially Irish, and no longer as Englishmen living in Ireland.

But those were mere local squalls and flurries compared with the tidal wave that was about to break over the western world, and to have far-reaching effects on the course of Irish history – July 1789, the storming of the Bastille; the French Revolution.

To the downtrodden everywhere it gave hope and encouragement, and indeed more, it scattered among them the seeds of rebellion and revolt. To crowned heads and landed oligarchies it caused fear and consternation. Before long it became clear that Western Europe was about to be engulfed in war, and leading British politicians saw that England could not fail to be drawn in, and that the situation in Ireland would be of great importance.

In Ireland, the debate on her future was given enormous impetus at all levels – from would-be revolutionaries to conservative constitutionalists – and was conducted without intermission. Here, if ever there was one, was a down-trodden community ripe for liberation from its disabilities – and a privileged oligarchy seeking to hold onto its possession and power.

The two most important subjects of debate were whether Catholics should be given the vote, and whether they should be allowed to stand as candidates for the Irish Parliament. At first the Government in Whitehall favoured giving them the vote only, while the majority of Irish Protestant legislators were against any political relief for the Catholics. That, as they saw it, could only lead in the end to the Catholic majority in the country becoming politically dominant, in which case the Protestants would be ousted from their lands. The Whitehall view prevailed and, in 1793, Catholics were enfranchised on the same property qualification as Protestants.

The more able Irish politicians, and the Viceroy, saw that in consequence it would be advantageous to give Catholics seats in Parliament as well. They had it in mind that those seats could be filled by a few remaining and, as they saw it, respectable and loyal, Catholic gentlemen of old Irish families whose absolute loyalty was assured, and who would not work against the interests of the Protestant gentry. It would be a class compact. The Catholic gentry members of Parliament would be mere ciphers. They had, in fact, already largely opted out of the political arena and debate, as the experience of our own family illustrates. The danger otherwise would be that, since the vote had been given to the Catholic 'rabble', it would inevitably lead to Catholics sitting in Parliament, and, sooner or later, if Catholic gentlemen were not manoeuvred into those seats, the 'rabble' voters would choose 'rabble' political leaders from among themselves.

The very thought that Ireland could be governed other than by the Protestant land-owning gentry, seemed to themselves inconceivable. They knew, and they were no doubt right at the time, that no-one else could do it so well. Despite the corruption, the jobbery, the nepotism, the sale and bartering of peerages, the so-called 'pensions', the drain of absentee office-holders, they were for the most part capable, serious, dedicated, hardworking and responsible men. They alone in Ireland had been educated and conditioned to shoulder those responsibilities. They were also very conscious of the fact that their ownership of the bulk of the land would be in jeopardy if the Catholics in general obtained any substantial measure of political power. They were, for reasons of expediency, prepared to let a few Catholics sit in Parliament with them, provided only that they too were property-owning gentlemen. It would indeed be a property-owning gentlemen's club. But Whitehall vetoed the suggestion of allowing Catholics into the Irish Parliament.

Nevertheless, although the Protestant gentry were determined to hold onto power, it is clear that there was a strong feeling in the air that change was inevitable. Among a good many ominous signs we may particularly note one. In one of his letters to London, the Viceroy commented that Members of Parliament were frequently met with the phrase, 'The lower Catholics already talk of their ancient family estates.' And a later letter from the Chief Secretary to London contained the phrase, 'The lower order, or Old Irish, consider themselves plundered and kept out of their property by the English settlers.'

It was clear in Whitehall that, after the measure of freedom gained by the Irish in 1782, the pressure was going to be on from the Irish Protestant leaders for complete independence. Whitehall was not prepared to allow that. Ireland could not be trusted to be independent, either ruled by Protestants or by Catholics. The Americans had not been Catholic, but they had allied themselves to Britain's enemies during the American War of Independence, and had seceded from the Empire. The Irish Protestants could no more be trusted than the Americans never to do the same.

The situation, in effect, was this. The lands of Ireland had been given to English Protestant settlers to occupy as a colonial garrison to keep Ireland safe and quiet. But after a century, the garrison was no longer English. It was very consciously, self-consciously, and proudly Irish – a new sort of Irish. And it now sought independent nationhood. Moreover, the garrison had now come to see that they could not hold down the native populace much longer, and must therefore come to an accommodation with them which would at least have the semblance of power-sharing. But English strategic interests dictated that she could not, and must not, allow control over Ireland to slip from her grasp, particularly as the settler garrison was weak numerically, and native Catholic power might somehow be regenerated in the future.

What was England to do? A word began to creep into the thinking on the subject during the last two decades of the eighteenth century. 'Union.' Unite the two kingdoms, abolish the Irish Parliament, and govern the lot from Whitehall. Give the Irish a minority of seats in the Whitehall Parliament, to enable them to feel to be, and indeed actually to be, represented in the legislation of their own country.

By 1793, the matter was no longer one for drawn-out political debate. England was now at war with France, and approaching a situation she had known before, and was to experience again, in the future – the lights going out all over Europe, and herself left alone, or almost alone, to fight a mighty tyrant single-handed. Furthermore, Irish dissidents, prominently led by Protestants – indeed in the cases of two of them, members of the Irish Parliament – were already in contact with the French. And there had for some time been evidence of possible resort to violence in Ireland. England was in no mood to be soft with the Irish.

By the middle of the last decade of the eighteenth century the Irish Parliament seemed, with the full accord of their Viceroy, Lord Fitzwilliam, to be on the point of legislating to allow Catholics to sit in the Irish Parliament. A 'Catholic Bill' had been prepared for debate in the Irish House of Commons. Whitehall firmly arrested those proceedings and promptly sacked the Viceroy. England just was not prepared at such a moment of national peril to place any political power in the hands of Irish Catholics. But the alternative of a single united kingdom of Britain and Ireland looked a poor starter. All the main elements in the Irish political scene were opposed to the idea of 'Union'.

Leading Protestant politicians in Ireland had formed a body named the Whig Club, to preserve for 'all time in Ireland a Parliament of her own within the realm,' and, as Henry Grattan put it, 'to prevent the Union.'

The Catholics were no less hostile to the idea. At a large meeting in Dublin called by the principal Catholic organization, the 'Catholic Committee', a resolution was passed:

That we are sincerely and unalterably attached to the rights, liberties and independence of our native country; and we pledge ourselves to resist even our own emancipation, if proposed to be conceded upon the ignominious terms of an acquiescence in the fatal measure of a union with the sister kingdom.

The British government could not prevent the Catholic Bill from coming before the Irish House of Commons, and it was duly debated. Had it been passed it would have emancipated the Catholics and given them seats in the legislature. The word 'emancipation' in this particular Irish political context had no other meaning than the admission of Catholics to Parliament. But no bill could pass the Irish Commons against the wishes of Whitehall. The House was packed with 'placemen' who for favours rendered, or promised, voted as instructed. As one member of the House put it during the debate:

> *In 1792 a majority decided against giving any further privileges to the Catholics. In 1793 the same majority passed the Catholic Bill (giving Catholics the vote). Everyone believes that a majority will vote against it now, and should the English Ministers in the next session wish it to pass, who does not believe that a majority will vote for it?*

In the debate on the Catholic Bill in 1795, George Knox, a descendant of a settler family, said:

> *The Irish Parliament justly thought that we could not be a powerful, prosperous, and happy people if three-fourths of us were ignorant and beggars. It opened the gates to knowledge and opulence, and by doing so created unexampled and rapidly increasing prosperity. But politically this was an act of madness unless carried further. In a few years, if trade increases, the Catholics must possess almost a monopoly of the personal wealth of the kingdom. If we drive the rich Catholic from the legislature and from our society, we force him to attach himself to the needy and disaffected. We oblige him to breed and nourish discontent. It is impossible that the question can rest there. Take, then, your choice. Re-enact your penal laws, risk a rebellion, a separation, or a Union, or pass this Bill; for the hour is nearly arrived when we must decide. The hour is already come when we ought to decide. If we continue to exclude and irritate the Catholics, we can have no real security but an unconditional surrender to Britain. But if we adopt the measure now, we shall gradually liberalise the Catholic gentry; they will see how much their property, their liberty, and their lives depend upon the Constitution.*

The Bill was, of course, defeated. A fateful moment in the history of Ireland. It was the sign for disaffection to begin to assume the characteristics of revolt.

There began a series of sporadic outbursts of violence. All communities with a grievance were involved – principally Presbyterians, other dissenters, also Catholics, and some Protestants. As in the seventeenth century, Ulster was the chief centre of disaffection. France was their model. An independent republic was their aim. And a French landing and supporting invasion was their hope. The form was the now common hideous Irish pattern. Clandestine, indiscriminate murder. Robbery of arms and treasure. Mutilation of cattle, and indeed of human beings. Arson of homesteads. Whispered threats, blackmail and intimidation of witnesses, jurors and magistrates. The voice of the Catholic church was ignored by the rebels, save in individual instances where, contrary to the injunctions of the Catholic bishops for moderation within the constitution, a handful of individual priests signified their approval of, or even gave encouragement to, violence.

Initially, although serious in places, these incidents were not on such a scale as to be especially alarming, and seemed unlikely to become critical without the support of a French invasion. Many parts of the country were unaffected, and at periods the violence died down to negligible proportions. The history of the period is confused. It was the time when the Orange Society was founded in Ulster. On the one hand Catholics and Presbyterians united to oust English influence. On the other, they assaulted each other with hideous savagery.

In December, 1796, came the moment that England had feared. The French, encouraged by Wolfe Tone and other Irish rebels, mounted an invasion of Ireland with a large force. Bad weather and bad seamanship scattered the fleet of French transports, but a considerable number of them hovered off the south west coast for several days. One settler landlord, a Mr White, together with his Catholic tenants and retainers, played an active and spirited part in preparations to meet the invaders should they come ashore. His elevation to the peerage, as Lord Bantry, was an ennoblement that he had no reason to be ashamed of. But his experience was typical of that of other responsible authorities in the south and west of Ireland. The Catholic peasantry showed every disposition to act under the leadership of their 'Gintry', and to serve with positive loyalty in the event of a French invasion.

It was the very moment that the British Government, with its customary lack of sensibility in handling Irish affairs, chose to announce that the emancipation of the Irish Catholics would be inconsistent with the security of Britain.

THE '98 REBELLION

Although 1798 was the year of the rebellion, considerable disturbances were already taking place in 1797. A large number of organizations and fragmented organizations were involved, and they had as many different axes to grind. But there were three main currents of disaffection.

Firstly the French Revolution gave encouragement to a caucus of revolutionary individuals of all classes – aristocrat, middle class and peasant; and of all demoninations; Protestant, Catholic and Presbyterian, – who joined together in a deist organization which became known as the United Irishmen, whose aim was to turn Ireland into an independent republic.

The initial inspiration came mainly from Presbyterian elements in Ulster, and not from Catholics. The most Catholic areas of Ireland were the least disaffected.

Apeing the French revolutionaries, the conspirators called their central body the Directory. They had direct links with France which promised them an armed invasion of Ireland in support of their revolt when the time came. It was to the United Irishmen that the two historic Protestant leaders, Wolfe Tone and Lord Edward Fitzgerald, belonged.

The second current of disaffection was a renewal of sectarian strife, particularly on the part of the Ulster Presbyterians. In 1797 they carried out a pogrom against Catholics in Ulster, very large numbers of whom fled to Connaught. Fear of the Orangemen became the bogey of the Catholics throughout Ireland.

The third cause of disaffection was the most basic. Genuine grievances. There were four main grievances. First, corruption, largely exercised by the British Government, to pack the Irish Parliament and to manipulate legislation. Secondly, the exclusion of Catholics from the government. But neither of those grievances was of major importance to the mass of the impoverished and ignorant peasantry. An unlettered peasantry is not so much concerned about who its masters are, as about how their mode of government immediately affects its daily life.

The other two grievances did touch the mass of the people, and particularly the Catholic peasantry, at their own level. The altogether unfair burden of tithes paid by the poorest to the Protestant church was one. The French Revolution had abolished tithes. The United Irishmen promised to do the same. The other was rents; burdensome rack rents imposed by the middlemen. The French Revolution aimed to destroy the land-owning aristocracy and seize their lands in the name of the people. The United Irishmen promised to do the same. The United Irishmen promised the same policies as France. The landlords were to be destroyed, and the lands returned to the people. The prospects of a French invasion could therefore be shown to be something to be welcomed as certain to bring those benefits in its train.

To add to the Government's troubles and the general confusion in the country, the central control of the armed forces was weak. The forces themselves, regular, volunteer and militia, were scattered throughout the land in penny packets. Discipline was lax. Troops were billeted on the populace. There was much misbehaviour and injustice, and frequent and widespread outrages were committed by the troops. They were particularly concerned to prevent the spread of arms among the people. Their methods of extracting information, and of intimidating the populace into giving information about the whereabouts of arms, were crude and brutal in the extreme, but it had to be admitted that they were often effective. Innocent and guilty alike were flogged publicly, and that could mean several hundred lashes with a cat o'nine tails, to make them talk, and it did make them talk.

Houses in which arms were found were burnt. Houses found empty at night were likewise burnt because their owners were judged to be absent on secret revolutionary business. Large quantities of arms were nevertheless discovered by these means. The population at large found itself ground between the upper and the nether millstones, for it suffered hardly less intimidation from the United Irishmen who just as readily murdered, mutilated, and burnt the property of those known or suspected of giving information to the authorities, or those who withheld their support.

Much of Ireland remained quiet, but the lawlessness in 1797 led in the early months of 1798 to a situation in which the authorities perceived that it was inevitable that the United Irishmen were going to launch a full-scale revolt, accompanied by the promise of a French invasion. There were few men of ability in the leadership of the United Irishmen. Their security was lax. The upshot was that the bulk of the central leadership was arrested in Dublin a few days before the revolt was due to start in May, 1798, including Lord Edward Fitzgerald – a foolish, romantic, unstable young man, the story of whose arrest, wounding and subsequent death in prison, which saved him from the gallows, has passed into the literature of historic tragedies.

The rebellion started on the night of 23–24 May, 1798, on the outskirts of Dublin. During the next fortnight, the central counties of Ireland were most affected. Sizeable bodies of United Irishmen attacked towns and garrisons, but the rebels were for the most part ill-led and ill-organized, and suffered a number of defeats. Central Ireland was soon pacified.

A more serious situation developed in the south-east, principally in Wexford. The religious aspect of the rebellion was confused. The Catholic bishops were explicit in their condemnation of the revolt, and urged the people to abide by the law, and support the constitution. But in the south-east, the rebellion began to take the form of an ugly vendetta on the part of the more numerous Catholics against the Protestants, and a number of the most prominent leaders were the lower class of priests, having themselves a peasant background. And the fears of the Catholics were deliberately inflamed by tales that the Orangemen were coming, bent on the annihilation of the Catholics. In a situation not far short of mob rule, a campaign to exterminate the local Protestant community descended almost to the level of a blood lust. Some horrific acts were perpetrated which rival the Black Hole of Calcutta, and the massacre of Cawnpore. But they are best forgotten. They were in part retaliation for the widespread brutal excesses of the military authorities, floggings, burnings and hangings, perpetrated against the Catholics, in their efforts to extract information before the rebellion started.

The rebels captured the town of Wexford and other towns, but it was not long before they were defeated, and the whole rebellion was virtually at an end in less than six weeks.

Civil war seems to call forth man's most brutal instincts. The '98 Rebellion, short as it was, is a loathsome tale of barbarism perpetrated by both sides. Thousands were killed, most of them other than in the set-piece battles. But amid the countless tales of horrors, there are also marvellous tales of heroism. As ever, the Irish faced death bravely, whether in the field, before the firing squad, or on whatever make-shift gallows were to hand. The Irish character seems to admit extremes of both cruelty and tenderness. There were incidents where Catholic servants played traitor to the Protestant gentry they served. But the aristocratic tradition dies hard in Ireland, and there were probably very many more occasions where masters and their wives and families, on the one hand, and their servants on the other, risked all to save each other.

If the map of Ireland is divided into four quarters, with the horizontal dividing line running through Dublin, then the rebellion was confined almost to the bottom right hand quarter – the south-east. The Catholic west, Connaught, and south-west, were almost unaffected. Ulster, too, except for two small incidents, remained quiet, which may seem curious, as the Ulster Presbyterians had been the main inspiration of the United Irishmen.

But alarm bells were ringing in the Presbyterian camp. The Presbyterians had given themselves a fright. They became aware that they had let a genie out of the bottle. The Catholic excesses against the Protestants in Wexford caused them to perceive a factor they had so far overlooked. Suddenly they saw the great Catholic mass of their fellow countrymen in a different light. Not as fellow-sufferers under a discriminatory government, which must, with the help of France, be overthrown and replaced by a republic in which there would be liberty, equality and fraternity for all, but as primitive, ancient Irish savages, rising from centuries of subjection to claim their own, – and with themselves, the Presbyterians, the foreign plantation 'Orangemen', their principal enemy – and the Presbyterians found it an ugly and frightening revelation, and one they were not disposed to encourage further. To conduct a nice little pogrom against the despised Ulster Catholics was one thing. To act so as to promote the ascendancy of the ancient savage beyond-the-Pale Catholic Irish as a whole was quite another. At that moment was born the modern antipathy that has haunted the two communities ever since.

No French forces arrived to assist the rebels during the rebellion but, in the late summer and in the early autumn of 1798, after the rebellion had been crushed, there were three French landings, or attempted landings on the west coast. In the first, over a thousand French troops landed and carried out some successful operations. They then penetrated as far as the Shannon basin where they were destroyed by an overwhelmingly stronger British force. They were a fine fighting body of men, and well officered, and they behaved with gentlemanly chivalry. They were accompanied by Wolfe Tone's brother, Matthew, who was captured and hanged.

The other two French expeditions were abortive. One was of one vessel only which landed for a few hours in the Aran Islands. The other, in mid-September, carried Wolfe Tone himself. It consisted of eight ships which had three thousand French troops aboard. It was met at sea by an English squadron, was defeated, and never reached Ireland. Wolfe Tone was captured and condemned to death, but committed suicide by cutting his throat with a concealed pen-knife. That squalid, melancholy end to the life of a brave idealist of none too great ability – despite the later mythology – came in November, 1798. Wolfe Tone, the Protestant, stands today in Irish folk lore on a pinnacle high above all the heroes of Catholic nationalist Ireland. Perhaps that augurs well for some sort of future rapprochement between the two communities.

With his death, apart from a few last flickers of the revolutionary flame, the rebellion was over. But the aftermath was to come, and was vastly more important then the rebellion itself, not least for the future of the landowning families of the Ascendancy.

THE UNION

Up to the time of the 1798 rebellion, the British Government had seen 'Union' – the incorporation of Ireland into the United Kingdom – as a future possibility, but not as an immediate aim. However, the rebellion reinforced the view in England that only direct rule from London could ensure that Ireland did not become a menace to British security. England was now virtually alone in the war with revolutionary France. The French were not just a threat. They had indeed landed, and attempted landings, in Ireland. The settler rulers were not only striving for a greater measure of independence than they had obtained in 1782, but were also actively concerned to make at least an apparent power-sharing compact with the Catholic gentry. The time had come to put a stop to all that, and to impose direct rule from Westminster. 'Union' was to be the means to that end.

A late eighteenth century document among Lord Castlereagh's papers gives the views on Ireland expressed two centuries earlier by Queen Elizabeth's counsellors, and adds that there was little doubt that they were views that had not altered two hundred years later.

'Should we,' said Elizabethan counsellors, 'exert ourselves in reducing this country to order and civility, it must soon acquire power, consequence and rule. The inhabitants will be alienated from England. They will cast themselves into the arms of some foreign power, and perhaps erect themselves into an independent state.'

To frustrate any such Irish ambitions had been England's consistent policy for centuries. Ireland must never become – indeed must never be allowed to be fit to become – independent, lest she pursue independent policies of her own choosing, and lest those policies be such as to expose England's strategic rear to a foreign enemy.

To force Ireland into a subservient union with Great Britain, legislation was now drafted and laid before the Irish Parliament, which was, in effect, asked to sign its own death warrant. Under the Act of Union, both houses of the Irish Parliament would be abolished. Instead, the Irish would be represented at Westminster by a hundred members of the Commons, twenty-eight representative peers, and a handful of bishops. All that they would be able to do was talk. They could not out-vote the English members. They could at times be a nuisance. They could at other times offer their voting strength to one of the English parties for some *quid pro quo* to their own advantage. But they would have no power on their own account. They could never be a majority party. Government of Ireland by the Irish would be at an end. Ireland would in future be no more than a province of the United Kingdom. The gentry could run their estates, and local affairs, subject to laws made at Westminster; what you owned in the eighteenth, and much of the nineteenth, century, you also governed – but that was all. They would be shorn of real power to influence the destiny of what they regarded as their own land.

But so unpopular was the prospect of Union that, despite the packing of the Irish House of Commons with placemen, the legislation did not at first succeed, and had to be postponed till the following session.

The British Government then indulged itself in a monumental campaign of corruption. By this time, a straightforward and honourable soldier had been appointed Viceroy – Lord Cornwallis; he was horrified at what he had to do, but felt it his duty to obey orders. His correspondence survives, so we know how he thought.

> *The political jobbing in this country gets the better of me. It has ever been the wish of my life to avoid this dirty business, and I am now involved in it beyond all bearing. How I long to kick those whom my public duty obliges me to court. I despise and hate myself every hour for engaging in such dirty work. Nothing but the conviction that a Union is absolutely necessary for the safety of the British Empire could make me endure the shocking task which is imposed upon me.*

The task consisted of dishing out a total, during his short period of office, of twenty-eight Irish peerages as bribes – sixteen of them explicitly for support in the Union debates. Six Irish peers were additionally given English peerages. And twenty Irish peers were raised in rank. And, at lower levels, there were all sorts of lucrative offices, pensions and so forth. Sixty-three members of the Irish House of Commons who were not prepared to vote for the Union were by one means or another dislodged, and their seats given to more acquiescent men. The bill was at length passed through all its stages in the Irish House of Commons, though by majorities which were disappointing, given the advantage with which the British Government had armed its bribed supporters.

One of the new peers was Arthur Magan the Younger's brother-in-law, Charles, Lord Castlecoote. Another connection of the family also received a peerage; and another, who was already a peer, received a step up in the Irish peerage and an English barony as well.

Many years later, Gladstone was to say of the Act of Union:

There is no blacker or fouler transaction in the history of man. We used the whole civil government of Ireland as an engine of wholesale corruption. We obtained that Union against the sense of every class of the community, by wholesale bribery and unblushing intimidation.

What the Act of Union did was to reverse the Tudor, Stuart and Cromwellian policy of pacifying and ruling Ireland through a garrison of Protestant English settlers. The settlers were no longer to be trusted. They were, in effect, dismissed; and Whitehall took over. The settler policy had failed, as it had failed continuously since the time of Henry II. If the modern – that is to say seventeenth century – settlers had not exactly gone native, they had nevertheless become too self-consciously Irish, and too independent.

To compound their corruption, the British Government also grossly mishandled the situation. Left to themselves, Irish parliamentarians, like Henry Grattan, would have carried out a raft of necessary and beneficial reforms. True they would have striven to keep power in their own hands, supported by a few property-owning Catholic gentlemen, but they would have actively tried to clean up the corruption in political elections; tithes would have been abolished, or commuted; there would have been amelioration of rent grievances. There would also have been proper administration and control of both Catholic and Protestant clergy. There would have been attention to the education of the mass of people. To do nothing – for England did nothing – after forcing through the Union, to carry through any such programme of reforms was neither honest nor sensible.

And so, having secured the Union, and emasculated her loyal Irish friends and loyal supporters, the Irish gentry, both Protestant and Catholic, England was content largely to ignore Ireland and let her stew, which indeed she did to bring forth in due season a brew of hostile demagogues from the ranks of the peasantry who were to be a thorn in her flesh for evermore.

But we have to remember that the focus of Britain's primary attention was necessarily elsewhere – on the mortal threat to herself and Europe from Napoleon; and that Ireland was, therefore, back in its role of Europe's pawn.

The Union of Great Britain and Ireland came into being on 1 January, 1801. It was the beginning of the end for the Protestant Ascendancy. But it was the leading Protestant gentlemen of Ireland who foresaw what the English failed to perceive – that it was also the beginning of the end of English domination of Ireland, and indeed the beginning of the end of the Empire.

Grattan, and a few others, had the prescience to see that it inevitably paved the way not just for an independent Ireland, but indeed for a native Irish independence, not the complementary independent loyal sister Kingdom to the larger island that had been the aim of the Ascendancy leaders. Grattan said:

The constitution may for a time be lost. The character of the country cannot be lost. The ministers of the crown may find that it is not so easy to put down for ever an ancient nation, by power and corruption, however irresistible.

But it is important not to confuse the concept of a union between Britain and Ireland as a general and desirable constitutional aim, with the corruptly enforced arrangements of 1801. The more general proposition had a much older history, going back to the seventeenth century; and, at the beginning of the eighteenth century, at the time when Scottish union with Britain was being negotiated, a century before the Irish Act of Union, the Irish parliament had petitioned Queen Anne in vain to consider bringing Ireland into the Union. Adam Smith, at the end of *The Wealth of Nations*, had also advocated the union of Ireland with Great Britain, both for economic reasons, and for the future national well-being of the Irish themselves.

Indeed, it must surely be the case that no solution of the Irish question is foreseeable outside some form of association, if not a union, between mainland Britain, the Republic of Ireland, and the Ulster loyalists, for which various patterns that have evolved within the Commonwealth might provide a starting point of precedence.

The otherwise corrupt Union with Britain, into which Ireland was forced, has one boast. It gave birth to the world's best-known flag. The red diagonal cross of St Patrick, so called, was added to the old Union flag to become the Union Jack. Why does the Republic of Ireland not use that beautiful cross as its emblem? The tricolour has particular nationalist associations as it was the Fenian flag which was run up on the spur of the moment over the General Post Office in Dublin during the 1916 Easter rising. But, as a banner, with its weak colour arrangement, it is not sufficiently distinguished or striking to do justice to Ireland. It would hardly have inspired the septs to battle.

A distinguished Irish flag would be a blue background with St Patrick's diagonal red cross and four superimposed golden harps, one in each angle of the cross – one for each province of Ireland. That would be mildly provocative and controversial, but never mind! Such a flag would be a worthy banner of the primary colours under which to kick your way to victory, and to glory, against the All Blacks – or England for that matter – and would be a symbol of unity, where the tricolour has become associated with disunity.

CHAPTER 26

The Roman Catholic Branch
of the Magan Family under
the Penal Laws

As a minor episode in Irish social history, the eighteenth century record of the Catholic branch of the Magan family is not without interest because of the extent to which the family successfully evaded, or avoided, the worst rigours of the Penal Laws.

They had made no bones about their Catholicism. Richard Magan the Elder had received a caution under the Treaty of Limerick. His son, Richard the Younger, had made a spectacularly Catholic marriage to a girl who was the daughter of one prominent Catholic chief, the Lord of Owney, and granddaughter of another, the O'Conor Don. And Richard the Elder was himself married to a D'Alton whose Catholic family had suffered suppression and dispossession of their lands.

Strongly and defiantly Catholic as the family thus continued to be, it was nevertheless not molested. It was not transplanted to Connaught. It maintained its landed gentry status. It remained in its old home Umma-More, and retained its estates intact – some of Ireland's prime lands.

It is as certain as can be that no-one ever dared to try to steal a horse from a Catholic Magan for £5. Members of the family continued to make advantageous marriages. Some even improved their status as landowners. And in defiance of the Penal Laws they succeeded to substantial lands under the will of their Protestant cousin, Thomas Magan.

It is clear enough that the well-calculated prudence that had enabled the family as a whole to survive the successive dangers of the sixteenth and seventeenth centuries, continued to guide it through the perils of the eighteenth century. Risks were unavoidable, but were well-calculated, and not rashly undertaken. The greatest was the risk the Protestant branch took to shelter and support the Catholic branch.

The effects of the Penal Laws are seen in the case of James Magan, a son of Richard Magan the Younger. Unable to live as a landowner, he became the first known member of the family to join a profession – the only profession open to him as a Catholic; medicine, which he practised in Dublin.

Dr James Magan's elder brother, Francis Magan, who succeeded to the Umma-More estate, married Mary Esmonde, a member of a distinguished Catholic settler family which had come to Ireland in Tudor times from Lincolnshire, and which had, early in the seventeenth century, been awarded a baronetcy and a peerage. Mary's father underlined the tough fibre of the Catholic Irish gentry by the manner of his death in a hunting accident at the age of ninety.

The old Irish Catholic families were assailed by an agonizing conflict of loyalties, from which the Catholic Magans were no more sheltered than other families. Thus Francis Magan and his wife Mary Esmonde had a daughter, Margaret Magan, who married a Tipperary Catholic landowner, descendant of one of Henry II's Norman knights. Margaret Magan's son, Colonel Hervé de Montmorency Morris, who subsequently succeeded to the Tipperary property, was a colonel, not in the British army, but in the army of France, serving against Britain at the time of the Napoleonic wars. He married a European noblewoman. When she died, his second marriage entailed an extraordinary conflict of loyalties. The time is still the period of the Napoleonic wars, and the event is the Irish rebellion of 1798. The story was first published many years ago.

Some twenty miles west of Dublin, and not far from each other, in the County Kildare, are two little towns which, on account of their names, are something of a joke in Ireland. One is named Clane (which is the way the Irish pronounce the word 'clean'), and the other is named Prosperous.

On the first day of the '98 rebellion, 24 May, 1798, a force of some 300 rebels attacked the little garrison at Clane. Although the garrison was greatly outnumbered, its commander, Captain Richard Griffith, drove the attackers off with a well directed fire, pursued them out of the town, killed many, burnt every house in which they took refuge, and took six prisoners, all of whom were summarily executed; such were the harsh realities of war and rebellion in those times.

On returning to the town with his small body of troops at five o'clock in the morning, Captain Griffith learnt that, three miles away, Prosperous had also been attacked. There the sentries had been overpowered in the dark. The small garrison of some fifty men were largely caught in their billets, to which the rebels set fire, burning the soldiers to death. Some who jumped from windows were impaled on the pikes of the rebels. Others who tried to cut their way out were mostly killed, as were some prominent citizens of the town.

On hearing that news, Captain Griffith rightly assessed that the victorious rebels from Prosperous would next seek to destroy his force, and to that end would invest Clane. He placed his small force in an advantageous tactical position, and was soon under attack from a large and ragged rebel force, whom his garrison put to flight with a disciplined charge and pursuit in which the rebels lost many killed, and abandoned large quantities of arms.

Captain Griffith decided then to take his wounded on carts, under escort of the remnants of his small force, to the larger garrison town of Naas. When the roll was called, many of his men were missing, including his first lieutenant who happend also to be a medical doctor. A yeoman who then strayed in from among the missing stragglers from the Prosperous garrison, told Griffith, to his amazement, that the first lieutenant had been the commander who had led the rebel night attack on the garrison at Prosperous.

No sooner was Griffith's force drawn up, ready to march out of Clane in the direction of Naas, than the first lieutenant rode up in clean uniform, fully armed and looking very spruce. He took his usual place in the line of march. Unaware that he was under suspicion, he rode into Naas in his rightful place as the second in command of the gallant little force. Once in Naas, Captain Griffith halted his troops at the gaol, and incarcerated the lieutenant. There was ample evidence of his guilt, and he was subsequently tried and hanged.

He was, like Dr James Magan, another Catholic gentleman who had sought a medical career. He was Dr John Esmonde, nephew of Mary Esmonde, who had married Francis Magan. And it was his widow, Helen, who married as his second wife the Irish-French Colonel Hervé de Montmorency-Morris, son of Margaret Magan and grandson of Francis Magan and Mary Esmonde.

And the loyalty convolutions of the children of Dr Esmonde take this dilemma of old Catholic Ireland to mind-boggling lengths. He had five sons – left to be brought up by his wife and her Irish-French Colonel second husband.

The eldest son succeeded to the Esmonde family honour. One son became an officer in the French army. Two sons became officers in the British Royal Navy. And one son became a priest. For whose victory did he pray? And if the sons came back to Ireland to visit their eldest brother at the family home – or to visit their Magan connections, for that matter – did they all sit down amicably to dinner in their various uniforms? And a grandson of the luckless Dr John Esmonde, a British army officer, was destined to be awarded a V.C. in the Crimea, and a later descendant, a Fleet Air Arm officer, received a posthumous V.C. in the Second World War. It is hardly to be wondered at that things Irish are neither very straightforward, nor easy to unravel.

That, by who now knows what contrivances, some Catholic families continued to flourish and to hold important offices, is a puzzle well illustrated by the descendants of Mary Magan, sister of Francis and Dr James Magan. She it was who married Cuthbert Fetherstonhaugh, descendant of the Catholic royalist who perished at the hands of Cromwell along with the Earl of Derby and others.

Six of the descendants of Mary Magan became High Sheriffs of the County Westmeath, several married peers and baronets. One male descendant married the daughter of a Privy Councillor, another became a Gentleman-in-Waiting to the Lord Lieutenant of Ireland. Another changed his faith and became an Anglican clergyman.

That members of Mary Magan's family became the Fetherstonhaughs of places with such names as Mosstown, Brackley Castle, Grouse Lodge, Rockview and Carrick, denotes the acquisition of landed property – all despite the Penal

Laws. One of her female descendants, Barbara Francis MacEvoy, became the wife of Sir Bernard Burke, the genealogist, thus linking him to the Magan family.

It is perhaps appropriate at this point to acknowledge the enormous debt of gratitude owed by any genealogical researcher into the landed gentry of these realms to 'Burke's'. Collation on that scale would be quite impossible for an individual writer. But more than that, much of the information would by now almost certainly have been altogether lost had it not been for the devoted work of the founder, early in the nineteenth century, Sir John Burke, and of his son Sir Bernard Burke – and their twentieth century successors.

Two of Mary Magan's female descendants who married baronets married in different generations into the same family, one to Sir Thomas Chapman, 2nd Baronet of Killua Castle, Co. Westmeath, the other to Sir Benjamin Chapman, 4th Baronet of Killua Castle. The baronetcy had been created in 1782. The 6th Baronet died in 1914. He had no son. His successor, as 7th Baronet, was Sir Thomas Robert Tighe Chapman. He was a grandson of the 2nd Baronet and therefore a great-grandson of Mary Magan who married Cuthbert Fetherstonhaugh.

This Sir Thomas Chapman, 7th Baronet, was in middle life when he succeeded to the title. He had married many years before and had had three daughters, but no son. He had then deserted his family and run off with his daughters' governess, a Miss Lawrence. By her he had a number of sons. One of them was Lawrence of Arabia, who thus had Magan blood in his veins from his great-great-grandmother, Mary Magan. The three deserted Misses Chapman, none of whom married, were not only kinswomen, but also neighbours, of ours as they lived together not far from our home at Killyon Manor, Co. Meath.

None of us ever met Lawrence of Arabia. Indeed, I never heard anything to suggest that he ever visited Ireland to meet his half-sisters – an act that would perhaps have been out of character, as there is some evidence that his illegitimacy was an acute embarrassment to him and preyed on his mind.

Like Baron Corvo, he will, for a long time to come, be an intriguing study for students of human nature. He was brilliant, eccentric, absurd; a genius, a poseur, a mountebank. Fellow of All Souls, and man of action. Erratic and psychotic, he was one of the world's outstanding compulsive egocentrics. He remains renowned as author and compiler – for not the least of its excellencies are the pictures – of *The Seven Pillars of Wisdom*, though his letters are more revealing of the real man. He craved publicity. To gain it he cultivated a pose of being conspicuously inconspicuous whether dressed as desert Arab or as Air Force private – 'hiding himself in the limelight,' as Bernard Shaw said of him.

Lily Montgomery, whose family home, Kilmer, was the nearest large house to Killyon, and who also was not married, acted as companion to the three spinster Chapman sisters when they became elderly. One of them, according to Lily, ruefully and nostalgically kept a copy of *The Seven Pillars of Wisdom*, by her bedside. What, we may ask, in sympathetic retrospection, might sisters, sensible and kindly Irish countrywomen, not have been able to do to alleviate the stresses of the poor tormented genius, before his life came to its untimely end in a tangled heap of motor-bike metal?

Among other descendants of the Catholic Magans, and among the families of their marriage partners were an Inspector-General of the Ulster Police, a Member of Parliament, two Treasurers of the County Westmeath, a Clerk of the Crown for Co. Westmeath, two Barons of the Court of Exchequer in Ireland, and a Recorder of Dublin – surely unexpected holders of office to find in the pedigree of an Irish Catholic family at the time of the Penal Laws.

But not all the Catholic members of the family found life tolerable in Ireland. A grandson of Francis Magan and Mary Esmonde who curiously, for a Catholic, was a Resident Magistrate, and who married a Fetherstonhaugh cousin, had six sons and two daughters all of whom emigrated, five of the sons to Buenos Ayres, Argentina, and one to Hamilton, Victoria, Australia. One of the daughters went also to Australia, and the other to Berlin.

The heir of Francis Magan and Mary Esmonde to the Catholic Magan estates, and the last but one male generation of the Catholic family, was Thomas Magan. He was born in 1759, when the Penal Laws were being relaxed, so he never knew their worst rigours. That the Catholic Magans were still worth marrying is revealed by the fact that his bride was Catherine Brabazon of – as the pedigreeist puts it – 'the house of Brabazon, Earls of Meath,' and his pedigree is unblushingly peppered with titles and peerages.

When he died in 1814, he was succeeded by his only son, another Francis Magan, born in 1791, the last male Catholic Magan in Ireland of the ancient Umma-More. Like his father, he also showed himself to be a desirable marriage partner for a very well-connected lady, Margaret Strong Hussey, descendant of a Henry II Norman settler, Sir Hugh Hussey. The pedigreeist once more harvested a splendid crop of related titles including no less than three dukes. Larding the Magan family pedigree with all that glitter was not, of course, just a decoratively frivolous conceit. Peers were, almost by definition, still very wealthy and influential and, in some cases, powerful. To be able to show that you moved in such a lordly ambience gave you, therefore, some additional muscle, and a boost to your own authority.

Francis, the last male Catholic Magan to live in Ireland, died in 1841. His only brother, William Magan, did not marry; and Francis's only son, Thomas, had died long years before as a child aged seven. Francis Magan is buried at the right side of the altar of the Roman Catholic church at Ballymore, which he largely built, although it was not finished until two years after his death. There is also a memorial tablet to him on the wall to the left of the altar, erected by his family. His predecessors are buried in the large, one-time Protestant, and now disused, graveyard, a few hundred yards away on the hill above the present village. It ceased to be used in the 1840s, since when burials have been in the churchyard surrounding the Catholic church. In the midst of the old graveyard stand the ruins of the Protestant church. The old graveyard itself is also in ruins, with fallen and buried headstones, graves fallen in, inscriptions effaced by time. It would now be difficult, if not impossible, to identify old Magan graves.

The Catholic church is a large, solid, stone building, in character with the enormous numbers of such churches built all over Ireland in the nineteenth and early twentieth centuries. They are not great works of architectural art, but they do reflect the enduring solidity of nineteenth century building; and the immense main spires of some of them, such as St Mary's Chapel, Athlone, must surely rank as considerable feats of architecture, engineering and building. The excellent quality of the stonework, too, is a memorial to masons of skill. Do not underestimate the native Irish. They can do it when they set their hands and minds to it. Go and look at St Mary's, Athlone. It may not be the world's most inspired building. But it is impressive. And they chose a fine site for it. It dominates the landscape for miles round. Those who built it were no slouches. And when its great bell rings out the Angelus, the sound carries miles upon the wind. And to this day the faithful bow their heads, remove their hats, make the sign of the cross and say their prayers.

That Francis Magan was in a financial position in 1841 to contribute largely to the building of such a church as the present Catholic Ballymore church, is further proof that the Catholic Magans had not only weathered the Penal Laws without undue hardship, but had also remained well-to-do, and had maintained their position as the leading family – or one of the leading families in that area. Another indication that that was so came my way not long ago. I wrote to the Roman Catholic Parish Priest at Ballymore in November, 1973, asking if there are any old parish records that might be worth research.

Almost by return of post I had a charming reply from Father Mahony, clearly so aged and infirm that he could only with difficulty hold the pen. He said that parish records do not go back beyond 1830, probably because before that Ballymore, like many other parishes, could not afford a resident priest. He added that in Dean Cogan's History of Meath Diocese it is recorded that in the early nineteenth century the Bishop 'often spent the night with the Magans of Emoe on his way to Ballymore for Confirmations.' I wonder whether the girls kissed him – perhaps only his ring. Father Mahony was kind enough to send me his blessings. I told him I was very pleased to receive blessings from the successor to those who must have blessed many of my ancestors.

I have consulted Dean Cogan's book. The remarkable Catholic Bishop of Meath at the turn of the eighteenth/nineteenth centuries, the Right Rev Dr Plunket, called the Magan home Emo, not Umma-More, and spelt it thus and not Emoe. He also spent at least one night with Francis Magan's bachelor brother, William, at his Streamstown home not far from Ballymore – yet another Magan Catholic property.

Although Francis Magan had no male successors, he was survived by three daughters. A word or two about them illustrates the extent to which even the Catholic gentry of Ireland had, by the nineteenth century, thrown in their lot with the Crown, the Empire and the Ascendancy.

One of the daughters, Margaret Magan married a man who was a Justice of the Peace for Co. Kilkenny, and for the Queen's County, and who became High Sheriff of Kilkenny. He was Michael Cahill of Ballyconna House, Ballyragget, Co. Kilkenny, and their family still survive there.

The oldest of Francis Magan's daughters, Mary Magan, who was born in Paris in 1819, was married at Umma-More two months after her father's death in 1841, to John Lentaigne, whose settler background was unusual. His father, a member of a distinguished French family, and an officer in the royal French army, fled the French Revolution – two of his brothers were guillotined – joined the British Army, qualified as a doctor, and settled and practised in Dublin.

John Lentaigne – Mary Magan's husband – had a remarkable career for a Catholic. He was a Justice of the Peace for the counties of Dublin and Monaghan, High Sheriff of Monaghan, Inspector-General of Prisons in Ireland, and a Commissioner of National Education in Ireland. He became, 'The Right Hon. Sir John Francis Nicholas Lentaigne, P.C., C.B., D.I.' He and Mary Magan, his wife, produced a family of nine sons, and four daughters of whom two became nuns.

One son became a barrister and rose to be Permanent Secretary to the Chancellor of Ireland. Another became President of the Royal College of Surgeons, Ireland, and was knighted. Another became a High Court Judge in Burma. One became a priest. Four of those Catholic sons were educated at the Protestant establishment, Trinity College, Dublin.

Major Edward Charles Lentaigne, son of the President of the Royal College of Surgeons, lost a leg, and was awarded a D.S.O. in the 1914–18 war.

Walter Lentaigne – known in the family and to his friends as 'Joe' Lentaigne – son of the Burma judge, became a General in the Indian Army and succeeded General Wingate, when he was killed in an air crash, as Commander of the Chindit force in Burma in the Second World War.

And there I shall leave the Catholic Magans – from the Catholic grazier chieftain Richard Magan the Elder, warned under the terms of the Treaty of Limerick, to his descendant General 'Joe' Lentaigne, Catholic Commander of His Majesty's Chindit Force, is a scrap of the convoluted pattern of the mosaic of the story of Ireland which perhaps suggests that we should not close our minds about future possibilities in Ireland. The unlikely may yet come to pass.

BOOK FIVE

The Zenith of the

Family as Irish

Landowners at

the Dawning

of Irish

Independence in

the Nineteenth

Century

CHAPTER 27

The Renaissance of the Real Irish

WE NOW ENTER THE nineteenth century, and usher in the most profound development in Irish history for two thousand years. At last, after all that time, the real Irish, the pre-Celtic Irish, were on the road to freedom from alien – first Celtic, then English – overlordship.

There were four key elements in this great national transition:
1 Politicians – the new nationalists.
2 The People – the real Irish.
3 Power – why it passed to the people.
4 The Priesthood – the source and nature of its enormous authority.

1 – POLITICIANS: THE NEW NATIONALISTS

The Act of Union effectively destroyed the political authority of the Protestant Ascendancy – the property-owning and landed gentry of Ireland. Even a family like the Magans, which had steered clear of direct involvement in politics at national level, was inevitably destined to be caught up in the deep effects this was to have on Irish life from the beginning of the nineteenth century onwards.

The Ascendancy did not immediately lose all authority or influence. Locally, its members remained powerful. They administered, but no longer governed. Government was from Whitehall, on a colonial pattern through a Viceroy, or Lord-Lieutenant, in Dublin.

Some of the officials were English, but the majority were educated Protestant Irishmen of the Ascendancy, as were the High Sheriffs, the judiciary, including Justices of the Peace, military officers, and other officials throughout the country, and as, later on, were officers of the police after the embodiment of the force which was to become the Royal Irish Constabulary. And, 'what you owned you ruled,' continued to apply in large measure to the locally powerful estate owners.

Westminster's authority was, however, now about to be challenged by a new brand of politician – initially educated, upper or middle class, but joined progressively by men whose origins were in the emerging peasantry. This new breed of politician represented the aspirations of the mass of native Irish, whose own origins were in the pre-Christian peasantry.

To speak of a challenge is hardly correct. The political emasculation of the Ascendancy had caused a power vacuum, and those were the two forces most naturally placed to fill it.

Policies, too, were reversed. Prior to the Act of Union the Protestant Ascendancy had striven for self-government for Ireland; Ireland to be wholly independent of Britain, a Protestant-governed country within the Empire. But when the Catholic majority began to demand the repeal of the Act of Union, the Protestant Ascendancy had no alternative but to oppose them, and to support the Union. The repeal of the Act of Union would mean the restoration of the Dublin parliament. The Catholics already had the vote. 'Emancipation' to give them seats in parliament could not be indefinitely withheld, and those seats would now go not to loyal Catholic 'gentlemen', but to the emergent peasant 'rabble' politicians. The repeal of the Act of Union would therefore lead to a 'native' Catholic parliament, and the end of the Protestant Ascendancy, and the seizure of their lands by the natives.

The Protestant landlords were, therefore, from then on, acutely aware that their salvation lay solely in the protection that the British government could, and would, give them against the rising power of the native Catholic majority; and that protection depended in its turn upon the maintenance of the Union with Britain.

At that point, therefore, begins that fierce loyalty to the British and Imperial cause which has ever since been such a notable feature of Protestant Ireland. In essence it was their own protection and salvation that mattered to the Protestant Irish loyalists, faced as they were by a numerically overwhelmingly superior native Irish Catholic population. But, for all that, they did not see themselves so much the dependants of British power, as an outpost of Empire, frontiersmen braving a latently hostile, greatly more numerous, population in order to uphold the Pax Britannica in the name of the Crown in this theatre so vital to the security of Britain.

The process of Hibernicization of the Irish Protestant Ascendancy ceased. From then on, while still regarding themselves as the elite Irish, it was just as important to them to be at the same time unequivocally British. The education and upbringing of their children, therefore, became such as to ensure that from the very cradle they grew up to be fervent loyalists. You will never see an Irish Protestant standing sloppily when 'God Save the Queen' is played; ramrods, all of them.

Hitherto, before the Act of Union, only the sons of the greatest nobles in Ireland had gone to England to school. Henceforth, the majority of upper-class Protestant boys and, later, girls would be sent to English schools, to be brought up in the British culture. Thereafter, a very large number of them were destined to enter the various services of the Crown, more especially the armed forces for which their active open-air life, the exceptional loyalty with which they were imbued, and their vigilant frontiersman attitudes to threats and dangers, made them particularly suitable.

The initial native Irish clamour at the beginning of the nineteenth century for the repeal of the Act of Union came to nothing. And even Catholic emancipation was not achieved until 1829. Irish Catholics then began to be elected to the Westminster Parliament. As the nineteenth century went on, native Irish influence and pressures of one kind and another, legal, illegal; violent, peaceful; were directed particularly at loosening the settler Protestant grip on the lands of Ireland. Concessions were gradually won by tenants, until, by the beginning of the twentieth century, a succession of land legislation had ensured the eventual total break-up of the great estates, except for the demesne lands – the home farms – and the restoration of the land to the people in the shape of owner-occupier farms, large, small and very small.

In the latter part of the nineteenth century, 'Home Rule' – 'Rome Rule' to the Protestants – became the demand of the native Catholic Irish, led by the Protestant settler-family landowner, Charles Stuart Parnell. The initial demand was not for independence. Home Rule was a limited concept of control of domestic affairs by an Irish parliament, ultimately subordinate to the British parliament at Westminster. It was, however, to be nearly another fifty years before a Home Rule bill reached the statute book. 'Home Rule' is not, however, in any sense 'Rome Rule'. The Fianna Fáil Party, which has governed Ireland for much of the past sixty-five years, has tended towards anti-clericalism and has not been influenced by the Roman Catholic Church or the Vatican. An authority on Irish politics has said this about it.

The Catholic Church in Ireland, powerful though it may be, has never been powerful enough to influence politics really effectively.

2 – THE PEOPLE – THE REAL IRISH

The English attempts to turn Ireland into an Anglicized, and Protestantized, country was, in the event, destined to produce a result as remote as it possibly could be from the intention. And that result was to mature in the nineteenth century, and to come to fruition in the treaty of 1921 between Britain and the Catholic Irish Free State which was thereby created.

The historic panorama was this. When the Celts reached Ireland they found it well populated. It had been well populated for three or four thousand years. The people were of mixed origin. But it is to be supposed that late-comers during the millennium or two before the coming of the Celts were few in number because, the land being already well populated, the indigenous people would not have suffered themselves to be overrun by large numbers of immigrants.

The likelihood, therefore, is that what the Celts found in Ireland was an essentially very ancient people who had been there for seven thousand years, and to whom the Atlantic cliffs had allowed no choice but to stay there and root in Irish soil, and become a distinct people. But within that broad general structure of the population of ancient Ireland, there was nevertheless a breakdown of tribal differences.

So, in general terms, we can say that before the coming of the Celts, Ireland was peopled by, and ruled by, the Ancient Irish. Thereafter, during the two thousand years or so following the arrival of the Celts, Ireland was ruled by two different successive hierarchies. First the Celts. Secondly the English Protestant Settler Ascendancy.

The Ancient Irish leadership was destroyed by the Celts, and the Ancient Irish people were held down as a peasantry first by the Celts and then by the English Settler Ascendancy. Drop-outs from the Celts and from the later English settlers, such as disbanded rank and file soldiers, were absorbed into, and became indistinguishable from, the Ancient Irish peasantry.

The first phase of new rulers, the Celtic phase, came to an end when the English finally destroyed the Celtic leadership in the seventeenth century.

The second phase, the rule of the English Settler Ascendancy, came to an end when the British Government progressively stripped them of their authority, and legislated to strip them of their lands, in the nineteenth and early twentieth centuries, and then abandoned them, powerless, to the newly formed Irish Free State Government, under the treaty of 1921 – the million Ulster Protestants being strong enough to hold out in six counties and to insist on remaining a part of Great Britain.

By destroying the Celtic overlordship, and then withdrawing her support from her Protestant settler garrison, what Britain had achieved was not the Anglicized Protestant state of her intention, but the restoration of their land and their rule, after two thousand years or more, to the Ancient, and by then Catholic, pre-Celtic Irish.

Although they are no longer so, the Ancient Irish were, at the beginning of the nineteenth century, and until well into the twentieth century – indeed up to the time when power in their own land was restored to them – a peasantry, and they had the abiding characteristics of peasants the world over.

In the context of their resurgence after two millennia, the most important of those characteristics – which the Irish had in full measure – is the peasant's ability to resist change over immensely long periods of time. Conquerors may come and go. 'Crowns and thrones may perish, Kingdoms rise and wane.' Marauding armies may trample and pillage. The peasant may be at the mercy of tyrants great and small. Adapting only as he must, he treats them all with as much indifference as he can. He has as little concern with them as he may. In the midst of battles, he ignores the transient combatant intruders, and tends his beasts and hoes his clods with changeless deliberation. He is capable of aeons of patient indifference to oppression and deprivation. Defenceless against greater force, and better trained minds, he can be cunning, crafty and secretive.

How many times has Persia been trampled over? But visit the threshing floors of remote Persian valleys; all is just the same as described in the Bible millennia BC. Visit the villages of the alluvial plains of the Indian sub-continent, fought over time and again by invading armies; life has scarcely altered in five thousand years. There are remote valleys in Italy where life goes on as it did in pre-Roman times. Not even the Roman Empire touched it or altered it. And thus did the peasantry of Ireland preserve within itself the soul of the Ancient people of Ireland.

The Celts changed the language and the laws, but we may be sure that they were themselves largely Hibernicized, and had their own language modified by, and themselves adopted many of the characteristics of, the Ancient Irish. The Christians changed the religion. The English again changed the language and the laws. But what are those holy wells, and the thorn bushes with the rags hanging on them? Surely a continuing survival of much older practices than anything Celtic, Christian or Anglo-Saxon; and they continue to have real inner significance for those who still attach importance to them to this day. Why do you never throw out a pail of dirty water after dark? Find an Ancient Irishman and ask him.

Until as recent times as the early years of this century, antiquarians could point readily to widespread practices, particularly in the west of Ireland, which had not changed for two thousand years, and for perhaps a great deal longer. But if those surface things did not change in thousands of years, it could not be otherwise than that there are deep characteristics in the people themselves which are no less changeless.

Can there be anyone who has lived in Ireland, who – even if brought up there, and calling him- or herself Irish, but not of peasant stock – has not had the experience of going into an Irish cottage, particularly in the evening, and finding there a murmuringly quiet group in the corner of the turf-smouldering hearth, and feeling that he has made an intrusion into an incomprehensibly deep, dark and profound stratum of elemental Ireland, fathoms down in antiquity from the surface Ireland of everyday life? We have, so to speak, chanced upon something secret and normally hidden from us.

It is not that there is anything secret in a conspiratorial sense, or in the sense of a cult. It is just that there is a deep rapport and understanding among the people which cannot be shared with any who are not of their origin and upbringing. It is the real profound essence of Ireland.

It is that indefinable shared ancient spirit of subconscious understanding that motivates the inner being of the Irish even now. It is not articulated. It is handed down within families and groups of families, within the community at large, at their mother's knee, by spontaneous, unconscious custom, attitudes and manners. In their looks. In their gestures. In the subliminal communication between mothers and their infants. In the atmosphere and quality of the almost sub-rosa murmuring round the turf fires after dark, even though the subject is only the calving of Pat

Murphy's cow. And it is millions of cultural miles from anything fully comprehensible to an Anglo-Saxon.

Peasanthood is not a genetic inheritance. It is a social state reflecting environmental circumstances. The peasant is a peasant because he cannot break the political and economic bonds that hold him in that condition. Subject to the worst oppressions that may be forced upon him, his lot may be terrible. At a less harsh level, as a peasant proprietor, his circumstances may be so relatively tolerable that he is content to continue in them for countless ages, as in the case with some of the more fortunate peasant communities of Southern and South-East Asia.

The term 'peasant' carries disparaging implications which are certainly by no means always justified. The ancient peasantry of the Punjab straddling the borders of India and Pakistan, for instance, are an exceptionally handsome, healthy, dignified and intelligent people. Much of the peasantry of South-East Asia are a very beautiful, graceful, artistic and intelligent people. Beside such peasant peoples, some of the 'civilized' city peoples of Europe appear loutish. Kipling said it of the Burmese girl:

> Tho' I walks with fifty 'ousemaids outer Chelsea
> to the Strand,
> An' they talk a lot o' lovin, but wot do
> they understand?
> Beefyface an' grubby 'and-
> Law! wot do they understand?
> I've a neater, sweeter maiden in a
> cleaner, greener land!
> On the road to Mandalay ...

The Irish, too, are a handsome and intelligent people, and visitors to Ireland are struck by their stylishness.

The peasant is the elemental human being; the elemental homo sapiens. Liberate him from his bondage to the soil, and he has the capabilities of his better-schooled brothers, even to fly, if need be, to the moon. He is cocooned man. Man of the chrysalis. Warm him in the sunshine of knowledge and a little affluence, and he will fly like a butterfly. Just consider the examples of Irish and Scottish peasantry successfully emerged from their peasant cocoon and into the wide emigrant world. The metamorphosis may take a little time, and more than a little schooling. It cannot always be achieved in a generation.

Because Ireland is a pastoral country, with hitherto very little industry, it has needed only a small workforce. Heart-rending emigration in huge numbers has been the lot of its youth, but destined often enough thereafter to prosper exceedingly abroad. The Irish have shown beyond contradiction that they can go out from their homeland, take on the world on level terms, and succeed. They are not a people to be underestimated or disparaged.

Artists, with insight, intuitively aware of truths often denied to philosophers who seek them by logic, have seen and described what I have here tried to say about the real People of Ireland.

John Betjeman, on visiting the West of Ireland, wrote:

> *Stony seaboard, far and foreign,*
>   *Stony hills poured over space,*
> *Stony outcrop of the Burren*
>   *Stones in every fertile place.*
> *Little fields with boulders dotted,*
>   *Grey-stone shoulders saffron-spotted,*
>   *Stone-walled cabins thatched with reeds,*
> *Where a Stone Age people breeds*
>   *The last of Europe's stone age race.*

And what else but the coming into their own of the ancient Irish are those spectral shadowy figures in the paintings of Jack Yeats, presaging unease, and dimly discerned, coming through the swirling mists and curtains of rain and cloud, riding and walking out of the half-charted wildness of bog and mountain towards the world of full focus.

We may forget about the 'Little People.' We may forget about the fairies. If we want to see leprechauns, we need look for nothing mysterious. We just have to look at the faces of Irish males. We will see leprechauns by the dozen. We may forget about the Irish being fey. We may forget about Irish mystics and mysticism. The reality is an ancient people emerging from two thousand years of oppressed peasant bondage whose peasant characteristics of crafty secretiveness enabled them to keep the profoundest fifth of their ancient Irish souls hidden within their own bosoms and comprehended only by themselves.

We may laugh at such an image if we apply it to a drunken corner-boy reeling out of a reeking Irish pub, or to a porter-smelling jarvey with a silver tongue coaxing money out of our pockets for another round of drinking, but surely we must look beyond those surface realities to the deeper reality beneath and, indeed, ask what are the ancient sorrows, sufferings, oppressions and indignities against which those two seek oblivion in an unworthy soak.

Nor, indeed, is the familiar picture of the drunken Irish anywhere near fair to the mass of the people. There is too much public drunkenness in Ireland, and the Irish seem to have a knack of bringing themselves into undeserved disrepute. The popular concept of the Irish as a race of lazy, lying, lay-about inebriates does not at all correspond with my experience of the marvellous and delightful working people of Ireland. A short roll-call of some who are now long dead will remind me, and members of my family, with affection and admiration, of virtuous folk of wonderful quality who peopled our early life. Such were, Jimmy Smith, John and Anne Curley, Tom and Ned Dooley, Biddy Nolan, Tom and Polly Shanley, Pat and Ellen Callaghan, Johnnie and Maggy Duffy, Biddy Green, Paddy Whittaker – I could go on and on without ever encountering a drunk or a good-for-nothing, and add the names of others still, happily, living. My family owed much to them, and not least for a wealth of warm friendship of the sort that Stephen Gwynn described. They were all capable, kindly, humorous and reliable people. None of them was lazy. What might they not have accomplished with better educational and other opportunities?

When the English withdrew from Ireland in 1921, the peasantry were not wholly abandoned to sink or swim as best they might. Important elements of the professional and commercial classes who remained in Ireland, and who are descended from highly qualified and competent settler stock, lent support. They did not, and do not, seek to rule. Rulership passed to the descendants of the pre-Celtic Irish. They, nevertheless, were leaderless, their ancient pre-Celtic hierarchy having long since been destroyed by the Celts, and they were left to throw up from among themselves a new hierarchy in an era of political democracy.

In the early stages of their emergence to power from their long ages of subservience, the Irish peasant people – as they then were – were much helped, and even led, by dissident members of the upper and middle classes whose mission to bring about the emancipation of the mass of the people of Ireland was as clear – and as dear – to themselves as it was to the most enlightened of those whom they were trying to liberate, and a sprinkling of men and women whose origins were in the middle and upper classes have continued up to the present day to involve themselves in the political, and the Catholic Church, leadership. Nevertheless, as the nineteenth and twentieth centuries progressed, power passed overwhelmingly into the hands of people whose origins had been in what was up to the beginning of the nineteenth century, and even later, the Irish peasantry.

They are, however, still handicapped – handicaps that are not ineradicable, but that equally cannot be dispelled overnight. There was the appalling 'unsettling of the nation' of the sixteenth, seventeenth and eighteenth centuries. The slow recovery of the nineteenth century was dashed by the terrible years of the famine, and the loss of nearly half the population in half a century, by death, emigration and lowered birth rate.

Irish scholars were very properly interested in rescuing and preserving such knowledge as they could of the Gaelic period, particularly because the language, as a living language, was fast approaching extinction. But that laudable effort was then turned into a chauvinistic political campaign. The more zealous nationalist politicians were concerned to give Ireland as distinctive a national appearance as they could. And in particular to emphasize her dissimilarity from England.

The original concept was, however, as I have already said, largely a piece of Anglo-Irish cultural romanticism. It did not spring from the real and ancient people of Ireland. The Irish people as a whole were not interested. They knew that there was no bread and butter in an attempted revival of the Gaelic tongue. And they had better reason than most to know the importance of bread and butter. Had they not insisted on their children learning English in the hedge schools? And had not the parents boxed their children's ears when they got home if they were reported for talking Irish instead of English in school?

It was thus not the will or the decision of the people of Ireland themselves to be re-Gaelicized half a century ago, and the programme has not worked. It is true that there are more people who know a smattering of Irish than there were then, but there are many less who now speak it as a first language. There seems indeed to be no question that Gaelic can ever become a first, or even second, language, spoken country-wide in the homes of the Irish. To have some knowledge of it gives interest and enjoyment to a few. But the Irish at large are not concerned to revert to the Irish tongue. And to keep an otherwise qualified person out of a job because he has not got a smattering of the Irish tongue is as imprudently wasteful of talent as it would be to deny him the opening because he was unable to stand on his head.

Nor have the Irish people shown any inclination to adopt antiquated Irish dress. They have stuck to their ordinary clothes and battered hats, and have no desire to revert to saffron nightshirts, or to wear the Irish variety of the kilt.

To preserve the Gaelic language, Gaelic dress, and customs, for reasons of history, culture, learning and pleasure, and for distinctively national symbolic purposes is laudable, but to try to make Irish the first language of the land, and Gaelic culture the mode of today, is about as sensible, and creates about the same image of the Irish in the eyes of other peoples, as if the English were to adopt Anglo-Saxon as their national language, and as if the British Foreign Secretary was to use it in public speeches at international conferences. As an Irishman, I feel that the Irish have been overdoing it.

But even if, for want of appropriate relics of an earlier epoch, the Irish must opt for Gaelic symbols of national culture, a glance at the chart on the page following is sufficient to underline their truly much more ancient origins, and to emphasize that the Gaelic culture was a late-comer, and was the culture of their Celtic colonial masters.

We take a visual view of history. Before the coming of the Celts, as we see it in our mind's eye, all in Ireland is dark and void. Irish history emerges into the light and begins with the Celts. Before that were what we think of darkly as pre-historic times. But they were pre-historic only in the sense that their history was not recorded. Men and women made history then, just as they do now. The Irish story does not start with the Celts. Before that, all is not a darkly pre-historic void. It is a much longer time than the Celtic period, and some of it was very creative.

9,000 BC	The Peoples of Ireland since the Ice-age
8,000 BC	Pre-man
7,000 BC	Post Ice-age Tundra
6,000 BC	
5,000 BC	Hunting and food gathering man
4,000 BC	
3,000 BC	Peasant farmers
2,000 BC	
1,000 BC	Bronze and Golden Ages
0 AD	
1,000 AD	Celtic Ascendancy
	Celts plus some Norsemen
2,000 AD	Celts plus Norsemen, Normans and English
	The English Protestant Settler Ascendancy

One of man's distinguishing features is his self-assured arrogance. It is a part of his innate optimism. But it causes him to inflate the importance of his own life and times. He fails to see himself in a proper historical perspective. He has an overweening belief in the comparative excellence of himself, and in the rightness and exceptional importance of his current works. It is a conceit that might be termed the arrogance of the present; the arrogance of currently living man who, despite the disorder of his own times, regards himself as so superior to his ancient forebears as virtually to deny them their claim to have existed as fully fledged human beings. Rather, perhaps, ought we more humbly pause to ask ourselves whether there will be anything worth-while left of the world when we of today have finished with it.

If we avoid the pitfalls of 'the arrogance of the present' in respect of our Irish ancestors; if we use our imaginations to enable us to picture Ireland throughout those tens of centuries before ever the coming of the Celts, then we can see that, just as now, the sun shone, the clouds rode white in a blue sky, the rain fell and, with the sunshine, gave life to the soil. The winds blew, men moved about the face of the land of Ireland, and were doing so for seven thousand years before the Celts came – three and a half times as long as from the coming of the Celts to today. The Celts were there for twenty hundred years. The real Irish were there for seventy hundred years before that. The Protestant Ascendancy for two – only two – hundred years. The Celtic period is short by comparison with the earlier Irish period when men lived upon the land, farmed it, husbanded their beasts, built themselves homesteads, married, reared families, worked out their corporate relationships, made beautiful artefacts, traded internationally, worshipped their gods, and talked together in the languages of their times which, if they could be re-discovered, would enable the Irish to give up the signposts in supposed Gaelic script. There was no such thing. The Celts did not write. It is a Latin script, just as the script of the rest of Western Europe is. Every Western European nation has just as much right to the use of some archaic Latin script. But they do not go to the lengths of using it to the confusion of nearly everyone, including their own nationals. As an Irishman, it makes me wince a little to look at those signposts. It would be more to the point to have them in Ogham.

A look at the chart should cause eighteenth century Ascendancy families to feel some modesty, even humility, when they compare the mere moment of time – two hundred years – when they were, 'Drest in a little brief authority,' with the long ages, the seventy hundred years, during which the Ancient Irish, the real Irish, ruled their own land even before the coming of the Celts.

Ireland is littered with eighteenth and nineteenth century buildings. But they are relatively very modern. Some of them have fallen down; a great pity, as a lot are worth preserving, a task that some devoted people have set themselves. There are some two thousand eighteenth and nineteenth century country houses to boast of. What will be left of them in three or four thousand years time? Will most of them have disappeared into total oblivion like the Tilson-Magan mansion, Eagle Hill? And what will be left of the eighteenth century artefacts? And will the totality of all that remains, buildings, artefacts and all, seem anything to boast of then compared with the many tens of thousands of still identifiable remains of sites once inhabited by ancient Irish man?

When we speak of our cultural heritage, we too often perhaps have the eighteenth century in mind. Surely we need a different historical perspective. The chart gives a graphic view of the ethnic history of Ireland. Look where the year nought AD comes. Seven ninths of the story, and of the works of the people who have inhabited Ireland, were by then already over. Though we have not got a recorded history of those early times, it is nevertheless the fact that people, dwelling in organized communities, lived out their lives over a period so long that it makes the long Celtic period in Ireland look short, and that those ancient peoples did not die out but are still there, the People of Ireland of today, halted there millennia ago by the Atlantic cliffs.

> ... *think ye see*
> *The very persons of our noble story*
> *As they were living ...*
> SHAKESPEARE

Just because they left us no history of themselves, we cannot ignore their existence as though they had never been, nor relegate them to some negligible status as 'early stone-age people.' Their descendants of today are the inheritors of the earth that by most ancient right of earliest and continued occupation is truly theirs.

In our mobile modern western society, people find it difficult to identify themselves with past generations. But that is not so everywhere. Go and meet those villagers of the great alluvial plains of India, and you will know people who, and whose way of life, have not changed significantly for at least five thousand years. In an Indian village you have no problem in imagining life as it was five thousand years ago. Likewise, in Ireland, certainly west of the Shannon, it is still not difficult to see what John Betjeman saw, a way of life that was lived not only two thousand years ago, but having much in common with life two thousand years before that, and yet another two thousand years earlier still.

Looking across the whole stretch of nearly ten thousand years of man's habitation of Ireland, and knowing the ancient Irish race to have been all that time cultivating a unique individuality of its own, which no others can fully comprehend, who can say what – now that it is theirs alone, for the first time in two thousand years and more, to work out their own fate – they may be capable of doing? Anything could happen. Nothing may happen. It is the longest capped dormant volcano that makes the greatest explosion when the cap blows off, and the suppressed and repressed and pent up energies are released. You may prefer to ask whether it is not more likely that a people who allowed themselves to be sat on for two thousand years will do no more than poke their noses over the rim of the crater, take fright, and return to the comforts of the bottle? A fair question. Only time will tell. Intelligence is related to vocabulary. We think in pictures, but we also think in words. Say 'Himalayas', or St Paul's Cathedral', and you see their image in your mind's eye. Come to some more abstract topic, and your vocabulary becomes your medium of thought. The very large vocabulary used by the ordinary people of Ireland, betokens an intelligent people.

But let not the Irish be too cocksure of themselves. Have they some deep flaw? Did they come to inhabit the outer fringe of the Indo-European world because they were the most enterprising and most adventurous of its peoples? Or was it because they were genetically the weakest – the ones who got shoved around, and pushed to the fringe of the comity of nations? In the gregarious mammalian groups of nature, it is the weaker members who are kept on the periphery of the group. They are the ones the lions get. Let the people of Ireland be cautious on this score. Kipling, with his poet's insight, had his doubts about the Picts. The last verse of his poem on them contains these lines:

> ... We are not strong,
> But we know Peoples that are.
> Yes, and we'll guide them along,
> To smash and destroy you in War!
> We shall be slaves just the same?
> Yes, we have always been slaves ...

3 – POWER: WHY IT PASSED TO THE PEOPLE

We approach the nineteenth century in conditions in which the Protestant Ascendancy still administered Ireland, was still looked up to as the 'Gintry', but in which power had been taken from them and removed to Whitehall, which was progressively going to withdraw its support from them, and finally to abandon, to whatever might be its fate, this most loyal group of all the subjects of the Crown.

In point of fact, when the real Irish took over power in 1921, not only did they not discriminate against the declining remnants of the settler Protestant Ascendancy, but in some respects accorded them particularly favourable treatment. And no objections were raised to their continued first loyalty to the Crown. Although mistakes were made, both sides, nevertheless, in this particular matter, behaved with commendable good sense and good manners. Only a very few Protestant gentry involved themselves in the politics of the new Irish state. But at the professional and commercial levels of society they have rendered, and have been left entirely free to render, most signal service to their country; and it is their country, their homeland, for they are Irishmen, and women, even though their undervests may be, and are well understood by the native Irish to be, Union Jacks.

Why did the Protestant landed and professional gentry of Ireland, if indeed they were 'one of the great stocks of Europe,' and since they were, and are, people of demonstrable ability; why did they, as Irish people, not seek to assume the political leadership of the newly independent Ireland? In a serious book written half a century ago – *The Riddle of the Irish*, J. Chartres Moloney blamed the failure of the Protestant gentry to fulfil what he saw to be their proper leadership role, on their exclusiveness:

> The natural leaders of the Irish people, the gentlemen of Ireland, did not lead, were not capable of leading. They were separated from the mass of

the people, and separated from one another. Each man ordinarily had an infinitely and absurdly exaggerated idea of his individual importance. Each man isolated in his country place expected the world to stand still.

But that misses the cardinal point. Wilful the landed gentry may have been in their lofty detachment; and they were not all that detached from their own retainers and tenants. But it was not that that prevented them from fulfilling the leadership role. They were not in fact, as Chartres Moloney says they were, the natural leaders of the Irish. The fact is that they never more than partly knew the Irish, and they did not regard themselves as, and indeed were not, Irish in the native sense. There was no better combination than native Irish troops led by mostly Protestant officers of the Ascendancy. There was no better police force in the world than the largely Catholic Royal Irish Constabulary, similarly led by Ascendancy officers. Its spirit was epitomized by its distinction of having been the only police force to send a volunteer contingent to fight in the Crimean War. But that is different from the leadership which tugs at the heart-strings, at the very soul of a nation. The Ascendancy were rulers and masters, but never in that sense leaders of the Ancient Irish, the real Irish, the pre-Celtic preponderant part of the people of Ireland.

The real soul of Ireland remained submerged far below any level of consciousness to which the Anglo-Irish Ascendancy's heart and mind could penetrate. And in the depths of her Irish soul, Kathleen ni Houlihan could never see the Gintry as other than a kind of English from whom she had always kept the deepest recesses of her ancient Irish spirit dark and hidden. And to the Anglo-Irish themselves there seemed always to be in the make-up of the native Irish a shadowy element, covert, shrouded, penumbral, obscure, mysterious, secretive and not without some suspicion of lurking menace.

Those were the ancient secrets of Irishness of which an understanding was for ever closed to those born beyond, or much above, the confines of an Irish cottage, and outside the embrace of the Irish version of the Roman Catholic faith, within which the ancient gods of Ireland are not denied a niche in the warmth of its hospitality.

There is also the very important fact that the settlers remained distinctively identifiable by their religion. The hazard of the separate religious badge did not menace the Normans in England. They merged into the community and survived. England is only now purging herself of their most baneful influence, arrogant exclusiveness. But the Normans themselves cannot be purged. They are unidentifiable. But the religious badge did, for instance, attach to the Moors in Spain who, after no less than five centuries, were isolated and expelled. It is dangerous to a minority, even though they be the rulers, to wear a badge, even after no matter how long a period of residence.

The old Celtic chiefs came much nearer to real leadership of the ancient Irish than did the Ascendancy Protestants. They were the same faith as the Irish. They lived largely communally with the native people. Those children of the chiefs who were fostered in the cabins of the native Irish must have come very near to a complete understanding. The old Irish chiefs did not talk in so detached a way as the Protestant Ascendancy about 'the natives', or 'the mad Irish,' or 'the wild Irish.' They were too nearly identified themselves with the natives. They had gone a long way down the road of complete ancient Hibernicization, but not quite all the way.

I have suggested that the Celtic incursions may not have amounted numerically to more than a dominant aristocracy of at most a few thousand families, together with a second rank of supporters. Their rule was to that extent comparable to that of the English settler Gintry. But it lasted ten times as long, and they thus became much more Irish than ever the English settlers did. They also became separated from their ancient European Celtic base, so there was no fount from which to continue to nourish their Celtic culture.

But, for all that, even the Celtic chiefs, in two thousand years, did not, I believe, fully penetrate that submerged fifth of ancient Ireland, cocooned, as it was, in the heart of the peasantry. Their identification with the ancient natives was never total. They continued to differentiate between themselves, the Milesians, and earlier inhabitants, some of whom, including earlier Celtic settlers who had 'gone native,' are, for instance, described in an ancient Celtic document as:

... black-haired, tattlers, guileful, tale-telling, noisy, contemptible, wretched, mean, strolling, unsteady, harsh, inhospitable, slaves, mean thieves, disturbers of every council, promoters of discord ...

in contrast to the Milesians, who were said to be:

... white of skin, brown of hair, bold, honourable, daring, prosperous, bountiful, not afraid of battle or combat ...

There seems, therefore, to be a valid case for drawing a clear distinction between those inhabitants of Ireland who descended from the Picts – the real Irish – and the Celts, and for recognizing that that distinction persisted throughout the whole period of Celtic domination. From the beginning the Celts acted, and then continued to act, essentially like a colonial power, but one that had settled there for good, and who had no other homeland, somewhat on the lines of the white South Africans, but with a much greater measure of integration with the natives. Having established their dominance by their martial superiority, and their perhaps more forceful character as a people, they retained and maintained it by honouring valour above all other qualities. In the manner of colonial masters they saw themselves as a superior people, and the Ancient Irish as inferior, and they assigned to the Ancient Irish a subordinate role in society. In the manner of colonists, they no doubt allied themselves to a chosen elite among the Ancient Irish who were prepared to throw in their lot with them. From them, again, in the usual manner of colonial settlers, they learnt and absorbed into their own culture much that had already become culturally indigenous to Ireland. In the manner of colonial masters, however, they imposed much of their own culture on the subjugated Pictish majority, and in particular their Celtic laws and language for purposes of administration.

The period of Celtic colonial rule in Ireland was a long one. It was two thousand years before it was finally extinguished. But throughout that period the much larger Pictish sub-stratum of the population remained the real essence of Irish life, just as the distinctiveness of the Spaniards survived nearly eight hundred years of Moorish Moslem rule, albeit with their language much adulterated; and just as many Middle Eastern cultural entities also survived five hundred years of imposed Turkish imperial power.

Thus it was that because the Celtic overlords remained throughout their two thousand years of colonial rule of Ireland an identifiable element – an exclusive aristocracy – it was possible for more powerful invaders, the English, to dislodge them by exile, reduction and assimilation in the seventeenth century. And thus it was, too, that, when the time came that England lost the will to govern through the Ascendancy, the real people of Ireland, freed at last from dominant alien overlords, chose to be led by politicians, on the one hand, and a priesthood, on the other, recruited from their own peasant, or near-peasant, ranks, into whose hands power in Ireland passed. But a cultivated leadership takes time to mature. That colourful Irish politician and wag, Tim Healy, immortalized the dilemma. When asked how it came about that the newly formed small Free State Army had so many generals, he replied, 'Well now, you see, its heredithary with them. Their muthers were cook-generals before them.'

4 – THE PRIESTHOOD: THE SOURCE AND NATURE OF ITS ENORMOUS AUTHORITY

Lecky's description of the two kinds of men who occupied the Irish priesthood around the turn of the eighteenth/nineteenth centuries, provides a key that opens the door to an understanding of the phenomenon of the people of Ireland emerging from an age old bondage and throwing up their own priestly leadership from among themselves.

As the Penal Laws allowed no instruction in Ireland for men destined for the Catholic priesthood, their training during the eighteenth century could be carried out only abroad and illegally. Lecky calls the first type, men of the 'better class'. They were educated in France, Italy, Flanders, or at the Irish college of Salamanca; men who came from Irish homes higher up the social scale than the peasantry, some from the landed gentry. He goes on:

They grew up when Catholicism throughout Europe was unusually temperate, and they brought back to Ireland with them a foreign culture and a foreign grace which did much to embellish Irish life. Their earlier prejudices were corrected and mitigated by foreign travel. They sometimes mixed with a society far more cultivated than an Irish Protestant country clergyman was likely to meet. This type of priest might be frequently met with in the last years of the eighteenth century, and the first quarter of the nineteenth century, and its disappearance has been an irreparable loss to Irish society. Mild, amiable, cultivated, learned and polite, uniting the meek spirit of the Christian pastor to the winning gentleness of the polished man of the world, these men were welcome guests at the tables of the Protestant gentry.

That sort of priest largely disappeared, partly because of the greatly diminished number of Catholic gentry families from which they could be recruited; and partly because the anti-clerical nature of the French Revolution, and the many following years of continental war, much diminished the opportunities for ecclesiastical education in France and on the continent.

Lecky has this to say, by contrast, about the other type of priest in Ireland in the late eighteenth century:

Boys, springing from the very humblest peasant class, learnt their letters and a little Latin in the hedge school, and then travelled through Ireland as mendicant scholars till they obtained the means of going to France where, by the performance of servile duties, they obtained their education for the priesthood. They usually returned to Ireland with a slight tincture of scholastic and controversial theology, a large store of extravagant legends, all the zeal of an impassioned missionary, and most of the tastes, passions and prejudices of an ignorant peasant. Their fanaticism, their credulity, their coarse, violent, grotesque sermons, their frequent pretensions to miracle-working powers, their complete sympathy with the ideas and feelings of the peasantry, gave them an influence much greater than that of the learned and polished ecclesiastic.

Those were the men who, from that time onwards, were to rule the Roman Catholic Church in Ireland, and largely govern the daily lives of the people. And because the Roman Catholic Church was where much of the future power – and some affluence – lay, it was the ambition of every small-time family to get a son into the priesthood and a daughter into an order of nuns. Even as late as the 1920s, an Irish writer was writing of the typical Irish Catholic parish priest that:

He is, almost invariably, himself of peasant extraction, and, almost invariably, he is just about as well informed as a well informed peasant.

It was that peasant priesthood that was destined in large part, in the nineteenth century, to fill the power vacuum left by the seventeenth century destruction of the Celtic chiefs, and the Act of Union emasculation of the Protestant Ascendancy.

But the peasant priest power that thus became the greatest force in Irish life has a much greater significance than its Catholicism or its clericalism. The fact of its origin in the Irish peasantry was bound to cause it to mould Irish life according to its own erstwhile peasant characteristics.

To describe the Irish priesthood of the past, and indeed of the recent past, as a peasant priesthood, is perfectly valid, but it would not only seem discourteous to speak of the priesthood of today as such, it would also no longer be accurate. Much of that stratum of society which formed the peasantry of even half a century ago is now a socially liberated and educated community from which is recruited the priesthood of today. What can be said is that it is nevertheless a priesthood 'of the people', not a middle or upper class priesthood. It is thus a highly democratically recruited priesthood which, in true Irish paradoxical fashion, has until very recently assumed a quite exceptionally autocratic role in almost every aspect of Irish life.

There are two reasons why the priesthood in Ireland acquired so much power. First, no man seeks ordination into any priesthood unless he believes himself to have leadership potential. The priest is not going to be one of the flock. He is going to be the shepherd. A humble priest is a contradiction in terms. His role depends on a sense of superiority over his flock. He preaches humility to them, but acts his own part magisterially. He may feel humble in the sight of his maker, but not towards his fellow men.

Consequently, in a situation where local leadership collapses, or is withdrawn, as was the case in Ireland, it comes natural to priests to assume additional, including temporal, power, and natural to their flock to accept their authority in matters secular as well as spiritual.

The second reason why the priesthood slipped into the power vacuum is that when authority breaks down in a state, it is the organized elements in society that are most advantageously placed to seize control – the armed forces, the police, the palace guard, even the tight-knit underground revolutionary movement. Clearly, those with arms are most likely to succeed. But the priesthood is also organized. If it has enough secular power, it may be able to seize the lead. We have, in recent years, seen Archbishops in power in Greece and Cyprus; a priest in power in Zambia, and priests struggling for power in Rhodesia; and the emergence of temporal priest power in Persia.

If a military authority, which seizes control, is strong enough it may, as happened in Russia, and some of the Eastern Bloc communist countries, take steps to neutralize the threat of latent priest-power. In other countries, particularly where the church has a strong superstitious hold over the minds of a largely uncultivated population, the authorities may feel it to be too dangerous to themselves to antagonize the priesthood, and may even find it necessary to compromise with them. Such today is the case in Poland, and in some Muslim countries, Libya, Algeria and Pakistan in particular, which have become fanatically Islamic, and where mediaeval Koranic law is being strictly applied.

In Britain, priests were shorn of their temporal power in the sixteenth century, but have never been discouraged from exercising as much spiritual and moral authority as people are prepared to accept from them. In England there have been srong lay checks exercised through local squires, lords of the manor, patrons, church wardens and people. In Ireland, in the nineteenth century, because the landowners and local administration were Protestant, and were hardly privy to what was going on within the Roman Catholic Church, and did not wish to meddle in that delicate field, such checks did not operate. There was thus a local extension of the power vacuum which the priests filled, taking upon themselves what were in effect, and even if not specifically sanctioned by law, substantial secular powers. Moreover, the Roman Catholic Church, being authoritarian and hierarchical, has both the will and the organization to impose its authority.

Writing in a highly reputable Roman Catholic journal in 1977, an American Roman Catholic Jesuit priest, who had spent five years studying the situation in Northern Ireland, said that although the Catholic grievance had been made clear enough, not many people had grasped what the Protestant grievance is.

He repeated the well worn and discredited Protestant code word for Protestant fears, 'Rome Rule'. And he added that it is not only Irish Protestants, but indeed Catholics from other parts of the world also, who are frightened of the pattern of clerical domination of Irish Catholic life.

The way Protestants see it, he claimed, is that if a Catholic falls out with his priest he is in such serious trouble that there is no future for him in his local community, and there is nothing left to him but to leave the district.

For a politician, an academic, or a professional man, to fall out with a Roman Catholic bishop, could mean the end of his career and of his future in public or professional life. People know better than to risk it. What the bishops might object to is never attempted. That means stagnation in public and professional life.

Those, the writer said, are the appearances as Protestants see them, but he added that, within Northern Ireland, 'the actuality is distressingly close to what we have described.' And he went on:

What we have said here amounts to asserting that the existing power-structure of Catholic church life is eventually the crucial factor behind the situation of violence.

That is certainly not true. The crucial factor behind the situation of violence is that a very small minority in the Republic of Ireland believe that a united Ireland can be achieved only by force, and the response in Northern Ireland is a small minority who are prepared illegally to use force to resist this.

I have not quoted that in any spirit of criticism, but simply to point to the fact that the power which the Catholic church in Ireland acquired over the people, and over every aspect of their lives, during the nineteenth century, extended far beyond the spiritual and pastoral, and into the social life of the nation at many points, and into the most intimate corners of the private lives of the people; a power greatly in excess of that held by any other church in Western Europe.

Even at the end of the eighteenth century it had become clear to Catholics and Protestants alike that a pattern of Catholic priesthood was developing which, if not forestalled and modified, would not be in the best interests of the people of Ireland generally.

What became evident in the 1970s to the American Jesuit priest was not unfamiliar two hundred years earlier. Commenting on the Irish Catholic priesthood in the last days of the eighteenth century, Lecky wrote:

In the English church the power of excommunication had long been disused. In Ireland it was lavishly employed. The excommunicated person is driven from society; no-one converses with him; no-one serves, no-one employs him. A Catholic who in his family read the English Bible, and who sometimes went to hear a sermon in a Protestant church, was publicly excommunicated. The immediate consequence was that he lost his business as house-painter and was reduced to poverty. At last he was obliged to flee the country.

The training that was provided for priests in Ireland after continental training was made impossible by the French Revolution, centred, and has ever since centred largely, although there are other establishments, on the seminary at Maynooth, in Co. Kildare, which was established with a substantial provision of public funds in 1795.

Three suggestions were made at the time that Maynooth was founded. First, that the education of the ordinands should not be exclusively Catholic. During the secular part of their higher education – their degree course – they should share the life and work of Protestant students and should not be exclusively taught by Catholics.

Second, that the staff at Maynooth should not be exclusively Catholic. A Catholic petition presented to the government at that time said that for the college of Maynooth to be exclusively Roman Catholic would be:

highly inexpedient, inasmuch as it tends to perpetuate that line of separation between His Majesty's subjects of different religions, which the petitioners do humbly conceive it to be in the interest of the country to obliterate; and the petitioners submit that, if the youth of both religions were instructed together in those branches of classical education which are the same for all, their peculiar tenets would, in all probability, be no hindrance hereafter to friendly and liberal intercourse through life.

The third suggestion was that the priests should be paid from public funds. That would have relieved the great mass of the people, the poorest section of a very impoverished community, of a considerable burden. It would also have given the government some control over the priesthood.

Those proposals were ignored. Maynooth did become a rigidly closed Catholic community. For the ordinands it is a strictly disciplined, testing, seven year period of instruction. About a third of the entrants fail to stay the course and do not reach ordination. Their training has hitherto produced doctrinaire, puritanical, austere, autocratic, domineering men. But they have been a force in the land, and a force for discipline among the people. That their emoluments have had to depend on the offerings of the people has caused them to ensure that virtually the whole Catholic population attends mass weekly and places something in the plate. On the other hand it has been damaging to the image of the priests that they have had to demand some payment in kind; firewood, for instance; or in labour, turf-cutting; and that they may have seemed to batten on the credulity of ignorant, superstitious and fearful parishioners in such matters as payment for masses to be said for the souls of the 'departed'.

Not only did the priesthood secure the exclusive education of its own ordinands, but indeed it came also in later years to dominate a great part of lay education in Ireland, most of the teaching being in the hands of lay brothers of the order of Christian Brothers. They, and the teaching nuns, are regarded for the most part as devoted teachers.

The priesthood in Ireland has never sought political office, but it has involved itself in politics. In the early nineteenth century, the most notable and influential nationalist leader of his time – a cosmopolitanly educated member of the lesser Catholic gentry – Daniel O'Connell said; 'I take my religion from Rome, but my politics from Ireland.' That may have sounded all very well to those who feared 'Rome Rule', but he involved the priesthood massively in whipping up the support he needed to force the British eventually, in 1829, to grant Catholic Emancipation.

But, just as it would be absurd to ignore the fact of priest power that came about in nineteenth century Ireland, so would it be an injustice to individual priests to imply that they were there solely because they were power-hungry men.

Every priest is first and foremost a pastor. Prayer, meditation and the offices of the church demand their time and attention, but, for the rest, they go about their parishes encouraging the strong and heartening the weak. No-one can overlook their genuine benevolence, and kindliness, not least for the distressed, the suffering, the sick and the dying. Even the Inquisitors, while primarily concerned to safeguard their own power base, were genuinely concerned for the souls whom they tormented in the name of the Lord.

And who has ever heard of a cowardly priest? If their flock is at war, they go unarmed into the heart of the battle to minister to the wounded and the dying, and to give faith and courage to the living. In the midst, too, of epidemics of pestilence and disease they do their unflinching duty, and perform their errands of mercy. Father Damian's self-sacrifice for the lepers was not the exception. He was the epitome of selfless, priestly devotion to the service of God and man. And it is the priests who are in the forefront of the ranks who may face martyrdom. In their scores they have died all down the ages, and they continue to die today, often suffering most hideous cruelty, for the sake of their faith.

But those, and other such considerations, must not cause us to shut our eyes to so important a phenomenon as the power and influence of the priesthood in Ireland during the past two centuries. It is, indeed, such qualities that make a priesthood so potentially, and so actually, formidable. And, whereas we might wish that the advice tendered at the time that Maynooth was established had been accepted, and that it had been set up as a less rigidly Catholic place, there may nevertheless be much to be said for the fact that whatever tends to emphasize the Irishness of Ireland may in the long run prove most beneficial to relations with England which has so consistently failed to recognize, or even to try to understand, the deep cultural differences between the two nations.

Lastly, it must be said that the assumption of power by the new nationalist-politicians and the priesthood, did not constitute a new aristocracy. That they could never be. Born of the people, they could never have the magic of an exclusive high-born caste. Moreover, it is questionable that there remains a valid place today in any widely-educated, and well-educated, community for an aristocracy with hereditary authority. But it so happens that a better educated community with a higher standard of living throughout Western Europe has been tending towards a more secular society, and this is true of the Republic of Ireland where the priesthood has not only been losing some of its authority, but also, in some instances, coming into public disrepute.

CHAPTER 28

The Family at the Beginning of the Nineteenth Century

AT THE VERY MOMENT when the grasp of the Protestant Ascendancy on Ireland was beginning to be loosened – the turn of the eighteenth/nineteenth centuries – the Magan family reached the peak of its material prosperity in the person of William Henry Magan the Elder of Clonearl, sometimes known as William Henry the Magnificent. Born in 1790, he was the second, and eldest surviving, son of Arthur Magan the Younger, and his wife Hannah Georgina, co-heiress with her sister, Lady Castlecoote, to her landowning parson father, the Very Reverend Dean Tilson.

The era of the Penal Laws was effectively over. The family need no longer have furtive fears for the taint of its former Celtic Catholicism. It could, and did, enjoy to the full the social fruits of its wealth and its secure niche in high society. With a quite unalloyed self-assurance, it took its place decisively in the ranks of the swanks.

William Henry the Elder, an eight year old boy at the time of the '98 rebellion, came into his inheritance ten years later when no more than eighteen years of age, on the death of his father, in 1808. At the age of twenty-seven he married, in 1817, a considerable heiress. Together they owned very large tracts of the best grasslands in Ireland, and other valuable properties, including one hundred and sixty-five acres of Dublin. By the standards of the time they were immensely rich. They built and staffed a great house, and filled it with treasures. Children were born to them, and in due course three of William Henry's four younger brothers married and had children also. The future of the family, as almost a minor principality once more, in the seemingly unshakably landlord-dominated society of the time, must have appeared very secure. But it was to prove otherwise.

William Henry Magan the Elder's line of the Protestant Magans was destined to die out with his children. The descendants of his next two married brothers were also to die out in the male line. We, the survivors, including our American cousins, are the descendants of the third of William Henry's four younger brothers. The fourth did not marry. Not only was the family to be thus diminished, but it was also to lose virtually all its lands and possessions.

William Henry's wife was a young widow, Elizabeth (Eliza) Georgina, relict of Colonel Thomas Lowther Allen of Kilmer, Co. Meath. Born in 1796, she was six years William Henry's junior, and had been married and widowed by the age of twenty-one.

Eliza was the daughter and co-heiress, with her sister, of Dudley Loftus of Killyon Manor, Hill-of-Down, Co. Meath. Her first husband's home, Kilmer, is three-quarters of a mile from, and within sight of, her home and property, Killyon. Killyon Manor was destined to be the last of the, at one time, numerous great houses which the family owned. As children, it was for my generation a second home, and my parents lived there altogether for the last thirty years or so of their lives.

Eliza's mother, before her marriage to Dudley Loftus of Killyon, was Lady Jane Gore, daughter of the 1st Earl of Aran. The Irish branch of the Gore family descended from one of those 'keep Ulster quiet' baronetcies of James I in the early seventeenth century. On the death of Dudley Loftus, his daughter Eliza inherited Killyon and considerable family estates there.

On her father's side, Eliza was descended from the great settler family of Adam Loftus. He it was who had roasted the poor Roman Catholic Archbishop's feet. Adam Loftus was chaplain to Queen Elizabeth I, and then to her Viceroy in Dublin, the Earl of Sussex. Aged twenty-eight, he became Archbishop of Armagh, and four years later Archbishop of Dublin. In 1578 he was appointed Lord High Chancellor of Ireland. He it was who was mainly responsible for establishing the University of Dublin (Trinity College) and was its first Provost. He died, in 1605, 'worn out with age', having been an archbishop for forty-two years. Five years later, his son, Sir Thomas Loftus, received, in 1610, a grant of the Monastery of Clonard, Co. Meath, which included Killyon, Eliza's home; and that was the estate that she inherited. And not far away was the home of her kinsmen, who also descended – in their case on the female side – from the archbishop, the family of which one son was the Duke of Wellington.

The great house that William Henry Magan the Elder built – for I think it was he rather than his wife who had in him a strong vein of obsessional grandeur – was Clonearl, near Daingean (formerly Philipstown), Offaly (formerly King's County), where it replaced the earlier dwelling in which the family had already been living for two generations.

It was a very beautiful neo-classical Georgian building of exquisite proportions built of dressed stone. He is said to have spent an enormous sum on it. He was a creative man, clearly of excellent taste. He followed the eighteenth century tradition of a classical country house, furnished with beautiful objects, and set in a landscaped park. Its principal living rooms were, in the fashion of that time, on the ground floor, rather than on the first floor, as in earlier times.

Clonearl survived only a quarter of a century or so. It was accidentally burnt in 1846. No doubt much of its contents were lost. But from time to time William

Henry's possessions turn up. There is a Magan fireplace in an Australian museum, and another in a Royal residence, Clarence House, London. They both came from his Dublin residence, 77 St Stephen's Green, and are thus suggestive of the standards he set for his principal residence, the palace of his properties, Clonearl.

Recently a half canteen of very beautiful silver, by Paull Storr, his exact contemporary, carrying his coat of arms, appeared for a very short time in a Dublin jeweller's shop before changing hands for, it is supposed, a substantial sum.

Clonearl belonged to the hey-day of the country house. At an earlier time country residences had been regarded by those who could afford town houses as little better than the rustic administrative centres of their estates where life, by comparison with the glitter, excitement and endless company of the society of the metropolis, was dull and cloying in the extreme.

But all that had changed by the early nineteenth century. Much better roads, and comfortable coaches and carriages, had put the country house within easy reach of town. People were ceaselessly on the move between town and country, and between one house and another. The great stable yard at Clonearl must have been a constant bustle of coming and going of coaches, carriages, vehicles of all sorts, and riding horses, as members of the family and visitors, the elegantly and colourfully attired cream of the fashion of the time, not only from Dublin and other great Irish houses, but also from across the water, endlessly came and went.

'Visiting' – staying in other people's houses – continued in Ireland on an enormous scale throughout the nineteenth century, right up to the outbreak of the 1914 war. The landed classes had ample leisure, and there were no telephones. There was much letter writing, particularly with the improved postal services after the mid-century. But, to keep in close touch with friends and relatives, you had either to be in town, or to visit in the country – or, more usually, both.

Clonearl would have been alive with people. There would have been a large permanent complement of servants, a butler and footmen in livery, and others of more menial office behind the green baize door; maids galore with their many different functions, and a fully staffed kitchen. Uniformed coachmen in the stable yard with a supporting posse of grooms; gardeners, of course; and the inevitable Irish hangers-on of no fixed role, self-recruited, and self-invited recipients of the never to be refused Irish hospitality, who did no more than they could avoid, but whose Irish drolleries provided an endlessly straight-faced penetrating commentary on the passing scene, and not least on their betters.

But that was just the sub-stratum of Clonearl's inhabitants. They were there only to serve the others, the family and the never ending stream of guests for which the house, its grounds, and the estate, were laid out to provide every kind of diverting entertainment and pleasure.

To lead an outdoor life, to appreciate nature – even, for the most soulful, to indulge in such fantasies as 'to commune with nature' – and to participate in outdoor sports, had become fashionable virtues. So, all that could be done was done to facilitate the innocent enjoyment by the many guests, both male and female, of walking and riding; shooting and fishing, for the men; and, in season, following the local pack of hounds.

Relaxed enjoyment was the key to the house-party life of the times. You could spend your time as you liked between a sumptuous leisurely breakfast and a great formal dinner. Breakfast was not only a large meal, and one that could be very late, but it was also a social occasion. An invitation card survives from the Duke of Leinster to Eliza Magan and her daughter to breakfast with him at 'Two o'Clock', at his enormous country mansion, Carton, at Maynooth.

If, after breakfast, you did not choose to go out of doors, strolling in the garden, or doing something more active, you could read or study in the library, write letters or your journal, practise the piano in the drawing-room, talk with the other guests, play cards or other games, or, if you were young and pretty, and of marriageable age, delight Mama's heart by showing, with all due modesty, some disposition not to resist the proffered company of the eligible young man she had contrived to have put in your way.

Dinner having at one time been served much earlier in the day had, by the nineteenth century, become an evening meal. It was invariably a ceremonial occasion preparatory to which the guests, in full evening finery, assembled in the drawing-room, whence they processed in precedental order to the dining room, where they drank from elegant crystal, and were served on the best plate and porcelain by servants in full regalia. After the meal the ladies withdrew to the 'withdrawing', or 'drawing', -room, where they were later joined by the men. Then there was more diversion, dancing, music, cards, and conversation till bedtime.

But, looking at that scene now through the hindsight of long historical perspective, Byron's words keep coming to mind:

There was a sound of revelry by night
...
The lamps shone o'er fair women and brave men;
A thousand hearts beat happily;
...
And all went merry as a marriage bell;
But hush! hark! a deep sound strikes
*   like a rising knell!*

The deep sound in this case was the ancient Irish peasantry mustering in the bogs and mountains, and on the Atlantic cliffs, who, led by their priests, and politicians of their own kind, and by a handful of visionary and prescient members of the Ascendancy itself, were to rise up and come again, after aeons of time, into their own, and to sweep away Clonearl and Carton and their glitter. At the summit of its glory, indeed before ever it was built, Clonearl was, unknowingly, already

9 Connaught – oil sketch by May Hamilton

10 Clonearl – water colour drawing by William Hayes

11 Thomas Magan

12 Morgan Magan

13 Susannah Magan,
(b. c. 1695)

14 *Arthur Magan the Younger,*
(1756–1808)

15 *Hannah Georgina Magan –*
wife of Arthur Magan the
Younger, (b. c. 1760)

16 *Lady Jane Loftus,*
(b. c. 1770)

17 *William Henry Magan*
the Elder, (1790–1840)

18 Captain Arthur Magan R. N.,
(1794–1858)

19 William Henry Magan the You
(1819–1860)

20 Georgina Elizabeth Magan –
later Mrs Bartlett,
(1819–1910)

22 *Augusta Magan, (1815–1905)*

21 *Eliza Georgina Magan,*
   (b. c. 1800, d. 1880) – daughter
   of Dudley Loftus – she inherited
   from him Killyon Manor, and the
   5,000 acre Killyon estate

23 *Killyon Manor – water colour by the author's wife, Maxine*

24 *Pat Callaghan at St Mark's, Lough Ree*

25 *Mary Callaghan and Irish cooking pot,*
    St Mark's Cottage

26 The author's
father and mother
(Colonel Shaen
and Mrs Magan)
at Killyon Manor

27 The author's father
and mother on the
Avenue bridge at
Killyon Manor

28 *Killyon Manor*

29 *The Avenue bridge at Killyon Manor*

30 *Colonel Shaen Magan and his wife, Kathleen, at tea*

an anachronism, though it, or its kind, would be a hundred years and more a-dying.

But that is not to suggest that the glittering life was all mindless frivolity. Beneath the superficial and pleasurable elegancies, was the solid sub-structure, which made it all possible – an efficient and well-run estate, a field in which Eliza was no less concerned, hardly less involved, and no less capable, than William Henry; and they remained great cattle people.

I think it probable that Eliza preferred her own old home and property at Killyon Manor, Co. Meath to the more pretentious Clonearl. She inherited it when she was only eleven years old, on the death of her father, in 1807. It was her beloved home.

It is a charming, rambling, friendly old house which has grown through the centuries, incorporating additions representing all periods of Irish architecture.

Its core is an ancient tower-house, now in the centre of the house and containing the main staircase. The top storey of the tower still remains a dwelling room.

The south wing is a typical late seventeenth century, partly fortified, substantial stone-built annex to the tower-house, with no passages, the rooms leading directly into each other and reflecting the days of little privacy.

The east wing, with powder rooms attached to the principal bedrooms, and stuccoed externally, and with a parapeted roof, has passages and is probably mid-eighteenth century. In its centre is the porticoed main entrance to the house, and to balance the height, and match the contemporary Palladian style, two great walls extend, one from each end of this wing, which became in the eighteenth century, and remains to this day, the main frontage of the house.

The splendid ballroom is probably later eighteenth century. There are remnants of older buildings – an old pigeon loft; and there is a late nineteenth century annex including a large kitchen.

There is only one alteration to Killyon Manor which I think might have been made by William Henry and Eliza during the early nineteenth century. Perhaps she preferred not to make too many changes to a loved childhood home. Unlike William Henry, she may have found warmer delights in the rambling, muddled old Killyon house than in the contrived and orderly grandeur of Clonearl. Perchance she felt at one with Herrick that its old disorder:

Do more bewitch me, than when Art
Is too precise in every part.

The one alteration is the addition of a three-storied annex to the west side of the tower-house which, half way up the stairs to the first floor, gives a charming open lobby with a large window which catches the mysterious western light of the Irish afternoon and evening.

It was there that my mother always sat in her later years in the afternoons and read or wrote letters, knitted and snoozed. It is Eliza's place, too. Unfortunately

I am not tuned in to ghosts, and have therefore not had the good fortune to encounter Eliza, but when her benevolent spectre is seen, she is seated in the lobby. It is hardly a room, having no door, and being totally open to the stairs. There is nothing grand about it, but it has an air of infinite repose.

No doubt there were great house parties and balls at Killyon – where there was an organ in the ball-room – just as there were at Clonearl. And to accommodate the horses and carriages, William Henry and Eliza built a magnificent stable yard, next to what was doubtless an ancient cattle yard. It has now been demolished. There is a ghost there too, invisible but capable it is said of opening locked doors.

The grounds of Killyon are typical of an Irish country house. A river runs through them a hundred yards from the house – the Deal, a tributary of the Boyne. The front avenue crosses it by a substantial double-arched stone bridge coped with massive slabs of dressed granite. Above the bridge, looking upstream to the house, there stood until recently a beautiful curved weir. But, like other civilized countries, Ireland is now plagued by the bowler-hat brigade of officials and the people have to suffer what Hamlet called 'the insolence of office'. Not long after the Second War, they defaced the weir by building a concrete salmon ladder onto the front of it. The salmon had been happily jumping the weir, and successfully taking their chances with poachers for 200 years. But the cement ladder could not altogether destroy the beauty of such a structure, particularly when the river was in flood.

However, the next squad of bowler-hats took care to complete the work, but not, I am glad to say, until after we had left Killyon. They demolished the weir altogether. It really was a pricelessly beautiful amenity, marvellously made of cut stone, so well fitted that it had endured two centuries of tearing water with no need for maintenance or repair, certainly not in my lifetime, and only very little natural wear and tear. And those Jacks-in-Office destroyed it on the nod.

Ireland, at the official level, suffers from a lunatic obsession with draining rivers. It does little good, and a lot of damage. It destroys precious water meadows which would otherwise receive annual dressings of marvellously fertile alluvial silt from the flood waters. It is, I suppose, a dying twitch from the seventeenth century days when they lost their common lands. Anything that gives the illusion of laying hands on even a little bit of land is some balm to the still raw wounds of bitter deprivation.

Until the demolition men arrived, there still grew the remnants of eighteenth century ornamental trees planted to show off the weir to its best advantage. Upstream of the weir the river had been widened and straightened by an eighteenth century landscaper to give a long and lovely stretch of tranquil water. That also has, of course, gone, and the river now runs through a deep ditch, where the little lake-like feature had been.

The whole place is redolent of history and the ancient past. Not far downstream of the house, the Deal joins the River Boyne, a major artery whereby early man penetrated Ireland, leaving the Boyne valley rich in prehistoric remains. My brother has a beautiful stone axe head found since the Second War at Killyon by my father's gardener.

The ancient Egyptians knew the Boyne. It features on the maps of Ptolemy. It was along the Boyne that Christianity came to Ireland. St Patrick – according to one account; there are contradictory claims – landed at the mouth of the river and raised his cross upstream at Slane. And Killyon itself has a perceptible air of ancient sanctity. It was clearly an associate part of the great ecclesiastical university and monastery founded close by at Clonard by St Patrick's successor, St Finnian, who in 520 AD became its Bishop. It was one of Europe's great seats of learning, having upwards of three thousand students, drawn not only from Ireland but from Britain and the Continent. It was from Clonard that Iona derived its religion and its architecture. On the site of the ancient monastery is a small Protestant church where, in the graveyard, my parents are buried. The fields round about are said to be full of ancient bones.

And in the grounds of Killyon, on the river's bank, and not far from the house, are the ruins of an ancient church, and an old burial ground, and nearby a holy well, still a place of pilgrimage on Lady Day since how many centuries back? Perhaps how many millennia? Long, perhaps, before Christianity itself.

And up the Boyne came the Vikings to despoil the Clonard monastery. And along its banks the Normans and the English built their forts at the boundary of the Pale. One such, known as 'The Battery', stands in the field behind the house. And what, but some old defensive earthworks, is the enormous ditch that runs behind the garden wall and along the rising ground of The Battery field overlooking the river? The walled garden itself is of three acres, open on its south side to the river. And in Anglo-Saxon times someone hid his money for safe keeping near the holy well. Of the hoard of 88 coins, dated about 955 AD, and found there about the year 1876, some are now lost, some were stolen, others dispersed. The rest are in the collections of Westminster School and of the British Museum. Only one other discovery of coins of that period has been made in Ireland.

And on the Lawn – the park-like field in front of Irish houses is often called The Lawn – there once appeared in a very dry summer the distinct outlines of the foundations of a very large building.

That was the Killyon that Eliza Magan loved. She made rides through the woods where she could drive her pony-trap, and she scattered flowers along their verges. And she built a stone two-storied summer house in 'The Island Wood' where the river had been made to run in artificial channels, and she planted flowers around it. One of the elderly women about the place when I was young, told me she remembered, when she was a girl, 'The Quality' being entertained at the summer house by the water for strawberry teas.

But while William Henry Magan and Eliza were busy with their estates and their public, private and social lives, other members of the family had chosen different paths. However agreeable country house life was in Ireland in the first half of the nineteenth century, there were other, and wider, opportunities offering scope and interest, and a varied life for the enterprising, in worthy company, and in particular for younger sons with private means to ease their path. It was no doubt such considerations that tempted William Henry's next two brothers into the armed forces of the Crown.

Arthur, although brought up in a rich home in the centre of Ireland, miles from the sea, joined the Royal Navy at the age of fourteen, in 1807, the year before his father died. He resigned in 1814, at the age of twenty-one, having already reached the rank of captain. Like his uncle, the major-general, he settled down in England to the life of an English gentleman, and was the first member of the family to take an English bride – and from beyond the circle of the landed gentry at that. She had the remarkably English name of Catherine Smith, and they had an only daughter, Georgina Magan – who plays a notable part in my tale. Georgina was the first member of the family to experience divorce. Her marriage in 1840 to a Royal Naval surgeon named Henry Brummell, ended disastrously within a year.

In retirement Arthur Magan lived a country house life at Brighton. He saw the Pavilion completed, and, as a retired senior naval officer, and because the Royal Family kept close personal touch with service officers, he no doubt received invitations to some of the extravagant functions and entertainment there.

His next younger brother, Thomas Tilson Magan, became a soldier, and was followed into the army by two of his sons. One of them broke new ground for the family by joining the Indian Army, and his son in turn became a soldier, Captain Arthur Tilson Magan, who has a prominent part to play later in the family story. Thomas Tilson Magan himself, like his sailor brother, retired early having achieved no higher rank than captain. He married twice. Both wives predeceased him, but left him ten children. He never had remunerative employment, but when he died, aged seventy-two, in 1870, he had not only brought up his children, but had also amply provided for them all and for two brothers-in-law and a sister-in-law. There was plenty in the Magan family for everyone. Once, when I was a boy, my father's eldest sister, my Aunt 'Blossie', said to me that it was her experience – which went back nearly to the mid-nineteenth century – that 'All Magans seemed to have money'.

The third and last of William Henry the Elder's married brothers was my great-grandfather, ancestor of all the Magans of today, George Percy Magan of Duninga, Co. Kilkenny. He was born about 1799, and married in 1824 Ellen O'Connor-Henchy, who, like the Magans, could trace her descent from the ancient O'Conor kings of Connaught.

When George Percy married, his father had long since been dead, but his mother, the devoutly Protestant Hannah Georgina, daughter of her parson father, can hardly have favoured the marriage, as Ellen O'Connor-Henchy was a Catholic. Hannah Georgina nevertheless gave my great-grandfather, George Percy, the Duninga estate in Kilkenny which she had inherited from her mother. It was a large enough estate to support him and his numerous family. She also gave him another estate to the west of the Shannon, in Roscommon.

She struck a bargain with him. He could have the properties if his sons were brought up Protestant. The Duninga estate was to provide in the future for his eldest son, and any others, except the second son, who was to get the Roscommon property. Daughters could be brought up Catholic.

There were sixteen children of my great-grandfather's marriage, nine sons and seven daughters, and yet the family survived by only the merest thread, because one only of the sons, my grandfather, Percy Magan, had a family, and he did not marry till he was thirty-seven years of age. In accordance with his grandmother's bargain with his father, he inherited the Roscommon estate of some three thousand acres. And one only of the girls married. She was my grandfather's sister Ellen who married an eminent psychiatrist, Dr James Jameson Dwyer, a Catholic like herself. They had three Catholic sons, all of whom were officers in the British army.

My great-grandmother, Ellen O'Connor-Henchy, may also be supposed to have been well off in her own right. Her father, Valentine O'Connor of Rockfield, Blackrock, Co. Dublin, was, according to my father, known as 'the copper-nosed Jew', supposedly because he shrewdly enriched himself at business. The Irish Catholic gentry, as so often with Jewish communities, having been a persecuted minority, denied the right to acquire real estate, had, of necessity, had recourse to commerce to amass wealth.

There was nothing very grand about my great-grandfather's home. There was no great house on the Duninga estate. The house in which he lived was large, but it did not belong to him – only the estate was his. He rented the house. And because he did not own it he was not much concerned to spend money on its appointments. Its pronounced shabbiness was in marked contrast to his eldest brother's magnificent life-style at Clonearl. However little 'civility' Edmund Gosse's mother might have found in George Percy Magan's house, she would have experienced a fair amount of at least innocent 'savagery' in the teeming rumbustious outdoor and indoor life with all that family of sixteen children on the romp. We can imagine the activity, the noise, the bustle, the many and varied interests, the youthful, liberated energy, the games, the fun, but some civility there also was, at least in the background. And the familiar quirks of Irish genealogy had contributed a very special savouring of civility to that particular family.

The mother of all that brood, my great-grandmother, Ellen O'Connor-Henchy, had a sister, Honoria, who married a British army officer of the celebrated 60th Rifles. He was of Irish origin, Peter Slingsby Fitzgerald. His brother was Edward

Fitzgerald, the poet, author of the English rendering of *The Rubáiyát of Omar Khayyam* – and a direct descendant of the Princess Nesta.

Did the shy Edward Fitzgerald ever visit the thronging Irish household of my great-grandparents? Did he sit with the children round the great log and turf fire at Duninga and tell them tales of the Persians? Did he recount to them first-hand stories of his literary friends, Dickens, Tennyson, Carlyle and others? Whether he did or not, he did something that left us an incomparable record of the life of the family in the Irish setting of the time. He steered his friend Thackeray to Duninga. The visit is recorded in Thackeray's *Irish Sketch Book*.

Thackeray went to Ireland in 1842, three years before the famine. It was in July, and was a blazing hot summer. At that time my great-grandparents had been married for eighteen years, and were surrounded by most of their sixteen children.

Thackeray went first to Dublin for a few days. Thence he set off by the inland route in a southerly direction towards Waterford, as the first leg of a clockwise tour of the country. He travelled by coach with a number of other passengers. Between Dublin and Waterford they had two night-stops, both at country houses. His account seems to be deliberately vague.

The first night-stop was a little south of Kilcullen, not far from the Magan property of Eagle Hill. It was at an Irish country gentleman's residence which Thackeray calls H – town, and the owner Mr P –. Possibly it was Halverstown House.

On leaving H – town House, the route to the second night-stop led through Carlow and Leighlinbridge. After passing through Royal Oak, 'our road branches off to the hospitable house where our party, consisting of a dozen persons, was to be housed and fed for the night'. Again, it was a country gentleman's home.

'Fancy,' Thackeray goes on, 'the look which an English gentleman of moderate means would assume at being called on to receive such a company!'

That hospitable gentleman was my great-grandfather, George Percy Magan. The house Thackeray calls the house of D –, and he refers to his host as Mr M –.

The writer of a travelogue has to be careful. He wants to record his experiences; but people whom he has met, and particularly those who have been especially kind to him, may not be used to, and may not like, publicity. In order not to offend them, he must therefore not identify them too closely.

In what he has to say about H – town house, and D – house, Thackeray does not repeat himself but dwells on different aspects of Irish life in each. He did not write the account of the two houses until later, when he reached Waterford. When we put the two together, perhaps we get the whole picture. This may have been a deliberate literary device used by Thackeray in order not to be too revealingly specific about either house. One particular point which leads me to suppose that this may be so is that the teeming family he describes at H – town house must have exactly matched the tumultuous Magan family which he would have encountered at D – house at just that time. At all events, let us have both accounts, and we shall then have a marvellous eye-witness picture of the life of an Irish gentry family of that period, the first half of the nineteenth century, which certainly, in part or in whole, reflects Thackeray's experience of my great-grandfather's home.

Describing his arrival at the first of those houses, he implies that his host was travelling with him, and his device for recounting the atmosphere within the enormous family is to relate the scene of the father's greeting from his children on his home-coming.

We drove through a neat gate-lodge, with no lions or supporters, but riding well on its hinges, and looking fresh and white, and passed by a lodge, not Gothic, but decorated with flowers and evergreens, with clean windows and a sound slate roof; and then went over a trim road (avenue), through a few acres of grass adorned with plenty of young firs and other healthy trees, under which were feeding a dozen of fine cows or more. The road led up to a house, or rather a congregation of rooms, built seemingly to suit the owner's convenience, and increasing with his increasing wealth, or whim, or family. This latter is as plentiful as everything else about the place; and as the arrows increased, the good-natured, lucky father has been forced to multiply the quivers.

First came out a young gentleman, the heir to the house, who, after greeting his papa, began examining the horses with much interest; while three or four servants, quite neat and well dressed and, wonderful to say, without any talking, began to occupy themselves with the carriage, the passengers and trunks. Meanwhile the owner of the house had gone to the hall, which is snugly furnished as a morning-room, and where one, two, three young ladies came in to greet him. The young ladies having concluded their embraces, performed (as I am bound to say from experience, both in London and Paris) some very appropriate and well-finished curtseys to the strangers arriving. And these three young persons were presently succeeded by some still younger, who came without any curtseys at all; but, bounding and jumping, and shouting out 'Papa' at the top of their voices, they fell forthwith upon that worthy gentleman's person, taking possession, this of his knees, that of his arms, that of his whiskers, as fancy or task might dictate.

'Are there any more of you?' says he, with perfect good humour; and, in fact, it appeared that there were some more in the nursery, as we subsequently had occasion to see.

Well, this large happy family are lodged in a house than which a prettier or more comfortable is not to be seen ever in England; of the furniture of which it may be in confidence said, that each article is only made to answer one purpose: thus that chairs are never called upon to exercise the versatility of propping up windows; that chests of drawers are not obliged to move their unwieldy persons in order to act as locks to doors … in fact the place is just as comfortable as a place can be.

Thackeray goes on to contrast the sort of welcome you may expect from an English, German, French or Irish host, and then concludes:

It is clear that for a stranger the Irish ways are the pleasantest, for here he is at once made happy and at home; or at ease rather; for home is a strong word, and implies much more than any stranger can expect, or even desire, to claim.

Nothing could be more delightful to witness than the evident affection which the children and parents bore to one another, and the cheerfulness and happiness of their family parties. But a great merit, as it appeared to me, on the part of these worthy parents was, that they consented not only to make, but to take jokes from their young ones; nor was the parental authority in the least weakened by this kind familiar intercourse.

Then, when he comes to D – house, Thackeray relates other aspects of an Irish home.

A pretty road (avenue) thickly grown with ash and oak trees, under which the hats of coach-passengers suffered some danger, leads to the house of D –. A young son of the house, on a white pony, was on the look-out, and great cheering and shouting took place among the young people as we came in sight.

Trotting away by the carriage-side, he brought us through a gate with a pretty avenue of trees leading to the pleasure-grounds of the house – a hand-some place commanding noble views of river, mountains and plantations. Our entertainer only rents the place; so I may say without any imputation against him, that the house was by no means so handsome within as without, – not that the want of finish in the interior made our party the less merry, or the host's entertainment less hearty and cordial.

The gentleman who built and owns the house, like many other proprietors in Ireland, found his mansion too expensive for his means. There were numerous sitting-rooms below; and a large suite of rooms above, in which our large party, with their servants, disappeared without any inconvenience, and which already accommodated a family of at least a dozen persons, and a numerous train of domestics. There was a great courtyard surrounded by capital offices, with stabling and coach-houses sufficient for half a dozen of country gentlemen.

So my great-grandfather, George Percy Magan, although he was the fifth son of his parents, and had no professional source of earnings, could afford to live in a mansion large enough to accommodate a family of a dozen or more, plus numerous servants, and take in for the night, without any seeming squash, another dozen coach travellers and their servants – even if he did not feel inclined to go to the expense of refurbishing the interior of the place. But he seems to have been a sensible fellow. Thackeray goes on:

> *Our host has wisely turned the chief part of the pleasure ground round the house into a farm; nor did the land look a bit the worse, as I thought, for having rich crops and potatoes growing in place of grass, and fine plots of waving wheat and barley. The care, skill and neatness everywhere exhibited, and the immense luxuriance of the crops, could not fail to strike even a cockney.*
>
> *Several men and women appeared sauntering in the grounds, and as the master came up asked for work, or sixpence, or told a story of want. It appears the good-natured practice of the country admits a beggar as well as any other visitor. To a couple our landlord gave money, to another a little job of work. I could judge thus what a continual tax upon the Irish gentlemen these travelling paupers must be, of whom his ground is never free.*
>
> *There, loitering about the stables and outhouses, were several people who seemed to have acquired a sort of right to be there: women and children who had a claim upon the buttermilk; men who did an odd job now and then; loose hangers-on of the family.*
>
> *Nor did Mr M – 's 'irregulars' disappear with the day; for when, after a great deal of merriment, and kind happy dancing and romping of young people, the fineness of the night suggested the propriety of smoking a certain cigar, the young squire voted that we should adjourn to the stables.*
>
> *There were still the inevitable half-dozen hangers-on: one came grinning with a lantern; another ran obsequiously to the stables to show a favourite mare – I think it was a mare – though it may have been a male, and your humble servant not much the wiser. The fellows with the candles crowded about. The young squire bade me admire her fore-leg, which I did with the greatest possible gravity.*
>
> *There was another young squire of our party, a pleasant gentlemanlike young fellow, who danced as prettily as any Frenchman, and who had ridden over from a neighbouring house: as I went to bed, the two lads were arguing whether young squire B – should go home or stay at D – that night. There was a bed for him – there was a bed for everyone, it seemed, and a kind welcome too. How different was all this to the ways of a severe English house.*
>
> *Next morning the whole of our merry party assembled round a long jovial breakfast-table, stored with all sorts of good things.*

Such was the home of my great-grandparents from which the 'merry party' took their leave on a glorious cloudless morning after breakfast, and continued on their way to Waterford.

The girls particularly took Thackeray's fancy. It is fair to say that he was very partial to young ladies:

A word with regard to the ladies so far. Those I have seen appear to the full as well educated and refined, and far more frank and cordial, than the generality of fair creatures on the other side of the Channel.

The charming gaiety and frankness of the Irish ladies have been noted by every foreigner who has had the good fortune to mingle in their society; and I hope it is not detracting from the upper classes to say that the lower are not a whit less pleasing. I never saw in any country such a general grace of manner and ladyhood. In the midst of their gaiety, too, it must be remembered that they are the chastest of women, and that no country in Europe can boast of such a general purity. They are as well dressed as Frenchwomen, and incomparably handsomer. Among the ladies' accomplishments, I may mention that I have heard in two or three private families such fine music as is rarely to be met with out of a capital.

The landlords of Ireland have come in for much criticism. Listen to Thackeray's description of the home-farm at H – town.

Mr P – farms four hundred acres of land about his house; and employs on this estate no less than a hundred and ten persons. He says there is full work for everyone of them; and to see the elaborate state of cultivation in which the land was, it is easy to understand how such an agricultural regiment were employed. The estate was like a well-ordered garden: we walked into huge fields of potatoes, and the landlord made us the remark that there was not a single weed between the furrows; and the whole formed a vast flower-bed of a score of acres. Every bit of land up to the hedge-side was fertilised and full of produce. In a turnip-field were a score or more of women and children, who were marching through the ridges, removing the young plants, and leaving only the most healthy. The owner said that this extreme cultivation, which gained him some reputation as a philanthropist, brought him profit as a farmer too.

We went into the cottages and gardens of several of Mr P –'s labourers, which were all so neat that I could not help fancying they were pet cottages erected under the landlord's supervision, and ornamented to his order. But he declared that that was not so. The only benefit his labourers got from him was constant work, and a house rent-free. The neatness of the gardens and dwellings was their own doing. By making them a present of the house he in effect made them a present of the pig and livestock with which almost every Irish cottar pays his rent, so that each workman could have a bit of meat for his support. With regard to the neatness of the houses, the best way to ensure this was for the master constantly to visit them.

There are some happy organisations in the world which possess the great virtue of prosperity. It implies cheerfulness, simplicity, shrewdness, perseverance honesty and good health. See how, before the good-humoured resolution of such characters, ill-luck gives way, and fortune assumes its own smiling complexion. Such men grow rich without driving a single hard bargain; their condition being to make others prosper along with themselves.

That place being not far from the Magan property of Eagle Hill, it is certain that it must have been known to the efficient William Henry Magan and his wife Eliza. We may therefore be sure that they, too, had their properties in something like that sort of good shape. And then, three years after Thackeray's visit, came the sudden, unexpected, devastating flash of *Phytophthera infestans*, the potato-blight, and that huge and beautiful 'flower-garden' of a flourishing potato field must overnight have been rendered a black stinking mass of putrefaction. How now were that 'regiment' of workers, and those smart cottages, to be maintained? I bet Mr P – both did his best, and got the blame.

Thackeray was depressed by the appalling poverty, and the enormous numbers of beggars, of whom I have already written. And he noticed the prevalence of the austere priests, and did not like it:

Whence comes that general scowl which darkens the faces of Irish priesthood? I have met a score of these reverend gentlemen and not one of them seemed to look or speak frankly, except Mr Mathew (Father Theobald Mathew, the famous founder of the Temperance movement) and a couple more.

He was no less critical of the Protestant clergy for their failure to involve themselves, as the Catholic priests had done, in the conduct of the new national schools and the spread of education, thus isolating themselves from the up and coming generations of young Irish Catholics. The result, as Thackeray saw it, was that national schools were:

directed and fostered by the priest; and as no people are more eager for learning, more apt to receive it, or more grateful for kindness than the Irish, he gets all the gratitude of the scholars who flock to the school, and all the influence over them, which naturally and justly comes to him.

One of the things that struck Thackeray was the astounding interest of the Irish in literature. Surely we can trace it back to ancient Irish traditions, and relate it to Irish eloquence.

A stranger must remark the extraordinary degree of literary taste and talent, and the wit and vivacity of their conversation. Who ever reads books in the City of London, or how often does one hear them talked about at a club? The Cork citizens are the most book-loving men I ever met. The young clerks and shopmen seemed as much au fait *as their employers, and many is the conversation I heard about the merits of this writer or that – Dickens, Ainsworth etc.*

I think, in walking the streets, and looking at the ragged urchins crowding there, every Englishman must remark that the superiority of intelligence is here in Ireland, and not with us. I never saw such a collection of bright-eyed, wild, clever, eager faces.

I listened to two boys almost in rags talking about one of the Ptolemys! and talking very well too. Both of those Irish lads had the making of gentlemen scholars, orators, in them.

One last excerpt from Thackeray. This, three years before the famine, might be called; 'The potato fairy tale'.

In the county Mayo a gentleman by the name of Crofton is a landed proprietor, in whose neighbourhood great distress prevailed among the peasantry during the spring and summer, when the potatoes of the last year were consumed, and before those of the present season were up. Mr Crofton, by liberal donations on his own part, and by a subscription which was set on foot among his friends in England as well as in Ireland, was enabled to collect a sum of money sufficient to buy meal for the people, which was given to them, or sold at very low prices, until the pressure of want was withdrawn and the blessed potato-crop came in.

Some time in October a smart night's frost made Mr Crofton think it was time to take in and pit his own potatoes, and he told his steward to get labourers accordingly. Next day, on going to the potato-grounds, he found the whole field swarming with people; the whole crop was out of the ground, and again under it, pitted and covered, and the people gone in a few hours. It was as if the fairies had taken a liking to this good landlord, and taken in his harvest for him. Mr Crofton sent his steward to pay his helpers their wages, and to thank them. One and all refused a penny.

My great-grandfather later moved from the Duninga property to Portarlington. The Roscommon estate on the far – the west – side of the Shannon river, he kept. Portarlington may have been chosen partly because it was nearer than Duninga to the Westmeath centre of the rest of the Magan family, and partly because of the good opportunities for his daughters to learn French there.

The Catholic daughters of the Irish gentry were left with few of their own kind to marry in Ireland. The history of the past two centuries had depleted Ireland of eligible upper class Catholic males. France offered better opportunities. And the Magan girls had strong French connections. One of their mother's sisters, Mary, was married to a French nobleman. Her uncle also was married to a French girl. And two of her female first cousins had married French noblemen.

Portarlington had become a French-speaking town when, during the persecution of the Protestants in France, following the revocation of the Edict of Nantes, in 1685, it was given to Henri, son of the Marquis de Ruvigny. He was a French soldier and diplomat who joined the British army, fought in many campaigns, rose to the rank of general, and was British ambassador to Portugal. He became the first Earl of Galway, and he established a large Huguenot settlement at Portarlington. The town grew to be noted for its French schools to which the matter-of-fact Catholic Irish eagerly sent their children to learn a language that would be a passport to jobs – and marriages – abroad.

My great-grandfather George Percy Magan, died in the mid-nineteenth century, in 1857, aged fifty-eight.

The Family in the
Mid-Nineteenth Century

AT THE TIME WHEN William Henry Magan the Elder – the Magnificent – died in May 1840, his devout mother, Hannah Georgina, had not yet completed the building of her church at Crinken with its Magan burial vault in the crypt. He was therefore unable to enjoy her gruesome hospitality and was buried elsewhere. She herself was the first member of the family to avail herself of that doubtful amenity on her own death two years later, in her eightieth year, in 1842.

William Henry the Elder was survived by his wife Eliza, and their three children. They were, his heir, William Henry Magan the Younger – known as William Henry the Bad –, and the second son, Dudley Loftus Magan, and their younger sister Augusta. And, with those children, the family was destined to sink, from the peak of its power and wealth in their father's time, into a decline which, within little more than half a century, all but totally extinguished, if not itself, at all events its ancient fortune.

Dudley Loftus, the second son, joined the Rifle Brigade, died young while serving in Ireland, and joined his grandmother on that uninviting shelf in her inhospitable vault under Crinken Church.

His older brother, William Henry the Bad, born in 1819, came, at the age of twenty-one years, into his enormous inheritance. He and my grandfather, Percy Tilson Magan, his first cousin, were the only two males of that generation of the family to continue to live the life of landed gentry in Ireland.

1 – WILLIAM HENRY MAGAN THE YOUNGER
(1819 – 1861)

De Mortuis nil nisi bonum, but I never heard any good of William Henry Magan the Younger. There can hardly have been other than solid grounds for the bad character given to him universally by his relations. It may be that it started with high spirits but, if so, it seems soon to have plunged into the abyss.

The early nineteenth century life, into which William Henry Magan the Younger was born, was very different from life in Ireland in the late eighteenth century.

The Act of Union had changed life for the Irish gentry. Parliament had gone from Dublin and, with its departure, much of the bright life had gone out of the city, even though the pleasurable life in the country houses continued as heretofore. Those who were still actively engaged in politics centred their town lives on London, together with those who liked, or regarded it as important, to be in the top social swim. Those who either were not politically active, or who could not easily afford two establishments, or who now found Dublin too provincial and tedious, retired to their Irish country seats and stayed there.

It is not altogether true that the shifting of the political and social hub to London created a great increase in absentee Irish landlords. At least as many returned from the now extinguished bright lights of Dublin to their country estates. And social changes in Dublin were not to the Ascendancy's taste. Because there was no-one else for the Lord-Lieutenant to invite to the Castle, he and Her Excellency began sending invitations to 'tradesmen'; and even for the formal Balls!

Not only had Dublin social life been spoilt for the landed gentry, but many of the Irish were also unhappy in London. The starchy English turned up their noses at them. The Irish were for the most part not rich enough to compete comfortably socially. In their attempts to do so, they impoverished their Irish estates. All the evils of absenteeism, with their harsh consequences for tenants and employees at home in Ireland, became only too hideously apparent. There was thus discomfort and disquiet for the Irish both in London and on their Irish estates.

In London, those who might have some trace, and some had a good deal more than a trace, of an Irish accent, were regarded as déclassé. The language of Ireland was still Irish. The gentry, of course, spoke English, but many of them spoke Irish as well. English was common, together with Irish, in the eastern counties. West of the Shannon, the majority spoke no English. No wonder the Irish gentry had Irish accents. Even Irish peers were looked upon in London as second-class noblemen; not much above Ruritanian counts. Irish aristocratic attitudes, claims or pretensions, cut no ice with the English. Who on earth did they think they were? Although I have called the English nobility technically plutocratic, it would be absurd to deny that their lifestyle was magnificently aristocratic. The great English peers were far richer than the Irish. The Irish were altogether put in the shade, and in their place, as in every way second-class. Ireland could, for instance, at that time, boast only one duke; the Duke of Leinster.

It took ten or fifteen years for the Ascendancy to sort out its social life after the Act of Union. But, long before William Henry the Younger invaded London, it had done so in Dublin, and the Irish had also learnt to accommodate themselves to London fashionable life. The Irish Ascendancy had by then made itself fully bi-cultural. It was equally at home in England, and in London society, as in Ireland and in Dublin society; and also in its aristocratic role on its Irish estates.

The activities of the Magans were not restricted by lack of money in London or in Ireland. They now had a number of country estates; a magnificent new mansion at Clonearl, as only one of a number of sizeable places; and a splendid town house in Dublin, 77 St Stephen's Green. But that was not enough. London was the place for people of fashion, and William Henry Magan the Younger was indeed a man of fashion. In the world of glitter, nothing but the top, and the best, was good enough for him.

If Edward Hayes, who painted a technically splendid portrait of him, was also an artist of real insight, what he depicted, despite the sage and crafty old Magan blood, and the tough ruthless Loftus blood that ran in his veins, was a weak, vain and scornful character. Perhaps he was a genetic sport. But he probably had a fatal charm and winning ways, for, in a small way, he got places.

Because Ireland had now become merely a province, and since the centre of all that mattered, and of everyone who mattered, was London, it was there that William Henry Magan spent much of his time. He bought himself a commission in a British cavalry regiment, the 9th Lancers, but later transferred, as a captain, to the 4th Light Dragoons.

He appears at one time to have had duties in connection with the royal household, because there is a story that, on an occasion when Queen Victoria was driving with the young Prince Edward sitting facing her in the carriage, the boy became convulsed with uncontrollable laughter. Something behind the Queen seemed to be causing these paroxysms. She looked out of the window and saw William Henry, who was escorting the carriage, making terrible faces. She shouted at him, 'Ride back, Sir'. The story has it that thereafter the escort was ordered always to ride several lengths behind the carriage.

He married on 4th August, 1849, at the age of 30, Lady Georgiana Charlotte Hill (née Keppel), 4th daughter of the 4th Earl of Albermarle. She was the wife of Captain Eustace Edward Hill, a stipendiary magistrate in County Longford. William Henry seduced her from her husband who divorced her.

She was not destined long to survive her marriage with William Henry. Five years later, in March 1854, she died suddenly. A fine needlework picture, on which she was said to have been working, and which remained unfinished on account of her untimely death, is still in the possession of the family.

Family tradition has it that William Henry strangled her. A contemporary local press comment, however, states that he was in London when she died in Ireland. If that was so, then he must be exonerated.

In the first edition of this book I mentioned another alleged murder when, to amuse some friends at Clonearl, he was said to have tarred and feathered a poor half-wit and set fire to him and failed to extinguish the flames in time to save the man's life.

I am now, however, greatly indebted to the Offaly Historical Society for a mass of contemporary documentation on the incident.

Not long after he inherited the estates William Henry had an all-male house-party at Clonearl of half a dozen or so young officers mostly from his own regiment. To entertain them after dinner on the night of 11 December, 1841, he engaged two pipers and a local man, James Flanagan, who was perhaps a good-natured simpleton prepared, for a few shillings, to give some entertainment, and possibly to be the butt for jokes.

The pipers played and Flanagan danced and, after the pipers had left the dining-room, Flanagan stayed and continued his entertainment, and it seems likely there was some horseplay with the officers in which Flanagan's coat was removed, and his shirt was pulled out of his trousers and opened down the front. There is no reason to suppose that the larking went beyond a boisterous officers' mess guest-night.

At about 11 o'clock Flanagan finally left the dining-room to go downstairs to the kitchen. There is little doubt that he had had more to drink than he could hold. Outside the dining-room was a table with lighted candles on it. Perhaps he leant against it to steady himself. At all events the back of his shirt caught fire and he was terribly burned. His shouts brought the officers from the dining-room, and servants from below stairs. William Henry seems to have been first on the scene, and wrapped his coat around Flanagan to extinguish the flames. The poor man died six days later.

There was a thorough examination of many witnesses by the coroner, the Resident Magistrate, and the police. The papers went to the Inspector-General of Police, the Attorney-General, and probably to the Lord-Lieutenant himself. All were wholly satisfied with the verdict of accidental death returned by the Coroner's Court, in which there was a jury of twenty-one people.

Not everyone agreed. The press called it a case of murder, and Sir Percy Nugent Bart later referred to William Henry as a murderer and adulterer.

I have turned Devil's advocate in the matter of these two murder allegations against William Henry, but I cannot rescue him from some of the electioneering records that have survived.

The 'Annals of Westmeath' has this to say about the 1852 parliamentary elections in Westmeath:

The late Mr Pollard Urquhart contested the representation of Westmeath in 1852, and the election was a stirring and memorable one in the history of the county. There were five candidates in the field, viz: W.H. Magan, the Hon. George Mostyn, son of Lord de Vaux; Sir Richard Levinge, Mr John Ennis, afterwards Sir John Ennis, and Mr P. Urquhart. The Hon. Mr Mostyn and Mr Urquhart were the choice of the Catholic bishop and clergy, but the majority of the electors and non-electors were in favour of Magan, as he had the sinews of war – plenty of money, and was generous about it. For weeks the county was in a state of turmoil and confusion. Large mobs assembled at Mullingar, Moate, Kilbeggan, and Delvin to support the man with the long purse. There were open houses for the distribution of drink in every town and village in the county, and it is needless to say that the lovers of John Barleycorn saturated themselves to their heart's content. On the nomination day special trains brought contingents from the neighbouring counties of Meath and King's County to shout for Magan, and to wield the cudgel on the craniums of his opponents if necessary.

If that is parliamentary democracy, then it can hardly be expected that a whole county can indulge in one gigantic democratic soak, aided by supporters from the neighbouring shires, without risking a hangover. And we do have an account of one episode in that hangover.

There is a press report dated 27 November, 1853, headed 'Fatal Affray – one life lost'. It states that a publican named Kelly who held an extensive farm on tenancy from William Henry Magan had kept open house for William Henry's 'voters and mobsmen' at the recent election and thereafter furnished William Henry with a bill for £74. William Henry declined to pay, offered half, but was refused. Kelly began proceedings for recovery which so enraged William Henry that he distrained Kelly's crops against rent due. The crop was then sold to raise the money, and William Henry himself bought it, presumably at a low price. It was removed to the land of a man named Green who was a sub-tenant of Kelly's and was thought to be hand in glove with William Henry. Kelly therefore tried restraint against Green. But William Henry, suspecting this would happen, marched on Green's farm with a large number of retainers. Kelly moved in too, and 'upwards of 500 men were assembled on both sides'. A fight took place and one of Kelly's men was killed. The police arrived and arrested Kelly and two of his brothers. Next day William Henry was provided with a military escort to remove the corn to Clonearl. The article ends. 'The feeling of the populace is very violent against Captain Magan; he cannot show his face in public unless when guarded ... He will do well now to bear in mind what his friend Mr Keogh hinted about the "long nights etc. ... "'

He was given, too, to acts of gross extravagance, and is said on one occasion to have shod his horse in gold.

The burning of Clonearl, also, is supposed to have resulted from one of his drunken orgies. It has been said that this was not true, and that the fire started accidentally in a maid's bedroom.

He squandered his patrimony to the point where the lawyers were forced to take charge of his affairs in order to settle with his creditors. When they had thoroughly examined everything and were able to assess his assets they told him that all that could be saved, and all they could allow him, was sufficient to bring him an income of £1,500 a year, a substantial income in those days. He is said to have retorted contemptuously, 'Why, that wouldn't hold my horses heads in the streets of London'.

How much of the estates was lost I do not know. But his businesslike mother, who long outlived him, had seen to it that her own Killyon and Clonard estates were intact. Moreover, she had advanced much of the cash he had squandered, against mortgages on his other estates, which thus fell to her. He died on 24 October 1861. Despite whatever damage he may have done, enormous properties still remained in the family. Two decades later, his sister Augusta Magan's estates were just on twenty thousand acres, and they included Clonearl and Eagle Hill, Co. Kildare, which had been his, and which his mother must have rescued or recovered.

William Henry the Younger died aged forty-two. I once, when a boy, asked my Aunt Blossie, what had caused his death at so early an age. She answered with one emphatic word; 'Divilment'. I asked for no elucidation. Delivered in the authoritative tones of a wholly morally confident, though very gentle and amiable Victorian, that splendidly damning word explained everything. That our institutions are sometimes in disrepute is hardly surprising when we consider that this man was High Sheriff of Westmeath, and was for a dozen years or so a Member of Parliament at Westminster, and a Justice of the Peace for the county.

He was interested in becoming a peer. In the summer of 1856, six years before he died, when he was 37 years of age, he wrote from London to Sir Bernard Burke, Ulster King of Arms, to enquire whether a petition on behalf of his mother would succeed in securing for her one of the Loftus family peerages. Clearly he had it in mind that he would in time inherit it.

Sir Bernard replied regretting that the Loftus family had three branches and only two peerages, and that two of the branches already occupied the Marquisates of Drogheda, and Ely, so there was nothing left for his mother who represented the third branch, that of Loftus of Killyon.

Had he behaved himself, and not died of 'divilment', he could, no doubt, with his wealth, influential connections and long service as an M.P., have contrived to get himself a peerage if that is what he wanted, and peerages were, of course, of great material value in those days. There is no information to suggest that his mother was at all interested in becoming a peeress. The probability is that, being an imperious woman, she did not feel at a disadvantage with anyone, and felt no need of any embellishment.

Let there be one little bit of commendation of William Henry the Younger, even though it is highly confected praise.

The Irish have always been prolific writers of ballads. Presumably the tradition derives from the ancient practice of homespun music, poetry and songs in the old septs. In the same way that many Persians doodle carpet patterns, so some Irishmen are liable to burst into a ballad at any moment; and everything, but in particular an 'heroic' act, is grist to the Irish balladier's mill. If you want to be immortalized in a ballad as the 'Brave Paddy X', all you have to do is to blow up a bank. There will be ten rousing verses in your honour in the morning. On the occasion of at least one election fought by William Henry, a rhyming ballad was composed and published to the honour and glory of 'Our Member, Brave Magan'. Its first verse gives a taste of the Irish balladier's art. It is an acquired taste!

To the people of Westmeath
Come all you People of Westmeath
  And listen to what I say,
Your Men you have again to choose
  Upon the Tenth of May
For twelve long years and upwards,
  Dispute this if you can,
Our cause was well supported
  By our Member BRAVE MAGAN.

If the paean of praise that followed had been the only record of him to survive, he would have a very different reputation from the appalling one which he has, and which he seems richly to have deserved.

Five years after William Henry the Younger had inherited the Magan estates at the age of twenty-six, the great Irish Famine began. It affected everyone in Ireland, and does so to this day.

2 – THE FAMINE

During the latter part of the eighteenth century, and the early part of the nineteenth century, there were considerable increases in population in England, Wales and Ireland. The influences that affect population fluctuations are not fully understood. Nevertheless, there were two linked factors in Ireland which must be assumed to have contributed substantially to the population increase. As we have seen, the population was probably about one million in the seventeenth century. By the end of the eighteenth century it was assumed to be approaching five million. A census in 1841 produced a figure of over eight million. That was almost certainly an underestimate. It is likely that the population was more than nine million by the time of the famine.

The first factor influencing this exceptional population growth was doubtless the potato. I have already called it a wonder food. With some milk and green vegetables, it was an easily cooked, easily digested, palatable, wholesome, nourishing diet. It needed only to be boiled. It was also a useful food for animals, particularly pigs and poultry. On an acre or so a family could just about live, with a spade ('shovel' in Ireland) the only necessary tool.

Turf (peat) was available nearly everywhere, for the effort of digging it ('cutting' it) for fuel. It smouldered year in, year out, on the hearths of the cabins – some fires perhaps never went out for centuries. It saw to the simple cooking needs, and kept the people warm in the comparatively mild climate, despite the inadequate rags which was all the clothing many could afford.

An important factor affecting the cause of the famine was that Irish cooking skills had virtually become limited to boiling; and Irish digestive ability to the potato. Such alternative foods as might therefore be made available were neither easily cooked nor easily digested, particularly by people who were already too ill from starvation and its consequent illnesses to be fit for more than an invalid diet.

As the population grew on the potato, so the available land for the swarming, often almost destitute, poorest section of the peasantry became more and more fragmented until some families were struggling to exist on perhaps no more than a quarter of an acre. The future was hopeless. No-one in the most congested areas could look forward to any betterment. There was no more available land. Marriages, therefore, got earlier and earlier. There was no point waiting for better earnings. They could never come. Irish girls have always been chaste. If they were going to be mothers, then they might as well marry young and get on with it. And the Irish are very fertile, and their families were large. The population increased rapidly.

I have already mentioned the starvation gap between the end of the consumption of one potato harvest and the beginning of the next. It was estimated that, by 1845, the first year of the famine, more than two million people were unemployed and at near starvation level during those months, and hence the people whom Thackeray saw begging for work, food or money at my great-grandfather's place in the month of July.

That was the situation when the disaster struck. It was not confined to Ireland. The blight, an air-borne fungus, which multiplies its spores at enormous speed, and destroys its host plants almost as quickly as a searing blast, first appeared in America in the summer of 1845. It had not been known in Europe before, or indeed identified or listed anywhere. No-one who has not seen a *Phytophthera* attack could believe its appalling, mercilessly complete, and wildfire devastation. It next appeared in the Isle of Wight. It spread rapidly through southern England, and on the Continent where there was also famine, but not on the Irish scale. Lastly it attacked Ireland, the most vulnerable country of all, because of the enormous extent of the dependence of the bulk of the population on the potato as the main part of their diet. It destroyed a very large part of the crop including much that had already been harvested. The devastation in the affected areas was as complete as if the land had been drenched in sulphuric acid.

I am not going to repeat the harrowing tales. Acute famine conditions continued for four years. In addition, the second winter, that of 1846–47 in which there was total failure of the potato crop, was also climatically the hardest ever remembered. Instead of the usual balmy Irish south-west winds blowing up from the tropics off the warm ocean, it was bitterly cold with snow and ice and continual winds from the north.

The following harvest, that of 1847, was largely spared the blight. It was, indeed, a good harvest, but pitifully small because the peasants had not had the money for seed, or the health to dig the ground, and so the famine conditions, and consequent epidemics, continued in the winter of 1847–48. The next harvest, that of 1848, was again totally destroyed by the blight. And, for years to follow, intermittent famine and epidemic disease continued in Ireland.

No-one knows how many people died during the four principal years of the famine. A million? Possibly many more. Starvation was not itself the main direct killer. Of those who died, possibly not more than ten per cent died of starvation. Up to ninety per cent may have died of disease, principally typhus, cholera and bacillary dysentery. Most of them would have starved, had not the epidemics released them prematurely. No part of the community was spared. All classes suffered. Doctors died by the score; as did devoted officials, and as also did heroic priests and clergy, who went among the people, at great hazard to themselves, doing what they could to alleviate the appalling miseries and distress of the poorest and most helpless, who, of course, suffered most.

The unstinting hospitality of the Irish contributed to the terrible spread of disease. Even the utterly destitute and starving turned no disease-ridden stranger from their door, but invited him in to share their warmth and their last half potato. Many eye-witnesses, coming fresh to the scenes, testified that, although prepared, by the tales they had already heard, for scenes of horror, the reality they experienced on the spot was dreadful beyond anything that anyone who had not witnessed it could have imagined.

Emigration during the famine years accounted for the loss of more than another million of Ireland's population. This, and the figure for deaths given above, are probably conservative. The more likely figure seems to be a loss in population from both these causes of two-and-a-half to three million. Large numbers emigrated to North America, particularly Canada, which was British territory, as the United States did not want them. Even larger numbers emigrated to Britain.

These Irish immigrants were extremely unpopular everywhere. In their famished state, they were for the most part useless and unwanted as citizens. They had no skills except to use a potato spade; little or no education; many could not speak English; they had never lived above the cultural level of a leaky cabin shared with their animals. They were destitute; at best covered in a few rags; at worst, and very frequently, diseased; and were thus all too soon to start epidemics of typhus and dysentery wherever they settled.

The bulk of eighteenth century Irish settlers in the United States had been Ulster Presbyterians who did not want this influx of Irish Catholics. But the immigrants managed to swarm in; some directly in immigrant ships; others simply by walking across the frontier from Canada. Wherever they came to rest, they greatly diminished the quality of life for everyone else. As an instance, the enormous number who reached the port of Boston, U.S.A., largely destroyed the prosperously cultural life that had grown up there. Their depraved state of destitution led them into every sort of crime and vice, to say nothing of the appalling health hazards that they imported for the inhabitants.

In Canada, Montreal, which became a terminus on the St Lawrence river for immigrant ships, suffered similarly from the swarms of these diseased, destitute and all but useless people. It took two generations for the Irish immigrant community to recover on the American continent. Their intelligence and abilities then began to flower. Henry Ford was the grandson of one of them. And, with their recovery, there grew, too, a hatred of England, to which they ascribed all their miseries; a hatred that has fired the large Irish American anti-British lobby to this day.

In Britain, famine immigrants were loathed, both for the reasons I have given, and because mid-nineteenth century Britain was, both at the level of church and chapel, a very strongly Protestant country which resented this invasion of priest-ridden, literally pestilential, Papists, talking a foreign tongue, living little better than animals and having outlandish ways. I recently heard a Roman Catholic priest say that 'the Protestant Church is much more English than the Catholic Church has ever been'. He put his finger on something very important. The English do not dislike Catholics, and do not dislike foreigners. But the Protestant Englishness of England is sacrosanct. That is what they do not want to see altered, even though they have themselves laboured mightily to Anglicize the rest of the world.

These swarms of Irish were both Catholic and foreign, and where they settled in large numbers they changed the character of England, and that was resented. Controlled, small-scale immigration of able-bodied Irish had been tolerated. They were prepared to do the most arduous manual work. They were the navvies who did the spade work, literally, that built the British and American railways. But these hordes of useless, diseased, emaciated Irish refugees from the famine were a liability, and one that was also a danger to the livelihood of the manual labourer both in England and America, because, when sufficiently recovered to work, they were prepared to do so for very low wages.

But despite American and English detestation of this literally pestiferous invasion, there was at first no lack of compassion for the terrible suffering which had been brought upon the unfortunate Irish through no fault of their own. Huge sums were raised in both countries by voluntary subscription for relief work. The private citizens of the two countries – Britain and America – between them subscribed something like a million pounds. That would be a large sum today for a disaster fund. In the 1840s it was a staggeringly enormous amount of money, the real value of which would be twenty times that sum today. It is also not to be overlooked that it fell largely to the English Treasury to furnish such food and relief as was provided during those years. At one time the Treasury employed upwards of three-quarters of a million Irishmen on relief work in Ireland to enable them to earn something. In addition there was a time when the Treasury was making food available for more than three million people. Ultimately, the people of England paid.

But the Irish largely destroyed the sympathy and compassion that had been felt for them. The last year of acute famine was 1848, the year in which Europe suffered a number of what would now be called 'left-wing' revolutions. A bunch of disparate Irish revolutionaries followed suit; not peasants, but intellectuals, country-gentlemen, priests, 'middle class' they might be called today, carried out a campaign of vilification of England, and of the gentry and others who were in some position to help, and who had striven, within their lights, to do so. This was followed by a totally abortive attempt at rebellion. It was all a lot of noise, but it forfeited sympathy. Voluntary subscription largely dried up. Why should anyone go on trying to help so ungrateful a nation? The British Treasury was experiencing a financial crisis, and severely limited further financial help to Ireland. The result was to pile desperation on disaster. It is for the Treasury stringencies of 1848, above all, that the Irish immigrant communities in North America have never forgiven England.

Estate owners in Ireland were not farmers, except for some who were graziers in a big way. Other than the home farm – the demesne – their land was capital, rented to tenants. Rents were their incomes. Over much of Ireland the tenants were rendered destitute by the famine. Not only were no rents paid, but landlords were under an obligation to try to support their destitute tenants with famine relief work, and relief in kind. Furthermore, in order to compel Ireland to strive to the uttermost to help herself, rates were raised steeply from which relief was to be provided for the destitute. But with no rents coming in from destitute tenants, the landlords had no incomes from which to pay the rates. In consequence many landlords were themselves bankrupted, and others nearly so.

There are no doubt those who might blame me for not devoting a paragraph to the iniquities of the landlords. They are the obvious target. Some made errors, some, or more often their agents, committed iniquities in their name. Detailed research would be needed to establish the truth of hostile allegations. If there were iniquities, it is equally true that there were many acts of generosity, much display of responsibility, much compassion and kindliness; and there were a great many landlords who were themselves all but ruined by the disaster. They were, of course, made the scapegoat at the time. Their lives were endangered, as were the lives of their agents. Among those murdered was a kinsman of the Magan family, Major Denis Mahon, of Strokestown, Co. Roscommon. He had, in fact, and at great expense to himself, been doing his best to solve the hideous problem with which the plight of his tenants faced him.

Many, officials, landlords and others, have been blamed for the part they played or failed to play. Mistakes, of course, were made. Some, no doubt, behaved unworthily. We can seek to place the blame where we will – the economic theories of the time, the change of government in England at a crucial moment in the famine episode, the ignorance of the peasants, the supposed rapacity of some landlords, the alleged indifference of the English Treasury, and so on – but the cap fits none of them.

There was one immediate cause, and one immediate cause only – the infestation originating in America of *Phytophthera infestans*. And, given that human society can never be expected to perform to perfection, the fact is that even angels could hardly have mitigated more than marginally the effects of so great a natural disaster.

Potato blight is still rampant, and, despite the now available scientific methods of control, still does enormous damage in years when the climate is favourable to its development and spread. And this would appear to hang a terrible, and undelineated, peril over mankind.

To move the wild potato root from the American continent to Europe; to plant it in large intensive areas away from the symbiotic associations of its natural habitat, was to change its environment. It failed to adjust itself quickly enough to the hazards of this environmental change, and was unable to survive the onslaught of the blight, with disastrous consequences to mankind in a small corner of the world. But, and here is the point, although there had been previous crop failures, it was not until three centuries after the first transplantation of the potato that man was overwhelmed by disaster.

It is not the only disaster of its kind that has occurred even in these islands. Exactly 500 years earlier, 1348–49, bubonic plague, the Black Death, swept a large part of the world, from China across Asia to the Atlantic. A quarter of the population of Europe is thought to have been wiped out. In England a third to a half of the population is estimated to have perished. It, too, resulted from man's modification of his natural environment. The cause was his development of international commerce throughout the Eurasian land mass. Together with his goods, he transported the plague-carrying rat. That commerce had been going on for centuries before plague struck so widely, so devastatingly, and again with wildfire speed.

But during recent centuries, and particularly in the twentieth century, mankind has made environmental changes on an enormous and hugely diverse scale. How many of them hold a similar delayed time-bomb in their grasp? We have vast resources of science nowadays to call to our aid, but what would the equivalent of a myxomatosis epidemic have done to mankind, before the antidote had been found? Both the potato blight and the bubonic plague struck so quickly and on such a wide scale that it is doubtful that even modern science could have mounted a counter-attack in time. And whatever the potential threats may be, they need not be in the nature of possible preventable or curable disease. They could be of any kind; even of kinds unimaginable. We tinker with our Earth's natural environment literally at our peril. It may again be 500 years before it comes, but another disaster will occur one day.

And one question must be asked about the Irish famine itself. Suppose that Ireland had been someone's dream of a Utopian state in which there were no landlords; in which land could have been freely accessible to everyone wishing to have a little holding, and his own potato patch, would not the tragedy then never have happened? Was it not *au fond* because the great landlords had hogged the bulk of the land that the disaster was made possible?

The answer is, no. The disaster would have been a great deal worse. If we turn to Ecclesiastes, we find that things were known then that we seem to have forgotten.

> *When goods increase, they are increased*
> *that eat them.*

One modern example – and there are many others – is Egypt. In the latter part of the nineteenth century, improved administration in the fertile delta resulted, within half a century, in trebled production. The population trebled in consequence, and the process has since continued. Many more millions of people continue to live at the same squalid subsistence level as in the past. They 'that ate' the increase, have themselves increased.

If Ireland had been fragmented into a mass of very small holdings, the population would have been enormous, and, in the circumstances of the time, would have still been largely dependent on the potato. Nor England, nor any power on earth, could have begun to provide the necessary relief. This is not an excuse for landlordism. Neither I, nor anyone else, knows what is the optimum desirable manner of land distribution. I am merely answering a hypothetical question which, even if not in quite so extreme a form, must surely occur to everyone.

The officials, that is the government, and the landlords, got the blame, and indeed they blamed each other. But the government, and the landlords, between them, organized relief. It can be said that this went wrong, that went wrong; this was stupid, that was inept; this was selfish; that was heartless, and so on. But if there had been no-one but peasants, no potent government machinery, no powerful landlords, to organize such relief as there was, things would have been worse, very much worse.

And yet, and yet, and yet, the question persists. That one man should have twenty thousand acres while millions scrape less than an adequate subsistence from as little as a quarter acre; is that a proper way for a society, and an economy, to be organized? In one form and another it is, of course, a question with which economists, sociologists, politicians, theologians, traditionalists, revolutionaries, and many others, have wrestled for centuries, and one that I am not going to tackle here. Many of the poorest in Ireland were not owner-occupiers of tiny patches of land. They were sub-tenants of sub-tenants of sub-tenants, struggling on the fragmented sub-lettings of, in some cases, large estates. Probably those who came off best were the owner-farmers of some substance, say thirty acres or more, who were not wholly dependent on the potato; and the farmer tenants of large and wealthy estates.

The whole of Ireland was affected by the famine. The west, where the holdings were much more fragmented than elsewhere, and where the population was largely dependent on a subsistence economy based on potato production on minute patches of reclaimed marginal peaty land, suffered much worse than other areas. Westmeath, the Magan country, and other areas of the great central grasslands, suffered least. It remained largely, as in Celtic times, a land of graziers with a smaller density of population to herd the cattle, and less wholly dependent on the potato. But to say that is no more than to say something relative about a generally desperate situation. Even in Westmeath, conditions were terrible. The fine market town of Athlone almost came to a standstill, and many of the well-to-do shop-keepers shut up shop and not only fled but emigrated and turned their backs on Ireland for ever.

All estate owners were beset with work and problems, near insoluble economic difficulties, and appalling threats to health and life itself, which affected their tenants, employees, and themselves and their families alike. It is not therefore surprising that no member of our family found time to write a journal of those years – or if one was written it has not survived. Nor have they left us any precise descriptions of their experiences at that time. The famine took place only sixty years before I was born. My grandparents' generation were alive at that time, even though as children. There were a great many people alive when I was young whose parents had lived through the famine. But it is a curious thing that no-one ever talked about it. In the days of my boyhood there was no radio, no television, no canned music, except some primitive gramophones that were not very common. In the evenings we sat round the fire and talked. Why didn't we hear endless tales of the famine? The only mention I ever remember was walls – the marvellous endless walls of Ireland – being pointed out to me as examples of famine relief work; and the remains of wide ridges in the fields that I was told were former 'lazy-beds', the wide ridges in which the potatoes had been planted in those times. Scotland has a similar memorial to her own terrible man-made tragedy of the 'clearances', which was contemporary with the Irish famine. The Scottish lazy-beds, where the small tenants grew their own staple food, oats, are clearly visible to this day along the mountain skirts.

Although William Henry the Younger, and his brother, Dudley Loftus, were both serving in the army, they must at least have visited the estates during the famine. Let us hope that they acquitted themselves creditably. Perhaps the bulk of the responsibility fell to their mother, Eliza. From what we know of her character, and her managerial skill and interests, we may be sure that she did her best – and that it would have been a good best – to alleviate hardship and suffering on the estates.

It must be at least possible that many of the tenants on the Magan estates fared better than the great bulk of the population. Because so much of the land, probably not less than ninety per cent, was grazing land, the tenants were probably for the most part at least reasonably substantial farmers, and in some cases large farmers, and not wholly dependent either for their incomes or their personal diet on the potato. On that account the family's own economy is likely to have suffered much less than that of others. The tenants, we may assume, were at least able to continue to pay some rent, thus enabling the estates to afford the higher rates and the relief work required of them.

3 – MRS ELIZA MAGAN (1796–1880)

When, in 1861, nearly a dozen years after the end of the famine, William Henry Magan the Younger joined his brother and his grandmother in the grim Crinken crypt, his mother, the former Eliza Loftus, was heir to whatever was left of his estates. She lived on and continued to control her enormous properties for another nineteen years. She was a diminutive woman, and a dynamic, energetic, managing person, though she may not have been very far-seeing. There is no evidence that she continued her husband's creative activities. She was forty-four years of age when he died, and still had nearly half her life before her, but she seems not to have done any more building, or to have carried out any further substantial changes. She lived mainly at Killyon – where no significant additions or alterations were made to the house in her time – and at her town house in Dublin. It is likely that she found a greater interest in the business management of the estates than in decorative improvements to her houses. She drove about in a pony-trap issuing her daily commands, and inspiring a good deal of awe. She was commonly known among the country people as, 'the four foot faggot', which is perhaps descriptive enough to need no elaboration.

That she should strew the verges of the woodland paths with flowers shows a lighter, gentler, and more feminine contrast to her managerial asperities. But, that she was at the same time capable of an imperious *hauteur* is illustrated by an amusing story about her.

Edward Cecil Guinness, the head of the brewing family, who was destined to become the 1st Earl of Iveagh, owned the next house to her Dublin mansion in St Stephens Green. He wished to improve his property. He therefore approached her through his agent to see if she would sell her house. 'What? Sell my house to a brewer? Not likely.' Ireland, as so often, was lagging behind England where the peerage was already eagerly marrying the beerage!

She died aged eighty-four years on 11 September, 1880, the year of my father's birth. The rather coarsely Irish sobriquet of 'four foot faggot' suggests that she may not have been endearing to everyone. We must nevertheless respect her. She was clearly a woman of character, with an impressive personality. Her family hadn't roasted archbishops for nothing. And she was seemingly ready to administer at least mild roastings herself to get her own way. In a world then dominated by men, in which handicaps were heaped upon women, she struggled and succeeded, and more than held her own, and there is reason enough to suppose that under her management the Magan estates tackled their problems with vigour, enterprise and credit to themselves, and to herself.

When she died, my Magan grandfather, Percy Magan, went to her funeral. It was, he said, an enormous, almost regal affair. To quote him, 'Even the coffin nails were of gold'. She lies in a, if I remember right, purple plush covered coffin, in her last resting place on that grisly shelf in the Crinken church crypt.

A question-mark hangs over the judgement of Eliza Magan. She lived twenty-nine years after writing her last will and testament. Why did she never trouble to amend it? Why did she not take some steps to secure the future of the estates? She must surely have known her daughter and heiress, Augusta, well enough to be aware beyond any doubt that she was not competent to be entrusted with so great a responsibility. By that neglect, all that she and her husband, William Henry Magan the Elder, had striven to build up, improve and safeguard was destined to come to naught.

And with that we will take our leave of Eliza, scattering flowers, let us hope, in Elysium.

CHAPTER 30

The Family in the Last Part of the Nineteenth Century

AFTER THE DEATH of Eliza Magan, widow of William Henry Magan the Elder, in 1880, there remained two land-owning branches of the family in Ireland. They were headed by cousins. There were also other cousins who had in effect ceased to be Irish and who lived permanently either in England or abroad.

Of the two land-owning branches in Ireland one was my grandfather Percy Magan's branch, from which the Magans of today descend. He had his estate of three thousand acres of not very good land in Roscommon.

The other branch was already in a cul-de-sac. It would inevitably come to an end with the death of its existing incumbent, Augusta Elizabeth Magan, only surviving child of William Henry Magan the Elder, and my grandfather's first cousin. Augusta was the sole, unencumbered and unfettered owner of virtually all the ancient Magan estates and wealth – twenty-thousand acres of some of the best land in the world, valuable houses, parts of Dublin, treasures and riches. She was fifty-five years of age, and unmarried, when she came into her inheritance, and not a little unstable. She was destined to live another twenty-five years; destined, too, to destroy or disperse all the material possessions that the family had built up, accumulated, and carefully husbanded over the centuries. With a stroke of her pen she did more damage than Cromwell, the Jacobite Wars, and the Penal Laws all put together.

1 – AUGUSTA ELIZABETH MAGAN (1825–1905)

Augusta seems to have been the antithesis of her mother. She lacked drive, energy and will-power to a marked degree. She was devoid of managerial capability. She grossly mismanaged the estates. When she died they were found to be in a dreadful state of neglect. Her houses likewise were a shambles; an awful state of clutter and dirt. It was an Augean task to deal with them.

A report by the official valuer who examined her properties after her death stated that at Killyon Manor:

Every passage and every room to which access could be gained was packed with parcels and packages of all descriptions. Piled on top of the furniture, underneath furniture, piled on the floors, were packages, deed boxes etc., on top of one another. The litter on the main stairs and vestibule was almost knee deep. It took the valuers three whole days to clear the deceased's bedroom alone of papers and rubbish which had been allowed to accumulate there. Every apartment in the mansion was in the same condition. The most astonishing discovery was that amongst this accumulation were found money and securities for money, jewellery, and valuables of every description. Bank notes for small and large amounts were found adhering to old newspaper wrappers, or thrown carelessly aside in wastepaper baskets. Sovereigns and coins of lesser value were picked up on the floors of the several rooms, or were lying about in tea cups or kitchen utensils, and in most unlikely places –

A euphemism for chamber pots according to the stories I heard. The account went on:

In almost every page of the valuer's report occurred such phrases as 'Found £5 note amongst rubbish'. Although the valuers went very carefully through all the papers and rubbish with which the house was packed, finding large sums of money and articles of value for several days, still, when the solicitor for the executors came to go in detail through the several boxes of papers, letters, etc., which had been sent up from Killyon, he also found large sums of money, uncashed cheques etc., which had been lying untouched and unthought of in many instances for upwards of 50 years. Amongst the valuables found hidden with piles of rubbish of years were some large chests filled with silver plate, and plated ware, valuable furniture and wearing apparel which had never been removed from their original packing. When the deceased's house in Stephen's Green was opened it was found to be, if anything, in worse condition.

My father and his sister, my Aunt Violet Magan, were appointed managing agents of the estates. They were thus officially and intimately involved in all the details of winding up Augusta's affairs. They told me that when the auctions of the contents of Killyon Manor and the other houses were held, it was judged unreasonable to undertake the task of emptying the clutter in some of the less important rooms. Their contents were therefore auctioned in each case as a single lot, unseen. The buyers, so to speak, took pot-luck on what they might get.

Although Augusta did not marry, there was a man in her life. It used to be said that she had been betrothed to a Capt. Bernard, a member of the Bernard (pronounced Bar-nard) family of Castle Bernard, King's County, and that he was killed riding in a horse race at Mullingar races in Westmeath. But the evidence does not fit that story. Among her surviving possessions there is a small portrait of him.

He had been born in 1822, three years before her. He fought in the Crimean War and was at the battles of Alma, Balaclava and Inkerman. He served at one time in the Austrian army. He held the post of Chamberlain at the Court of Dublin under two Viceroys, the Dukes of Abercorn and of Marlborough. In 1859, three years after the end of the Crimean War, at the age of thirty-seven, he married Ellen Georgina, widow of the Hon. Henry Handcock, 5th son of the 2nd Baron Castlemaine of Moydrum Castle, Athlone, Westmeath.

Colonel Richard Wellesley Bernard died in 1877, at the age of fifty-five. Augusta was then fifty-two years old. Richard Bernard's wife, Ellen, lived another thirty years. She outlived Augusta by a year or so.

Since Colonel Bernard died when he was fifty-five years old, it is at least questionable that he would have been riding in a horse race. Whatever the cause of his death, his body – and it really is a bizarre story – was at one stage wheeled along the platform of Mullingar railway station on a station trolley. Augusta Magan got hold of the trolley and lived with it in her bed-sitting room – for she lived in only one room at Killyon – for the rest of her life.

In strict mid-Victorian times, and under the dominance of a strong-willed mother, who was still alive at the time of Colonel Bernard's death, it seems unlikely in the extreme that Augusta could have had a serious love affair with a married man. No-one of my father's generation, all of whom knew this story, ever suggested that any scandal attached to Augusta's association with Richard Bernard.

It is therefore at least curious that Augusta should have been so closely involved in the disposal of Richard Bernard's remains as to have gained possession of the humble station vehicle which transported them for so minute a part of their sad last journey. It is also curious that she should have been so deeply affected emotionally as to have felt unable for the rest of her life to be parted from so unusual, hideous, cumbersome, and useless a piece of furniture as that railway station barrow, and so grim a reminder of that abnormal and grotesque cortege which, in its own crazy way, also serves to epitomize the great nineteenth century era of steam locomotion.

We do not know the facts of this affair. The most likely supposition is that Augusta fell in love with Richard Bernard at a time before he married, and that it was then that he gave her the portrait, for it is of a mature but not yet middle-aged man. That he gave it to her at all suggests a close association between them, but not necessarily that they were ever betrothed, which on the whole seems unlikely. Perhaps the truth is that he preferred Ellen, whom he married, to the eccentric Augusta, despite her wealth, but that Augusta never lost her infatuation for him, while nevertheless managing outwardly to keep on conventionally friendly terms with both him and his wife.

There seems no question that Augusta's heart had been touched, and it is certain that Richard Bernard's death preyed permanently upon her mind. Such lingering manifestations of affection and grief were common at the time. Queen

Victoria's tributes to Prince Albert were in the same vein. And an exaggerated description of a similar case is drawn round the person of Miss Haversham by Charles Dickens in *Great Expectations*. It has even been suggested that Dickens learnt of, and drew on, Augusta's anguish for his story. But the dates do not fit. *Great Expectations* was written before the unfortunate Colonel Bernard was trundled his last along the Mullingar platform of the Midland Great Western Railway.

After her mother's death Augusta lived alone, moving from one to another of her great houses, but probably spending more and more time at Killyon. Although she did not go mad in any sense of that term suggesting a mind deranged to the point of not knowing what she was doing, she became progressively more eccentric. She bought enormous quantities of useless goods; useless in the sense that she could make no possible use of them. These, as we have seen, were piled, often unopened, in every room and corner of her large houses. The ballroom at Killyon, a very large room, was stacked with unopened packing cases of bed linen, kid gloves, and all manner of things.

And, when Killyon was opened up after her death, there came to light a grim memento to her brother Dudley Loftus Magan. In the small room, the head of the former old tower, at the top of the stairs to the upper floor of the east wing, were his hunting clothes, laid out ready for him the moment he arrived home. But he never came. He went instead to the military hospital at Portobello in Dublin, and there died. Sixty years later, still altogether undisturbed, his pink coat, buckskin breeches and top boots continued to await his return.

For some reason known only to herself, Augusta once turned the servants out of Killyon and hid the family jewels, supposed to be of great value. They have never been found. No inventory of them now survives, but there is a picture of her wearing enough of them to set 'the boys' ' mouths watering in gangster land. It was thought by my father's generation that they could not have been stolen because they would have been instantly recognized had they come on the market at that time. We were never bored at Killyon. There were too many interesting things to do. But if ever there was a spare moment, 'looking for the jewels' was a perennial occupation. My sister Maureen had an exciting moment. Near the house, leading a horse with Tommy Shanley, a boy who worked on the place, grandson of a former steward, Tom Shanley, the horse sank one hoof into a hole. Maureen and Tommy dug, and disclosed a casket. It contained a dog's bones.

I never heard an ill word of Augusta. I heard often of her kindnesses. One of the elderly women about the place at Killyon told me that when she was a girl, she and others of the cottage girls often went up to the big house to see her. She was always pleased to see them, and very kind. She was enormously wealthy, and she seems to have been conscious of it. She once said to one of the men, who recounted it to me, that she could pave 'The Lawn' (eleven acres) at Killyon with £5 notes and not be at the end of her loose cash.

My father's eldest sister, my Aunt 'Blossie', was exceedingly fond of her. When Blossie was very old and her mind was full of lucid recollections of her childhood years, she described to me in detail the trouble Augusta had gone to to take her to her first ball, and she recalled every detail of the dresses they had both worn.

Every starving tinker's donkey could be sure of Augusta's hospitality. She bought them and turned them loose on her lands. When she died, parts of her neglected estates were like a nature reserve. There were untended, unshod donkeys and ponies with curled up hoofs a foot long. There were ancient and half wild bullocks with long shaggy coats. Gipsies and tinkers I met many years later in the lanes around Killyon used to talk of her as 'Lady Magan'. Perhaps they thought the additional courtesy might be worth another half-crown.

It will be hard for future generations to realize that in mid-Victorian times there was no escape for a woman from a subordinate domestic role at home except through marriage. There were no professions, and there was no work open to women of the upper classes except such as they could find, or create, for themselves in the home, which is one reason for the elaboration and clutter of home life at that time. Such of their handiworks as have come down to us, samplers and needlework pictures, are not so much a tribute to their skills and industry, as a memorial to the appalling extent of the tedium of their excessive and frustrated leisure. Such must have been Augusta's life.

For the twenty-five years she lived after her mother's death, she appears essentially as a lonely figure. A modest, reserved, kindly person, thrown more and more in upon herself until she became a virtual hermit living alone in that one room at Killyon in an indescribable state of filth, with the ghoulish railway station barrow for her companion. The room was the ground floor, north room on the east front of the house. To a world full of want it might seem that she had all and very much more than any human being could desire. But perhaps, as a kindly and affectionate woman, she lacked the most important thing of all; someone with whom to share her life and her affections. Liberated tinkers' donkeys are an inadequate substitute for the beating of another human heart. Was it that, or was it that she was at least in part deranged?

While she was pursuing her more and more lonely and eccentric way toward that eventual Crinken shelf, her other land-owning first cousin, my grandfather Percy Tilson Magan, was, in parallel, leading an essentially different life in that he was far less well-off and was surrounded by a large family whom he had to support. He and Augusta were exact contemporaries. Born in 1828, three years later than Augusta, he was destined to die two years before her death. They knew each other well, and kept in close touch throughout their long lives.

2 – PERCY TILSON MAGAN (1828–1903)

My grandfather, Percy Tilson Magan the Elder, was one of that noisy cheerful throng of children who greeted Thackeray's coach on its arrival at Duninga. The second son of George Percy Magan, he was destined to be his heir. I have said that, his mother being a Catholic, there was an agreement that her sons should be brought up Protestant. Nevertheless the time had come when Protestants did not leave such matters to chance. The days of the continentally-educated priests who were welcome at the tables of the gentry were over. Maynooth had been in existence for more than thirty years turning more rustic material into disciplined, assertive men who harboured a genuine inner conviction that a heretic Protestant converted was a soul saved; and who did not overlook the earthly advantage of getting a well-to-do and influential landowner for the Church of Rome; and it was perhaps seen as no less an Irish duty, than a sacred duty, thus to help restore the land to Catholic ownership. On that account, Percy's very actively Protestant grandmother, Hannah Georgina Tilson, showed positive concern to ensure that the Catholic Church did not catch this innocent. But there is a story that he was, nevertheless, very nearly lost to the Protestant faith.

It is told that one of Percy's Catholic sisters whisked the infant off to the Catholic priest and had him baptized into the Roman Church. That cannot be accurate as his oldest sister was no more than four years of age when he was born, and it would be stretching credulity beyond bounds to credit such an escapade to so young a maiden. Nor does it seem likely that any priest would have lent himself to such a caper. Nevertheless, that someone, perhaps a zealous nursemaid, did hatch some stratagem to save his little soul, does seem at least possible, for he used to say; 'They tried to get me when I was born; and they'll try to get me when I am dying'. Whatever the truth, the general purport of the tale is of interest in serving to illustrate Protestant fears of the growing power of the native Irish Catholic Church so relatively soon after the founding of the Maynooth seminary.

My grandfather remained a well-to-do bachelor until he was thirty-seven years old. He did the Grand Tour of Europe, or something like it, and returned with art acquisitions that were more pretentious than valuable or interesting.

His first known residence, Marfield, near Gorey, Co. Wexford, in the south-east of Ireland, was not far from his father's old home at Duninga. It was a sizeable, well-built, stone house, with attractive terraced gardens, which he rented, together with its home farm, from the Earl of Courtown.

He married, in 1865, Annie Catherine only daughter of the Rev. Edward Richards, Rector of Clonallen, Co. Down, Ulster. She was a sweet-natured person, and a much loved 'grannie' to my generation. They were a devoted couple. For her wedding present her reverend father gave her a splendid Bible which weighs 7lbs 7oz. She treasured it greatly and bequeathed it to my father. It is beautifully printed and a joy to handle and read. But I hope her father also gave her something for her material comfort.

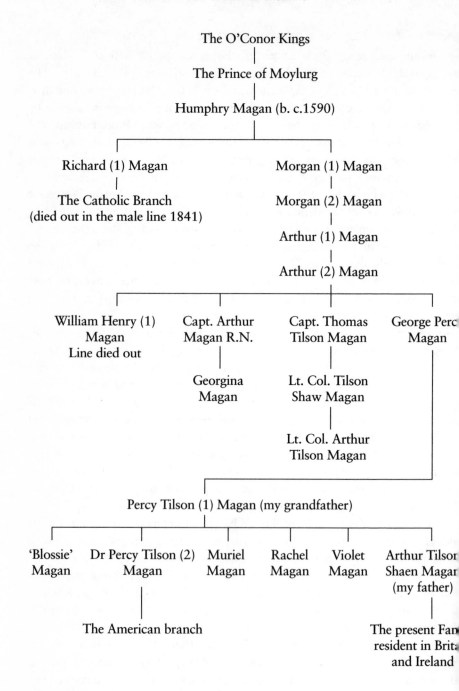

The O'Conor Kings
|
The Prince of Moylurg
|
Humphry Magan (b. c.1590)

Richard (1) Magan
|
The Catholic Branch
(died out in the male line 1841)

Morgan (1) Magan
|
Morgan (2) Magan
|
Arthur (1) Magan
|
Arthur (2) Magan

William Henry (1)
Magan
Line died out

Capt. Arthur
Magan R.N.
|
Georgina
Magan

Capt. Thomas
Tilson Magan
|
Lt. Col. Tilson
Shaw Magan
|
Lt. Col. Arthur
Tilson Magan

George Perc
Magan

Percy Tilson (1) Magan (my grandfather)

'Blossie'
Magan

Dr Percy Tilson (2)
Magan
|
The American branch

Muriel
Magan

Rachel
Magan

Violet
Magan

Arthur Tilsor
Shaen Magar
(my father)
|
The present Fan
resident in Brit:
and Ireland

My grandmother's grandfather was Solomon Richards, a celebrated doctor who was President of the Royal College of Surgeons of Ireland. He was also a landowner who had acquired, among other properties, the estate of Ardamine, Gorey, Co. Wexford, not far from my grandfather's residence, Marfield. Surgeon Solomon Richards' grandson, my grandmother's first cousin, Solomon Augustus Richards, and his wife Sophia, built the little church by the sea at Ardamine, which was consecrated in 1862. With the church built at Crinken in 1840 by Hannah Georgina Magan; the church built at Ballymore in 1843 by Francis Magan; and the Ardamine church in 1862, my family contributed one Catholic and two Protestant churches to Ireland in a little over twenty years in the nineteenth century.

Our Richards ancestors were a settler family, described as, 'springing from Wales of a very ancient stock'. They were settled in Kent and Southampton County in the reign of Henry VII, and one of them was Vice-Admiral – equivalent of High Sheriff – of the Isle of Wight in the reign of Edward VI. Our first Irish Richards ancestor was Solomon Richards, an Irish Commissioner, and Governor of the town of Wexford during the usurpation of Oliver Cromwell. He received a grant of three thousand acres of land at Solsborough in Co. Wexford. He raised the 17th Regiment under William and Mary, and was its first colonel. He died in 1691, the year of the Treaty of Limerick, and is buried in Westminster Abbey. So there is a drop or two of our blood within those sacred precincts.

And thus, in the marriage of my grandfather, Percy Magan, to Annie Richards, did the Montagues and the Capulets come together; a descendant of the Catholic Celtic grazier chief, Humphry Magan, wed to the descendant of Cromwell's hated Governor of Wexford.

Although the Richards were a landowning family, they were even more pronouncedly an example of those gentry families whose main contribution had, since the sixteenth century, and particularly in England, been in the professions; and they must have bequeathed us a strong dose of professional inclinations. A head-count of the Irish Richards family covering a couple of centuries or so, throws up twenty-one parsons, including a bishop, twenty-one service officers, including four generals and an Admiral of the Fleet, barristers, doctors, members of parliament, a genealogist, a university don, seven high sheriffs, and numerous Justices of the Peace.

The Richards' family home at Gorey, Ardamine House, was destroyed in 1921 by the Irish Republicans who had, since the Easter Uprising of 1916, been conducting a widespread campaign against the Government, including incendiarism against the homes of the landed gentry. According to a contemporary newspaper report, the caretaker and his wife were given time to remove their private effects, but were refused permission to touch anything belonging to Major Maudant-Richards. The house and its valuable contents were totally destroyed, and there was much consequent loss of employment to the considerable staff whom he employed.

My grandmother, Annie Richards, also brought us a dash of erstwhile French blood, as her mother was Emily Saurin, a member of a distinguished Huguenot family. One of my father's sisters, my aunt Rachel, gave me many years ago, miniature painting of Emily Saurin. My great-grandfather, the Rev. Edward Richards, had the right idea about girls. She is an irresistibly sweet and feminine young lady – but to get rapturous about one's great-grandmother might seem a some what unnatural, if not unlawful, piece of eccentricity, so I will leave her at that.

My grandparents kept in touch with their French relations on the Saurin side of the family, and also with the French relatives of my grandfather's own mother. There was therefore a certain cosmopolitan flavour to their Irish life, which was not just one of rustic insularity. They used to go for holidays to Jersey where perhaps they met their French relations.

Percy and Annie Magan, my grandparents, had six children, four girls and two boys, my uncle and aunts and my father. Their joint life-spans suggest a longevity gene floating around in the family. Despite the fact that one of the daughters died relatively young, the average age of them all was seventy-five. Three, if not four, of those who topped eighty had malfunctioning hearts – so, if we are feeling pressed by labours yet uncompleted, piles of unsorted correspondence, or undarned socks, and if we have a heart that does not work very well, we may take comfort, for there may be some grains of sand in the hour-glass yet!

Five of the children were born at Marfield House, but one, the third child, Muriel, was born in the parish of Granville, Jersey, and 'being very ill', was baptized privately on the island by the rector of Gorey. One wonders, consider ing the rigours of travel in those days – 1870 – what my grandmother was doing in Jersey when there was a child so imminently on the way, but she was a placidly imperturbable person, and may have decided to take a 'sporting chance'.

My grandfather must, during his early married life, have been busy with farming both at Marfield and on his Roscommon estate which was more than a hundred miles away, a considerable journey in those days of horse transport. Farming has its endless problems and worries, and he had more than his fair share of them. Expenses, too, were rising with a growing family. A well-to-do bachelor's circumstances must have been much altered by another seven mouths to feed, and another seven bodies to house, warm and clothe, and all the additional staff to see to their needs. My grandmother, too, must have had her time fully occupied with six children and a considerable household to look after. She was very well versed in household duties, and had her own manuscript book of excellent homely recipes. In Ireland, by the way, they do not pronounce the word 'recipe' as it is pronounced in English. Indeed, to Irish ears, that pronunciation sounds a rather refined affectation. They pronounce it receipt – exactly the same as an acknowledgement for a payment.

But whatever the burdens, responsibilities and anxieties my grandparents had to shoulder, I have the impression that, apart from the disharmony which was to arise between my grandfather and his eldest son, they were a happy family, showing more internal affection towards one another than was, I think, common in upper class Irish homes. Earlier, I drew attention to the saying that the women of the Irish Ascendancy put their dogs and horses first, and their servants and children last. Perhaps, in my grandmother's house, the warm French blood of her mother brought a gentler influence to bear. There was certainly nothing horsey or doggy about her. She was a country woman, and enjoyed all those things that went to make up a country life. But she was first and foremost a mother to her family, and to the extended family of the estate. She was an unforgettable personality, but to me as a boy she was a warm lovable person, and nothing was more joyous to me than staying with her in her home, which I often did.

I remember her only as an elderly person of seventy years or more, but I knew her for a long time as she did not die until I was eighteen. She was tall and slim, but in no way angular. She had an authoritative dignity, but was not at all stern or austere. She had a rather round and benign face which proclaimed her gentle nature. Her marvellous auburn hair never turned grey. Being widowed before I was born, she always wore, as was the custom of the time, black or dark grey, usually with an upright white lace collar and white cuffs which set off her beautiful hands.

She had a very soft, sweet voice. She never raised it or laughed loudly. She wore at times a chatelaine's keys on a silver chain round her waist, and round her neck she always wore a long gold chain on which hung a small gold hunter watch which, as very small children, we used to enjoy the pretence of opening by blowing on it. She spoke with that barely perceptible, but softly pleasing, trace of Irish intonation, not uncommon, but also not universal, in the Irish gentry.

She was the epitome of open, innocent, sensible simplicity. She loved jokes and fun. She practised no artistic talents. Her life was spent in the service of her family, of the country people, and of her friends and neighbours – but not pietistically. It was just a natural discharge of the duties and responsibilities that life placed before her. She took a positive and practical interest in my grandfather's farming and estate management. She kept open house for young people.

She was religious. She went to church on Sundays. While her children were growing up, she had morning prayers. They were held in the front hall. Sometimes the postman knocked, and my father, as a boy, used to shuffle on his knees to the door and take in the post still kneeling. Hers were not long-faced religious observances. She had a simple, unshakeable Christian faith which, to her, was just part of the decencies of life. She was always warmly welcoming to me. I do not suppose that, as a boy, I troubled to keep letters, and an itinerant life since has ensured the loss of much of my personal junk, but I have one letter of hers written to me when I was a boy at school. After commiserating with me for being in hospital, and giving me some news, she goes on:

Of course, dear, I shall be delighted to have a visit from you at X-mas, and I hope Roscommon will be quite enough for you to have some sport in. In old

281

days I always thought the wild shooting there was the very best, and kept my larder well stocked.

And then, after some more chat about the family, she finished by warmly repeating her Christmas-time welcome to me.

To those of the older generations who will thus give us a warm place in their lives when we are young, we owe not only glowing recollections but also an increased sense of security to help us through life.

When my grandmother was very old, I used to sit and talk with her. When I greeted her or left her, I always held her hand and kissed her cheek; and her skin was so soft and so fragile that I was almost afraid that to touch her might hurt her. Her mind wandered a little in her great old age, but at the end she was absolutely lucid and calm. She bade her family goodbye, and gratefully and knowingly closed her eyes for the last time.

Fifteen years after their marriage, my grandparents left Marfield and moved to Kilcleagh in Westmeath, a very agreeable late Georgian house a few miles east of Athlone near the Quaker town of Moate, and not far from my grandfather's estate to the west of the Shannon.

An impression of my grandmother, in her role as mother at that time, survives in a letter written after her death in 1927 by her elder son, Percy, from America, where he had been living for more than forty years. Writing to his sisters he said:

I was away in San Francisco when your cable came telling that sweet old Mistress had passed away ... as I entered the hotel, the Desk Clerk, whom I know very well, handed me a telegram ... relaying the message from you ... It would be in vain to ponder over the thought as to whether it is harder for you dear women who have been so close to Mother for so long or for one who has been absent over a toll of nigh onto forty-three years, with but two brief glimpses between. I have tried to write you several times during the last few days, but somehow or other I could not do it. I felt so badly and sad, and so many things that I would love to do or say kept crowding into my mind ... Of course I have nothing recent to recall, so naturally my mind drifts back into the twilight of years long since faded and gone.

The Red Room at Marfield when Violet was born, with its huge bed and valence round the base, and the rest of us being brought in to see the new baby. I can see her there with her beautiful hair in long plaits down her back while Nurse Ferguson and Rosy herded us youngsters around.

I remember her so well on the occasion of the last time I came home from School in England. It was a pretty hard trip. I had arrived at the North Wall (The Dublin dock) early in the morning, but something was not working right about the trains and I was stranded in Dublin during a cold and wet Sunday. I went to a wretched little hotel, the name of which I do not remember, so as to keep dry and half-way warm. I don't just remember, but I believe I only had a few shillings in my pocket, and the Master (his father) had warned me not to spend a penny more than necessary as times were close with him, so I did not buy any breakfast or dinner and took the train in the late evening without supper. Din met me in the pouring rain at Moate with the dogcart and drove me home. It was very late. Everyone had gone to bed except the Mistress. She was up and waiting for me. Nothing would do but that I must be fed, and I can see her yet sitting so kindly beside me in the dining-room at Kilcleagh, and feeding me bread and ham and beer. Then she took me up to the Red Dressing room and stayed with me while I went up to bed, and got a hot water bottle of some sort to get me warmed up.

While living at Kilcleagh my grandfather built himself a substantial house at Correal, his Roscommon property. The family moved there in 1888, having been at Kilcleagh for eight years. For those times Correal must have been an unusual house as it was all on one storey at ground level. It was destroyed by fire in the 1920s.

Correal was a wonderful place for young people. That part of Roscommon is rolling open stony grassland. Almost all fences are walls of loose stone. The fields are small because the walls are not only divisions but also a way of disposing of the enormous quantity of loose stone lying on the surface of the land. As one Irishman said of the hunting there: 'It would make you seasick with leppin' '. Between the low hills are bogs, marshes and lakes, full of duck, snipe, plover and other wild game.

Only six miles to the south-east, a not excessive bicycle ride in those days before motor cars, was the fairly large town of Athlone straddling the Shannon, a considerable river at that point. Athlone housed a large garrison of British troops, which meant unlimited sport and fun, in which the Services always take a lead; athletic and sporting activities of every possible kind by day, frequent dances and parties by night.

Two miles by water up the Shannon, north of Athlone, and only four miles from the family home at Correal, was Lough Ree, a large lake, eighteen miles long and seven miles wide. It is a beautiful lake lying between low hills. The water is clear, but stained porter-brown from the bog-lands it drains. There is a very large number of islands, bays and inlets, giving great interest to the whole expanse of water and wooded shoreline. It is also steeped in history. The ancient Egyptians knew it. Just as he showed the Boyne on his map, so Ptolemy showed the Shannon river (Senos) and Lough Ree (Ribh).

There are many remains of early Christian religious settlements on the islands and on the shore. The earliest is said to be on the island of Inchbofin where St Rioch, son of St Patrick's sister, Darerea, established a monastery in 450 AD. Rioch's brother, Mel, became bishop of Ardagh, where, nearly thirteen hundred years later, my ancestor, the Very Rev. Louis Saurin, became Dean. In Ireland, walking the fields, rowing a boat, whatever we may be doing, we live with the visible and tangible remnants of the ancient past as a part of our everyday life, which nourishes our deplorably long sense of history.

About the year 520 AD, the year in which St Finnian founded Clonard, near Killyon, another Irish saint, St Dermot, founded a similar great monastery on the island of Inch Cleraun in the centre of Lough Ree. It was one of the Irish seats of learning and religion that kept the light of civilization burning on the fringe of Europe through the long centuries of the Dark Ages. St Finnian was mentor to Ireland's favourite saint, St Columba, who founded Iona. Could his popularity be due to the fact that he was a prince, a chief, a man being groomed for the highest kingly office – in short an aristocrat? And is there some special balm for the human soul in, on the one hand, the Cinderella theme, the rejected maiden turned princess and, on the other, its reverse, the prince turned, or at least disguised as, monk or mendicant?

I myself, as a boy, spent much time on the dark waters of Lough Ree, with the silver sunshine glinting on it from the west, sometimes rowing with long strokes through a calm surface, at others pulling hard into steep waves. Sometimes I would pole the boat rustling through the reed-beds in the shallows where a sudden swirl would proclaim the disturbance of a basking pike. Often I fished and, in those days, I usually had everything and everywhere to myself. And I would go ashore on an island, or elsewhere, and examine the screaming gulls nests in the spring, or lie in the sun in the summer, throw stones in the lake, play ducks and drakes, or pick blackberries or crab apples. And we had lovely picnics when we were fishing or boating, with a fire of driftwood between two rocks and the kettle astride them singing, and a loaf of Irish brown bread, and a lump of Irish butter.

There was a small community of people who lived altogether on the islands. They were always spoken of as 'the Islandmen'. They kept very much to themselves. They had a few beasts and did a little husbandry, but their main occupation was fishing; eels, caught on long lines, being an important part of their economy. Their lives can hardly have changed in thousands of years. I recall a letter from my Aunt Violet to my father telling him that one of the ancients among the Islandmen had died. She had watched his coffin being ferried through the white-capped stormy waters for burial on the mainland. She added that, since he had spent his life on the water, it would have seemed more appropriate, 'had he been buried at sea'.

It was in, and around, and on, Lough Ree that, during the last twenty years of the nineteenth century, my father and his sisters, when they were growing up at Correal, spent much of their almost semi-aquatic lives. The lake provided endless interest for the young, with wonderful boating, sailing, yacht racing, fishing and swimming. It was a great school in hardiness and self-reliance for those who lived near its shores. Every vacant house within reach of it, and within reach of Athlone, was rented by a military officer's family. The sailing has always presented a special challenge because of the many submerged rocks and shoals, and the far from easy winds.

The life my father and his sisters led at that time also reflects one of the most notable features of the nineteenth century – accelerating personal mobility, and increasing personal independence. In 1756 John McAdam was born in Scotland. At the end of the century he began his experiments in road-making. In 1815, as Surveyor-General of the Bristol roads, he was able to build roads according to his new methods which were then generally adopted and led to the enormous improvement in road-making known as macadamizing. Hard, durable stone roads, such as the Romans had enjoyed, even though the construction was different, replaced muddy rutted tracks, and made travel faster, safer and much more comfortable.

Steam locomotion on railways began at the same time. Richard Trevithick's plate way in South Wales in 1804 was the first steam railway; and railway development became rapid and widespread during the nineteenth century.

More important than railways, from the point of view of personal, individual mobility, in about 1800 the first experiments with a bicycle were made, even though Leonardo Da Vinci had foreseen this invention centuries earlier. But it was in 1889, when my father was nine years old, that the bicycle really came into its own when the pneumatic tyre, invented the previous year by John Boyd Dunlop, a Belfast veterinary surgeon, came into general use.

Before that, wheels had had solid tyres, excessively uncomfortable on the roads of those days, which, even when macadamized, which by no means all of them were, were rough enough, and often pot-holed with wear. By 1893 the bicycle had been stabilized to the pattern which we know today; two wheels of equal size, chain drive, pneumatic tyres. The free wheel came into use in 1896, when my father was sixteen, enabling the machine to coast along, for instance down hill, without the pedals going round. He and his sisters all became vigorous and enterprising users of the bicycle.

This modern-type bicycle brought enormous personal liberation. On foot, the comfortable limit of a day's journey might have been five miles out and five miles home, by horse ten miles each way. The bicycle enlarged that to twenty-five miles out and home, and it did not have to be fed or watered or held by the head while its rider went shopping, and it did not go lame. A pump and a puncture mending outfit was all that was needed to sustain this marvellous extension of personal liberty. And when combined with rail travel, that extension was almost unlimited. Shove the 'bike' in the guards van, which you could not do with a horse; get out at any station you liked; go up to twenty-five miles in any direction you fancied. Catch the evening train home and sleep in your own bed.

This new boon was quickly seized with both hands by rich and poor; men, women and children. There were no motor cars. The first self-propelled car with an internal combustion engine was made in 1884. It was not until a decade later that a very small number of petrol driven vehicles began to appear. And so, for a time, the cyclist was free to spin along, the wind in his or her hair, no fumes in the lungs and no fear of being run over. No aeroplane had yet flown. It was not till 1903 that the first powered heavier-than-air machine was to rise from the ground. There was no noise, save that natural to a farming countryside – the birds, the animals, wind, weather and the shout of a ploughman to his team; and country scents still prevailed, flowers, trees, plants and new-mown hay, and all could be enjoyed from the skimming bicycle.

One particular feature of the golden era of the 'bike' was its liberating effect on women. They were no longer largely dependent on men for their transport, as they were in an equestrian world. The bike made them as free as men to move about at will, and in that sense the equal of men. It is hardly fortuitous therefore that the coming of the cycle-age saw women joining widely with men in physical sports; tennis, hockey, golf and so on. And that in turn influenced female fashions. Women took to wearing men's clothes, in particular men's shirts, collars and ties, and men's jackets. There are pictures of my aunts wearing such clothes. Skirts, however, remained decorously at ankle length, and so the bicycle had to be specially adapted to the female skirt. Some daring girls did anticipate their grand-daughters by wearing trousers for cycling, in the form of male knickerbockers.

And so the bicycle brought not only more mobility, but also a degree of social restiveness. More people would be away more from home, and more often. Women would fret for release from home restrictions, would demand more free-dom of movement, more opportunities to be out of the home. Was it the case perhaps that, riding on the bicycle, women's emancipation was on the way?

Could it, for instance, be that there was more than coincidence in the fact that it was in 1889, the year the pneumatic tyre was introduced, that Mrs Pankhurst founded the Women's Franchise League, the Suffragette Movement, which, like the velocipede itself, was to gain such velocity in the next two decades as to ensure for women in Britain an undreamed of degree of liberation? Perhaps history has yet to wake up to the enormous influence of the humble bicycle on the affairs of social man.

My grandparents were just too old to benefit from the liberating effects of the bicycle. They may have ridden the earlier uncomfortable and unsafe models, but my grandfather was already sixty-one years old when the pneumatic tyre came into use. Their transport at Correal therefore was still the riding horse, traps, gigs, horse-drawn carriages and coaches of various design.

At Correal, my grandparents were hard up for money. Although my grand-father's three thousand acre estate remained intact he was perennially short of spending cash. Perhaps the expenses of a large family, and the large household, conventional in those days, to support it, in addition to the outlay on the build-ing of Correal, had depleted his cash resources. But, according to my father and my Aunt Violet, he was also extravagantly concerned to keep up appearances. My father was known as a boy as 'Tats' because his clothes were always in tatters while, so he used to say, the unnecessary footmen had plush breeches. The eldest son, Percy, too, described his father as a spendthrift who lived beyond his means.

But there was also probably a more radical cause, which may not have been so clearly discernible at the time. In the 1870s there was a catastrophic collapse of British agriculture. There was a series of bad seasons. But a deeper cause was the opening up of the American prairies as grain-growing areas, which, together with the contemporary development of steam transport, railways and ships, enabled American farmers to undersell the British farmers even in British markets. Stubborn political belief in Free Trade did the rest, and the British landed gentry were decimated. In the last quarter of the nineteenth century the area under corn in England and Wales declined by two million acres; 25 per cent of the total. There was a corresponding increase in pasture but not in livestock because of the recent development of the refrigerated ship which caused that market to be undercut by cheap frozen meat from Australia and New Zealand.

Those were the conditions in which my grandfather had to survive on farming with a growing family. He could be blamed by his children for some extravagance, but ought he not more properly perhaps to be praised for surviving, and for contriving somehow to maintain what, in the context of his own time, he no doubt considered to be high standards which ought not lightly to be abandoned? None of us, as children, can – at any rate at the time – properly understand our parents' difficulties, or appreciate their labours and contrivances to overcome them. Nevertheless, my grandfather was doing an imprudent thing. In the changed circumstances in which he found himself, he was in fact pretending to be richer than he was. It is a very hard and painful thing to have to cut your standard of living. In his own time, many landowners in the British Isles generally were forced to sell up; and many more have had to do so since. The last thirty years of his life must have been much marred by financial anxiety, but when all is said and done, we have to give it to him that, battered though he may have been, he survived and kept his property intact.

He died at Correal on Boxing Day, 1903. He did not reach great old age. He was seventy-five. But he had become senile. Johnnie Lane, a contemporary of my father and my Aunt Violet, whose family were small tenants of my grandfather's, and who lived and worked on the estate, told me, when he himself was an old man, that, as a boy, he worked in and about the house at Correal. He said my grandfather used to meet him in the morning and say:

'Have you seen Johnnie Lane anywhere?'

Johnnie would reply, 'Yes Sir. It's me'.

My grandfather would then give him orders for the morning which would involve more work than could be done in a fortnight, and promptly forget all about it.

Johnnie told me one of his daily duties as a boy in winter was to lay and light fourteen fires in Correal house. Save for the cooking stove, the kitchen 'range', as it was called, heating in houses had not changed since the fifteenth century.

There was no electricity, no gas, no oil, no central heating, no air conditioning. Open fires of wood and 'turf' (peat) were the rule. Up to the fifteenth century the smoke from such fires had gone up through a hole in the roof. In the fifteenth century chimneys began to be built. They did not become general until a hundred years later when, in Tudor times, coal began to be more generally used. Possibly a little coal (still, when I was a boy, called 'sea-coal', the name given to it in London in the fourteenth century because it was shipped by sea from Tyneside) was used at Correal, but there were still never any coal fires at Killyon up to the time of my parents' death in the 1960s – nothing but wood and turf.

Johnnie Lane was an exceptionally attractive, gentle, quiet-spoken man, of great charm and natural courtliness, and he was a life-long friend of my father and my Aunt Violet. They grew up together, shooting, fishing, and larking around Correal. Like a true Irish countryman a scare-crow would not have thanked him for his clothes, and he wore an ancient battered hat at an angle; but he had an innate courtesy and dignity combined with a real warmth of friendliness. And he spoke in a quiet Irish voice, not volubly but with enviable eloquence. When my father sold the estate, I believe he gave Johnnie the house his family had lived in, together with some land. I am still in touch with the same family.

CHAPTER 31

The Family at the Turn of the Nineteenth/Twentieth Centuries

THE TURN OF THE nineteenth/twentieth centuries was the time when my four Magan aunts, and their brothers, my Uncle Percy and my father grew up. However much I might try, I could not do my Irish Magan aunts justice. I can neither re-create the marvellously free, natural, friendly, light-hearted atmosphere in which they led their fundamentally responsible and serious lives, nor can I adequately describe the nature and the depth of my own affection for them. As a boy, I knew them very well indeed. I saw them frequently and often stayed with them. Of course I did not then think of them in these terms. They were a part of the furniture of life as I knew it. But they were always a most agreeable, amusing, enlivening and interesting part of it. There was nothing emotional about my relationship with them. That would have spoilt it. They weren't that sort of women. We never kissed each other. We would have thought that absurd. They never used extravagant terms of endearment. I was never called darling, or anything of that sort. That might have smacked of condescension. Beyond calling them Aunt, and treating them with the natural courtesy due to aunts, our association was that of close and relaxed friendship full of laughs and jokes.

They were late Victorians, but truly the late Victorians were not, or were certainly not all, as stuffy, old-fashioned and dull, as the image that has been pinned on them. I knew them, so I can speak for them. There were Victorian restraints, but there was a tremendous liberation of the spirit in the late nineteenth century which was no less exhilarating than the restraints may have been stultifying. The image, therefore, of prudish, dull and unbending nineteenth century aunts, does many of them, certainly my Magan aunts, a great injustice.

The art of an age depicts its character. Think of the sparkling authors of that time, and the light-hearted things they wrote: *Three Men in a Boat*, *Alice in Wonderland*, *Ruthless Rhymes*, *The Wind in the Willows*, Conan Doyle, Stevenson, Kipling. Nothing stuffy about them. Or the music of Western Europe: Gilbert and Sullivan, Offenbach, Verdi, Rossini, the Strauss family, and many other composers, as well as dozens of other song and dance tune writers, pouring out music and tunes that were going to set centuries of their fellow human creatures whistling and beating time with joyous hearts. And the painters: need one say more than, 'Impressionists'. They lifted the spirit of art till it soared in the sunlight. And whenever before was there such vigorously joyous entertainment as the bright and light gaiety of the late Victorian music halls?

There was an uplifting of the spirit, a light-heartedness, and a zest for life, such as there had never been before, and has never been since. It was as though the butterfly of humanity had at last emerged in all its gay glory from the chrysalis. Would its flight prove to be all too short? That's another question.

History will perhaps come to see the closing years of the nineteenth century – the years of my aunts' maturing as young people – as one of the great pivotal points in human affairs. The coming of the cycle, the motorcar, the aeroplane, the telephone, telegraphy, wireless, antiseptics, the liberation of the talents and energies of women from much domestic drudgery; and of nearly everyone in large parts of the world from ignorance and lack of opportunity; above all, the release of a vast accretion of energy in the exploitation of oil resources. This was the take-off point for these and many other innovations which have in a century brought about enormously greater changes in human life than in its many tens of thousands of years of earlier existence. It was an exciting world to live in. No wonder it lifted the spirit and gave energy to those who experienced it.

The three eldest of my four Magan aunts were Emily Georgina (Blossie), born 1866, followed not long after by Muriel and Rachel. I will come later to the exceptional story of Violet, their youngest sister. These girls grew up in an age of social conscience; an age when upper class young ladies were emancipating themselves from mid-Victorian domestic bondage, and were not content merely to smoke cigars and enjoy the freedom of the bicycle, and to participate with men in outdoor sports. Under the leadership and inspiration of Florence Nightingale and others it began to be accepted that unmarried young ladies should learn useful occupations, and be able to support themselves.

Even though such ideas were gaining ground, they were not universally accepted, and it cannot be other than to the credit of these sisters that, given the landed gentry background in which they had been brought up, they all devoted themselves to useful work.

Blossie became a trained hospital nurse and practised that profession. Being tall, she had a splendid air in uniform of professional competence. Muriel also I think had some medical training, and then spent many years looking after a retired sailor at Capel in Surrey. Rachel devoted her time, talents and energies as a young woman to trying to improve the lot of the people of rural Ireland – the peasant proprietors and small tenants. It was a very evident need, daily before the eyes of Irish country-dwellers like my aunts, in view of the widespread poverty of those times.

She joined the Hon. Sir Horace Plunkett's 'Irish Agriculture Organisation Society' (IAOS) – as did her younger sister, Violet, and her younger brother, Shaen, my father. It was not a charitable organization. Its aim was to help people to help themselves through the acquisition of better and new skills, up-to-date methods, better stock and seed, co-operative purchasing and marketing, and corporate protection against those, like the 'gombeen men', whose role was comparable to that of the Indian bania, and who preyed on them ruthlessly.

It was non-political and non-sectarian. The founder and head, Horace Plunkett, was the rich son of a Protestant nobleman and landowner, Lord Dunsany. One of the other, most able, active and inspiring moving spirits was a Catholic priest, the Rev. Father Thomas Finlay. And although there was a strong accent on the co-operative nature of its activities, it was not socialist-inspired. As Father Finlay said:

The Co-operative Community is one in which humble men combine their efforts, and to some extent their resources ... We make no war upon capital or capitalist ... We aim at being capitalists ourselves, and amassing for the group the capital necessary to the operations carried on for the common benefit ... In doing so, we concede the same right to everyone. The idea of a war of classes is wholly alien to our movement.

In his recent book on the Irish Co-operative Movement, Mr Patrick Bolger includes pictures of Rachel and Violet Magan as young women, and refers to them as 'the beautiful sisters' who established Co-operatives in Roscommon and Westmeath – Magan country.

An editorial in the Irish Agricultural Organisation Society's weekly journal – *The Irish Homestead* – included this passage:

Miss Rachel Magan has succeeded in establishing a most successful Home Industry Society for girls of the district in which she lives, and at the present time a large number of young girls, who might otherwise have emigrated, are being employed in lace making at a house provided for the purpose, near Correal. Miss Magan procured an excellent teacher, and has visited the classes personally almost every day since they have been started.

My grandfather, Percy Magan, made no bones about his concern to uphold Protestantism in the face, as he saw it, of the menace of the Roman Catholic Church. In his will, for instance, he explicitly threatened to disinherit any of his daughters who might either turn Catholic or marry a Catholic. It may therefore seem surprising that Father Tom Finlay was not only a welcome guest at Correal, my grandfather's house in Roscommon, but was indeed so welcome and frequent a guest that a room was set permanently aside for him, and was known as 'Father Finlay's room'.

Despite the ascendancy of the Catholic Church in Southern Ireland in the past century and a half, there has never been any animosity on the grounds of religion between individual Protestants and Catholics. In the sense of upholding his own faith no-one could have been more staunchly Protestant than my father, even though he may not have been particularly religious, but nothing pleased him more than a social call from a local priest, particularly if the priest had been in the mission field and had interesting tales to tell of far-off lands.

And so, to a Southern Irish Protestant, there seems nothing strange about my very positively Protestant grandfather keeping a special guest room always ready for a Catholic priest.

Rachel's interests were more intellectual, and her tastes more feminine, than those of her sisters. She was more concerned about her dress; more interested in pretty things. It was she who ran my grandmother's flower garden. It is characteristic that it was she who instituted the lace-making.

She was young enough to have come under the spell of the beautiful dark waters of Lough Ree. She learnt to sail, and had a dashing scarlet sailing boat of her own.

In Ireland it is always as well to expect the unexpected. There is a story of how Blossie, the eldest sister, dealt with such an event.

At the gate of Ardaghcourt, the house just outside Athlone where my grandmother lived during the closing years of her life, there was a railway bridge. After the withdrawal of British rule from the south of Ireland in 1921, the newly formed 'Free State' army posted a guard of very green soldiers on the bridge. Blossie walked down the avenue to post a letter. As she reached the gate, a bullet whistled past her. She went up to the sentry who had fired it and asked:

'What did you do that for?'

He was trembling.

'She went off on me' he gasped.

'Well, mind her,' Blossie replied. 'She nearly went off on me.'

'Yes, Ma'am,' touching his cap peak with his forefinger. Military salutes were not yet second nature to him.

In the mid-1930s, when flying was still a rare experience for ordinary people, Sir Alan Cobham, the celebrated aviator, who at that time had a business giving people short pleasure flights in open cockpit light aircraft, brought his aeroplane to Athlone and gave flights from a field at Glynnwood (where I was born) near Moate. Nothing would do Blossie, then around seventy years of age, but to have a 'flip'. So, arrayed in all the clutter of an elderly lady of the time, umbrella, handbag, mackintosh and so on, she repaired to Moate, paid her money, and mounted the aircraft. But if Alan Cobham thought he was going to get away with a few circuits of the field he was mistaken. Blossie had her own ideas, and Cobham was politely but firmly ordered to fly to Lough Ree, and to circle some of her favourite spots on the lake including St Marks, then owned by her sister Violet. She belonged to the generation epitomized by the vignette of conversation overheard between two elderly ladies in a tea-shop ' ... the most exhilarating thing I know, dear, is harpooning whales'.

Muriel, like Blossie, did not marry. She had a warm heart, was always good humoured, and invariably amusing, and she was safe and comfortable. She had a very positive personality, and innate authority. There was about her a quite unselfconscious aura of assurance that could not but cause others both to respect her, and to feel absolute confidence in her. Albeit with a light touch, she could have run anything. When my grandmother had grown too old to look after her house, it seemed natural that Muriel, when she was there, should slip into the role of chatelaine. Things just quietly happened. There was no bossiness.

I was away at school when she died – too young at fifty-five years of age. I received a postcard from my mother telling me that 'Aunt M.' had died unexpectedly. I clearly remember reading it with a numbing incomprehension of the works of God, as I walked across the quadrangle to tea.

Rachel was the only one of the sisters to marry. At the time when she died during the Second World War, I was overseas. That led, after the war, when I was at home for a short spell, to a curious little incident. Her husband was her Roman Catholic first cousin, Hugh Dwyer, one of the three soldier sons of the famous psychiatrist who had married my grandfather's sister. Hugh was probably a lapsed Catholic – I never saw him go to church – and Rachel remained staunchly Protestant. They had no children. A regular officer of the Connaught Rangers, he was invalided out of the army from the Mesopotamian campaign during the First World War.

Thereafter he grew into an amiable eccentric. He was short, somewhat portly, benign and cherubic. He always wore a winged stiff collar. He was clean-shaven, and clean nuts about sun-spots which were accountable for everything, earth-quakes, railway accidents, floods, droughts, miscarriages – the lot. He had a great store of worthless information collected largely from crank astrologers, doubtful astronomers, quasi-scientific journals and the like, which he recounted with relish and plausible conviction. His idiosyncrasies were boundless. He was prepared always for the worst. If he went for a walk, he took both coat and waterproof, and two hats, one a waterproof to cover the other; an umbrella always, and I believe a stick as well. Although genial, he was enormously suspicious, but his suspicions were directed not so much at those around him as towards anonymous, shadowy, malevolent beings waiting to catch him unawares. He did not like writing letters for fear of eavesdropping. When he did write, he often wrapped the text, for protection, in several sheets of plain paper before putting it into the envelope.

When I returned to Britain after the war, following my Aunt Rachel's death, he asked me to lunch with him at a well-known London hotel. During lunch he told me that Rachel had wanted me to have some small pieces of family silver which she had, and which he had brought with him and would give to me.

After lunch we went into the 'foyer'. The hotel was a particularly cosmopolitan one, and no doubt bristling with house detectives. I waited while Hugh went to the cloakroom, whence he returned with a small locked black leather bag of rather sinister appearance. He was at his most furtive and suspicious and, taking me over to the wall, turned his back on the foyer and began rummaging in the bag, fishing out silver teaspoons and shovelling them into my pocket. I expected to be arrested at any moment, but the operation was successfully concluded without our having to 'give an account of ourselves'.

Although she was the eldest, Blossie outlived Muriel and Rachel, and died, aged eighty, in 1947. I am much indebted to her for the bequest of a very small attaché case of newspaper cuttings and other family papers which have been useful to me in compiling this memoir. My father said of her that she had a very strong old-fashioned loyalty to the tribe. She kept a journal, many volumes of which have survived; and her scissors snipped away throughout life at the 'hatches, matches and dispatches', and other cuttings – grist to the mill of Irish historical urges. I only regret that I did not adequately tap the enormous amount of family information stored in her mind. She had in her make-up something of the instincts of an ancient Irish bard.

The youngest of my grandparents' four daughters was Violet Augusta Magan, born 1876. She was young enough, when my grandfather moved into his new house on his Roscommon estate, to feel that it was truly home to her. Home was that open wilderness of rolling grassland hills, and small fields; that chequerboard of loose grey stone walls, and boggy bottoms, not far from the ever changing, with wind and calm, shine and rain, night and day, great dark waters of Lough Ree. She lived at one with wild nature; the call of the plover and the curlew, flocks of wild duck, skeins of migrating geese, the drummings of snipe at nesting. These and all the other country sights, sounds and scents were a part of her. And she was more competent in a boat than many a seaman, and no less familiar with the considerable local fishing industry. Great quantities of fish were caught both in the lake, and at the eel weir at Athlone; and later in life she owned her own draw-nets on the lake.

A more distant, but ever present, influence, was the garrison town of Athlone, six miles away; a thriving market town with good shops, a junction for two railways, straddling both banks of the great Shannon waterway, with a vigorous and renowned woollen industry, and all the bustle and fun of the soldiers, and the symbol that they were to the Ascendancy of its deep loyalty to the Crown. Athlone and the lake remained the background to the whole of Violet's life, a background of water almost as much as land.

What was the magic force that Violet radiated? We are all different. But there are few so rare as she. Shakespeare must have had such a one in mind as the image of his 'lass unparalleled'. She was slightly built. She was quiet. She was modest. She never obtruded herself. She was never theatrical, dramatic or emphatic. She was much too innately natural, and far too exquisitely humorous, to be capable of any pretensions. She was wholly unassuming. She had a great, but quite unsentimental, and unromantic, love of country things, and affection for the cottage folk of Ireland. An obscure country girl one might think, happy in an atmosphere of dogs and horses. But I suppose that if you had mentioned 'Miss Violet' anywhere in the counties of Roscommon, Westmeath or Longford, in much of Meath, Kildare and the King's County, and many other and more remote parts of central, west and southern Ireland, there would have been no doubt in anyone's mind whom you meant. There could be only one 'Miss Violet'; and deep affection would have welled up with the mention of her name.

Respect for her did not stem from external trappings. She needed no trappings, and was not concerned to have any. She did not drive in a carriage and pair. She went everywhere, indefatigably, perfectly naturally, and covering enormous distances, in often rough country, and rough weather, and alone, on a bicycle.

What was the secret of this rather frail girl? With what capacities, what talents, what gifts, what flair had nature endowed her? She was, of course, clever, but not intellectual. I do not think she had read much. Indeed, almost her only reading appeared to be local country papers, and sporting journals such as *Horse and Hounds*. Because schoolmen are necessarily for the most part intellectual, cleverness and academic intellectuality have come to be confused. Violet's cleverness was penetrating insight and balanced judgement. Her inner computer and gyroscope were both of the highest quality and perfectly attuned. Although the least obtrusive member of the family, she was the most influential. It was almost automatic within the family not to take an important decision until one 'had had a word with Violet'. I think she would still have been the focal point of the family even had her more assertive older brother Percy remained in Ireland.

She got her own way in a pretty wide field of affairs, and did so not because she thought she was more right than others. She was too modest for that. She got her way because she was right, and demonstrably so to everyone else. And because, like the Duke of Wellington and Nelson, and all others who rightly judge the priorities, she rolled up her sleeves and did the job herself when she had to, or couldn't trust anyone else to do it right.

When she joined Sir Horace Plunkett's Irish Agricultural Organisation Society, she made poultry her speciality. Every Irish cottage kept poultry – 'hins', in the vernacular. They were the province of the wife. Her normal way of cashing the surplus eggs was to barter them at the nearest store for groceries. The tradesman got two profits, one on the value of the groceries, the other on the sale of the eggs. The wife got an exchange of goods, but no profit. Better breeds of poultry, better feeding for them, increased egg laying, better grading, co-operative marketing and purchasing of feeding stuffs and equipment, could enormously increase the egg production of Ireland and the economy of the hen-wife in the cottage, and that was Violet's message.

She travelled the rough lonely roads of remote Ireland endlessly on her 'cycle.

She stayed anywhere she could get a clean bed. She lectured, advised, helped, informed, encouraged and involved herself in setting up local organizations to keep the good work on a permanent basis. She was in and out of every cottage. Poultry was not her only interest. She did whatever useful work she could to further the benefits of the co-operative movement. She was as wholly unpolitical as was the movement in Ireland.

After her father's death, she and her mother and sisters moved from Correal, and from Roscommon, and settled on the other shore, the east, or Westmeath, shore of Lough Ree. She therefore relinquished the secretaryship of the local co-operative movement in Roscommon. *The Irish Homestead* burst into print again:

> *We believe Miss Violet Magan has, as a volunteer worker in the co-operative movement, done as much or more than any volunteer worker in Ireland to forward its aims, and, if we only had one Violet Magan in every county, we could generate a vital warmth and kindliness in it which is not too present always.*

In addition to her work in the co-operative movement, she and my father and two close friends, George Moony of the Doon, and the Hon. Arthur Handcock, established an estate agents and auctioneers business in Athlone. For one reason and another, all the men had, by degrees, to relinquish their interest, and my Aunt Violet continued to run it single-handed till she was seventy years of age.

In whatsoever undertakings Violet involved herself, hers was the leading role. It was not that she tried to exert, or wished to exert, or even did exert, any special authority. It just was that everyone was drawn to her because she put forward the most good sense. She did not try to lay down the law, did not pretend to be better, or know better, than others. She quite naturally treated everyone else with friendly equality, and conversed quietly with them, but what she had to say was all pure gold and salted with delicious wit and humour.

Her influence was enormous. But she was not motivated by abstractions or theories. There just were an awful lot of things under her feet in Ireland that needed to be done, and she got on with it and did them. She had lived cheek by jowl with dreadful poverty and want in Connaught. She told me, for instance, that, when she was quite a small girl, there was a typhus outbreak. She was not allowed to go into cottages where people were affected, but her mother used to give her bowls of cooked and warm food which she used to carry out and place on rocks near the cottages and then call out that it was there. And she told my sister Mollie that she had once witnessed an 'eviction', a sickening spectacle, such as she hoped never to see again. There was endless work to be done for the rural people of Ireland, which, for the most part, with her help and encouragement, they would be able to do for themselves.

She had wretched health and had a number of serious illnesses and underwent a series of severe operations and other surgery. But all that seemed to make no difference to the energy and vitality with which she led her life.

She was always well and quietly dressed, but had little interest in pretty, feminine things. She had no feminine romanticism. She told my sister Mollie that she had not felt attracted to marriage. She liked animals. She always had a horse or two, and a dog. They were her friends, not her belongings. But she was not horsey or doggy. Towards people she was highly compassionate, but without sentimentality. She saw the funny side of everyone and of all situations.

While she remained essentially feminine, there was a masculine cast of objectivity about her thought processes that caused men to accept her on equal terms in their affairs, and to respect her judgement. She was shrewd and never fooled. Rogues, blackguards and scamps were by no means unknown to her, and she was well able for them. It was to fall to her to run the Magan estates, and the Biddulph estate of my mother's family, as well as other estates. In that work, and in the administration of the co-operative movement, not only did she have to work with men, but she was for the most part in control of them, and they were more than ready to accept the sensible policies she formulated.

She enjoyed hunting; not with swanky packs, but almost exclusively with the little local pack kennelled just outside Athlone, the South Westmeath Hunt, of which she was for many years the Honorary Secretary of the Hunt Committee. In other words she ran it. It was run on a shoestring. The only paid hunt servant was the kennelman. The whip, Paddy Fitzpatrick, a real Irish genius with horses and hounds, was a volunteer. If additional whip services were needed, several members of the field were ready to oblige. They had a large and varied country on both sides of the Shannon, and showed good sport.

She was a really brilliant helmswoman. There she could outclass the men in the by no means easy sailing conditions on the Shannon lakes. There was a day when, in a series of different boats, she won every race on the card.

She and my father were inseparable friends all their lives. It was said that she spoilt him, which was true. But he had immense respect for her and her brains. She was the only woman whom he regarded as the equal, and even the superior, of males. She did not shoot, but she enjoyed going with him on his shooting days.

With children she was a Pied Piper. They found her irresistible. She took very little notice of them unless they sought to involve her in whatever they were doing, or wanted to involve themselves in whatever she might be doing. She just let them get on with whatever they were at, and did not frustrate them. Children knew instinctively that they could trust her not to be what they would think unreasonable. They gave her their confidence unreservedly. They also found her ever amusing, and always interesting. She for her part, was, at the same time, shrewdly understanding.

She was unflinchingly courageous. Following the 1916 rebellion, Ireland had a decade of 'troubles'. In land-hungry Ireland, the landlords and their agents became prime targets for the most ruthless and brutal of the citizenry. Ireland reverted to murder and arson. And because Violet was managing a number of estates, mostly for friends and relatives who, through age or incapacity, were unable to do so for themselves, she was in the firing line, and knew it. She had many warnings. She also had among the country people many friends in the right places who gave her information valuable for her safety. But she was not going to be deterred from the work that had to be done. She continued to pedal the lonely roads on her bicycle. She had a motor vehicle, but the 'cycle was often the better mount, for many of the roads were made impassable to heavier traffic by blown-up bridges, felled trees, and other obstacles and obstructions. Usually one could get by with a 'cycle.

Then came a dark December day in 1924. My maternal great uncle Middleton Biddulph's beautiful house, Rathrobin, in the Kings County, had been burnt and bombed and totally destroyed by the I.R.A. some months earlier, on 18 April, 1923. Middleton Biddulph and his wife were both old and invalid and were living in London. Violet Magan continued to run the estate, and visited it frequently. That day, 8 December, 1924, she went there. As usual, she took her bicycle on the train from Athlone to Tullamore, and from there cycled the seven miles of lonely road to Rathrobin. On the way she called at Screggan Post Office, half way to Rathrobin. While there, a man enquired who owned her 'cycle which was leaning against the wall. The man had been seen at the post office a few times before.

Violet did her work at Rathrobin and, in the darkening December afternoon, set off for her lone return ride through the desolate countryside to Tullamore to catch the train back to Athlone. She had not gone far along the road between the hamlets of Mountbolus and Screggan when she was set upon by three armed men, pulled off her bicycle, knocked down, her mouth forcibly opened, and poison, in the form of green paint, poured down her throat. She was then tied up in sacks, thrown into a wood, and left for dead.

She managed to struggle free from the sacks and ropes and, though terribly ill, to crawl back to the road. A passing man found her and went to Ross House, not far away, where lived a Doctor O'Regan, to whom the man said that he had found a lady lying unconscious by the roadside. The doctor immediately got out his motorcar and went to her. He found her sitting semi-conscious with her bicycle leaning against the bank beside her. She asked to be taken to her friend Dr Kennedy in Tullamore, which Dr O'Regan did. Dr Kennedy put her to bed in his house, and treated her as best he could, though he did not know what particular poison had been administered to her.

When she did not return home on time, the family, knowing the constant dangers she ran, became anxious. Michael Hopkins – 'Mike' to everyone far and wide – who had been a member of my grandmother's household ever since he grew up, was the only man in the house. He set out to look for her, and his enquiries took him eventually to Dr Kennedy's house in Tullamore.

She never wholly recovered. Her mind and body were both affected. For some years her mind worked only very slowly, and she could talk only with some difficulty. Her already frail body became more so. But she would not give in. Slowly she returned to adequately good health and, as she regained her strength and faculties, she gradually resumed all her former activities, and defied the gunmen, and continued her estate agent work for another twenty years.

The Irish Free State judge who subsequently tried one of the men, and who must by then have been well used to the worst excesses of Irish brutality, described this as an appalling act, and said he 'did not think it would be possible for such savagery to exist anywhere'. Neither he, nor my aunt, nor anyone else who knows the Irish, would judge the whole nation by such an act.

The last years of her life she lived at her lovely property, St Marks, beside her beloved Lough Ree, and was looked after by Mike Hopkins and his marvellous wife Lena. She said to me that the lake helped to dispel loneliness – which she felt after Blossie's death. The lake, she said, was always alive, always changing, even with every cloud, always full of movement.

From there, during the years of the Second World War, although she was by then an elderly woman, she carried on her estate work from her office in Athlone. St Marks is some nine miles from Athlone. There was no petrol for motor cars. So she did the journey daily by bike, or sometimes part by boat and part by bike.

I last saw her when I spent a night at St Marks in the autumn of 1950 just before I returned from leave to Egypt where I was stationed at the time. Although she was very frail, she insisted when I left that she would come in my car with me up the long avenue which runs along the brow of the hill and along its entire length overlooks the wide, sparkling, island-dotted lake, away to the Roscommon shore, and the setting sun. She said she would walk back and shut the gates. Although we neither of us said anything, we both knew why she did it. We knew it was the last time.

She died the next year, aged seventy-five, on 9 September, 1951.

That, then, ends my small and altogether inadequate tribute to my splendid Magan aunts. They were such wonderfully sensible and natural and unaffected people. None of them had any vices. Drinking and smoking they thought an absurdity. Gambling they considered the height of folly. They had been sickened by their father's experiences of the extravagances of keeping up appearances. They were a good influence on everyone. Above all they were funny.

My Magan grandparents had two other children; the oldest and the youngest; the two boys; my uncle Percy, and my father, Shaen Magan. As Percy emigrated, I shall leave his exceptional story for a few pages more. Now, I must describe my father. Filial obligations dictate that he must have a chapter to himself. Anyway, he would not have been satisfied with anything less! He differed from the others. He was the most colourful; and he meant to stay that way.

My Father

ARTHUR TILSON SHAEN MAGAN, my father, was the sixth and last child of my grandparents, Percy and Annie Magan.

Both my father and mother were unusual and interesting people who, throughout their very long lives, were well known in Ireland both in the society into which they were born, and also to a much wider field of people of all classes. Rather, therefore, than let them sink into characterless oblivion, I shall take the risk, with due deference to the proprieties, of trying to tell of my father, and later of my mother, as they really were.

Anyone reading this who knew my father may at this point be holding their breath. There is, they will think, a certain difficulty in giving a rounded and truthful picture of him. How is that going to be overcome without embarrassment? I do not think it so difficult. I shall grasp the nettle and get it out of the light straight away.

A. J. P. Taylor, the historian, comes of a Lancastrian family. He has said that Lancastrians regard themselves as honest, but, honest or not, he holds that Lancashire men are without exception romancers. His father he says never gave his mother an absolutely accurate and truthful account, throughout their married life, of what he had been doing, even if he had only gone out for half an hour. An embroidered yarn was more interesting to himself and, he might have hoped, to her, than the truth. Even if he intended to be truthful, things were bound to come out distorted. By that account my father might have been a Lancastrian.

I find nothing offensive in A. J. P. Taylor recording that of his father, or indeed of Lancastrians in general. On the contrary, it adds a dimension to our interest in them. It means we are likely to be dealing with people who are more colourful than dull.

Like the Lancastrians my father was all his life given to flights of fancy, and was most emphatically more colourful than dull. In business matters, and other affairs of practical importance, particularly where money was concerned – no doubt like the Lancastrians than whom none could be more hard-headed about 'brass' – he was perfectly factual and precise. In other matters he gave his imagination free rein. His romancing was innate to him. However much he had been schooled or disciplined, something of it would have remained. But he did not use it to deceive. He used it to entertain. It was a theatrical performance in the guise of everyday life. 'All the world's a stage' was true for him. He did not want to cheat you. But he did want to make his world more entertaining both for himself and for you by dramatizing it, with himself the principal actor. And he did indeed succeed in making it seem very interesting and exciting for his audience. Nor would he have been at all concerned to reform himself. He was very well pleased with himself the way that he was. Perhaps there was here something of the hyperbole of the old chiefs, and the histrionics of the ancient bards. At all events, he was a uniquely striking character whose large figure and exceptional personality were very well known in central Ireland throughout the active years of his adult life, and he was very well and widely liked.

It would be nonsense to write about him and to seek to gloss over this universally known characteristic. But that said, it is nevertheless a trait that does have a danger. In less tolerant societies than the Lancastrians or the Irish, or if the romancer comes up against a rigid, uncomprehending, intolerant puritan, he may be more harshly judged, dubbed a liar, and therefore, *ipso facto*, not to be trusted in any matter; and then there may be trouble, unwarranted perhaps, but serious nevertheless. That was to be my father's misfortune.

He was born on 21 May, 1880, at Gorey, Co. Wexford when his father was fifty-two years old. It was the year in which my grandfather moved from Marfield to Kilcleagh, Moate. My father's early boyhood was therefore spent at Kilcleagh. But when he was eight years old the family moved to the west of the Shannon, to Correal, Co. Roscommon in Connaught.

He was never sent to school. He never attended any school of any sort in his life. Because he lived in a wild, sparsely inhabited area where there were no near neighbouring children of his own sort, he had everything his own way. He did, of course, know the country boys, and some of them were his lifelong friends. But that was not the same thing. They were hardly in a position to apply the chastening restraints we receive from our peers.

He received some lessons from the rector at Moate, and I suppose had similiar instruction at Correal. There were no doubt governesses, and perhaps tutors. But the net result for my father was a poor education. Apart from reading and writing, his only formal academic knowledge was some mathematics. Curiously, in that day and age, and taught partly by parsons, he had no knowledge of the classics (except in English translation); and he learnt no foreign languages, though he had a smattering of Irish, which was still quite widely spoken in Roscommon at that time. He had literary tastes and interests, which remained unfortunately uncultivated. Coupled with them he had an exceptional memory for English verse and prose. To the end of his life he could quote voluminously and accurately. He also found some interest in the political history of the late eighteenth and early nineteenth centuries. He liked to quote the epigrams and aphorisms of Burke, Pitt (father and son), Castlereagh, Napoleon, Wellington and others of that period.

By inclination he was magnetically drawn away from his rural roots, and towards the world of professional men whose influence in, and importance to, the weal of the Realm had been growing ever since the end of the Wars of the Roses; and he subscribed at heart to their codes. But his lack of formal education, together with the circumstances of his early life, which necessitated that even in adolescence he should both earn his living and involve himself in propping up his father's tottering estate, ruled out any chance of his obtaining a professional qualification. It was to be a lifelong handicap to him that he did not acquire the personal and intellectual disciplines that schooling, higher education and professional training gave to so many of his contemporaries in his own stratum of society. His aptitudes were not academic, but he had a quick, enquiring and inventive mind. He had a natural numeracy. He was attracted in particular to mechanics and engineering, and to finance. Given the education, there is little doubt that he would have chosen a professional career in engineering, banking, stockbroking, or some comparable field. There was one job that he might with a bit of luck have had which would have suited him well and which he would have done well, but that was not to be.

Throughout his life he felt himself to be at a disadvantage among men who had had a formal education, and particularly because it was an age when education had become part of the social armament and equipment at any rate of those who wanted to be accepted on equal terms by the English upper classes. In Ireland he was safe. He was known for who he was. To Englishmen of his own class he was – and I am sure felt he was – apt to be seen as someone who had not been to a public school. They were times when you could still just about get by socially with, 'educated privately', but it was better to have been at Eton or elsewhere, and he talked a good deal vicariously about life at such great schools based on what he had heard from his friends.

He never came to terms with this problem. On the contrary he tried to put a seemingly bold – but in fact absurd – face on it by adopting the attitude, 'look at me, as an example of a man all the more successful for never having been to school'. It may have been reasonable for William Blake and others to claim that geniuses are better for being unschooled, but the modern man of professional competence, the lawyer, the doctor, the engineer must, I fear, be equipped with a comprehensive education. Genius alone isn't enough.

My father's life was, indeed, a mass of contradictions. As the youngest child, and only boy at home, following his elder brother Percy's emigration to America, he was the centre of the considerable interest of his mother and four older sisters, and of an ageing, and perhaps by then somewhat indulgent, father. He could hardly have failed to develop a sense of personal importance which was even further underlined by being the son and heir of the local landowner. Throughout the remainder of his working life the innately heaven-born aristocrat struggled within him with the contradictory, uncomfortably insecure, inadequately tutored, man of professional aspirations.

Finally, at the age of fifty-four, he gave up the struggle, retired into Killyon Manor, reverted largely to ancient Irish type, fattened a few cattle, planted some timber, engaged in a little dilettante horticulture, shot, fished, tended his investments, and lived largely in a world of fantasy. He dreamed of himself as an educated, professional man, and talked of engineering, business, and financial affairs as though personally involved in some undefined way. He quoted verse, held court when he could get an audience, talked about the classics, claiming to me one day that he was glad to have time to read Greek in the original – even though he knew that I knew that he knew no Greek – and became progressively more eccentric. The aspiring modern professional man lapsed by default into the image of an idiosyncratic Irish chieftain even though he himself scorned and ridiculed the very few who consciously adopted that role with their saffron kilts, bagpipes and so forth.

Brought up in his formative years in the wild, undulating, rocky hills and marshlands of Roscommon, he was bred a countryman. His rural interests were, for all that, limited. He did not like horses. He did not hunt. In so colourfully spectacular an arena as the hunting field, only one place would have been tolerable to my father, the centre of affairs; the focus for all eyes; the man with the horn; the Master. But he could have afforded neither the time nor the money. Nor would he have been any good. He lacked the necessary instinctive rapport with, and interest in, animals. Horses and hounds could never have captured his enthusiasm. They bored him.

He did not become a fisherman till late in life, and fished rather indifferently, but with fair success. He had a real interest in estate management, but his only special farming interest, and it was genuine and life-long, was in fattening cattle on grass. The blood of the ancient graziers was in his veins. Late in life he developed an interest in forestry. He enjoyed boating and sailing, but was not especially competent. I once asked his sister Violet how good a helmsman he was, for he boasted a good deal about his early sailing days. She said he was too 'hysterical' to be really good. 'Hysterical' was her choice of word.

He used to tell a nice sailing story about himself, which incidentally revealed something of his excitability. He and Violet jointly employed a boatman, Johnnie Duffy, a very competent man in a boat. They sailed together for many years, and most successfully. At a critical moment in a race, my father, running down the boat to do something or other, found himself obstructed by Johnnie.

'Get to hell out of my way, Johnnie,' he yelled.

Johnnie, who was as phlegmatic as my father was excitable, replied dryly.

'And I might be in your way there, too.'

My father's chief country interest was shooting. He was a consistently very good shot, with never an off day, well able to hold his own with the best shots in the British Isles. He was an excellent cover shot. But his heart was in the wild bogs in which he had spent his boyhood. Wet to his knees from early morning to sundown, he tramped, and waded, and jumped 'drains' – as the Irish called ditches – indefatigably, with one or two kindred spirits like Arthur Handcock, shooting snipe, duck, golden plover and woodcock mostly. In the half hour of dusk there was always the duck and golden plover flight. The plover he called on a whistle made for him by a poacher when he was a boy. He had a real hunter's knowledge and understanding of wind, weather, the lie of the land, and the reactions of the birds to these elemental influences. He never carried waterproof clothing. If it rained hard enough he sheltered under a bush. Otherwise he took no notice of it. He had an uncanny sense of weather. When we were sheltering under a thorn bush, he would suddenly say: 'Come on. It's over now.'

It would seem to me to be raining as hard as ever, but sure enough it would clear up in a few minutes.

He was no games player. He was too unco-ordinated physically. He used to talk of his boxing and rugby football prowess in early life, an almost sure sign that he had had, as I would suppose, little aptitude for either. But on his feet, walking, and more particularly strolling at slow pace, and especially in his venerable years, he had a most distinguished appearance. He was almost 6 feet 5 inches tall, and his stoop added, if anything, to his imposing figure. He was spare of flesh, but large of frame, and well-proportioned. A splendid ploughshare nose, and noticeably fine hands, put the finishing touches to a striking and near-regal appearance.

But there was nothing of coronets and ermine about his dress. He had a smart suit or two of great antiquity. He was always spotlessly clean. But his daily clothes were ancient and well patched. His favourite jacket was made for him by a country tailor in the year of his marriage. He used to say, 'It will see me out'. It did; but was more patches than original. That sort of attire, together with old shoes, baggy grey flannel trousers, and the whole ensemble crowned in his later years by a discarded, battered shooting hat left behind at Killyon by an old friend, did nothing whatever to detract from the rugged dignity of this Irish *grand seigneur* whose striking personality, on his own ground, in the Irish countryside, together with his strong ringing voice, which was seldom silent, cut a figure twice as large as life.

He had no artistic leanings, but he sang hymns in church with vigorous enjoyment in rich, vibrant tones, more or less tunefully, and more or less in time. He liked good rousing tunes and melodies. A good refrain excited him into beating time energetically, while inexpertly emitting a kind of hissing whistle in imitation. But his greatest pleasure was talking. He was innately loquacious; and his capacious memory, quick mind, genuine, if superficial, interest in a wide variety of subjects; his excited enthusiasm for whatever had caught his fancy at the moment, and his endless capacity for plausible invention and embroidery, together with considerable histrionic talent, all combined to enable him to talk interestingly about almost anything under the sun, provided his audience was not too well informed about the particular matter in hand.

He was, however, no fool. He was careful in these matters, and did not leave his exhibitions of conversational prowess to chance. He had a technique of verbal scouting to discover the holes in his audiences' knowledge. He would then concentrate on their weak subjects and avoid topics about which they might be better informed than himself. He preferred women as an audience. They were safer than men, and they liked him. He knew how to flatter them, and did so, and enjoyed their response. He was quite openly, but in no way improperly, flirtatious. He was, indeed, very good company, and warmed irresistibly towards other people.

He was totally undomesticated. He could hardly boil a kettle. Babies he ignored. Doting mothers could expect no satisfaction on that score. But, instead, they would get the full treatment on their own account, and so were probably quite content to settle for what they got. For small children he had no time. They were in competition with him. They wanted what he wanted – constant attention. He was essentially very masculine. Children in their middle years, and young people generally, were a splendid, safe and uncritical audience whom he enjoyed, and they loved to listen to him. And if any boy or young man wanted to be taught about shooting, my father would go to endless trouble.

He certainly had in him something of a great teacher. No-one would have stayed away from school, lest they missed something too good to lose. He would have been unendingly interesting.

Many men, too, if they were not over-critical as to fact, and particularly if they had the customary Irishman's tolerance, found him very good company, and his talk engaging. Those pedantic enough to prefer precision and unvarnished truth, might have found his embellishments, embroideries, and theatricality irritating, but I am not sure. He was so extraordinarily plausible that even I, late in life, could be readily taken in by him. Perhaps he should have been an actor, but I doubt that acting requires histrionic virtuosity so much as rigorous disciplines; and that would not have suited my father. He would have kept *ad libbing* himself into the limelight.

He had indeed a seemingly compulsive need for the limelight, and for anyone to challenge his right to it was palpably displeasing to him. If someone else seemed to be holding the conversation, he could go to childish lengths to attract attention back to himself. He would sulk visibly, or start making noises, or try to change the topic of conversation to one of his own choosing. But there were times when he would submit to turn audience himself if he thought he could pick up something of interest to add to his own repertoire and store of colourful knowledge. Anyone 'in the know'; anyone 'home from the wars'; anyone from far-flung foreign parts; anyone with something new up his sleeve, a doctor with a new cure, a surgeon with some account of up-to-date surgery, a manufacturer with a new product, an adventurer fresh from a new adventure. All my father needed was a few new facts from such people. He could supply the rest, and mould the whole to his needs.

As a boy, I developed a great affection for him. I think I was just the right kind of audience. I was a magpie for general knowledge, and, having an elephantine Irish memory, I amassed a great store of superficial and useless information – a sort of walking *Guinness Book of Records*. I greatly enjoyed my father's endless talk. He took me everywhere with him, and regaled me with information – often exaggerated, and not too accurate – about everything under the sun. At his best he was a wonderful companion, if you were not too critical, and I was not. Also, by temperament, as a boy, I was endlessly patient, and could, and often did, *faut de mieux*, wait hours while he talked without ceasing to other people when he was going his rounds.

Long before I was old enough to carry a gun, I was taken on all his shooting expeditions. I carried a bag. I don't know what it sometimes weighed with a mixed lot of pheasants, wild duck, rabbits, snipe, golden plover, woodcock. But it was a point of honour that I staggered on all day through bogs to my knees, bracken to my waist, gorse and thorns over my head, scratched, torn, wet and blistered, and did it cheerfully and without a grumble. But males like hardship. It has its own secret satisfaction. And I enjoyed it. And at the end of the day, my fingers so cold I couldn't undo the laces of my boots or my buttons – gloves were not allowed; they were for softies; only mittens – it would be a blessed relief to get into the shelter of some welcoming cottage and change into dry things – and my father would still be talking and puffing at his pipe.

But in later life he did often strain even my affection for him to near breaking point. He could not bear that any of his family might seem to outshine him. As his own powers and vitality waned, and those of the younger generations correspondingly increased, his efforts to hold the centre of the stage became increasingly bizarre. In the end, all that was left to him was to be a nuisance. His demanding egocentricity caused him to develop a technique of deliberately and consistently, and often subtly, annoying other people in order to focus attention upon himself.

As a man in his sixties, and still in full command of his faculties, he had to undergo an operation in a Dublin nursing home. During the succeeding ten days he had many visitors, and his lady friends came and petted and comforted him. After that, the novelty wore off for everyone. The visitors were fewer. My father got bored. There was no stage: no limelight: no drama: no audience. But his instinct for the histrionic did not fail him. He decided to die. At any rate, if he said he was going to die, no-one could safely ignore him, or deny him the spiritual comforts of a dying man. So he acted out the part, and gasped out a request for the last rites of mother church, and demanded that they should be administered by no less a person than a bishop; nothing but the best would do for him on so solemn an occasion. And that is what he got. It was a triumphant success. After

31 *Violet Magan*

32 *Colonel Shaen Magan and his cattle*

33 *Mrs Kathleen Magan fishing
   at Killyon Manor*

34 *Assheton Biddulph M.F.H.*

36 Motor-car picnic – Colonel Middleton Biddulph, his wife Vera (left) and her maid 'Weston', 1920

35 Florence, wife of Assheton Biddulph

37 Rathrobin from the lake

*38 Ass cart picnic –
Rathrobin, 1902*

*39 Going to church
in a side-car,
1902*

*40 Vera Biddulph
(with dog) and
friend,* au jardin *–
Rathrobin, 1904*

41 Vera Biddulph
(left) and friends,
1904

42 Middleton Biddulph
(wearing cap) afloat, 1911

43 Vera Biddulph
with Paul Wallace
coachman

44 Edwardians among the cattle – Rathrobin, 1902

45 Mares and foals – Rathrobin, 1903

46 *The Ascendancy goes to church – Rathrobin, 1902*

47 *Tea time for the Ascendancy, Vera Biddulph (left), 1901*

48 Irish country people, 1902

49 Irish schoolgirls, 1901

50 *The author, aged 11, with his father at Rathrobin*

51 *The author as a young man fishing an Irish river*

that the nurses bundled him off home. He was becoming a nuisance.

With his great height and large frame, he was physically larger than life. He was an outstanding figure whom no-one could overlook or ignore. And he not only was larger than life, but he himself felt larger than life. And everything associated with himself must also be larger, or interestingly smaller, than reality.

My sister Mollie once met a man in England who, learning that she was Shaen Magan's daughter, said to her: 'Ask him if he remembers me. If he does he will tell you either that I am the most brilliant man in the world, or the worst fool that God ever poured into a pair of breeches.' It is thus little to be wondered at that, even in Ireland, he had a reputation for hyperbole.

If he went into a shop, which he seldom did, he expected the whole place to stop in its tracks and attend to him, a result he usually contrived to achieve. He would quickly create an occasion to draw particular attention to himself. He would tell a little story, or recite an apt little piece of verse. He would address himself warmly to the shop attendants and treat them with great courtesy. A little imperious he might seem, but certainly not aloof. After wasting ten minutes of everybody's time, he would take his regal departure having bought two-pennyworth of nails.

He was a frugal man. A lifelong teetotaller, he ate sparingly, but liked sophisticated dishes, of which he got little enough from my mother who was a spartan in all things. One of his memorable aphorisms was:

There's one thing you can say for the French. – They've damned good grub.

In money matters, it is not too much to say that he was almost obsessively prudent; some might say excessively tight-fisted. The iron of his father's seeming extravagances, and perennial financial difficulties, had entered into his soul. He did not share his money with anyone, not even his wife. If he had been doing his calculations, and he did not leave them long undone, he would shout across the table at her: 'Kathleen, you owe me a penny halfpenny for a stamp I put on a letter for you.' He shouted because she was very deaf. He thought she heard better if he shouted. He never learnt, what I think we children learnt instinctively, that pitch, or wavelength, was much more important than volume of sound.

Like his sisters, he worked when he was young for the Irish Agricultural Organisation Society in which he had the status and emoluments of a temporary civil servant. He is commended in Patrick Bolger's book for his valuable work. He spent some of his time in Dublin at the headquarters of the Society, and was well acquainted with Sir Horace Plunkett – for whom he and his sisters had an enormous regard – and all the other senior people connected with the Society. A lifelong friend of all of that generation of the family was Sir Patrick Hannon, a colleage in the Agricultural Society, and later for many years a Westminster Conservative M.P., a notable business man, and a pillar of the Catholic Church. George Russell (A.E.) the poet, mystic, philosopher and painter, was the secretary of the Irish Agricultural Organisation Society. My father owned a picture painted by him, which I suppose A.E. gave him.

His early years, around the turn of the century, were busy ones. In addition to the Co-operative Society work, it fell largely to him to run the estate for his ageing father whose mental powers were failing. And it was during those years that the estate office in Athlone was set up.

Unlike his elder brother, Percy, he seems to have had a good relationship with his father. He always spoke affectionately of him as the 'Governor', and he did not complain, as Percy did, of his sternness. He only ever told me one story suggesting that he might have been unreasonably strict, though he did not himself complain of that. One morning, as a boy, having spoken to his father in his study, he went out shooting. After he had tramped several miles, one of the men came panting after him. 'The Master wants you, Master Shaen.' My father tramped home again, took off his boots, put on his house shoes, went to his father's study and said, 'You sent for me'. All that his father said was: 'Shut the door.' My father said that thereafter he always remembered to shut doors.

Although, on his father's death, my father became an estate owner at an early age, it was not of great or immediate benefit to him. There was legislation hanging over all Irish estates which involved their gradual break-up and sale to their tenants. The Roscommon estate had, moreover, to support his mother and sisters. With their agreement, therefore, it was sold off to the tenants. The girls took their portion outright in cash. My father kept the house at Correal and a small fully stocked home farm of a couple of hundred acres; and the remainder, which belonged to him, went to support his mother for life.

St Marks, a beautifully situated house on the east side of Lough Ree, with a magnificent view of the lake, was taken on a long lease for my grandmother – and bought out at a later date by my father's sister, Violet. There was some seventy acres of land with it, and some fine timber in the grounds, a really lovely old sheltered walled garden, and a stable yard incorporating part of the ancient St Marks' monastery walls which are probably well over a thousand years old. St Marks' had its own boat house, harbour and landing jetty. There was a grass tennis court, and in the days of the British garrison in Athlone there was a thriving social life. St Marks' nearest village is Glasson, encompassing Auburn:

Sweet Auburn! loveliest village of the plain.

of Oliver Goldsmith's *The Deserted Village.*

So, by 1906, the Roscommon estate had been sold and my father's mother and his sisters were installed in St Marks, while he remained on his farm at Correal on the other side of the lake, and there I shall leave him for the moment while we follow his brother across the ocean.

CHAPTER 33

Percy Tilson Magan the Younger

IF THE TURN OF THE nineteenth/twentieth centuries
aw the end of what had been my grandfather Percy Magan's Roscommon estate,
also saw the beginning of a robust new phase in the life of his family, launched
·y his eldest son, my father's older brother, my Uncle Percy. He was one of those
/ho take a conspicuous interest in their own lives. His life, consequently, is well
ocumented. He kept virtually all his correspondence. He regularly kept a journal.
˙he archives of the movement to which he devoted his life are no doubt very full
·f material reflecting his work, and written by him. And much has been written
bout him.

He did not get on with his father, whom he described as harsh and impossible
o satisfy. His schoolmasters he criticized in similar terms. None of the other
hildren made any such criticism of their father, or of their mentors. It must
herefore be at least possible that the iron will and great abilities that Percy was
o show later in life may have been at the root of a perhaps somewhat rebellious
·oy who, at the same time, was more than usually sensitive, and appears to have
ad a tendency to introspection and self-pitying; witness the pathetic – if evocative
account of his journey home from school, which was a common sort of
·ccurrence for all of us Irish children who had our education in England; and, like
he rest of us, he had doubtless imprudently over-spent his journey money in the
arly stages.

When he was just sixteen years of age there came a permanent breach with
is father. He returned home from school and, according to himself, things were
o bad between his father and himself that the father went so far as to exclude him
rom the family Christmas festivities at their home at Kilcleagh. It was decided that
·e should leave school and leave home.

A few months later, when he was no more than sixteen and a half years old,
ɪ the spring of 1884, Percy bade a sorrowful farewell to his dearly loved mother,
isters, and the family staff, and sailed for the United States of America. And so,
s with countless other Irish families, we must cross the Atlantic, at least for a
ew pages of this book.

His father had arranged for him to be apprenticed to an emigrant Irish cattleman in the mid-West by whom he was to be taught American cattle ranching methods, and who claimed to be able to set him on his way to making a fortune, whereafter he could return to Ireland to resume the life of an affluent country gentleman.

But it is clear that Percy's departure for America was intended by his father to be permanent, because his will, dated six months after Percy had sailed to America disinherited him, and made his younger son, my father, at that time a four-year old infant, his heir. It seems an extraordinarily harsh and unnatural sentence to have passed on a son who had hardly even reached years of adolescence.

Percy had an introduction in New York, and another in Chicago where his contact kindly offered him a place in his business. But he was concerned to honour his father's contract with the cattleman, and so set out by train southwards for Red Cloud, Nebraska.

Now he was on his own, a stranger in a vast strange land, heading into the heart of the American continent. If he knew, or sensed, that this was exile, not just a temporary adventure, the journey, and his arrival at the small prairie settlement of Red Cloud, a frontier-type place little more than a dozen years old, must, for a sensitive sixteen-year-old boy, have been a benumbingly desolate experience.

The Irish cattleman, whose ranch was a dozen miles from the township of Red Cloud, turned out to be bogus, and Percy spent a seemingly unprofitable year on the ranch living in squalid circumstances, working long hours, and doing the most lowly of menial work in primitive farming conditions.

At the end of the year he found work in Red Cloud with an elderly banker and his wife who were good to him and allowed him the civilized amenity of the use of their library. They also introduced him to neighbours who happened to be members of the Seventh-day Advent movement to which he became attracted and of which, a year later, he became a member. Here was a community that offered him something of a home from home, a wider family to which to belong and into which he could come in from the cold of his state of exiled loneliness.

The Seventh-day Advent Movement has now spread its influence throughout much of the world. Its membership, world wide, is more than three million, while in the United States and Canada membership is not far short of 1 per cent of the population of North America. Any cohesive religious body, mustering 1 per cent of the population of the world's most powerful people, must be counted a very substantial force. That it has achieved so potent and influential a place in the world, is in no small measure due to the ability, inspiration, and unremittingly dedicated work and activity of my uncle, Percy Magan.

Early in the nineteenth century a widespread revival in Europe and America of interest in the Bible prophecies began to give rise to expectation of the second coming of Christ – the Advent. A certain William Miller, an American, a Baptist, a soldier, and an honest doubter, became convinced through his studies of the

Bible that the time of the second coming of Christ was nigh, and, in 1831, started to preach publicly.

By the end of that decade he had aroused a good deal of interest, and his followers began to call themselves 'Adventists'. In 1844, his movement suffered two blows from which it failed to recover. He had preached that the second coming of Christ would be between 21 March, 1843, and 21 March, 1844. When it did not take place, the movement was shocked. Another date was calculated; the 22 October, 1844. When that prediction also failed, the movement was doomed.

But Adventism as a belief had aroused such widespread interest as to enable it to survive those set-backs; and it was the Seventh-day Adventists who took up the torch. A re-examination of the prophecies convinced them that Miller's date predictions had been accurate. The error was that they related not to the coming on earth, but to events in Heaven preparatory to the second coming at some unspecified future time. Satisfied with that explanation, the movement revived.

The use of the term 'Seventh-day' derives from the Adventists' rejection, as an early Roman pagan innovation, of the keeping of Sunday, the first day of the week, instead of Saturday, the seventh day, as the holy day of rest. The Adventists therefore reverted to a Saturday sabbath.

From the time that Percy joined the movement, he became active in it, and indeed began to live his whole life within it. From the first he displayed a precocious ability. At that time, pioneering was still a way of life for many in America, and particuarly so within the still young Adventist movement. Consequently, there were few restraints on energetic youth. There was work and responsibility, and to spare, for all who were prepared to shoulder it. By the age of twenty, he was already preaching publicly for his new faith; and it was then that he made up his mind to seize the opportunities for higher education offered within the movement.

At Battle Creek, Michigan, some 50 miles east of the southern part of Lake Michigan, where the Adventists had set up their headquarters in 1855, they had also established their own college, offering University degree courses. It was there that Percy enrolled himself as a student in January, 1888, when he was twenty years of age. To pay his way, as he was short of funds, he worked in the sanatorium.

The following year, 1889, one of the Elders of the movement took him as his secretary on a round the world tour. It was typical of Percy that he armed himself in advance with an adequate facility in shorthand and typing.

During the tour he visited his family at Correal in Roscommon in Ireland. He was received with rejoicing and affection by his mother and sisters, but said that his father treated him coldly. It was the last time father and son were to meet.

Thus launched into the Adventist movement, the tempo of Percy Magan's life became extraordinary. He worked throughout the best part of sixty years at a pace and intensity that most men would nowadays expect only to exert in time of war or some great emergency. The Sabbath was by holy writ a day of rest; but

311

one on which Percy saw no reason to rest from religious exercise, preaching and so on. For the other six days, week in, week out, year in, year out, there was no rest, no limit to the daily hours worked, no day off, no half day off, no annual holiday. He virtually took no holidays throughout his life until advancing years forced upon him a little remission from his lifelong restless working pattern. It was the essence of his life that it was led wholly in a religious context.

Two years after his return from his world tour, he became a teaching professor at Battle Creek College, and in the same year he married, at the age of twenty-four, a fellow-student at the College, Ida Mary Baxter.

For the next ten years he taught at the College, holding at the same time a senior administrative post. But he was much more than a preacher, teacher and administrative academic. An immensely powerful vein of practical common sense informed all that he did. He believed that his students should be Christians, but that they should be practising Christians, and that practising meant having practical abilities and skills that they could use and exploit; and that meant not only secular, as well as religious, teaching, but also vocational training as well as academic learning; and no-one was readier than himself to take off his coat and get down to a physical task. His year on the cattle ranch was, after all, not for nothing; his sanatorium work to supplement his student income held as valuable lessons for him as anything he had learnt in the classroom.

Students, too, needed recreation from their books, so why not teach them practical skills, rather than games? So, when, in 1897, farming operations were begun as a sideline to more formal college activities, Percy drove the team of mules that ploughed up the recreation ground to sow it with potatoes. Farming was only one of many manual skills and crafts that were taught. Handicraft resulted in products; products needed a market. So Percy, and his equally staunch leading colleagues, were in business as well, seeking and finding market outlets. And, by contrast, the diversity of his activities is underlined by the fact that it was also in 1897 that he was ordained a minister in the Adventist movement.

A few years later, he was the moving spirit in founding another college. He and his close colleagues had themselves to clear the land. They then had to farm it to help it pay its way. They had to design and, with their own hands, do much of the work of building the primitive buildings while, at the same time, conducting campaigns to raise the necessary funds.

All this was accomplished with extraordinary speed. Within a year or so the new college was accepting students. Percy was appointed Dean. The title sounds grand, but conditions were primitive. There was a shortage of everything, including such basic comforts as reasonable warmth in winter, adequate running water, and bathing facilities. But it was part of Percy's philosophy that the men and women he was training were destined for the mission field where they would need to be experienced in, and content with, the most rudimentary living conditions. But he did not neglect anything he considered important. He thought there should be music, so he founded an orchestra and, typically, learnt to play two instruments himself.

But such almost frantic undertakings were not accomplished without disagreements and dissensions with, and criticisms from, his more cautious, or faint-hearted and less dynamic or adventurous colleagues.

In 1904, his wife died, leaving him with two young sons. Weary with work, sorrowful, and at times near to despair at the difficulties with colleagues, he received a tempting offer which would not merely have relieved him of the penury and physical hardship of his life as an Adventist missionary, but would have made him an exceedingly wealthy man.

One of the farming families in the Battle Creek area who were closely involved in the Adventist movement, and who were well known to Percy, and who recognized his exceptional ability, were the Kellogg family. And it was from the Kellogg food company that he received a management offer. But he did not take it. His innate compulsions could find full satisfaction only in a life of service.

In August, 1905, he married again, a person as versatile, able and energetic as himself, Lillian Eshleman, and as nice as she was modest, and as good as she was capable; and she bore him another son. He had known her since her student days at Battle Creek. She had graduated in medicine five years before their marriage.

She, too, knew the Kellogg family and, in particular, Dr John Harvey Kellogg, leader of the Health Reform Institute in Battle Creek which became a world-famous health clinic. Many years ago she, or some member of the family, told me this story.

Food was seen to have a religious connotation, and Dr Kellogg saw cereal foods as beneficial to both body and soul. Puffed wheat, grape nuts and other such foods had already been developed under religious stimulus. Maize had hitherto been regarded as animal fodder of which there were at times embarrassing gluts. But it was known to have been used by other communities for human consumption, and it seemed possible that investigation along those lines might solve the problem of surplus maize. Because of her interest in nutritional medicine, Lillian Magan was asked to try to develop this idea, and it was she who, as a result, came up with the idea of the corn flake.

In addition to all his other work, and because of his belief in medical missionary work, Percy enrolled himself for a medical course at the age of forty-three, and four years, and a bout of pneumonia, later, he qualified as a doctor. His wife said he was a brilliant diagnostician.

When, during the First World War, the Adventists' claim for a non-combatant role met with scant sympathy from the American government and public, Percy was chosen to negotiate their case at Federal level which he successfully did with great skill and tact.

He continued actively in office up to the age of seventy-five, and in his later years held some of the most senior posts in the movement.

All his life he was hard up. Nevertheless, after he had qualified as a doctor, he protested at being paid more – and it was little enough – than ministers and church officials of the movement. He even tried to insist on having his salary cut, but it involved too many administrative problems. Although he was frugal and abstemious, it is said that he did enjoy good food and creature comforts when well-wishers were good enough to put them in his way. In the colourful words of his very colourful oldest son, the late Dr Wellesley Magan, 'if there were silk pants going in the family, he saw to it that he had them'. Was he human enough to have had a trace of my father's old Irish humbug about him?

He demanded high standards and good behaviour in others. To that end he was concerned to set a high example himself. As he said, he could truthfully tell his students that he had never even been to a circus. To the students themselves he appeared as a man of exceptional and striking dignity, but one, nevertheless, who was always approachable.

Percy was a small, rotund, genial man with a sparkling intelligence and an ever present sense of humour. Below the surface he was a serious, purposeful man of Napoleonic energy and, despite a genuine humility, a Cromwellian belief in himself as the chosen instrument of the will of God. I say advisedly *the* chosen instrument. His Bible reading had convinced him that God does not inform a whole community or company. He chooses one of their number and makes known to him His will. And Percy clearly saw himself as that man. Had the aristocratic inheritance of the Irish chiefs come to root in America; that certainty of your God-given superiority; your mistily conceived descent from the very gods themselves?

He was in the best sense of the word, a visionary. He had the gift of clear-sightedness and, coupled with it, immense resolution. In his very early days in the Adventist movement, he came to see with clarity that its most important future role would be, and ought to be, that of an evangelical, medical movement – men and women of God, morally and technically equipped and hardened to meet whatsoever difficulties, going out into all parts of the world to minister to the souls and bodies of those in need.

From the moment he saw that vision, he became a man in a hurry. Life would hardly be long enough to do what he had to do. And indeed, despite the unremitting, almost breathless, efforts of a lifetime, his final undertakings, the White Memorial Hospital and the Loma Linda Medical School at Los Angeles – later to become a university – were achieved only in the nick of time. No wonder that he was not infrequently at loggerheads with more cautious and less daring colleagues of less faith. It often seemed to his less venturesome colleagues that he was attempting the impossible, and that that must lead to disaster. Percy had called his father a bigoted Protestant. Scratch a bigot, and we find a zealot. Zeal was the essence of him. Nor was he himself noticeably tolerant of religious views – or any other views for that matter – that differed from his own. Perhaps the problem between him and his father was not that they were too dissimilar, but that they were too alike. They might even, in the language of those times, and 'in all humility', have got around to accusing each other of spiritual pride. Maybe the quality that enabled his father to survive the hard times, scarred perhaps, but nevertheless intact, when other landowners went under, was the same that caused Percy time and again to attempt, and to achieve, the near impossible.

His humour was commented upon universally by all who knew him. It was a profound part of his humanity. The man of innate humour is not just issuing pleasantries. He is giving special point to whatever the subject of the moment. The absurd, the bizarre, the droll, are as much a part of life as its other characteristics; part of that deeper feeling that can strike laughter, as soon as tears, from the human heart.

He died in 1947, aged eighty. His death attracted widespread notice for the end of a great life of service. One of his old friends was moved to quote Hamlet:

He was a man, take him for all in all,
I shall not look upon his like again.

Another had said of him:

Percy Tilson Magan was born, and has been intrinsically at all times, a gentleman.

He said of himself, 'I somehow always had a desire to give my life to helping souls whom others did not want to help. I do not think it is any credit to me. Maybe it was a kind of vengeance more than godliness, but people who are in sorrow and trouble always appeal to me.'

He bequeathed to America not only the tangible monuments to his work as an Adventist – as essentially a medical Christian missionary – but also an energetic, capable and very nice family of descendants, many of them devoted to medicine.

BOOK SIX

The Twilight of
the Protestant
Ascendancy

CHAPTER 34

The End of an Ancient Inheritance

AT THE MOMENT when my father was completing the liquidation of his Roscommon estate, an event of great importance in the family occurred. Augusta Magan died on 26 October, 1905. The consequence for the family's ancient landed inheritance was as profound as any former event in its long history.

When she died no will could be found. She was assumed to be intestate. Captain Arthur Tilson Magan, a serving British Army officer, was the senior living male member of the Magan family. He claimed the inheritance, and entered into possession and enjoyment of it. He was my father's second cousin.

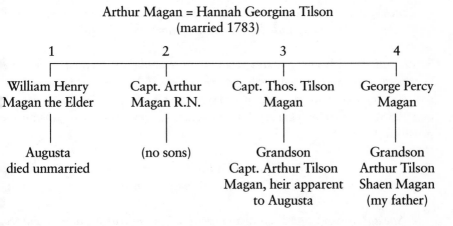

On taking possession of the estates, Arthur, who had never lived in Ireland, wisely turned to my father and my Aunt Violet Magan to be his agents. He could not have been more fortunate. They had unsurpassed knowledge of rural Ireland. They were widely known, and well liked, among all classes, and not least among the country folk on account of their work for the Irish Agricultural Society. They understood estate management. They also were both scrupulously honest and honourable, and had Arthur's best interests at heart.

Six weeks after Augusta's death, a will was found among the mounds of paper, clutter and filth in the single room in which she had lived at Killyon Manor. It had been signed in 1881, twenty-four years before her death. No later will ever came to light.

Augusta's will is the ultimate example of her inadequacy to assume the responsibilities which had fallen to her. Although she had inherited a very large estate, and great wealth, it seems she did not regard the making of a will as a matter of any importance. Indeed, it appears likely that, had she not been prompted, she would not have made a will at all. The occasion that caused her to do so was recounted in the court proceedings which followed her death, and was reported in the press in the following passage:

Miss Magan was well known in the County Meath. The circumstances under which she made her will are rather peculiar. A solicitor, one of the executors, who was a great friend of the deceased and other members of the family, happened to be in the neighbourhood at the time on a shooting expedition, and, in conversation with her, it being shortly after her mother's death, on which she inherited the property, he suggested to her that she ought to make a will. She, it appeared, said she had never thought of it, but agreed that it would be a proper thing to do, and asked him to prepare a document for her. She stated that she wished her heirs to inherit the property at her death, and informed him that she also wished to leave some legacies, and he, at her request, drew up a will, leaving to her heirs at law all her real, freehold, and chattel estate of every description.

So the solicitor, who presumably recounted the above story twenty-five years later, went away and drafted a will in accordance with her supposed instructions. It was a very short will. In single-spaced typescript it occupies only half a page of quarto. She left some legacies. Otherwise there were only two substantive provisions:

1 *I leave to the person or persons who shall be my heir or heiresses at law at my decease all my real freehold and chattel real estate ...*

2 *She appointed Capt. F. Gore and the solicitor her trustees and executors. 'I leave them the residue of my personal estate to build or assist in building - hospitals ... one ... to the memory of my mother another to the memory of Dr Fleming and the third to the memory of Colonel Richard W. Bernard ...'*

When, after she died, the will was disputed in the courts, as such a will was bound to be, the judge, it has been said, commented that whoever drafted it must have been drunk. In effect it was an invitation to Augusta's relations to fight it out among themselves after her death to establish who was her most rightful heir or heiress.

And so it turned out that when Augusta Magan died, aged eighty, or thereabouts, one part of her legacy to posterity was a vast and chaotic mess, encompassing the material ruin of her family; the other was a very substantial endowment to the hospitals of Dublin from which countless people, and particularly less fortunate members of the community, have since benefited.

The will itself suggests very clearly whom she thought to be her heirs. The only members of the Magan family living in Ireland were her first cousin, my grandfather, Percy Magan, his wife and their family. Augusta knew them well and was very friendly with them, but she did not leave a sausage to any of them, not even a few trinkets to the girls, not even a brooch to my Aunt Blossie of whom she was especially fond. But she left large sums of money, and substantial legacies, to more distant cousins on her mother's side of the family who lived out of Ireland, and with whom she cannot have been as closely acquainted, and other legacies to people who were not even relations. Being a simpleton she assumed my grandfather and his family to be her heirs. Who else? No need to leave them anything as they were going to get the lot anyway.

In effect, the first substantive point in the will meant that all her enormous real estate and her many houses would go to her 'heir or heiresses'. The second meant that all her considerable amount of cash and investments, her private possessions, the contents of her houses, must be realized to build hospitals. One of those to be commemorated, Dr Fleming, was her private physician. Another was her old flame of the railway station barrow, Colonel Bernard. She also left a substantial legacy to his widow, 'Mrs Colonel Bernard'.

But what in the name of all that is wonderful did the solicitor think he was doing? He was a professional man. It was his duty to draft a sound will. He must have asked her whom she had in mind to be her heir. Why did he not name that person?

He was not a purposeless man. He appointed himself as executor. The other executor, Captain Frederick Gore, was Augusta's second cousin on her mother's side of the family, and was a serving soldier in the British Army, and did not live in Ireland. As an executor for this Irish estate he would therefore be as much use as a sick headache. Thus, as the sole effective executor, the solicitor to this huge estate held all the strings.

When, twenty-four years later, Augusta died, and no will could be found, why did he not divulge the fact that there was indeed a will? Why did he allow her to be declared intestate? He must have been aware of the possibility that once Arthur had installed himself there would be a challenge to his claim to the estates?

As soon as the twenty-four-year-old will was found, steps were taken to obtain probate. But the will was immediately contested by four Magan cousins all of whom lived overseas. Their purpose was to test whether it had been properly executed, and whether Augusta understood what she was doing when she signed it. Probate was granted.

That was the beginning of court proceedings. But the will itself was so equivocal, the estate so large, Augusta's affairs in such disorder, and the interested parties so diverse, that legal proceedings of one kind or another, relating to it, were dragging through the Irish courts at the highest level for the next five years with fat fees for the lawyers.

While the will was making its tortuous way through the courts, life had to go on down on the estates. Arthur Magan, the presumed heir, and my father and his sister Violet, set about bringing some order into the properties. Clearing the houses was like nothing so much as opening Tutankhamen's tomb. In an earlier chapter I quoted passages from the report of the official valuer. The newspapers had a fine time reporting the case under headlines such as: 'Secrets of a Mansion.' 'Stranger than Fiction.' 'Remarkable Discoveries.' 'Sovereigns in tea cups.' 'Bank notes in waste paper baskets.' The room in Killyon Manor in which Augusta finally lived and slept together with the railway barrow, was so filthy that my father and my aunt had it completely stripped, and they even removed and replaced the timber floor.

The landed estates, as I have already indicated, were in no better shape. No doubt good tenants had in their own interests looked after their farms and holdings. But those parts of the estate that were in hand were a shambles. The aged and neglected donkeys and ponies had to be dealt with. And the half-wild bullocks that snorted at my father over the untended hedges and fences were soon to find that they had met their match. Cattle were in his blood, and he understood them, and they had better be docile when he was around. No snorting at him!

Despite Augusta's neglect of the estate, and despite the fact that the liquid assets and cash were to go to build hospitals, there was still a huge income, and Arthur Magan did not have to worry about money.

He decided to make Killyon Manor his principal residence. To that end plans were drawn up to enlarge the already rather large house. Those plans were exhibited at the Royal Academy in London in 1907. Fortunately they were never executed. Not only would the much bigger house have soon become a white elephant, but the character of the old house would have been entirely spoilt. The present charming half-ruinous conglomerate which in its various parts, additions and alterations, visibly tells the history of centuries, would have disappeared into, and been smothered by, a pretentiously large shell of Edwardian bad taste.

While the arrangements were being made to enlarge Killyon, Arthur built the pebble-dashed house which stands on the corner opposite the front gate of the Killyon demesne. There he lived for two years. It was a time that was particularly remembered by those who knew it, for the splendid shooting parties conducted from the house which my father must have much enjoyed managing. He was a very good commanding officer on a shoot. He could instantly, and accurately, sum up the weather and other conditions of the day, and quickly dispose of guns, beaters, stops, dogs etc., to the best advantage, on each beat. At moments when quiet could be dispensed with, he made his large presence felt with much shouting and histrionics. His obituary from a one-time beater at Clonearl was: 'He was a great hollerer!'

Arthur's eventual plans involved a massive gradual reduction in the size of the estates. My father and my Aunt Violet well understood that the days of large estates in Ireland were over. The various land legislation enacted during the past half-century had ensured that. It was inevitable that, unless the trend of legislation was to be reversed, of which there could be no reasonable expectation for deep-seated political reasons in land-hungry Ireland, there would in due course be nothing left to estate owners but their home farms; their demesne lands.

While Arthur and my father and his sister were thus busying themselves with the management of the estates, the solicitor was diligently discharging his executorial responsibilities and, in particular, was active in Dublin and elsewhere in pursuit of a rival claimant to the properties, and in due course produced out of the hat a female contestant to the succession. She had never been in Ireland. No-one in the family had heard of her for fifty years. She was ninety years of age, and in good health, and lived a secluded life in Devonshire. She was Georgina, only child of the sailor of a century earlier, Captain Arthur Magan R.N., who had lived at Brighton. As such, she was the senior member of the family because Arthur, who had claimed the estates, descended from a younger brother of the sailor.

When the solicitor brought her to light, she bore the name of her third marriage, and was Mrs Bartlett.

Arthur Magan = Hannah Georgina Tilson

1	2	3	4
William Henry Magan the Elder	Capt. Arthur Magan R.N.	Capt. Thos. Tilson Magan	George Percy Magan
Daughter Augusta (died unmarried)	Daughter Georgina (The heiress)	Grandson Capt. Arthur Tilson Magan (Claimant)	Grandson Arthur Tilson Shaen Magan (my father)

Married 1 John Henry Brummell (Dissolved)
Married 2 John Rofe (Died)
Married 3 Joel Bartlett

My father and my Aunt Violet were informed. Their assessment was that Mrs Bartlett did not seem disposed to press her claim, and that if everyone acted discreetly nothing might happen to disturb Arthur Magan's possession of the properties.

They broke the news to Arthur, advised him to leave things to his lawyers and advisers, and to carry on as though nothing new had arisen. They urged him strongly to say nothing to his wife.

My father and my Aunt Violet thought her 'rather soft in the head'. She had been used to a sparse and frugal life as the daughter of an army officer, and wife of another. The wealth and prestige of the Magan estates had quite gone to her head. It was the view of my father and his sister that if she was told that Mrs Bartlett had been found to be alive, she would be so disturbed by the thought of the danger to her new-found grandeur that she might do something foolish which would risk precipitating a crisis.

Arthur told her.

A crisis there was.

His wife, without telling anyone, took the boat to England, and went to see Mrs Bartlett. What prompted her to do so? Whether or not anyone suggested it to her; and what she intended, is not known. She was indeed frightened, and at best must have had it in mind to plead with Mrs Bartlett not to dispossess her husband. Mrs Bartlett was prepared to see her. Just how the interview may have started is also not known, but we know how it ended.

Arthur's wife lost her head. She began to be abusive. She accused Mrs Bartlett of malevolent intentions to strip her husband of his rightful inheritance, and more in that vein.

Mrs Bartlett was a copper-haired woman. She was the only child of a father who had been brought up in the house of wealthy landowning aristocratic Irish parents, and she was her well-to-do father's heir. It would be surprising if in her bones she felt other than heaven-born, and doubly so when she could justifiably raise herself to commanding heights of moral indignation.

Mrs Bartlett did become very angry. She silenced Arthur's wife, and then went on in some such words as these:

'You dare to come before me dressed in silks, satins and furs which you know to be bought with my money; and you have the effrontery to insult me in my own home. Now let me tell you. I have been well aware all along of my just claim to this estate. But I am old, and I and my family are in no need of money. I had therefore made a deed gift of all these properties to your husband, Arthur.'

and then the crushing blow, perhaps drawn out emphatic syllable by emphatic syllable.

'And now I shall tear it up.'

Following Mrs Bartlett's decision, the whole majesty of the law got to work. Wigs and gowns assembled in force; and good Magan money poured into the coffers of the lawyers. The press rubbed its hands in expectation of splendid court scenes. 'A big bar has been engaged,' one of the papers reported in advance of the hearing. Big it was. No less than six King's Counsellors, together with their Juniors, and four firms of solicitors. The solicitor had rendered a signal service to his bewigged brethren of the law.

Judgement was found in favour of Mrs Bartlett, and its centuries old accumulated substance passed out of the hands of the ancient Irish Magan family and to English owners, and was largely demolished and dispersed.

It must be altogether out of the question that that is what Augusta intended. But it was what the solicitor contrived for her. Even his greatest admirers can hardly claim it to have been a very creditable contrivance.

It was in the year 1908 that judgement was given in favour of Mrs Bartlett, and against Arthur Magan. It was the year of my birth. Less than two years later, on 6 February, 1910, Mrs Bartlett died, aged ninety-two.

The estates then passed to her married daughter by her second marriage, Mrs Toppin, and were thereafter known as the Toppin estates.

It was agreed that Arthur Magan should keep such family furniture, pictures, silver and other goods as he had bought in at the sales of Augusta's personal effects. It was also agreed that he should keep the surplus income standing to his account at the time; a very large sum at today's value.

There was no enmity between the Toppins and the Magans. Everyone behaved in a civilized way. The Toppins wisely asked my Aunt Violet and my father to continue to administer the estates on their behalf. This they did until the outbreak of the Great War of 1914–18, when, on 4 August, 1914, my father immediately joined the forces, in which he served until demobilized in 1919. During the war my aunt administered the estates single-handed, travelling about the large areas they covered mainly on her 'cycle. She continued to do so after the First War.

The properties were gradually reduced by sales, mainly to tenants. Finally, under the land legislation of the Free State Government, in 1926, virtually all large properties were taken over by the Irish Land Commission and broken up for the most part into very small peasant-proprietor holdings. At that point the estates ceased to exist.

Did this dissolution of the Magan estates and fortune matter? Not much, perhaps. It may even have been a beneficial tonic to family members to make better use of any talents they might have.

But in two senses it did matter somewhat. Violent assaults on the accepted customs of an ordered society are damaging to the fabric of that society. That is not to say that there should not be change. It was at that time the custom in our society for large estates to pass more or less intact to heirs male, if any, provided there was no significant defect of health or character such as to warrant that they be debarred. That practice had evolved in order to give society social and economic stability. Otherwise, in cases where there was no heir male, estates were commonly shared by co-heirs female. Heiresses were likely to be married, and thus to attach their portion to the estates of their husband. In either case, therefore, in so far as provision could be made, there was a good assurance that the properties would remain with the successors male or female of the family and continue to be properly administered in the family tradition, and remain relatively undisturbed.

The forms of society we had in the past were far from perfect, but they were relatively stable. The world is going to pay very dearly for the footloose society we have been creating during the past few centuries. In that sense, what happened to the ancient Magan family business of large-scale rural management, in its evolving forms, did matter.

Arthur Magan was the heir male. He was a sensible man. That he planned to rebuild and enlarge Killyon is evidence enough that he intended to live in Ireland and maintain the family tradition there. And it was his intention, in the event, as it turned out, of his having no children, to ensure the succession within the family by making my father his heir.

The second respect in which the destruction of the estates mattered was that all the proceeds passed to England, and were lost to Ireland. My father and my Aunt Violet had, as we have seen, a great concern for the real Irish, the country people of Ireland, to whose betterment and welfare they devoted their early lives, and indeed, if less directly, the whole of their lives. If, therefore, the estates had remained in the family's Irish hands there can be little doubt that, in so far as seemed prudent and sensible, the proceeds of the land sales over the years would have been invested in Ireland for the good of Ireland and its people.

The story of William Henry Magan the Elder's senior branch of the Magan family in the nineteenth century, and the destruction by its last member, Augusta Magan, of the ancient family fortunes, was so close in time to my generation of the family when we were young, and had been so much a part of the early life of my father and his sisters, that it was still an endless topic of interest. As children, we discussed it interminably with them over the fire. But never did my father, or any of his sisters, once suggest to me that they had had any expectations, or were at all surprised, or put out, that nothing had come to them. Nor had any of them acted as though they were expecting to come in for a fortune. Long before Augusta died, they had all found themselves occupations to which they were single-mindedly dedicated. They all had a strong sense of self-reliance, and self-sufficiency. The speed with which Arthur Magan was informed, and took over the estates during the period of intestacy, suggests that it was well understood within the family before Augusta's death, that he, as the senior male member of the family, would be her probable successor.

Nor did any of them ever express any regrets at the passing of the Magan fortunes. Although none of them were socialists, or political, or social, theorists, they were well up to, if not ahead of, their time in social thinking. They had, since childhood, living in a poor part of Ireland, accepted that a better deal was overdue for the less well-off people of Ireland, and that that could only come about at that time by them having a greater personal stake in Ireland's richest lands.

I said earlier that there was one job that would have suited my father had it fallen to him with a bit of luck, and it was clearly a very near miss that he did not get it. It is a pity Augusta did not explicitly leave the estates to him as she had evidently intended. It would have given him a splendid job that would have suited him. His own judgement was pretty good, and he would have had the invaluable help of his sister Violet. He would have enjoyed the detailed administration. He would have had enough scope to absorb his pretty considerable energies, but within the rural world which was his element, and not in competition with qualified professional men. The pressures on him would not have been too great for his rather excitable and highly-strung nature. He would have made a good deal of heavy weather, and there would have been endless fuss and contrived dramas. But he would have enjoyed himself enormously. He would have known very well how to run those Irish estates in an Irish way.

He would have had the sporting opportunities he enjoyed. He would have given shooting parties and warmed to the companionship they would have given him. He would have tramped the estates endlessly on foot, talking his head off. He would have talked for hours to his tenants and employees, in gateways, in cornfields, in pastures full of cattle, in yards full of manure, by haystacks, by cornstooks, at turf banks, among gorse bushes, in woods, by lakeside and river and sitting in their cottages and houses, anywhere and everywhere that he could pin down an audience.

He would have seen to their welfare. He would have been fair, but also mighty careful of the money. He would have been chairman of not very arduous local committees, and would have felt important; and that would have given him innocent pleasure. He would have been a good and helpful neighbour to all, great and small. He would have done many kindnesses to those in need of help. A large countryside would have found him endlessly helpful, engaging, interesting, and companionable to all, of whatsoever class. His own eccentricities would have been a positive advantage to him.

During the Second World War, he applied for war service with the British forces, but was turned down on age. He was in his sixtieth year. He was greatly upset at being rejected, but instead he looked after their properties for a number of his younger friends who were serving the Crown. One of them, Sir George Mahon, on the occasion of my father's funeral, told me with modesty and gratitude that his property had been better run by my father than at any other time.

And even though the big estates were broken up under the various Land Acts, my father would no doubt have contrived, as others did, to keep enough land to absorb his energies and keep him interested and occupied in his later years.

Nor would he have minded the progressive reduction of the estates by sales of farms to tenants. He had already done it with his Roscommon estate. He had a high regard for the small and medium-sized Irish farmer and his working family, and he knew many of them intimately. He knew them to be proficient and hard-working people. He believed the time had come when they should own their own lands, helped, when there were no longer big and rich – and sometimes capricious – estates to do so, by such national organizations as the Irish Agricultural Society. He also felt that Irish farming had a special virtue which should be encouraged and preserved. It was not, he always said, primarily a money-making business. First and foremost it was an agreeable way of life, even though, at times of year, it meant long hours of hard work for the whole family.

But, although the properties passed out of the family, we, the last of the family living in Ireland, continued to have the enjoyment of them all the time the Toppin estates existed. My father had the use of the shooting and sporting rights of all the thousands of acres of former family property. As a boy, I accompanied him on his shooting expeditions all over central Ireland from Roscommon to Meath. In particular, Killyon Manor, adequately furnished for holiday purposes, was our second home. Until 1926 there was a large home farm there, and a good many people employed.

Life at Killyon was primitive, but we loved it. Log and turf fires warmed us. Candles and a few oil lamps illuminated us. There was no bathroom. There was one 'pull-the-plug' only. The kitchen was a vast vault. Cooking was on the wood-burning black iron range. Food – marvellous, healthy country food – for the dining-room had to suffer a long cold obstacle race including an open courtyard and a dark dog-leg passage with some low stairs in it, and finally the stone-flagged hall. The water supply was a hand pump on a well in the courtyard by the kitchen door. Cold, it was delicious to drink. As children we had scant use for it warm, but if a wash in warm water became a must, the water had to be heated on the kitchen range and carried in pails. I once estimated that we burnt sixty tons of wood annually, in addition to turf. All the wood was fallen timber, most of it beech.

Outside, the river, particularly the weir, and the woods, and the farm and garden, were sources of perpetual interest and pleasure. And for me there was the altogether endless joy of wood-chopping. All the wood was cut up by hand, first into short lengths by a two-man cross-cut saw. Then it had to be chopped into smaller logs. That was one of my favourite occupations. I chopped for hours on end with a two-handed axe. Beech, seasoned or unseasoned, chops like cheese. And making neat piles of the chopped logs gives almost as much satisfaction as the chopping. It must be one of man's oldest occupations, and is embedded deep in his instinctive self. The smell of the stuff. The feel of the stuff. Beautiful! And it warms you four times; when you saw it; when you chop it; when you cart it; and when you burn it – and by the light of a candle or two and the flickering flames of the fire, with our Aunt Violet Magan talking like pages out of Somerville and Martin Ross, telling us deliciously funny tales of Irish life in general, and of our eccentric and dotty old cousin Augusta in particular; those were lovely times.

The game-keeper John Curley, and his wife Anne, acted as caretakers in the house, and Anne Curley cooked for us all when we were there. There was also a farm and house carpenter, Jimmy Smith, who was a special favourite with us when we were children, not least because of his extraordinary facility for novel expressions and quaint sayings. He was a quite exceptionally nice and attractive person. Joe, the hunchback, who worked in the garden, was a lifelong friend. And not least Tom Shanley, the steward, and his, to us, beloved wife, Polly. The last of the old Killyon hands, Jimmy MacLoughlin, who looked after the horses with that knowledge and understanding that few others than real Irish horsemen have, was going strong until a year or two ago, and in his mid-nineties was still riding his bike and tending his garden.

After the estates were finally disposed of, my father bought Killyon Manor and the park-land round it. He did some modernization, and he and my mother lived there for the last thirty-five years of their lives.

Some two miles from Killyon is the Hill-of-Down railway station. The railway had been built in the nineteenth century through Magan property. One of the conditions on which the land was transferred to the railway company was that the Magans should have the right to stop any train, express or otherwise, at the Hill-of-Down station, for their own convenience, either to board it or alight from it. My father did in fact exercise that right during his later years.

The Hill-of-Down, where the railway line and a canal – long since disused – run parallel through a land of rich pasture, red bog, gravel hills – remnants of the ice-age – and noble stands of timber, consists of nothing but the small railway station, and very small post office-cum-sweet shop, and a small pub-cum-general shop. Otherwise, there is no village for miles. The pub-cum-shop was typical of its kind in rural Ireland. In a very small compass it sold across its one dark wooden counter everything from plain country food, to useful hardware. There were goods on the floor, goods on shelves, goods hanging from the ceiling that could only be dimly seen through a blue haze of plug tobacco-smoke. It smelt of everything; bacon, onions, bread, tobacco, and that indefinable compound smell of ages that is part and parcel of such a place. But most of all it smelt of that sweet sickly smell that oozes from the doors of pubs into every Irish street, porter; Irish stout. Half a century ago it had a crafty old bearded pub-keeper who used to boast, and it was probably no idle boast, that his three yards of pub counter was worth more than three thousand acres of the best Meath land.

I have said that the Magan estates case dragged through the courts for years. The personal effects were auctioned in 1906, but it was more than five years before the money was apportioned. Augusta Magan's will required the proceeds to be used to build three new hospitals in Dublin. The executors of the will recommended three hospitals, but it was thought that there might not be enough money for so grandiose a plan. The courts therefore adopted the compromise of adding wings to three existing hospitals.

If any Magan wants a bed in a Dublin hospital, they would be likely to be welcomed in any of the three that benefited. Augusta's bequests enabled the family, particularly my Aunt Violet and my father, during the next half-century or so, to obtain beds in those hospitals for their employees, people from the estates, and country people of their acquaintance who might be in need of such special treatment as could hardly be obtained at that time in Southern Ireland other than in the Dublin hospitals, and a few of the larger towns.

And so, after many centuries, came the end of the large-scale landowning and cattle grazing of one old Irish family.

CHAPTER 35

The Huntsman's Daughter

ALTHOUGH THE END of the ancient Magan estates was precipitated by the ill management of Augusta Magan's affairs, it did in fact do no more than foreshadow the shape of things to come, for the shadows were indeed closing in upon the Ascendancy itself – a fact that was to be graphically illustrated by the fate of the family into which my father married a few months after Augusta Magan's death.

My mother's father was Assheton Biddulph M.F.H., perhaps the most renowned Master of Foxhounds of his day in Ireland, and one of the best-known huntsmen in the United Kingdom. For the greater part of his adult life he was the owner, master and huntsman of the King's County Hounds, which his father had hunted before him.

Assheton Biddulph, and his wife Florence, had four daughters and a son. It was with Kathleen Jane, the eldest daughter, that my father fell in love.

The Biddulph family background was altogether different from the Magans. This was no Celtic family with an ancient chieftainly grazier past. The Biddulphs were settlers through and through. They regarded themselves as the elite Irish. But there was probably not a drop of old Irish blood in their veins. Their typically settler ancestor, John Biddulph, had come to Ireland in 1670, and carved out an estate for himself at Rathrobin in the King's County, and not untypically was murdered, but not before he had a son to carry on his line. Rathrobin, at the time of which I write, was still the seat of the head of the family, the huntsman's oldest brother, Colonel Middleton Biddulph; and it was in the protection of his interests at Rathrobin that, two hundred and fifty years after John Biddulph's murder, my Aunt Violet Magan nearly met the same fate.

Although the Biddulph family's Irish roots had been in Rathrobin for two and a half centuries, its deepest roots of all, as with many Irish settler landed gentry families, were still in England. The Biddulphs remained innately conscious that they descended from William the Conqueror's standard bearer, and that the family name derived from lands he was given at Biddulph in Staffordshire – lands recorded in the Doomsday Book. Home in its profoundest sense to the family was the remnants of Biddulph Old Hall, the great family Tudor house reduced by Cromwell when their Royalist ancestor had been slain fighting for his king. These, and other such heroic traditions – a forebear who bore a standard at Agincourt – another who sheltered Mary Queen of Scots when she fled to England – a midshipman drowned with admiral Kempenfelt in the sinking of the *Royal George* – a clerical hero, their kinsman 'Taylor the Martyr', Cranmer's secretary, burnt at the stake – and many who had spent their lives in the service of the Crown – made it almost a mandatory part of their loyalty to their sovereign for my mother's father, Assheton Biddulph, and his brother, Middleton, to take commissions in the British Army when they grew up. Moreover, their mother was a rich English lady who had given an English upper class cultural flavour to their young lives.

Assheton Biddulph spent only a few years in the British Army, and then settled down to a life of fox-hunting. At the age of thirty, he married an English wife, Florence Boothby. She was as active and energetic as himself, and a fine horsewoman. Hunting was in her blood. She was of the same family as the celebrated Squire Boothby who founded the Quorn Hunt in the seventeenth century, and whose son, 'Prince Boothby,' acquired hardly less notoriety when, after breakfasting off cold tea, he blew his brains out, because he had tired, 'of the bore of dressing and undressing'.

The home of Assheton and Florence Biddulph, Moneyguyneen, in the King's County, was beautifully situated at the foot of the Slieve Bloom mountains, and there Assheton built himself new kennels.

Kathleen, my mother, was thus brought up to a widely varied country life. It was centred on the Hunt, but there was also wonderful mountain walking, mountain streams to fish, and the beautiful and interesting boglands in the lower lying areas. And it was not an uncultured life. She was at school in England. Her mother was an accomplished pianist, and Kathleen herself was a good violinist and studied music in Dresden.

In those days fox-hunting in Ireland was not just a lark for the rich, and a social parade for the elite. It had a natural appeal for the pastoral and horse-loving Irish people. The Ascendancy took the lead and provided the sport, but the whole country shared its enjoyment either through active participation or widespread general interest. Many in those days owned horses of necessity, and used them, if so minded, for hunting. Also there were numerous foot and 'cycle followers. A press account of one meet records that on a December day:

... in delightful weather, genial and dry, and with just a touch of frost to make the air feel bracing, Mr Assheton Biddulph, the esteemed M.F.H., met at Corolanty a host of followers who could be counted by the hundreds.

There is another account of a meet attended by more than a hundred cyclists.

They were times when people had to find their life, their work, and their recreation locally. Masters of Hounds, therefore, in contributing to those needs, performed a valuable and valued service. Moreover, they gave the public a common link and bond. In consequence, they occupied an honourable, and honoured, and respected place in society and, together with their families, took a lead in most aspects of social life. They rose early, worked hard, and were expected to, and did, set a high example generally in their behaviour, and in the discharge of their duty, and not least in the courage and hardihood they displayed riding over difficult country in long, and often cold and wet, days in the saddle. And they were acutely concerned to respect the feelings of the public. Here is an instance:

Mr Assheton Biddulph had arranged to commence cub hunting on Saturday 20th September upon the summit of the Slieve Bloom mountains. But he postponed the fixture to enable all to foregather at the graveside to pay a well-merited tribute to the remains of General Sir Robert White of Aghaboe, one of the last of those who rode in Balaclava's brilliant and disastrous charge.

They were the days before horse-boxes and hound-vans. The Hunt travelled on foot. For a distant meet, the Master and his family, his hunt staff, and horses and hounds, would spend the previous night at the country house of some follower. Next day, if the hunting was good, the pack might cover up to twenty miles of country. There might then be a ride of as much as thirty miles homewards along mountain roads, much of it in the dark, and perhaps in the wet.

At best, the long rides home might sometimes be briefly broken by a little rough and ready hospitality. The end of a day in the Queen's County, for instance, might take the Master past Roundwood, the Hamilton home, where a blast on his horn produced a conventional flagon of ale and a lump of well-buttered bread eaten in the saddle, with another twenty miles yet to go.

The day's work was not over when you got home. By the light of stable lanterns hounds had to be put up, inspected for wounds and fed. Horses, too, had to be dried, cleaned, rugged and fed. It was a point of honour – and good management – that these last tasks were not just left to the men. When all was done, and only then, was it time to change your own wet clothes for dry, and finally enjoy the comfort of a large log and turf fire, and of mellow candle-light.

Bad weather was no bar to hunting, except snow and ice. There was a day when a snowstorm brought disappointment to Mr Thomas Walpole of Monadrehid. He had been hoping for a good run as it was his eightieth birthday, but the meet had to be cancelled. A few days later, however, hounds were out again, 'and Mr Walpole had the satisfaction of occupying a forward place in a good hunt'.

Some of the bad weather that the Hunt endured and my mother experienced in those times, has become historic.

The winter of 1895 was one of the coldest ever recorded. Ice was as much as two feet thick. An ox I think was roasted whole on the Thames. In the scrapbook which my mother kept as a girl, her father wrote in his own hand:

Hounds never went out hunting from January 25th till March 2nd owing to Hard Frost and Snow. [His capitals.]

If a fox took to the Slieve Bloom mountains at anytime in cold weather, the Hunt could run into snow. There was a day when hounds followed a fox high up into the hills and ran into a considerable amount of snow. In the end three and a half couple had to be left out, lost. The Master and staff and family rode home across the hills in a snowstorm, and the hounds found their way back next day.

Then there was the great storm of February, 1903. When I was a boy, a landmark in time in Ireland was 'The Night of the Great Wind'. A birth date or a bereavement would be remembered because he or she was born, or had died, on 'The Night of the Great Wind'.

The scrapbook records that on Thursday, 19 February, 1903, it was 'a terrible wild stormy day on which hounds found a fox in Harristown Gorse, but pursued and pursuers alike were absolutely bewildered by the storm. Hounds could hear neither one another nor their huntsman; all was soon chaos and it was with difficulty that the pack was collected.'

Two days later, 'Saturday was another dreadful day, when the same pack met at the Cat and Bagpipes, and the great wonder was that so many came out to meet them.'

Assheton's elder brother, Colonel Middleton Biddulph, recorded that, in one of his woods of seven acres of larch, out of about three thousand trees, only two hundred and eighty-six were left standing. An enormous amount of timber, including some very beautiful old trees, was blown down elsewhere on the estate.

For the first thirteen years of his mastership, Assheton Biddulph never missed a meet, and he paid scant heed even to his own injuries. He was recorded on one occasion as hunting with one arm 'bound up with a stirrup leather' after an accident – no nonsense with black satin slings.

The hunting life was far from soft, and it needed a disciplined and well-planned routine to ensure that family, staff, horses and hounds were all fit and up to the work. Lame horses, hounds with road-scalded pads, blown staff, and drooping family could not render the service that it was their chosen duty to give. It needed a good skipper the whole year round to keep it all in condition. As Jorrocks said:

Oh, gentlemen, gentlemen! None but an 'untsman knows an 'untsman's cares.

The end of the hunting season was by no means the end of the ' 'untsman's cares', or those of his family and the hunt staff.

There was his farm to look after. It was his habit to rise and begin the day at 6 a.m. except in cub-hunting when he was much earlier. He would come in from the farm and the kennels at 9 a.m. for a large breakfast. He would then return to his farm and hound work and much else that he had to attend to as Master. He had no lunch, but came in finally at 6 o'clock in the evening, when he would have his whiskey, which he called his *angelus*, before preparing himself for dinner.

The 'angelus' was the beginning of the evening ritual, the core of which was dinner at 8 o'clock. It was an absolute rule that all members of the family and any guests in the house had to attend, changed into formal evening clothes. No matter what you were doing, no matter how far from home, playing tennis, fishing, or anything else, you had to be back in time to be on parade changed for dinner. In the summer it could be an appalling bind for the young.

The dinner itself was interminable, and its centrepiece was Assheton Biddulph's ritual drinking. He drank large quantities of whiskey at the table. I believe as much as a bottle – in the form of hot whiskey punch which he himself mixed, followed by port. All had to sit through the ceremony. It must have been a dreadful bore. Nevertheless he seems to have defied Jorrocks's aphorism that hunting and drinking are two men's work.

He had a cold bath every morning. He no doubt needed it. There were of course no bathrooms. He had it in a round hip bath on his dressing-room floor. One morning he threw his sponge in preparatory to immersing himself, but the sponge bounced. He rang for whoever valetted him and complained that the bath had not been filled, only to have it pointed out to him that the water had frozen!

He was an unconventional man who did what suited himself and seemed to him sensible. Thus he did not, as was the general rule, put his hunters out to grass in the summer. They were hitched to farm carts and implements and did farm work. Instead of getting soft on grass, it kept them fit, and it made economic sense. They gave a return for their keep.

The hounds needed particular attention in the summer. They had to be kept exercised and healthy; and there were the puppies to be bred, and put out to 'walk' with those hunt supporters who liked to take care of them. Assheton Biddulph was well aware that the two most important ingredients in fox-hunting are the skill of the Master and the quality of the hounds.

That was the life to which my mother was brought up; and it had another side. There was the Hunt point-to-point, a largely social event in those days, with the officers of the local British regiment providing a band and a marquee well furnished with refreshments; and there was the Hunt Ball, a glittering occasion in late Victorian and Edwardian times. There was the Hunt puppy show in high summer. Accounts of it read like a verse from John Peel – Boaster, Bondsman, Bouncer, Boundless; Landlord, Lasher, Lavender, Lawless; Parasol, Passive, Parable, Paragon. The Master bred his own hounds and horses.

There were, too, locally arranged theatricals and other entertainments. An account of one such shows that the 'Quality' were all there, and 'a gay appearance was given by the hunting costume of Mr A. Biddulph M.F.H.'. His ladies did even better:

> Mrs Biddulph played accompaniments with the skill of a very superior pianist. A vocalist like Mrs Frend and a violinist like Miss Franklin and the talented young daughter of Mr and Mrs Biddulph [my mother], were sufficient guarantees for a musical treat.

In addition to being a good violinist, my mother sang well enough to be in demand at local concerts. Those talents brought her into friendship with the gifted, versatile and well-known writer, artist, musician and entertainer, Percy French, the author of *The Mountains of Mourne*, and many other favourite songs. She used to accompany him on the stage at charity concerts. On those occasions he would do trick lightning sketches, some with the aid of the smoke from a candle. The stage used to be littered with them, and my mother often said afterwards that she wished that she had thought to preserve some of them. There survives one charming little water colour sketch of his of an Irish bog scene at sundown. Perhaps it was one he gave her. His first song was that splendid refrain, sung and whistled from one end of the earth to the other, *Abdallah – Bulbul Ameer*, written when he was an undergraduate at Trinity College, Dublin. He published it locally, but omitted to copyright it. It was immediately pirated by a London firm of publishers who took out a copyright for their only slightly altered version, and scooped the pool.

As well as the more formal local entertainments, there used also to be much music and other homespun fun in people's homes. The Moneyguyneen visitor's book is witness to the good cheer in the house. Most visitors just wrote their names and the dates of their stay, but some added a few words:

> The jolliest month for eleven years.

> The rain is on the river, and on the hills all day, but the sunshine is in Moneyguyneen.

> Short and sweet, like a donkey's gallop.

Wrote Lynwood Palmer, the horse painter, a kinsman of Assheton Biddulph, who stayed at Moneyguyneen and painted his horses:

> Always have good luck when I come here.

'Made the "Hoighth of Ireland" one stone higher,' is a succinct description of a local mountain climb.

There were also many other activities that were part of the pattern of rural life. Fair days, the visiting circus, garden parties, flower, fruit and vegetable shows, exhibitions of handicrafts, poultry and dairy shows, and much else besides. My mother as a girl developed her own little dairy and invariably won the prizes for butter and cheese.

Thus it was that my mother had a wonderfully full and enjoyable life as a girl and as a young woman, with the added interest of her duties as the eldest daughter of a famous M.F.H., and living in the upper class stratum of society at a time when its gaiety and elegance were at their zenith – and she had many admirers. But:

Will fortune never come with both hands full?
SHAKESPEARE, *HENRY IV, PART 2*

Not, alas, for my mother.

CHAPTER 36

The Elopement

IT WAS IN THE MOST important matter of my father's life that his proclivity for romancing tripped him up – his marriage. His prospective mother-in-law, Florence Biddulph, was not only a resolute and capable woman of strong character, but she was also rigidly English to the core, and did not understand an exaggeratedly flamboyant Irishman like him.

Just as the Biddulphs were rooted essentially in Norman England, so was Florence Biddulph rooted in her Boothby origins, traditions and characteristics. Like the Biddulphs, the Boothbys had been great English landowners, with their name likewise linked territorially with the soil of England in Boothby-Pagnell. Of pre-Norman noble Danish stock, they claimed descent from Alfred the Great and Charlemagne. The Doomsday Book, the Revolt of the Barons against King John, and many other episodes in the long pages of English history were part of their family lore. But there was more to it than that. Florence Biddulph was the conscious product not only of her ancient past, but also of the times she lived in – times that gave her little stomach for what, at best, she saw as my father's very doubtful Irish peccadillos.

The time was the zenith of British imperialism. Her great English upper class was wealthy and powerful and was ruling a large part of the world. The Englishmen she knew were conventionally and strictly brought up in the pattern of imperial pro-consuls – men fitted to render selfless service to the Crown and the empire in one capacity or another; men of absolute integrity, undeviatingly committed to a spartan code of high and impeccable conduct. That a daughter of hers should contemplate marrying anyone who did not have the particular and peculiar English educational and social trappings of that sort of man, was for her altogether out of the question.

The boys of her own Boothby family were at that time receiving their education at Eton, and Oxford and Cambridge. The class to which they belonged was a largely exclusive, closed society whose rigid, conformist values were the negation of that kind of individuality, eccentricity, and personal idiosyncrasy which the Irish have never been concerned to inhibit or suppress, and which Shaen Magan exhibited so exuberantly and unashamedly. Unschooled, lacking in reticence, deficient in modesty, conversationally self-assertive, boastful, and more than a little prone to hyperbole and colourful embroidery and exaggeration, he was to Florence Biddulph 'not one of us'. He did not conform to her starched code, and therefore was unfitted to marry her daughter.

She could not, of course, be expected to see that that code was already starched to the point of near ossification, or that it was to be due before long for considerable modification and relaxation. Nor was she able to see that the difference lay only in the degree of starch, and not in the code itself. Shaen Magan's code of stoicism and rectitude did not differ from hers. Indeed it was in some respects stricter. In her circle it was fashionable to be seen at the races, and to do a little punting on the horses. He never had a bet in his life. It was also fashionable in her circle of male acquaintances to be able 'to hold' a fair quantity of liquor. He was a lifelong teetotaller.

We must, however, take it that she felt herself to have genuine, serious and honest misgivings – misgivings which caused her to go so far as to doubt his probity.

The upshot was that she forbade the marriage, or, rather, that she persuaded her husband, Assheton, to do so, probably against his better inclinations, being himself an Irishman. But, having taken his stand, he was then, as an Irish autocrat, committed stubbornly to assert himself within his own domain.

In the comparative isolation of Irish country homes, the heads of families went largely unchallenged, and expected to have it all their own way. It is therefore more than likely that the Biddulphs did indeed believe that their daughter would show a proper filial submissiveness, and bow to parental dictates; and also that Shaen Magan, brought up in just such another home, would respect this principle of domestic governance and not meddle further within Assheton's realms.

But that was to mis-judge the situation. Shaen Magan was no less an Irish autocrat than Assheton Biddulph, and no less concerned to have his own way; and Kathleen was no less resolute than her mother. Moreover, the two young people were confident that they were morally in the right. They had given their troth to each other and no-one else could undo that. Yet they were not looking for trouble. They were prepared to be, and indeed were, patient, in the hope that Kathleen's parents would come to their senses and relent.

For two years they waited. Separation was imposed upon them. They were subjected to moratoria. Kathleen was sent abroad for a time. They took it all calmly and in good part, and did nothing to aggravate the situation.

Nevertheless, the Biddulphs remained obdurate, and in the end my father warned Assheton that if he did not consent, he would marry Kathleen without her parents' agreement if she was still willing. But the Biddulphs would not relent.

A week later my father arranged for an old friend of the family, Dean Verschoyle-Campbell, to conduct the wedding service at his church, St Mary's, Athlone.

My mother went to stay locally with friends – a common practice in those days. From their house, on 21 January, 1906, she was fetched by another friend George Enraght-Moony, to his home, The Doon, half-way between the Biddulph home and Athlone. My father and his sisters Blossie and Violet were waiting at The Doon to receive her.

The Biddulph parents were given a last chance. An invitation was sent to them to visit The Doon, where they would have been asked to bury the hatchet and come to the wedding. Blossie's diary records:

We waited all day for Mr and Mrs Biddulph to come over as they had been invited, but they did not come, but sent the carriage and Miss Baker (a governess) at 5 o'clock with furious letters to fetch K. home, but she would not go.

Blossie's comment, as she closed her diary that night, was:

Almost the longest day I ever spent.

So, that was that. Next day they were married, and Blossie wrote in her diary:

Went to bed early and had a good sleep.

Assheton Biddulph never spoke to my mother again. He showed an extraordinary lack of charity. She had been his favourite daughter. Of the last day's hunting they had had together before all this blew up, he had written; 'She rode close on the back of her father, so we were there or thereabouts throughout the day' So had it always been with them, whether walking the hills and bogs, or fishing the mountain streams.

It was years before her mother was prepared to be civil to her again. And neither she nor Assheton were ever prepared to see my father.

They had made a terrible mistake. They had thrown out of their lives, and out of their home, not someone who would have been a liability, but a man who would have been as exceptionally dutiful and attentive a son-in-law, as he had been a tireless help to his own parents, and as, throughout his life, he was helpful to many other people.

He would have got real satisfaction and enjoyment out of doing what he could for them. And when bad times came for Florence, after she had lost her husband and her only son in the same year, and Ireland was beset by long years of I.R.A troubles, directed in part against the landlords and the gentry, he would have been literally ready to risk his life to help her, in the same way that his sister Violet was prepared to risk hers to protect the interests of Assheton's brother Middleton Biddulph, at Rathrobin.

Moreover, because he was Irish – which was, in effect, what she held against him – and because he knew the country and the people in a way that she never could, the people would have trusted him and his sister, being Irish, as they would never have trusted her, being English. He therefore could, and would, have done things for her that she could not do for herself.

Despite Assheton's unnatural ill-treatment of them, my mother and father never bore him any ill will. They often spoke of him with affection, told stories about him and repeated his amusing sayings. But my mother never spoke voluntarily of her mother, and it was hard to get her even to mention her. And it would be a splendid understatement to say that my father, who was in no way a vindictive man, or one to harbour grievances, could never bring himself to speak charitably of her.

When all is said and done, my father must surely be judged to have been unlucky. Almost all women could be guaranteed to fall for his charms, and not to be much concerned about his foibles. My stony-hearted grandmother, Florence Biddulph, was the rare exception.

The Victorian Locum

AFTER MY PARENTS' marriage, Assheton's older brother, Colonel Middleton Biddulph, asked him what it was that he had against my father. Assheton was never prepared to tell the truth about it. He had put it about that his objection was that he regarded my father as insufficiently well off to marry, which was palpably denied by my parents' married lifestyle. On this occasion, however, he told his brother that it simply was that he did not know Shaen Magan well enough to feel that he could agree to the marriage.

One day, finding himself with time on his hands at Assheton's house, Moneyguyneen, awaiting the return of Assheton and Florence, Middleton read through the visitor's book and found entry after entry of Shaen Magan's name.

That caused Middleton, who had no children of his own, to decide to take my mother under his wing, and to place himself *in loco parentis* to her. He made her a personal allowance for herself during his lifetime, and designated her his heir to Rathrobin, his estate and his fortune – arrangements which were revised after the I.R.A. had burnt Rathrobin. Middleton and my father became close friends, and my father was able to give him much help in running his estate and his private affairs.

Thus did Middleton Biddulph, and his English wife Vera, come to have an enormous and pervasive influence on the Magan family. He was the nearest thing I had to a grandfather, as my father's father had died before I was born, and my mother's father, Assheton, was not prepared to own me.

Vera never ceased to be what, in Ireland, we are used to calling 'very English'. She and Uncle Middleton Biddulph injected into the family a huge dose of late Victorian prosperous, English upper-class, high-principled, almost arrogantly self-confident, blinkered, yet genuinely conscientious and benevolent stuffiness that created a highly starched atmosphere in marked contrast to the easy-going ways of Ireland. In my very young life, 'Uncle Middleton' loomed larger in the background than anything else on earth.

In Middleton and Vera we encounter settler characteristics a world apart from those of the Celtic grazier chiefs, but characteristics which, nevertheless, were becoming increasingly common in the Ascendancy, and which could hardly have been more divergent from the rising Irish nationalism of that time. These features of the Ascendancy were the result of its ever closer links with imperialist late-Victorian England of which Middleton's and Vera's case was typical.

His father had died when Middleton was nineteen years of age. He did not, however, settle down to the life of an Irish country gentleman. He took a commission in the British Army and joined the Northumberland Fusiliers, The Fighting Fifth. He was a dedicated soldier with the ambition of every officer – the only ambition of many – some day to command his own regiment. His regimental soldier's work done, he could then retire to the enjoyment of his Irish estate. When that time came he renovated and enlarged Rathrobin and made it into a fine house.

He was in character a well-to-do, straight-laced, upper-class Victorian. From a position of Olympian confidence in the divinely ordered state of society in which he lived, and which decreed the innate superiority of the gentry over all others, he tended with meticulous humanity and sense of duty to the welfare of his tenants, employees, staff and servants. And we can feel assured that he did no less for his soldiers, and in loyal duty to his queen.

I have a vivid recollection of a particular act. As a small boy I was staying at Rathrobin with my mother. On Sunday morning we were taken to church in Uncle Middleton's closed carriage – a brougham. My mother and I were shut up in this conveyance in quite terrifying proximity to the great man and his statuesque wife Vera. It smelt strongly of leather and horse, and it swayed and rumbled along the uneven road with Paul Wallace, the coachman – and I think a lad – outside and above us on the driving box.

At a dismal, leaky, tumble-down, thatched cabin by the side of the road, Paul Wallace, a hardly less dignified figure than his master, stopped the carriage, got down from the box, leaving the boy to keep the horse steady, and came to the window of the carriage. At the same time an ancient, sickly, ragged woman appeared at the half-door of the cottage. Uncle Middleton let down the window and, producing a bottle of medicine from somewhere, gave it to Paul who took it to the woman. For all I know there may have been a few shillings wrapped up with it. The old lady was pathetically grateful. She'd been 'murthered' with the cough, or whatever it was.

The horse was persuaded to pursue its clopping way towards the church, and we moved on in a shower of Irish gratitude:

God bless your honour, and your lady, and God bless you too, Mr Wallace.

It was little enough, no doubt, but in those days if the gentry did not feel a sense of obligation to do what they could, there was no-one else to do it. I expect dozens of bottles of at least psychologically beneficial medicine and other gifts and comforts poured out from Rathrobin. It may not have been the best way to run society, but hitherto no-one had improved upon it.

Uncle Middleton was also a true Victorian in the extent to which he sought to preserve the old, the tried, and the good, particularly in manners and the humanities, while striving at the same time to keep abreast of all that was beneficially modern, adventurous, exciting and new.

He liked scholarship. He continued to read the classics in the original. He built up a splendid library at Rathrobin of several thousand books. It was a beautiful room panelled with teak which he had brought back from Burma. But the classics were not his only interest. He kept up to date with the moderns of his day. Darwin, Ruskin *et al.*, were on his shelves. But he was not tempted to discard the old Gods. His religious observances were conventional. His carriage, or his sidecar, and its horse clopped and swayed their way dutifully Sunday after Sunday to the church at Mountbolus. There, of course, he sat in a special pew – apart. And he did his civic duty. He filled the offices appropriate to a well-off country gentleman – Justice of the Peace, Deputy Lieutenant, High Sheriff of the King's County.

His interest in the exciting inventions of the Victorian era was not just academic. It took an essentially practical form. He had a quarter-plate camera and took large numbers of photographs, many of which survive, and even managed some indoor photography. When he moved into Rathrobin, he installed a carbide gas plant to provide lighting for the house. He also introduced modern plumbing. He was an early motorist and, even before the First War, was already a two-motorcar man. One was an enormous, closed black Wolseley Limousine Landaulette. The other an open De Dion Bouton, blue I think, with frighteningly low doors, and very sumptuous buttoned leather seats.

There was an occasion when Paul Wallace – black boots, leather gaiters, riding breeches, gauntlets, goggles and peaked cap – and I drove alone in the De Dion Bouton to Dublin from Rathrobin. Crossing the Curragh – the combined Salisbury Plain and Newmarket Heath of Ireland – God bless you Mr Wallace whacked her up to 45 m.p.h. I hung on for life, the wind streaming through my hair, a boy's wildest dream of thrilling speed in those days.

The brass carbide lamps and other lavish brasswork on those cars were solidly and splendidly ornamental as well as usefully functional, and Paul Wallace saw to it that they were kept spotlessly polished. Paul was my great-uncle's major domo. He was coachman-cum-chauffeur but could, in the absence of John, the butler, fill that role as well. P. G. Wodehouse's Jeeves is an only slightly exaggerated caricature of such polished, dignified, self-assured, versatile, wholly reliable and competent men.

And, with the motorcars still in mind, I must mention a particular piece of modern equipment with which my great-uncle had provided himself – or Paul Wallace. It was a most efficient, powerful and easily worked hydraulic jack with which to raise those monsters in order to change the often punctured tyres. There was also a maintenance pit in the garage floor.

Uncle Middleton was, too, an early user of a farm tractor. He was a diligent farmer. He renewed all the gates on his home farm. They were hand made of wrought iron, each with his own peculiar monogram ʒ incorporating his initials M. W. B. As he went about his home farm on foot he always carried a manual thistle cutter, and made war on weeds.

He used to tell a story against himself of one of his military innovations. He came to the conclusion that a modern invention, or development, could do away with the enormous amount of time wasted in the army on 'pipe-claying' white leather to keep it clean. White leather belts were worn with scarlet tunics, and were very smart. All that was needed was to substitute white 'patent leather' for it. So he had a white patent leather belt especially constructed and tailored for himself, and, unannounced, appeared on parade in it. The regiment was more shocked than impressed.

He used to terrify me when he asked me questions. As a small boy I was always top of the class at mental arithmetic. But if Uncle Middleton suddenly asked what are eight nines, nature introduced into the proceedings the same physiological trick with which she has armed the stoat to freeze the brain of a rabbit.

Then there was my unforgettable and dreadful solecism. I was staying with my father and mother at Rathrobin. It must have been soon after the First War as I was just about old enough to be allowed to stay up to dinner. There were no guests. Uncle Middleton and my father and I sat on at table after Aunt Vera and my mother had withdrawn. I was concerned to be as quiet, immobile and inconspicuous as some creature at the bottom of the ocean. I did not want to be asked any questions. But suddenly I was most unwillingly projected into the full glare of the limelight. Uncle Middleton addressed me:

'Would you please fetch the port from the sideboard.'

My father being a teetotaller, I knew nothing of the mysteries of drink. I had been made aware that it was dangerous stuff, and that was about all.

So, from my sort of mental camouflage of frozen immobility, I now had to rise and walk the length of the dining room with, so to speak, all eyes upon me. It was a long, imposing, panelled room. Such rooms can have an overwhelming effect on children. If I could get there without falling over my feet, or my knees giving way, I was going to be lucky. If I could then get back with the added handicap of bearing the full responsibility for the safety of the precious decanter of port, it would be a miracle. Knees knocking, off I went, made the sideboard and grasped the decanter.

There was one piece of knowledge in which I was safe. I knew what to do with dangerous liquids. 'Shake the bottle!' So, as I turned to start the return journey, I gave that decanter a vigorous shaking such as it would never forget – nor I. Cries of horror! Somehow I made the table again in utter confusion, and a great deal more shaken even than the port. I was lectured on the proper and respectful handling of port. It taught me a lesson – always to make sure in advance that people know what to do and how to do it before you entrust them with a mission. But, on this occasion, Uncle Middleton was at a disadvantage. He, poor man, had no children. He had not experienced their genius for doing the unexpected. Perhaps he had paid me the dangerous compliment of expecting adult attitudes and capabilities of me, including a well-instructed and respectful handling of vintage port. The occasion is so graven on my mind that I even remember the year of that vintage. 'Cockburn '96.'

In 1891, Middleton, aged forty-two, married Vera Josephine Flower, fourteen years younger than himself, sister of a very junior brother officer, and a member of the Stratford-on-Avon brewing family. Her father was Sir William Henry Flower, Director of the Natural History Museum, and President of the Royal Zoological Society.

Middleton's younger brother, my grandfather Assheton Biddulph, had by then already been married more than ten years, so Middleton's was the role of cadet in this marriage business. He confided his intention to brother Assheton.

'And who's the lucky lady?' asked Assheton.

'Vera Flower.'

'And who's she?'

'The daughter of Sir William Flower.'

'And who's he?'

'Really, Assheton! You're an incorrigible Philistine. You don't know who Sir William Flower is! He's the Director of the Natural History Museum.'

'Well, I wouldn't know him even if he was Director of the British Museum.' A pause, and then, 'By the way, Middleton, who is the Director of the British Museum?'

Middleton was just that much too serious, and liable thus to trip himself up. He was always scolding the family for their Irish brogues, and Irishisms. One day, when she was a girl, my mother and other members of the family were lunching at Rathrobin. Uncle Middleton had been out rabbiting. He was late returning, and it was decided not to wait for him. In the course of lunch he arrived, profuse with apologies. He couldn't help it:

'The ferret lay in on me' – a real Irishism. The younger members exchanged surreptitious knowing glances around the table.

Once after my mother – by then a long-since married woman – had written him a long letter, he sent her a dictionary to improve her spelling. It didn't; or my father's either; any old spelling was good enough for both of them.

And while on rabbits. Not only were they so prolific in Ireland in those days that it was necessary to keep their numbers down by waging constant war on them, but they were also a good and cheap source of food, and were part of the staple diet of nearly every Irish house, however grand. At the end of a visit to an Irish country house, Dean Swift was asked to write something special in the visitor's book. He said he would do so if they would promise not to open it until after supper. The moment came and, their mouths watering with anticipatory literary salivations, they read this:

> *Rabbits young, rabbits old.*
> *Rabbits hot, rabbits cold.*
> *Rabbits tender, rabbits tough.*
> *Praise the Lord! I've had enough!*

I have mentioned the influence that Uncle Middleton's marriage to Vera Flower had on the Magan family. This stemmed from her background of what might be called romantic high Victorianism. Her mother descended from the famous Elizabethan adventurer, John Smythe, who founded Virginia, and was rescued from death by the celebrated Princess Pocahontas. Her grandfather, Admiral William Henry Smythe, a rigorous self-disciplinarian who rationed himself to five hours sleep, was hardly less distinguished than his famous forebear. He had charted the Mediterranean, was a leading astronomer and numismatist, and an enormously versatile scholar of limitless ability associated with a large number of intellectual and scientific societies.

His three sons, Vera's uncles, were no less distinguished. One was Astronomer Royal for Scotland, and carried out researches into the Great Pyramid of Cheops, and the other two both received knighthoods. His daughters, Vera's aunts, likewise earned distinction. One was the mother of a number of distinguished sons of whom one was Lord Baden-Powell, founder of the Scout Movement, Vera's first cousin who used to visit her at Rathrobin.

Vera's mother, Rosetta Smythe, Lady Flower, I knew as a very old woman in her nineties. To me she was awesome on account of her antiquity, and because she had known Queen Victoria. I suppose her name, Rosetta, derived from some association of her father's with the Rosetta Stone during his Mediterranean service. A family joke about her was her supposed saying: 'Queen Victoria always has three cups when she comes to tea.'

Admiral Smythe's wife, Vera's grandmother, had, as a small girl, been the only 'lady' present at a dinner given by her father, the British Consul in Naples, to Nelson and his captains after the Battle of the Nile. She was disapproving of one of them who gave her a kiss. Nelson said, 'You must not mind. His name is Hardy; he is captain of the *Audacious*.'

On Vera's father's side, her great-grandfather, an ardent eighteenth century reformer, despairing of adequate reform in England, had sold his country estate, chartered three ships and, with his whole family, his menservants, his maid-servants, his oxen, his asses, six couple of fox-hounds and two deer-hounds, sailed, like the Pilgrim Fathers, for America, and there founded a Flower dynasty.

One of his sons, Vera's grandfather, returned to England and founded the brewery at Stratford-upon-Avon. His third son, William, was Vera's father.

As a boy, William Flower collected specimens and created his own personal museum in a box. He studied medicine, and early in his medical career volunteered for service in the Crimea where he suffered severe frostbite. Back in England he had, by the age of thirty, made a significant name for himself as a surgeon and scientist, and had attracted the attention of men such as T. H. Huxley. It thus came about that when he applied for the post of Director of the museum of the Royal College of Surgeons, he was chosen from a large number of candidates.

Three years earlier, he had married Rosetta Smythe. He was twenty-seven years of age, she was twenty-three. He had known her since she was fifteen. He met the Smythe family in his student days while on a walking tour in Wales. The rigorously disciplined Admiral of the rationed five hours sleep had been impressed when he had learnt that the young man his family had met at a dance proposed to have no sleep – simply to change his clothes, and then to walk twenty miles across the hills, presumably carrying his luggage, to catch a coach from Caernarvon. William Flower, for his part, was no less impressed and delighted with the vigorous physical and intellectual atmosphere and environment of the Smythe household. It was a marriage made in heaven. William Flower and Rosetta lived in devoted partnership until his death forty-one years later.

With his young wife and two babies, he moved into the spacious dwelling house that adjoined the museum in Lincoln's Inn Fields, and there Vera, and the other children – seven in all as the years went on – were brought up with skeletons, skulls and bottles of 'wet' specimens as an ever present part of their lives. Such affection did they have for the place that one of the girls said later that it had been her unfulfilled ambition as a child to sleep a night alone in the museum.

In Lincoln's Inn Fields, William Flower, while still only a young man, achieved by his ability and integrity, and his agreeable personality, a position at the very hub of the scientific and artistic world. All the great names were his colleagues, friends and visitors at the museum, and guests of the family at his house – Darwin, Lister, Huxley, Longfellow, Tennyson, Browning, Dean Farrar (*Eric, or Little by Little*), Charles Kingsley, are among those mentioned almost by chance in a short biography written after his death. A very close friend was the Dean of Westminster, Dean Stanley, whose wife was a daughter of the Earl of Elgin of the Elgin Marbles. At Lincoln's Inn Fields, and later at their house in Stanhope Gardens, when William Flower had become Director of the Natural History Museum, this procession of notables, including royalty, both our own royal family, and foreign royalty, to be conducted, instructed, consulted and entertained, was a ceaseless part of the life of the family. His home enjoyed, and his family experienced, nothing short of a parade of the great Victorians.

Those – together with the skeletons, skulls, and wet specimens – comprised the company, and theirs the table-talk, in which my great-aunt Vera grew up. She was brought up a town girl. She was brought up a London girl. She was brought up in the sheltered upper class urban, intellectual, scientific, literary and artistic heart of the first city of the world. It was an altogether different ethos from the life of the pastures, hills and bogs of Ireland.

Nor was it all London for Aunt Vera and the Flower family, or all science and seriousness. There were holidays and fun. A deliriously diverting time on one holiday collecting fossils, and on another studying extinct volcanoes. And light-hearted and entertaining parlour games no doubt, acrostics, double acrostics, anagrams, historical arithmorems, peppered perhaps with hilarious Latin puns.

Those were the influences that Aunt Vera transported with her to Rathrobin, and which emanated so strongly from her into the far less stringent, softer Irish atmosphere. It was, as we see, a background of marvellous interest, of impeccably good behaviour, of devotion to the highest duty, of time spent in the pursuit of excellence. But it was not quite a wholly rounded life. It lacked direct contact with mother earth herself, and with those fellow human beings who live nearer to the soil. The Irishness of Ireland had no appeal for Vera. Many English women fell for it and its ways, at least in part, and sometimes in large part. Vera's exclusive, English upper class, ruling class, fastidiously reserved demeanour of refinement and distinction was never so much as even slightly dented by laxer – I might say, more human – Irish ways. She remained, throughout her Irish life, firmly wrapped in her English class attitudes, quite impervious to any moderating influences. She was aesthetically beautiful, with a statuesque immobility of feature, and a distant manner, that had 'don't touch' written all over it.

Thus, with Aunt Vera anticipating Rupert Brooke, Rathrobin became 'a corner of a foreign field that is forever England' – and well-starched, upper-class Victorian England at that. It was the epitome of English Victorian drawing-room, smoking-room, billiard-room, library, conservatory conventionality; and it had an atmosphere that permeated an aura of disapproval of everything that did not meet its own impeccable standards; and the disapproval was real. Accents, deportment, table-manners, table-talk, dress and address – the course of life was absolutely strewn with bunkers for the uninitiated and the unwary.

I have many photographs – snapshots – taken of Aunt Vera by Uncle Middleton. In only two of them is there even a ghost of a smile. In almost all of them she is most beautifully – and one would suppose for the Irish countryside, unsuitably – dressed. She had a truly wonderful sense of clothing, and she wore her clothes like a queen. She had a marvellous figure, and the countenance of Nefertiti, and a posture compared with which the most prized model would look graceless, and always a regally imperious and abstracted look in her face.

Yet, while she thus exhibited a lofty poise, was she perhaps, at the same time, the victim of her circumstances? Hospitable though the Irish country gentry may have been, to a stranger theirs could seem a very closed society. They knew each other well, and had shared common, and very Irish, interests since childhood. And if your interests were not theirs, and did not include the more vigorous country pursuits, you could feel very much out of things. Possibly it was the case that the whole Irish scene was distasteful to her. Of course, by her strict code, she would have been too polite to say so, and too stoical to do other than endure it. Perhaps, deep in her heart of hearts, 'sick for home, she stood and wept amid the alien corn', pining in silent resignation for those dear old 'wet specimens'.

That as it may be, to visit Rathrobin was a special and constrained experience, like going to church – and wholly unlike a visit to my Magan aunts.

You were going to be lucky to get through it without reproof. Not from Uncle Middleton or Aunt Vera themselves but from those who were anxious that we should not let the side down. Aunt Vera and Uncle Middleton were not unkind. I still feel warmly grateful to him for the half-crowns he used to give me.

He was living in London, old and in poor health, when he heard that I, as a fifteen-year-old boy, acted as my father's bodyguard carrying his revolver on my knee as we drove in I.R.A. times to Rathrobin on similar supervisory missions to those carried out by my aunt, Violet Magan. He promptly sent me £100 which in those days was riches and, safely invested, brought in what to me was a handsome income.

Although they were not themselves unkind, nor were they spontaneously warm. Indeed spontaneous or impulsive behaviour of any sort were human frailties which they had long since strictly disciplined and repressed. It just was that it was a strongly alien, and severely restricting, atmosphere. The tang of Stanhope Gardens hung heavily about Rathrobin, and from there seeped into all our lives.

My own technique was to excuse myself from the presence as soon as I could and go ratting in the straw stacks with Uncle Middleton's terrier Risk, who was my friend – Aunt Vera kept lap dogs which were much less to my liking – or to go to the kitchen for tit-bits, and if they could spare me a little time, a lark with the servants. They, too, were my friends. With them I felt quite safe and at home.

I am not aware that Aunt Vera inherited any of her father's zoological interests, but in that connection there is a nice little story about Middleton.

He was innately didactic, and my mother one day overheard an exchange between him and his gardener. Johnnie was being interrogated on knowledge he had been vouchsafed on the life-cycle of a butterfly:

'And now, Johnnie, what happens to the chrysalis?'

After some puzzled head-scratching,

'I think, yer honour, she bursts'.

But there I must leave Rathrobin, and its powerful influences, and what to me is the immense interest of having had such close personal contact with, and such a strong whiff of, the world of the great Victorians. There were of course others of the same sort, friends of the family, whom I met, but Rathrobin was different. It was an ever present family influence and eminence overshadowing all our lives, indeed, as it seemed, overshadowing the world. It was an outpost of the leviathan battleground between Darwin and Bishop Wilberforce, and the shake and rumbling thunders of that encounter, and all that it stood for in the clash between enlightenment and obscurantism, were palpable there.

Early in the 1920s, ill health forced Uncle Middleton to live in London, where he and Vera had a house, or flat in Cheyne Walk. Soon afterwards Rathrobin was burnt by the I.R.A. They bombed the beautiful library just to make sure that nothing survived. Uncle Middleton died in 1926, in his seventy-seventh year. Aunt Vera lived on in England until 1938, when she died on her birthday, aged seventy-five. A part of the Ascendancy was gone.

CHAPTER 38

My Mother, Kathleen Jane Biddulph

I HAVE NEVER KNOWN a more contented person than my mother. There was nothing feigned about it. She was just naturally serenely contented.

She refused to worry. She had a saying – she had lots of sayings; my brother Francis collected some of them into a little book – 'Why worry? It may never happen', and with her it usually didn't. When we were children we lived surrounded by water. We were out in boats till all hours of the night. She went to bed, and soundly to sleep. She never worried about us. Despite some near misses, none of us drowned.

She was dreadfully handicapped by deafness from an early age. She got measles at school in England. The story is that her father insisted on her coming home too soon so that she could attend the Hunt Ball. Complications leading to deafness were the consequence. But she never complained, and never talked about it. On the contrary, she used to say, 'Aren't I lucky not to be blind'. When I was a boy I asked her whether there was anything she specially missed. She said 'Yes: the birds singing'. I think I never discussed her deafness with her again.

She lived all her life in the country, doing country things. She was no gardener, but kept a minimum of flowers to give a semblance of a garden and some colour. She did not like cut flowers. Any cut flowers in the house were usually presents from other people. She thought flowers had as much right to live out their lives as the rest of us. To her they were living things which she had no right to murder. She liked to keep a few fowl for eggs, and ducks, and sometimes geese to eat. She did not mind having them killed. But in her later years, when she was old, she did not bother with them. She could always buy fresh eggs, as all the cottages in Ireland keep fowl ('hins').

One Christmas she heard of someone who had good turkeys. Arrived at the cottage, she found a hedge along the road. It was dominated on the far side by a fine country face under a battered hat giving the hedge a pre-Christmas trim-up with a pair of hand-clippers.

'Are you Mr Malone?' asked my mother.

'No, ma'am. I'm his brother.'

No wonder the exile feels pangs at times.

My parents, until they were very old, always kept a couple of cows for milk for the house. My mother never lost the pleasure and interest in her dairy which she had developed when she was a child, and she continued to keep a dairy until she was too old to churn the butter herself in the wooden churn she had had for most of her life. She never allowed anyone else to do the dairy work. It was a part of the pattern of her simple lifelong country routine.

The milk to be skimmed for cream was poured into large shallow enamel bowls. When the cream had collected on the surface she skimmed it off with slightly concave, handled and perforated discs, into earthenware jars. The residue, the skim milk, was fed to the calves and pigs, or sold to the cottagers who had many uses for it. Some of the cream was used for the table, some was churned by my mother once a week to make butter. The residue, the buttermilk, was used to make bread. We were encouraged as children to drink the buttermilk, but it was watery and sour and we did not like it. The butter was patted into little balls and other shapes with serrated wooden spade-like 'butter pats'. It was never served on the table in a lump.

Some of the cream was allowed to go sour, and was made into white cream cheese. It was squeezed out in muslin bags, hung up to drain, and then placed on a plate with another on top, and a brick on top of that to flatten it. The resulting cheese was usually circular, about five inches in diameter, and one inch deep. It was placed on the table always decorated with a stinging nettle. It was delicious, and could be eaten with honey.

The dairy had a cool atmosphere of clean, wet, but drying wooden implements, washed and drying muslin cloths, and clean milk-pans standing on end against the wall waiting to be used the next time. My mother cleaned her own dairy, and herself kept the churn and all the rest of the dairy equipment scrupulously clean. That was part of her childhood routine that accompanied her through life.

She enjoyed hunting, and the long days in the saddle. She kept horses, and hunted, until she was in her fifties. But she was not horsey. Indeed she never rode except to hunt. She did not like racing. She had an idea that it asked too much of horses.

She loved fishing, particularly brown trout fishing. Brought up on the mountain streams at her home, she particularly liked wet-fly fishing for small trout. But she was also a good dry-fly fisher.

Mountains, too, she loved. She was born at the foot of the Slieve Bloom mountains and climbed them endlessly. She was not a technical mountaineer, but she was an indefatigable and very experienced mountain walker. She was one of those deceptive people who climb steadily and fast with a seemingly slow pace. You were soon panting to keep up with her. At the age of eighty, she and her youngest sister, Ethne, paid a visit to Iona. My mother saw an irresistibly nice looking mountain. Ethne, who could be bossy, said she was not to climb it. My mother insisted. It almost came to fisticuffs, but she climbed it.

She was not in any scientific sense a naturalist, but she knew the trees, the birds and the wild flowers. She was not sentimental about them, but, together with herself, they were a part of nature. Just to be out of doors in the country was satisfaction enough for her. She did not mind what the weather was like. She would go out in all weathers. Her unhurried country life was one that might seem to some to be dull. An acquaintance who met her one day in Grafton Street in Dublin said, 'I can't think, Kathleen, what you do with yourself all day, buried in the country'. 'Neither can I,' my mother replied. 'I only know that I never stop doing it.'

She did not often go away on holiday, though she and my father sometimes went to the west of Ireland for salmon and sea trout fishing. On any other sort of holiday, she liked very simple things, paddling in the sea, hunting for sea shells, the wonders of rock pools. The unusual always caught her eye – a plant growing where you would not expect to find it. The exceptional, whether terrestrial or celestial, always held great fascination for her.

She did no original thinking. She lived by a code of cliches and conventions that nevertheless stood her in good stead. Her attitude to life was uncomplicated and straightforward. She recognized no moral dilemmas. Things were either right or wrong.

Part of my mother's conventionality was religious fundamentalism. She was not obsessively religious. We did not have grace at meals, daily family prayers, Bible readings, or anything of that sort. It was simply that she took for granted that every word of the scriptures was literally factual, and that was the rock-like foundation of her whole way of life. Certain observances, too, were an indispensable part of her conventional routine. There was nothing soft about the Almighty. He demanded a stern code. I learnt from my mother the sort of religion that was hers. Children, at a very tender age – they were not themselves encouraged to be very tender – must learn the Lord's Prayer, the Catechism and the Ten Commandments. I knew them all by heart by the time I was about six years of age. Most of it was meaningless to me. I dare say much of it was to her too. What mattered was that it was part of life's holy drill.

Routine went hand in hand with her regulated attitudes. Her whole life was governed by simple routines. They were not slavish, or inflexibly rigid. Their purpose was to make life easier, not more difficult. Stick to the tramlines and the tram would largely look after itself. And, by and large, it worked very well.

She rose daily at the same time; had routine meals by the clock, and returned to bed at the same time nightly. She was quite wonderfully placid, and her routines, which were not exacting to herself or anyone else, were calmly and quietly carried out, and with unhurried deliberation. She didn't believe in fussing herself or anyone else. Life could be, and should be, a leisurely affair. The mornings were devoted to looking after her home, and she and the servants had their routine jobs.

She had been brought up in the conventional arts of country-house housekeeping. She had plenty of old-fashioned wholesome recipes, and a good bit of the morning was spent in the kitchen with the cook where she took some hand in the cooking, particularly cake-making, and jams and puddings. Meat and vegetables were more exclusively the province of the cook, until the meat got to the mince stage. Then my mother involved herself to ensure that nothing was wasted. My father's sister Violet used to say that whenever she arrived at our home she would be sure to find my mother scraping old bones. My mother used, too, to go herself to the garden and gather for herself the fruit and vegetables she wanted. She liked doing that, and was much more interested in the vegetables and fruit than in flowers.

She was very thrifty. Nothing was wasted or thrown away. My sister Maureen said that the weekly meat routine consisted of hot meat, cold meat and old meat. The old meat not infrequently became rissoles which, as a boy, I enjoyed. The Irish cook used to call them 'mystery balls'.

Irish country houses in their beautiful parklands – the demesne lands – may often have looked imposing, but life within them was very practical, simple and unpretentious.

My mother's thriftiness was such that the string of a parcel must never be cut. That was wicked waste. It must be carefully un-knotted, tidily rolled up, and kept. The paper must likewise be folded and preserved. I am sure she never needed to buy brown paper, and it must have been a rare occurrence for her to buy a ball of string.

Letter paper was another economy. Letters were always written on folded paper in those times. A short letter left the back fold blank. My mother carefully tore them off and kept them for use to particular correspondents, such as her children at school, who might occasionally be surprised to get a letter with a stray date, such as 1895, lingering in some corner.

Her thriftiness did not have a mercenary basis. It was just prudent housekeeping. She had no love of money. Indeed she positively disliked it. If she did not think it the root of all evil, at least she had a sort of Bible-based distaste for it. Of course she could afford to have over-simple views on the subject. But, in general, her view was that people ought to get along with what they had by living carefully and economically, and not go spending all their time trying to grab more money.

Her afternoons and evenings were free more or less. She would sew and knit, read and write letters. In her early married life she used to make clothes for herself and her children. Later she did less sewing, though she did a lot of mending. Until she was very old, she knitted endlessly. She did it while she read. The male members of the family were kept generously supplied with beautifully knitted socks and stockings. Our country life demanded thick woollen stockings and socks.

She always kept a dog, but never a pampered lap dog, and she was not doggy. I think her dogs were always mongrels. She would go for a walk with it in the afternoons. Dogs are specially good friends to the deaf, the dumb or the blind. There is a curiously close affinity. Dogs seem to know, and care. In the summer, she might take her rod and go fishing, but usually in the evenings for the evening rise.

She read *Blackwood's Magazine* from cover to cover all her life. Her book reading was light. She liked adventure, true adventure if possible, stories of mountaineers, mariners, aviators, explorers, big-game hunters, pioneers, missionaries, medical men, engineers, soldiers and sailors in wild, distant and outlandish places. That was part of the fare that Blackwoods served up with unfailing regularity and in delicious good taste. Books on Ireland, too, she found endlessly fascinating; also books on the peoples who lived outside and beyond the conventions of settled civilization, gypsies, tinkers or nomadic tribes.

But she also enjoyed fiction. There was a splendid crop of adventure story writers in the late nineteenth and early twentieth century – before the world went mad on sex, violence and psychology. *Beau Geste* (P. C. Wren). *Riders of the Purple Sage* (Zane Grey). That was the stuff for her. Then there were Henty, A. E. W. Mason (*The Four Feathers* – right up my mother's street), Stanley Weyman (*Under the Red Robe* – what a book!), and others – but that's enough. The shelves of Killyon were full of them. But we must have *The Thirty-Nine Steps* and *John Macnab*.

Because gypsies and tinkers were part of her local landscape, and because Walter Starkie was a Fellow of Trinity College, Dublin, his delightful book *Raggle-Taggle* was among her favourites. There was the day when she stopped to talk to a tinker encampment and was delighted to find that one of the men had held commissioned rank in the Royal Air Force during the Second World War. But 'home' to him was an Irish ditch with his pots and pans and tin-ware, and an even more rudimentary shelter than was customary among the meanest dwellings of the old Irish septs. People can still, even in the twentieth century, and even in our own islands, live contentedly in such conditions today – do, indeed, live in them for preference – even though they may have known the comforts of a British officers' mess.

In her later years, her taste for the extraordinary led her into the quasi-religious field. She became an ardent British Israelite. She believed implicitly in the so-called pyramid prophecies, which were in tune with her burning Irish Protestant loyalty to the British Crown. She was also innocently attracted to the mysterious and the occult. Pictures jumping off the walls as harbingers of death in the family, or ghostly coaches rattling up the drive at dead of night on a similar gruesome mission, were not matters for doubt or question.

Living as she did largely by code and precept, she was, of course, stubborn, though nicely so. She could not easily be shifted from any course on which she was set. Here her deafness was to her advantage. It was difficult to argue with her. The strength of her unimaginative determination to keep things according to the rules is well illustrated by the story of her encounter with the I.R.A.

It was in the morning. She was going hunting. She had just finished getting into her hunting clothes. She came down stairs to find a party of rough-looking men pushing their way into the hall. They were, it was later confirmed, the I.R.A. What they were proposing to do will never be known. They were not given time to explain themselves. Brandishing her whip, my mother went for them immediately and ordered them out of the house. 'Out! The lot of you – at once!' And they went. My view is that what passed through her mind was, 'what on earth do these dreadful people think they are doing coming in through the front door, of all places, and in their muddy boots. Don't they know that the kitchen door is the place for them?'

Of course, as a member of the Protestant Ascendancy, she was heaven-born. But that did not make her personally proud, lofty or haughty. You just were, by courtesy of the Almighty, placed by birth above the commonalty, and that was understood to involve more obligations than privileges. She was born into an hierarchical society whose social grades were just as natural to those who lived in it as is the caste system to most Hindus.

Nor did the country people much think to question those attitudes. The aristocratic tradition lingered on in most of rural Ireland. Moreover, it was still something more than a mere echo and legacy of the past. The big house continued to give a certain cohesion to rural life. At its best it was felt to be a source of protection, comfort, support, help and advice in time of need.

There would have been no good the egalitarians thinking they could make someone like my mother equal. They failed to do so with Charles I. They might batter her, and beggar her, but they could never change her. The regicides had to cut off Charles's head. Logically, they were right. There was no other way of ridding it of the certainty of his God-given superiority. What God had ordained, man could not disclaim. They would have had to cut off my mother's head, too, to purge her of that God-given sense of superior birthright.

She was very interested in her children, and uncritical of them. Not only was she never condescending, but, on the contrary, was herself so modest that she was inclined to think that whatever we did, however ordinary, was wonderful. But I think her interest was much deeper than her affections. If one of us had killed ourselves in a particularly spectacular way, and if a picture had hopped off the wall at the same time, or a ghostly coach appeared, the dramatic uniqueness of the circumstances of our demise would, I believe, have caused her to regard the event as more interesting than doleful.

In a practical, though sometimes unimaginative, way, she was marvellously attentive to us. She wrote a weekly letter to each of her five children all the time we were at boarding school, and indeed, I think, in later life as well. I myself certainly had a weekly exchange of letters with my parents, and particularly with my mother, throughout the twenty-three years that I was abroad, after joining the army – except when circumstances made it impossible. My mother's was a neat, open, round, legible handwriting – as patently honest and uncomplicated as herself.

That some of us went abroad for many years at a time was a hardship for her, though I don't think my father minded. But there was a certain glow of compensation for my mother in the fact that we went to the sort of, to her, exciting places where there might be sharks, crocodiles, wild animals, strange peoples including, with any luck, witch doctors, and even cannibals. Worry on that score? Of course not. One did not worry about anything.

To be spartan was almost a part of her religion. Excessive warmth – or much warmth at all – was un-Christian. All her life, she never had any heating in her bedroom. I truly believe she would have thought it sinful. If we had colds as children, we were turned out of doors. 'Nothing worse than stuffing in fuggy rooms.' The rooms were not all that fuggy. Sitting in them in a chair was cold comfort. You needed some sort of human spit to keep turning you in front of the inadequate fire even to stop your teeth chattering. It didn't suit my father. He liked 'roaring' in front of a roaring fire.

She did everything in moderation, and nothing in haste or to excess. In those ways she was the antithesis – should I say the complement? – of my father, to whom scenes and fuss, rhetoric and drama were the very stuff of life. In anything my father did he involved as many other people as he could muster, and, even if it was no more than hanging a picture, it was done to the accompaniment of a crescendo of noise, shouting, orders, counter-orders, and as much dramatic action as could be contrived. My mother, by contrast, would do it quietly by herself, standing on a chair, when no-one was looking. For my father every event, whether it was examining a herd of cattle, or marking trees for felling in a wood, had to be turned into a pantomime.

She was very hospitable, and both she and my father gave to all friends, relations and visitors a very genuinely warm welcome to their home. There is nothing that would please me more than to be able to arrive home again to the warm greeting I always received from my parents under the pillared portico at Killyon – where you risked half a hundred weight of rotten stucco falling on your head. Sitting in his chair, perhaps reading the paper, however inattentive my father might appear, he always in fact had one ear cocked for an arriving vehicle if anyone was expected. When he heard it coming up the avenue, 'There they are,' he would cry out, leaping as best he could from his chair, and hastening to the hall door in order to be there as soon as the sound of rattling gravel was heard on what he always called 'the sweep' in front of the house. The arrival of 'an audience' was a matter of real pleasure and excitement for him. He would fling open one of the heavy double oak doors. My mother would manage to be there as well, and the visitor, family member or anyone else, would get as genuinely warm a welcome as they might encounter anywhere in the world in a twelvemonth.

CHAPTER 39

Farewell the Ascendancy

WHEN WE BADE FAREWELL to the chiefs, it was the Ascendancy that took their place. Now, some three centuries later, the Ascendancy's own turn had come.

1913 witnessed a special event at Moneyguyneen. On 5 August – mark the date – my aunt, Ierne Biddulph, Assheton and Florence Biddulph's second daughter, was married from home, at Kinnity church, to Captain John (Jack) Goold-Adams of the Leinster Regiment.

A press report describes the moment of departure of the bride and bridegroom after the reception at Moneyguyneen:

As the bride and bridegroom left the door, her father, the M. F. H., unexpectedly blew a double 'Gone Away' on his horn. The hounds in the kennels immediately answered and helped to swell the chorus of cheers.

And as the guests waved the parting couple out of sight, and turned again for a last stroll on the lawns in the warmth of that summer evening, none was to know that the long drawn quavering final note on the Master's horn was near akin to the knell of an epoch. Within little more than a year Assheton's horn and hounds would be silenced, their music never more to echo through the valleys of the Slieve Bloom mountains. In 365 days to the day, the world would be struck, on 4 August, 1914, by a greater disaster than anything known for seven centuries, since Jenghis Khan and the Mongols had laid waste half the world. Many among the guests that day would soon lie dead on the field of battle, and the bridegroom and Master's only son were not to be spared. The whole pattern of the last phase of the Irish Ascendancy's existence, that I have been trying to describe in these pages, would be swept entirely away. It was farewell to the Ascendancy.

Ireland was effectively a colony, ruled, since the Act of Union, of 1801, from Whitehall, and garrisoned by troops of the Crown. Between the loyalist country gentry, and their upper professional and business counterparts, and the officers of the garrisons, there was a common bond that gave its particular flavour to the social life about which I have written here. The Act of Union itself, together with Catholic emancipation, had long since dissipated the political power of the landed gentry, and recent land legislation had spelt the coming diminishment – indeed dispersal – of their estates. For four decades, since the first Home Rule bill, the sword of Damocles had hung over this social scene, but few had expected it to fall, just as today few expect the atomic Armageddon.

But the 1914–18 World War brought the climax and the end. The Home Rule bill tabled in 1912, with the determination of the British Government that it should succeed, made it certain that a substantial degree of independence for at least the predominantly Catholic areas of Ireland was not far off. Had it not been for the war, it might have been delayed a little longer, but the cataclysmic social, political and economic upheaval of the Great War so weakened Britain's position in the world, even though she was one of the principal victors, that it can now be seen that she was not for much longer going to be able to retain her empire. Ireland, as Henry Grattan and other Irishmen had foreseen a century earlier would be the case, was the first stick in the imperial log jam to give way. India would clearly be the next, and talks to that end were soon vigorously under way. The Second World War washed the rest away.

Of the end of the Irish Ascendancy, it can be said that, with the disappearance of a large part of the hardy, free-spirited, mildly eccentric, self-assured and incontestably loyal Irish gentry – the Gintry – Britain has lost a not altogether negligible component in the constitutional fabric supporting the integrity of the Crown.

Lecky, in his great history published nearly a quarter of a century earlier, in 1892, had had this to say about the dissolution of the Ascendancy which had then already begun:

> *The soundest elements in Irish life are those which are least represented. The most peaceful, law-abiding, and industrious classes, are so completely out-voted by great masses of agricultural peasants, that they are virtually disenfranchised. Grattan clearly foresaw that this might one day be the fate of Ireland.*

He added that this had, 'contributed to a marked and lamentable decline in the governing faculty of the upper orders in Ireland'.

Those are sentiments familiar and comprehensible to all – and among them many Irish people – who have played a part in the conduct of benevolent colonial administrations, and who were whole-heartedly of one mind with Dr Johnson when he said:

> *It is our first duty to serve society ...*

Those whose lives had thus been devoted to good order and good administration, in a tradition in which they had been carefully schooled, and in which they believed, and which, in so far as they could make it so, they conceived to be the best of its kind, could not, like Lecky, be other than at least saddened, and more probably made apprehensive, to see themselves on the point of being supplanted by others, some, at any rate, of whom they believe to have standards rendering them less than fit to succeed to the hitherto near sacred charge now to be surrendered to them. Nor does the deplorable state into which some of the erstwhile colonial world has lapsed make such sentiments seem, in retrospect, by any means unjustified.

But there are other points of view. Curzon, towards the end of the nineteenth century, said of the Persians that he had come to the conclusion that they would far rather misgovern themselves than be well-governed by others. Perhaps, too, there are beneficial tensions in society that a benevolent colonial rule tends to suppress lest they escalate into disorder. There is also the fact that if the colonial power is to respect the ancient customs of the local people, as it must if it is to remain acceptable, it becomes a force for reaction, inhibiting change or progress.

That the deep cultural differences between the native Irish and the English should cause the Irish to conduct their affairs in ways less acceptable to Lecky than those of the Protestant Ascendancy, is understandable. Nevertheless, it was necessarily to be supposed that means and methods conforming and comfortable to their own characteristics would not work, but rather that they would work in their own Irish way.

Would it? – the question is inevitably asked in the context of all colonial situations – would it not have been better for colonial powers never to have become involved in the administration of other peoples? The answer is that that option was not open. As in the case of Ireland, so also elsewhere; the three-masted ship made involvement inevitable. Sailors could not stand offshore for ever. Once contact was made, a multitude of different interests, opportunities, ambitions, beneficial and deleterious, began to develop. The process could neither be prevented in the first place, nor halted once it had begun.

Following Ierne Biddulph's wedding one normal season's hunting remained, during the winter of 1913–14, and one more round of concerts, point-to-point, Hunt Ball, puppy show, and all the rest of the social calendar, but thereafter, the declaration of war was immediately critical for hunting.

There was some hunting in the King's County in the winter of 1914–15. But the 12 March 1915, heard the last long blast of the Master's horn fade away into the hills. Never would it disturb the Slieve Bloom foxes more. Let us then take leave of the Hunt with a short contemporary account of one last sparkling run – the last entry in the scrap-book:

Harristown held a brace of foxes. Hounds ran hard on a great scent past Harristown House, and over the big mearing fence into Ross. Then crossing the big pastures, they passed Ballyedmund House, went over the road and Whitewall Hill, going on through the old covert of that name. Skirting the bog and crossing the Galway Road, the fox passed the Rookery for Coolacutta, then went down to the river Goul, which was reached just opposite Mr W. Haughton's house at Glashare. The river was in high flood, and, worse still, was wired at the only fordable places, so followers had to watch the flying pack streaming away over a grand stretch of country. The field divided, some going to the right, some to their left, and both divisions picked up hounds who hunted their fox to the Rock Covert where they were stopped, the place being in the Kilkenny country, and hounds twenty-five Irish miles from their kennels. The time was an hour and ten minutes, and but for the river it would have been the run of the season.

So, in 1915, the horn fell silent. Instead, 'the trumpets sounded on the other side', both for the Master himself who died on 16 January, 1916, in the sixty-sixth year of his age, and for his only son, my uncle, Bertie Biddulph. He served for ten months in the trenches, but, after returning to England, contracted rheumatic fever, and died on 19 November, 1916, aged twenty-five. And Ierne's husband, Jack Goold-Adams, was killed at Ypres.

Had the world continued its pre-war course, Bertie would, without doubt, have followed his father as Master of the Hunt. His inclinations were the same as his father's, and he shared the old man's hardihood. From school, he went to Oxford. There, not surprisingly, we find him first whip and secretary to his College Beagles, and he had taken over the Mastership when war broke out. For three years running he won the College 'grind' – steeplechase. He was in the University Officers' Training Corps, and with the Special Reserve of 'The Bays' he won for the Regiment the subaltern's cup for 'Skill at Arms' in March, 1915.

Tucked in the back of Bertie's 'game book' are the Oxford University Greek and Latin papers for the Hilary Term, together with a series of questions on Logic. The Irish gentry were not just fox-hunting Philistines. Thackeray, in his *Irish Notebook*, had written:

Nor am I in the least disposed to sneer at gentlemen who like sporting and talk about it: for I do believe that the conversation of a dozen fox-hunters is just as clever as that of a similar number of merchants, barristers or literary men.

After the deaths in 1916 of her husband, Assheton, and her only son, Bertie, my grandmother, Florence Biddulph, lived on at Moneyguyneen for the remainder of the First World War, and for a few more years.

Thereafter, because she was English, because of the insecurity in Ireland due to I.R.A. threats, because there was no question of keeping the Hunt going, and because her daughters, other than my mother, preferred to live in England, she decided to sell Moneyguyneen and move to Sussex.

Thus ended the Irish life of one old settler family.

CHAPTER 40

The Aftermath

MY PARENTS LIVED on together until within ten weeks of their diamond wedding, when my father died on Armistice Day, 11 November, 1965, and that would have pleased the old loyalist mightily. Only if you are an Irish loyalist can you extract the last ounce from all that it means to be a loyalist – another Irish paradox. And although he was only an amateur soldier and, in the eyes of his mother-in-law, nothing but a bog-trotter, he was as well able as every other member of the Ascendancy to assume the role of 'an officer and a gentleman', and his services in the British Army in the First War earned him a C.M.G. and three mentions in dispatches, and an affectionately, and appreciatively, inscribed piece of silver from the officers serving under him.

Earlier I said that his life was a mass of contradictions. And even the last event of all was as paradoxical as had been so much of it. I was in England when he died in his bed at Killyon. By the time I reached Ireland after his death, others had been good enough to make all the funeral arrangements, including the choice of music, and thus his coffin was solemnly carried from the little former Killyon estate church at Clonard to the admittedly haunting and very moving strains of the Cortege of Bacchus. What a send-off for a lifelong teetotaller who had spent his time colourfully and forcefully deprecating the evils of what he habitually called, 'filthy liquor!'

A few months after my father's death, my mother's doctors demanded that, for her own safety, she must be moved from Killyon Manor to a nursing home. Fortunately her diminished state of mind was such that the move did not distress her. In all the complicated circumstances of the time, it became no longer possible to keep Killyon going, and the last old Magan Irish home passed out of the family. My mother died three years later in her eighty-eighth year.

The passing of people like my parents marks to a great extent the passing of the Ascendancy itself, for even its remnants are now largely ceasing to exist, albeit in the powerless state into which it had lapsed.

At the turn of the nineteenth/twentieth centuries *Burke's Landed Gentry* (1904) of Ireland included some twelve hundred families. The 1976 edition, now called

Burke's Irish Family Records, contains no more than five hundred and fourteen families, not all of them descendants of the landed gentry. The heads of one hundred and fifty of those families do not live in Ireland. The remnants of the old Ascendancy still resident in Ireland are thus reduced to three hundred and fifty senior branches of families. Of those, something over seventy families are in Ulster. This comparison with 1904 cannot be taken as absolute. The figures depend on a number of factors including changes in editorial policy in Burke's but there can be no doubt that there has been a massive decline in the number of old Irish landed gentry families, with the disappearance from Ireland of perhaps seventy-five per cent in three-quarters of a century.

There was inadequate opportunity left in Ireland for all that mainly English educated, Anglo-Irish, talent, enterprise, energy and endurance, and it has taken itself elsewhere, where it could find more scope. Besides, its *raison d'être* in Ireland had largely disappeared. It was shorn of its estates; and the opportunity to serve locally in Ireland in the services of the Crown, to which it owed its loyalty, had disappeared from the twenty-six southern counties when their colonial status came to an end. The departure of so many of the gentry is a loss to Ireland. An objective Irish writer has recently made the point that the Anglo-Irish are apt 'to have sterling qualities for which the average Irishman is not usually conspicuous'. And it is a loss in other ways. Something deeply good goes with it.

When my generation of our family was young, we were well acquainted with Kilkea Castle, Co. Kildare, a splendid ancient Fitzgerald Norman stronghold in which lived the Duke of Leinster's unmarried uncles and aunts. They were elderly people, and they allowed us to fish their river, and to shoot over their estate. Not very long ago, my sister Mollie, happening to be nearby, went to look for William English, the Duke's gamekeeper, whom we had known well and with whom, as children, we used to roam about the estate shooting and fishing. She learnt that he had died not long before at a great age, but she visited his brother, an old man in his nineties. He welcomed her warmly, and, with tears in his eyes, bewailed the passing of the old times, 'with the gintry all gone'. Although we live in times conducive to a more classless society, some of the older Irish, at all events, are perhaps, even to this day, pining the departure of their chiefs.

But my sister's mention of this episode made me think of Sunday mornings at Kilkea. The little church is at the castle gates. The old folk, Lord Frederick Fitzgerald, Lord Walter, Lady Alice, Lady Nesta (that magic name) walking slowly down the avenue to the church, dressed in their somewhat rustic Sunday best. They knew everyone, and everyone knew them. We were all in our Sunday best. Some of it may have been a bore, but it was a leisured and well-ordered small corner of life. Today the castle is an hotel. Transient blue jeans no doubt scamper up and down the avenue of a Sunday morning. That may be nice, and liberating in its own way. But the old sense of order, permanency and stability is no more. Something good has indeed gone.

Lord Walter every summer used to take a scythe and mow the grass from the spot in the churchyard where he wished to be buried. One summer's day he did not return to lunch. Willie English found him. He had done his work and had lain down to end his life upon that spot of his own choosing, with the summer smell of new-mown hay all about him. For some people it does happen nicely, and how better for an old Irish country gentleman?

Wherever they have gone the Anglo-Irish will be useful citizens and will flourish. If they were not, as W. B. Yeats said, 'One of the great stocks of Europe', then they ought to have been, descended as they were from a mixed brew of Celtic monarchs and war-lords, Anglo-Saxon overlords, Viking chieftains, Norman barons, and every conceivable amalgam of that wide variety of vigour and leadership, laced and spiced doubtless with a seasoning from the older stockpot of Roman rulership, to say nothing of even earlier leadership material. If there is anything in the hereditary principle – and there must be something because our genes come from our forebears and not from thin air – then the now largely scattered old Irish chiefs and 'Gintry' must have bequeathed to their descendants two particular characteristics: durability; they stuck it out through thick and thin, and held their own century after century; and a willingness to take responsibility. They were deliberately born and bred to take charge, whatever the risk to themselves – and they led from the front.

A computation of the decline in numbers among the members of that other, and important, part of the Ascendancy, the Protestant professional gentry in the towns and cities of Ireland, is more difficult to make than for the landed gentry, because we have no such accessibly valuable and useful record as *Burke's Landed Gentry*. But, given that the towns were at one time mostly Protestant, it is significant that in Dublin, a Protestant city in the seventeenth and eighteenth centuries, the Protestant population now numbers only five per cent of the whole.

Those gentry families that remain, and who have been trying to maintain their large houses stripped of the estates that once supported them, have doubtless in many cases been becoming progressively less well off. Unless something happens to reverse that trend, they are unlikely much longer to be able to afford to send their children to school in England. Those who are educated in England will be inclined to seek more expansive lives and careers outside Ireland still further depleting the stock in Ireland. Those who are not educated in England will become more and more Hibernicized and, like the old Norman settler families of the twelfth century, and early English settler families, will be likely to become assimilated into the native Irish scene and culture.

BOOK SEVEN

The Reckoning:
Ireland Today

CHAPTER 41

The Great Ocean Wave
of Freedom

HERVE DE MONTMORENCY Morris, the Catholic Tipperary landowner – and grandson of Francis Magan of Umma More – was a colonel in the army of France when, on 18 June, 1815, the French forces were finally routed at Waterloo. But neither he, nor any other of the Irish soldiers who shared that day in the French disaster, is likely to have had the prescience to foresee that Napoleon's galloping coach, fleeing into the gloaming from the carnage of the field of battle, was doing more to bring about the liberation of Ireland from the suzerainty of England than any other event since Strongbow and the Welsh Normans had landed in Wexford. It was indeed to be another seventy years before the great oceanic wave of history set in motion by the French Waterloo defeat was to wash up perceptibly on the Irish shore.

In the year 1885, Gladstone, being temporarily out of office, allowed himself a short respite in Scandinavia. There, freed momentarily from the crowded pressures of political life at home, he had rather more than usual time for reflection and contemplation. He had been much involved in the Irish question. At the very moment when he first became prime minister, in December, 1868, he had had to deal with serious Fenian violence. He had disestablished the Irish Anglican Church in 1869. And his later administration had been responsible, in 1881, for extensive Irish land reforms which had gone some way towards relaxing the grip of the settler Ascendancy on the lands of Ireland. Moreover, he had lost the 1885 election to the Conservatives through his failure to court the Irish lobby in the House of Commons.

Influenced by the Scandinavian experience of seeing for himself a number of small countries living out their lives in viable independence, he became confirmed in the view not only that Ireland could well do the same, but also that nothing less would ever satisfy the Irish.

The Conservatives were not prepared to contemplate Home Rule for Ireland, so Gladstone manoeuvred himself into power again in January, 1886, and introduced the first Irish Home Rule bill into the House of Commons. In doing so, he probably never gave a thought to Waterloo. But, at last, after seventy years, someone in England had woken up to what the Waterloo defeat of the French had meant in the Irish context.

With the French defeat there was no longer any danger of a great and hostile European Catholic power allying itself with Ireland against England. There was, therefore, no continuing strategic security reason or necessity to hold Ireland in subjection. Ireland could safely be freed.

Yet it was not to be. Gladstone, like so many Englishmen before and since, did not understand Ireland. He saw the Protestants there simply in political terms as a voting minority who, as good democrats, must bow to the votes and the will of the majority. While the Protestants, with much influential support from England, not only from the Conservative Party, but also from within Gladstone's own Liberal Party, saw themselves as an essentially British community threatened with extinction by an alien native Irish culture and creed. The 1886 Home Rule bill was thrown out by the House of Commons. It had foundered on the issue of the Ulster Protestant community.

Gladstone tried again in 1893 with another Home Rule bill. It passed the Commons, but was rejected by the Lords. It was clear that no Irish Home Rule bill would ever pass the Lords unless there was parliamentary reform to reduce their power to block legislation.

For nearly another twenty years Irish Home Rule remained in limbo. It then became an issue in one of the local squalls of history. Asquith, seeking to curb the power of the House of Lords with his Parliament Act, had been forced to rely on the eighty or so Irish nationalist votes in the Commons. Their price was Home Rule; and a third Home Rule bill was tabled in 1912. This time there was to be no failure. Under the procedure then in force, the bill was bound to become law in, at the longest, two years. The king had been prepared to create enough new peers to force the Parliament Act through the Lords. That threat was enough to ensure their eventual capitulation on the Home Rule issue as well. And the armed forces were to be used to quell any physical Protestant opposition in Ulster. The English, once more, failed to understand Ireland.

The bill had a long and stormy passage during which formidable resistance built up outside parliament. A large volunteer force was recruited in Ulster and armed. Such influential people as Field-Marshal Lord Roberts and Lord Milner gave active support to the opponents of the bill in Ulster. Kipling subscribed a huge sum of money, and wrote a stirring poem in support of the case of the Ulster Protestants. Retired senior army officers commanded the Ulster Volunteer Force. The leader of the Conservative opposition gave explicit support to the loyalists. At the time of Gladstone's first Home Rule bill in 1886, Lord Randolph Churchill, Winston Churchill's father, had championed the cause of Protestant Ulster. Their old cry had been 'Home Rule is Rome Rule'. Randolph Churchill added another ringing cry. 'Ulster will fight, and Ulster will be right.' Loyalty to the Crown had been Protestant Ulster's very *raison d'être* for three centuries. She was determined now to go down fighting rather than be dragooned into submission to a 'papist' government in Dublin.

To Ulster loyalists, 'Home Rule is Rome Rule' was not just a catch phrase. It was a graphic and accurate reflection of their conviction that, in a Catholic majority government in Dublin, it would not be the will of the citizens of Ireland that would prevail, but that of the Vatican and the Roman Church, and nothing that has happened since has shaken that conviction to this day.

The least Ulster was prepared to contemplate in 1914 was an independent Protestant Ulster state within the Empire and under the Crown.

The Irish nationalists, for their part, were not taking Ulster hostility to the Home Rule bill lying down. They were recruiting their own corps of volunteers.

By the spring of 1914, the parliamentary stages of the bill were still incomplete, but things were reaching boiling point in Ireland. The two opposing volunteer forces contained the incipient seeds of civil war. Troop dispositions, threatening to Ulster, were being made by the British government. Lord Randolph Churchill's son, Winston, by then First Lord of the Admiralty, and an enthusiastic Home Ruler, was moving naval units threateningly against Ulster.

But there was a fly in the British ointment. Many officers in the British forces, particularly in the cavalry, belonged to Irish gentry families. They were becoming restive at the prospect of being used against their Protestant Irish brethren in Ulster. Any who felt strongly were given the option to resign their commissions, but were told that if they did so their resignations would not be accepted. They would be dismissed, unless they were themselves Ulstermen. That led the Brigadier-General and fifty-seven of the officers of the 3rd cavalry brigade, stationed at the Curragh, in Co. Kildare, to tender their resignations during the weekend of 21 March, 1914.

So massive a display by the officer corps of dissent from the government's Home Rule policy put altogether out of the question any further consideration of the use of military force to coerce the Ulster loyalists into a united, independent Ireland. And 'independent' is indeed too comprehensive a word, since Home Rule involved only internal affairs – defence, foreign affairs, trade and other subjects were to remain reserved to Westminster; and Ireland was to continue to be subject to the Crown.

No significant progress was made in the months following the Curragh incident and, by August, 1914, England was at war with Germany. By common – if on the part of Ulster very grudging – consent it was agreed to let the Home Rule bill complete its passage through parliament, but no attempt was to be made to bring it into force until after the war. Royal assent was given to the bill, which reached the statute book on 18 September, 1914.

At the time, it was no more than a formality. Irishmen from North and South, Protestant and Catholic alike, sank their differences, flocked voluntarily to the forces of the Crown and, although a higher percentage of Protestants than Catholics volunteered, large numbers of both communities fought and died side by side loyally and most gallantly throughout the whole period of the war.

By the time the war was over, the 1914 Home Rule bill was irrelevant. In 1921, the twenty-six counties of Ireland received their total independence within the Commonwealth. Six of the former nine counties of Ulster, where the loyalist majority was not prepared to become subject to the nationalist government in Dublin, became an internally self-governing province of the United Kingdom.

From those events it can be seen that, as long as a hundred years ago, in 1886, England – or at least a very influential body of opinion in England – had concluded that she could afford to give Ireland back her freedom, even though the measure did not succed in parliament. That view, and that intention, were endorsed by the Home Rule bill of 1914, and they have been repeated since.

The facts therefore are, that for a century past England has been disposed to facilitate the Irish nationalist aspiration to govern themselves; but the loyalists of Ulster have remained emphatically determined not to be united with a nationalist government in Dublin.

England's role in this matter has been much misunderstood. England did not create, and has not wished to perpetuate, partition. Partition was the consequence of the deep divisions which exist among the Irish themselves. England would have preferred a united and independent Ireland on the lines of Gladstone's Home Rule aspirations. The Government of Ireland Act, 1920, contains this passage:

> ... the Act contemplates and affords every facility for union between North and South, and empowers the two Parliaments by mutual agreement and joint action to terminate partition and to set up one Parliament and one Government for the whole of Ireland.

And the following words occur in the Sunningdale Agreement of 1972 between the British Government and the Government of the Republic of Ireland:

> ... if in future the majority of the people of Northern Ireland should indicate a wish to become a part of a United Ireland, the British Government would support that wish.

All that Irishmen have to do is to sink their differences and Britain will be happy to withdraw.

It is, of course, the case that H.M.G. has equally undertaken to support the wishes of the majority in Northern Ireland should they wish to remain within the United Kingdom, but that does not, and is in no way intended to, invalidate the absolute freedom of the people of Northern Ireland to join in a union with the South if and when they should wish to do so.

So, a century or so ago, 'the Irish question' became essentially, and has remained essentially, 'the Ulster problem', rather than the centuries-old British problem of safeguarding herself from an Irish-based threat to her sovereignty from a hostile continental power.

The Ulster Problem

THE ULSTER PROBLEM IS in outline this. The bulk of the inhabitants of Ireland did not become integrated into the Anglo-Saxon culture. Their basic culture crystallized during the Iron Age, about one or two centuries BC, into an amalgam of Ancient Irish cultures much overlaid, and fused together, by Celtic cultural modes. In the sense that in the period of the exclusive Celtic ascendancy – that is to say approximately the second century BC to the twelfth century AD – the population of all Ireland belonged to that cultural grouping, with common laws, a common language, and a common religion, it can be said that the map of Ireland was at that ancient period wholly green. They were people of a common culture, though loyal to separate chiefs, and not united under a single government.

Then came the Normans acting as clients for the Holy See in Rome, and the Anglo-French Crown. They started spattering the pure green with pink. But that did not greatly alter the cultural complexion of Ireland, because most of the Norman and early English settlers became assimilated into the Irish culture.

In the seventeenth century, the English seized the best land in much of the north of Ireland – what is now Ulster – and large areas there were settled with aliens – English and Scots. Extensive parts of that northern, and north-eastern, area thereby became solid pink on the map, and have remained so.

It can be argued that many of the seventeenth century Ulster settlers were ethnically akin to the Irish, and are not therefore an alien people to Ireland. Some had their origin in the Scottish Picts, a kindred people, and others in the Celtic Scots, who had been Irish settlers in Scotland. But common ethnic origins – particularly if there are no strongly distinguishing physical features, such as skin pigmentation – are much less binding than cultural uniformity. The root of the difference between those northern settlers and the native Irish was, and remains to this day, that the Ulster settlers did not, like the Normans, early English settlers and Danes, become Hibernicized, but followed, and still continue to follow, Anglo-Saxon cultural traditions, and are Protestant and not Catholic.

It is crucial to an understanding of the Ulster problem to appreciate that the principal divide is cultural. The northern loyalists are culturally Anglo-Saxon –

whatever their diverse ethnic origins. The remainder of the population of the whole of Ireland (except for the small number of culturally Anglo-Saxon mainly Protestant people living in the South) is culturally Ancient Irish – again, whatever their diverse ethnic origins right back to seven thousand BC. Ireland digested and assimilated culturally the bulk of the invaders prior to the Ulster Plantation, save for some domiciled within the Pale who retained their Anglo-Saxon culture. But the seventeenth century Protestant settlement of Ulster has not been culturally digested. It is still, so to speak, stuck in Ireland's cultural gullet.

In the twentieth century, by the treaty of 1921, came the restoration of the map of Ireland to pure green again, all except the top right-hand part which remains pink, and under British suzerainty – is indeed a part of Britain.

Southern Ireland wants that top right-hand part back; wants it pure green again, free from alien jurisdiction, and under her own rule; wants the whole map of Ireland to be solid green once more. That is the native Irish case. That is the Irish dream.

The descendants of the Scottish and English settlers in the top right-hand part are, however, determined to remain pink. They say they will fight to resist any attempt to turn them green. That is the Ulster loyalists' case. That is Ulster's nightmare.

England would have liked to see the two communities united, but has not since 1914 shown any disposition to try to force the issue.

The green Irish, for their part, have not pressed the matter too hard. They do not deny an Irish identity to the northern loyalists, despite the Anglo-Saxon tinge of their culture. They recognize the intractability of the problem, and have both treated it with long-term patience, and made some political capital out of it, without explicitly acknowledging the danger which they probably see to the green area in any attempt by either Britain or themselves to force the issue. At worst, that would lead to a dreadful civil war. At best, the green area would be faced with the unwelcome prospect of trying to digest a million tough and hostile Protestant Ulster citizens.

But a third party has intervened in the Irish government's policy; the I.R.A. They are not quite a third party. They have a cousinly relationship with the green fraternity. They have created a dangerous situation both for the green and the pink parts of Ireland, and for Britain, and indeed for Christendom, by trying to precipitate the very conditions that would result in the explosive situation between the North and the South that Britain and the government of the Republic have been at pains to avoid.

Glancing back through history, the evolutionary steps leading to the Ulster problem are plain. When the epicentre of Eurasian civilization shifted, at the turn of the fifteenth/sixteenth centuries, from the general area of the Eastern Mediterranean to the Atlantic seaboard, the new self-consciously independent Protestant island nation-state of England felt compelled to secure herself against her Catholic continental neighbours. A pressing danger was the threat to her western approaches from a possible alliance between Catholic Ireland and a hostile Catholic Spain or France. England's plan to avert that danger was to suppress the Irish, and to people Ireland with a loyal Protestant population. The plan failed, save in Ulster where the early seventeenth century Plantation did achieve just that objective. There, England is now hoist with her own petard. She wanted a loyalist, Protestant population, and that is what she has got. She 'unsettled' a nation, and it is still unsettled. The English of today are not to be blamed for that, but they are nevertheless stuck with its consequences.

Since the 1921 treaty, which gave the southern twenty-six counties their independence, a united Ireland has all along been the aim of the Southern government, but its policy is explicit that it shall be brought about by political negotiation and by consensus of all the people, North and South, Catholic and Protestant, and not by force. The people of Southern Ireland have, during the past half-century, endorsed that policy overwhelmingly by denying their support to the I.R.A.'s political nominees.

The I.R.A., for their part, reject the non-violent policy of their government and fellow-countrymen – indeed do not recognize the validity of their government – and arrogate to themselves the right to use force and violence. Because the I.R.A. is thus in breach of Irish law, the government of Southern Ireland has declared it an illegal organization. The political wing of the I.R.A., the Sinn Fein Party, is not proscribed, but receives no significant support from the public. It seldom wins a seat at an election in the South, though it may on occasion attract some temporary sympathy as during the most emotional period of the 1981 hunger strike.

The most militant I.R.A. members have always had a tendency to break away and form their own more violent splinter groups, but, for convenience, I use the term I.R.A. generically to include all Catholic nationalist groups engaged in violence even though, for tactical reasons, the I.R.A. may from time to time declare a ceasefire.

Looked at from the point of view of the Northerners, history might seem to suggest that there is some innate justification for a separate Ulster. It is an historical fact that Ireland has never in known times been a politically united nation under a single government, except when forced into a unified colonial system by the British from the late seventeenth century to the early twentieth century. But that is of no current significance except as a talking point for those who reject claims for 're-uniting' Ireland on the grounds that it was never united. The Irish were in Celtish times a distinct and broadly homogeneous people. Ulster in those early times was a part of that cultural whole, but was separated from the remainder of Ireland by a wild frontier of lakes, bogs, forest and mountains; obstacles which in modern conditions are irrelevant.

In the final six years of fighting against the forces of Queen Elizabeth, at the end of the sixteenth century, it was Hugh O'Neill, Earl of Tyrone, the great Ulster chief, who, with his Ulster Irishmen, led the all-Irish forces against the English Froude wrote of him: 'He held the Irish together more successfully than any insurgent leader had succeeded in doing before him.' It was he who won the famous all-Ireland battle over the English of 'Yellow Ford'. And it was he who with his all-Ireland force, together with the Spaniards, was finally defeated at the disastrous – for the Irish – Battle of Kinsale, in 1601, which was the beginning of the end of the long rule of the Irish chiefs. There can be no doubt that the Irish at that time saw themselves as one people.

It is not, therefore, a tenable claim that Ulster was always a separate state, even though she has, since the earliest pre-historic times, had close affinities with her near neighbours on the Scottish mainland. Ulster had for centuries been an integral part of the culturally homogeneous mosaic of Ireland and of Irish life. To the extent that Ulster may be a separate nation today she is so because she is the product of the seventeenth century influx and plantation of Scottish and English settlers, with a culture that is not Irish, and it is that that is at the heart of today's dilemma.

CHAPTER 43

The Elements of the Ulster Problem

OVER AND ABOVE THE cultural divide, the Ulster problem is a compound of complex ingredients. The first is the question of allegiance. The loyalists of Northern Ireland are unshakably loyal to the Crown. They are wholly unprepared to transfer that allegiance to the President of a Republic in Dublin or, as they see it, in part at least, to the Pope in Rome, though this is not the case.

The Southern Irish nationalists have no such precise focus of allegiance. The allegiance that tugs at their heartstrings is not to their President, or to their flag, or even to their faith. It is to their homeland, to a romantically idealized Shamrock Ireland.

The next factor is cultural patriotism. You almost need to be Irish to understand this point subjectively.

The Ulster loyalists' cultural patriotism is three dimensional and intertwined. They regard themselves as Irish. Indeed, like the old Ascendancy, they believe themselves to be a superior kind of Irish, a hard-working, thrifty and efficient people, much superior to the 'natives'.

Secondly, and even more so, do they feel essentially British. They are integrated into the widely varied cultural entity that is the Anglo-Saxon culture. Their Irishness is wrapped inside their Britishness. But, culture apart, their loyalty is to the Crown, not to England. If the Irish rugger team is playing England, Ulstermen will be playing in, and Ulster supporters will be rooting for, the Irish team.

The third dimension of Northern loyalist patriotism is the most potent. Above all they see themselves as Ulstermen. Their principal loyalty is to themselves, to their own community, because they believe that in the last resort only total self-reliance could save them, and they fear that some day they might be faced with that last resort.

The nationalist Irish view of themselves is altogether different. They do not, of course, 'feel' in anyway British. They 'feel' Irish, and they are Irish in the sense that I have described of being at least one-fifth innately endowed with the cultural traditions of very ancient Ireland, superimposed upon which is the long Celtic tradition which the English generally do not share, even though Celtic traditions were strong in western Britain until the tenth century AD, and are not negligible even today. The culture of the Irish is in that sense quite distinctly Irish. Theirs is a misty and amorphous sort of cultural patriotism which lacks any such focal point of identity as the monarchical traditions of Britain.

The Papacy in Rome is a part of their loyalty symbolism but is too distant, too foreign, and too different from the lives of ordinary people, to take the place of a monarchy. A lay monarch, a family person and a fellow countryman, is felt to have much domestically in common with the people, and is readily accepted as head of the greater national family. A celibate foreign Pope remains a revered figure, but one with whom ordinary people can less easily identify themselves and their lives personally, even though Pope John XXIII and Pope John Paul II have shown a remarkable talent for the common touch.

It is not, therefore, so much the Pontiff who is part of Southern Irish patriotism, as Catholicism itself. Catholicism has been the badge of Irish nationalist loyalty and patriotism for four centuries.

The very foundation, therefore, of the nationalist Irishman's cultural patriotic identification of himself is his 'feeling' of Catholic Irishness. To do anything counter to it has the semblance of being traitorous, and that has important consequences for Southern Irish attitudes towards the I.R.A.

That is what the Northern loyalists, and the Southern Irish, 'feel' about themselves. How do they see each other?

The extreme Northern loyalist view of Southerners is of an inferior, feckless race living in superstitious dread of their swarming priests.

The extreme Southern view of the Northerner is of someone who is not inherently Irish at all. He is still seen as a transplanted Scot, a coarser, more materialist breed than the sainted and poetic Irish, and an ebony-hard Protestant at that, usurping a corner of dear, soft, evergreen holy Catholic mother Ireland, ancient land of saints and scholars.

Those images may be an exaggeration but they underline the extremes of bigotry that can exist. And I have put it that way because it is of importance not to underestimate the effect of even very much more restrained versions of the same attitudes. It takes only a very little to leaven the lump. Thus it is that, in varying degrees, opinion is pretty generally at least somewhat tinged by stereotypes along those lines. And that is well illustrated by Protestant opinion in the South, which does not altogether lack something of the Southern nationalist view of the North.

Thus, the Southern Irish Protestants – the real Irish Protestants, as they see themselves – allude with at least a touch of superior self-satisfaction to 'the bigoted North'. The implication is that they themselves, the 'civilized' Irish Protestants of the South, unlike the stubborn northern bigots, know how to reach a satisfactory accommodation with their Catholic neighbours.

Meanwhile, in the eyes of the Northerners, the Southern Protesants overlook the price they have had to pay for their accommodation with the Catholics. More than half the Southern Protestant population has been lost in a little over half a century.

The principal causes of the decline in the Protestant population of Southern Ireland are that many Protestants preferred not to remain in Ireland under the Republic, and that the remainder, scattered for the most part in penny packets, cannot find enough Protestant marriage partners. They either remain unmarried or emigrate, in both cases depleting the Protestant population, or they marry Catholics. In that case, in accordance with the policy of the Catholic Church, the children are usually – though not invariably – brought up Catholics, thus further depleting the Protestant population. The Vatican introduced some relaxation of the Catholic marriage rules a few years ago, but Irish Protestants complain that that made little or no difference to the strict, and indeed, insistent, attitude of Irish Catholic bishops.

That then is the abstract line-up of how the Northerners and the Southerners see themselves, and see each other in stereotype. But the concrete realities – those of everyday life that face the man in the street – are different.

The border between the North and South is in fact open. There is some mild customs control. That is all. And the people largely disregard even that. There is an enormously wide range of contacts at all times between South and North. If, therefore, you are a Southerner, you may have many Northern friends and acquaintances. They, of course, are not a bit like the stereotype. They are the exception. Very decent, nice people, not at all bigoted, not a bit like the general run; and, as for business, rather any day a straightforward deal across the table with those down-to-earth chaps in Belfast, than a hole-in-corner wangle under the counter in a smoke-laden Dublin pub.

And if you are a Northerner, you are frequently in the South, particularly to enjoy its amenities. Thus the people in the little fishing village you usually go to are quite the exception. Nothing inferior about them. Open, friendly, man-to-man people. No-one more charming, amusing, kindly, helpful or hospitable. You wouldn't miss your usual fishing holiday in the South for all the world, with the warmth of greeting you get from the hotelier and his wife, the marvellous days in the droll companionship of Mick the boatman, and the welcome from old Mrs Flannagan when you visit her cottage to buy the dozen fresh eggs you always take home. Despite the rain and the 'misht', the whole experience sets you up with a sunny inner glow that keeps the cockles warm for a twelvemonth. And not the least of the glow comes, God help you, from the nice old parish priest, Father Kelly – quite exceptional, of course, not like the general run of priests. He is always so pleased to see you back. Gives you his blessing for a good holiday when you arrive, and again for a safe return when you leave.

Moreover, it is almost universal for the two communities to treat each other with courtesy. In the South it comes naturally. In much of the North there is between individuals more often than not, an almost exaggerated attitude of consideration in order to avoid offence.

The final factor affecting the attitude of the Northern loyalists to a united Ireland is the more particular religious divide. It is mainly a Protestant/Catholic divide. But it is not quite as clear cut as that. There are in Northern Ireland many Catholic loyalists. A third of the vacancies in the Royal Ulster Constabulary were from the beginning open to Catholics. Although the percentage of Catholics has never been as high as that, large numbers have served in the force, including many distinguished Catholic officers and other ranks. It may seem ironic that fully integrated co-operation, and comradeship, between Catholics and Protestants, is nowhere more in evidence in Northern Ireland than in that supposed instrument of Protestant oppression, the Royal Ulster Constabulary. It is because there is a substantial body of Catholic loyalists in Ulster that I more often use the term 'loyalists' than 'Protestants' for those inhabitants of the province who do not wish to be a part of the Irish Republic.

There has, too, always been a sprinkling of Protestant nationalists, from whose ranks have come some of Ireland's ablest nationalist leaders.

Religious sectarianism introduces the factor of minority fear. The population of Northern Ireland is approximately one and a half million; a million Protestants and half a million Catholics. In the twenty-six counties of the Irish Republic there are, in round figures, another three million Catholics. That situation gives rise to a treble minority fear.

Serious minority problems and fears do not occur because there are minorities. They occur either because minorities are very large numerically, and therefore appear to pose a potential threat to the majority; or because, being small numerically, they succeed in acquiring positions of power, wealth or authority altogether disproportionate to the numerical strength of their community, or because they can be regarded as the spearhead of some threatening external power. Thus, in Northern Ireland, Catholics, being a third of the total population, appear a dangerously numerous and threatening minority. Similarly, the Northern Protestants are a quarter of the total population of Ireland, and would, therefore, seem a threateningly large minority in a united Ireland.

The Southern Protestants, being only three per cent of the population of the South, are not felt to be any danger to the South. That, and not the more mature attitudes of Southern Protestants towards Catholics, is why there is no abrasion between Catholics and Protestants in the South. But if there were a million Protestants in the South, or if the Protestants were so politically assertive as to have captured fifty per cent of the seats in Parliament, and important ministerial offices, it would be a very different matter. Catholic apprehensions would be deeply aroused. As it is, there can be genuine accommodation with the Protestants – a

Protestant Senator or two, a few M.P.s, even an occasional minister, and two much respected Protestant Presidents – without the least fear of even the slightest dent in the fabric of the Catholic body politic of Southern Ireland.

The first of the three Irish minority fears is that of the minority of nationalist Catholics in the North who fear the loyalist Protestant majority, and with good reason. Historically, at moments of high tension, the Catholics have suffered grievously at the hands of fanatical Protestants. Moreover, the Catholics have had a quite inadequate voice in the affairs of the province.

But Protestant discrimination against Catholics has itself been the product of the second minority fear – the loyalist fear that the large Catholic minority is a ready-made Trojan horse for their greatly more numerous Catholic co-religionists south of the border. It was this fear that resulted in the virtual exclusion of the Catholics from local government. In the early 1920s the electoral system permitted the election of Catholic local councils in Catholic areas of Ulster, but, in the view of the loyalists, they conducted their business more as though they were part of the administration of Southern Ireland than of Ulster. The electoral arrangements were then changed to ensure that virtually all local government would be in the hands of loyalists.

The Catholic minority was to be given no rope or scope. It must not be allowed any of the reins of power, or any other substantial influence. That would simply start a process of grandmother's footsteps of encroachment into the North by the 'papist' South. So went the loyalist reasoning. And the emotive, pejorative 'papist' label comes more readily to mind in Protestant Ulster than the milder term, 'Catholic', which is more generally used by Protestants in the South.

And such reasoning has been accompanied by more than a suspicion of old Ascendancy attitudes towards the 'natives'. The 'Bogside' at Derry – a low-lying Catholic ghetto, overlooked by the old Protestant citadel – was good enough for them. They were not fit to be treated as equals.

That is not to criticize or condemn the attitude of Ulster Protestants. It is simply to nail an element of objective reality. The fact is that they remain in an eighteenth century situation, and are the inescapable inheritors of eighteenth century attitudes. They continue to be born, and to remain, the top dogs, and are innately conscious of the fact from the cradle onwards.

The third minority fear is the Protestant fear of being in a minority of three to one in a united Ireland.

It is not just differences of opinion, religious, political or cultural, that divide the two communities. As both communities in Ulster see it, there is nothing less at stake than survival. All they have, all they are, is seen to be at total risk. As the Protestants of Ulster see it, the Catholics want nothing less than to absorb them into the Catholic environment largely subordinate to the dictates of the Vatican which, of course, it is not. As the Ulster Catholics see it, they live under the perpetual risk of being hounded off their lands and out of Ulster as they were in the seventeenth century and the late eighteenth century.

There was in the past a fourth minority fear. It is dormant, but still latent below the surface. That was the nationalist Irish fear of a menacing England. Its actuality was removed by the tabling of the first Home Rule bill a hundred years ago, demonstrating England's growing willingness to get off the back of Ireland.

But there is yet another fear; one that is deeply felt by individual Protestants. It is the fear of the Roman Catholic Church *per se*. The American priest, whom I quoted earlier, drew very pointed attention to it, and made the point that in Ireland the reality bore a strong resemblance to the Protestant view of the bogy.

To discuss the problem of Ulster without a reasonably frank reference to religion would be absurd. I must therefore take the risks involved in making any such reference. I hope I shall offend no-one. I believe in everyone's right to worship as they like, or not at all if they prefer. To anticipate the helpful criticism of well-wishing pedants, I had better say that I am well aware that the 1662 Prayer Book nowhere speaks of the Protestant Church, but refers to the 'Church of England' as the 'Catholic Church'. I shall nevertheless follow the normal colloquial usage of calling the Roman Catholic Church the 'Catholic Church,' and of using the term 'Protestant' generically for those churches that became separated from the Roman Catholic communion in consequence of the Reformation.

Thackeray, on his tour of Ireland, voiced the Protestant fear of the Catholic Church thus:

> *I went into the Catholic chapel not without awe for, as I confessed before, I always feel a sort of tremor on going into a Catholic place of worship. Candles and altars, and mysteries, the priest and his robes, the nasal chantings and wonderful genuflections, will frighten me as long as I live.*

Kipling expressed it in the Ulster context in his 1912 poem 'Ulster', from which the following is one of the six verses:

> *We know the wars prepared*
> *On every peaceful home,*
> *We know the hells declared*
> *For such as serve not Rome –*
> *The terror, threats and dread*
> *In market, hearth and field –*
> *We know, when all is said,*
> *We perish if we yield.*

That Catholics might deny any reasonable cause for such fear, is beside the point. Rational or not, the fear itself is a reality to Protestants.

In many situations there are two actualities. There is the objective actuality itself, and there is what people think or sense the actuality to be, and that may be different. You have never been sailing before. Your friend takes you out in a fresh wind. The yacht heels over and the water comes foaming along the gunwale. Your heart goes into your mouth. You wonder if you are going to capsize. Your fear is real. But it is groundless. There is no danger whatever. Your experienced friend knows he could sail the boat with perfect safety much closer to the wind in much heavier weather.

So are Protestant fears of the Catholic Church – very real, at any rate to individual Irish Protestants in Ulster.

CHAPTER 44

Catholicism: What is it that Protestants Fear?

THERE HAS BEEN a number of elements in Protestant fears of Catholicism. One of them has now largely disappeared, or is at least much diminished. It is the one that seems most to have concerned Thackeray. It sprang in some part from a lack of understanding of the Catholic Church Latin service – fear of the unknown, or of the uncomprehended.

The seemingly monotonous mumbling – even, as it sometimes appears, gabbling – of an incomprehensible Latin text, together with high church ritual, the use of holy water, the lighting of candles, the tinkling of bells, the swinging of incense censers, the apparent veneration of relics, replicas and statues, had for Protestants a mystical content which they found disturbingly awesome – and, of course, it is the fact that, in ancient times, powerful priesthoods were concerned to develop rituals calculated to strike awe into the hearts of the people. The bishop's mitre, for instance, makes him taller, adds a cubit to his stature. The Ancient Egyptians knew that trick.

But the Second Vatican Council changed the atmosphere of Catholic services. Now that they are held in the vernacular, and Protestants and Catholics go freely to each other's churches, even in Ireland, lay people have been struck not so much by the differences as by the quite unexpected similarity in the texts of the liturgy of the two Churches. They begin to wonder whether there has not been a lot of fuss over the centuries about nothing, or about not very much, for the laity know little, and care less, about the deep doctrinal differences which still divide the Protestant and Catholic Churches.

It is, then, no longer Thackeray's genuflections, chantings, mysteries, candles and so on, that frighten Protestants. They are beginning to be regarded by the laity as what Queen Elizabeth I called them – 'trifles'. Theologians can have fun arguing about them till the cows come home, and about how many angels can dance on the head of a pin for that matter. The laity are not interested.

Residual lay Protestant concern about Catholicism rests on two other counts. The first is that raised by the American Jesuit priest – the power of the Catholic priesthood. Catholic bishops are concerned to be obeyed. But no Protestant fears a bishop. And Protestant bishops do not seek obedience from their flock. Nor would their flock obey them. They pay due regard to sound reasoning from their bishops, but in no way regard their pronouncements as mandatory. Benevolence, not authority, is what Protestants expect of their bishops. To be seen as 'the dear bishop' is more in character with the Protestant image of a bishop, than to be regarded as a stern and unbending episcopal Father in God. Moreover, the Protestant clergy have no power, and the Protestant laity is determined that it shall stay that way, even though some of the Anglican priesthood may cast longing glances Rome-wards, where power lies.

But Catholic bishops, by contrast, are explicitly authoritarian, and Catholics accept that it is right and proper that they should be. Catholics have a more romantic regard for their church than have Protestants, and they like to be able to look up to their bishops as holy fathers. And, whether or not the bishops themselves are concerned to be loved, they are more often than not concerned to be feared, or at least very deferentially and reverentially respected, and always to be obeyed. And even though mainland British Protestants may often be scarcely aware of the existence of the Roman Catholic Church in Britain, or of its characteristics, and may feel no current need to defend their faith against Roman Catholicism, Ulster Protestants are highly conscious of the proximity of a very authoritarian Catholic episcopacy in their midst, and do, on their own account, as the American Jesuit priest stated so frankly, feel acutely menaced by the Church of Rome.

The essence of Ulster Protestant belief is that the Reformation freed them from a foreign-dominated, superstitious, religious tyranny which, in their view, still exists, is still powerful, is un-reformed, is eager to grab them back within its fold, and is thus still to be dreaded by those who value independence of spiritual life, thought and worship, and who are concerned to be totally priest-free if they prefer it that way. Theirs to read their own Bibles in no way beholden to what they see as an autocratic, disciplining priesthood.

The other source of Protestant misgiving about Catholicism is not religious but political. It is still what it was in the past; what Henry VIII conceived it to be – a question of political sovereignty. In mainland Britain it is a part of that potentially dangerous field of controversy that the Catholic community has been at pains since the end of the Jacobite Wars not to bring into question, and it is, therefore, a part of the Catholic–Protestant question which remains dormant, and may appear to be hardly more than a technical constitutional question. It is, however, an issue which is dormant rather than dead, and one that even today in England were best let lie and not put to the test. But to Ulster Protestants it is a matter of burning and immediate concern in the context of any debate about Irish unity. It is at the very heart of the argument.

The crux of the matter is that the Papacy in Rome is foreign. When we are considering how the ordinary run of the Protestant laity see it, it would be pedantic to differentiate between the Papal State, the Holy See, the Pope himself, the Vatican Secretariat and so on. To the Protestant laity it is simply that the Pope is the head of an external foreign religious organization, with its centre of power and administration in Rome, to which Catholics owe a degree of allegiance. This can raise a suspicion of divided loyalty.

Ulster Protestants therefore find it impossible to believe that the policies of the Catholic government in Dublin do not in some degree reflect the influence of Rome. And Ulster Protestants are determined never to come within the ambit of that alien influence. 'Home Rule is Rome Rule' is an Ulster Protestant factual comment on the, to themselves, horrendous actuality that a foreign religious potentate – and even more so his secret secretariat – is meddling in, and in some degree formulating, the secular domestic policies of Ireland which, of course, is not so.

It is of course the fact that 'Vatican Two' allowed for a measure of decentralization of autonomy for Roman Catholic Churches within their own national jurisdiction, but the Church still remains very much centred on the Pope himself and upon the Vatican Curia. Moreover, the efficiency of modern communications must tend to operate against the decentralizing intention of 'Vatican Two'. Major policy is enunciated by the Pope. Local churches cannot but feel constrained to maintain close touch with Rome in detailed questions of its interpretation.

Whether or not popes may be concerned not to interfere in the secular policies of other states, it is nevertheless the fact that they do make – and cannot avoid making – pronouncements which do amount to at least an indirect involvement in temporal matters within the jurisdiction of other realms. Unless they are to emasculate themselves, other than in the strictly theological field in which the laity feels hardly concerned, Catholic bishops, and not least the Pope, must express themselves on at least some matters of political, social and economic consequence. There is, then, no way in which the Pope can avoid some degree of involvement in the political affairs of states having a Roman Catholic community. But the nub of the matter is whether or not such pronouncements are advisory or mandatory. Are popes and bishops recommending to their flock a course of action, or are they charging their flock to follow a course of action?

It is here that the difference lies between the Protestant and the Catholic Churches. If Anglican bishops condemn abortion or contraception, they are offering a moral opinion, which Protestants can reject at will. But the Catholic Church, being an authoritarian church, if the Pope condemns abortion or contraception, he is in fact forbidding them, even though they might be legal in many states. And he expects Catholics to obey him, and bishops and priests, wherever they can assume enough authority, to police his policies as best they can, whatever the temporal law of the land. Thus may papal pronouncements – however benevolent – cut across the secular laws of other lands.

In these days of easy movement, popes travel extensively. When they visit foreign lands they do in some degree – and I suppose quite naturally and deliberately, and particularly in Catholic countries – treat their foreign Catholic flocks as their own subjects, which indeed the First Vatican Council (1870) claimed them to be. Furthermore, their public comments on social, and even economic, conditions in the countries they visit go well beyond anything that would ordinarily be regarded as conventionally acceptable from a visiting head of state. That it may nominally be a pastoral visit scarcely masks the fact that the Pope is also in his other capacity a head of state.

What they have to say on those occasions may be morally right. The manner in which they say it may be distinguished by courtesy, tact and studied diplomacy. But it may, for all that, carry – and indeed be intended to carry – political implications amounting technically to an interference in the sovereign rights of the country in question. It may be implicitly, or even explicitly, concerned to encourage local Catholics in courses not favoured by the local political authority. It may implicitly carry advice to local governments to amend their political policies. Such host governments, being usually Catholic, have little alternative but to tolerate such Papal courses, whether or not they allow themselves to be influenced by them.

The only lay head of state who has acted thus in recent times was de Gaulle, and he received immediate and very short shrift from the Canadian authorities.

The Papacy sees this role as a wholly proper one, and not only may it be right that there should be in the world – and particularly in the numerous Catholic countries in which some sections of the population regard themselves as suffering intolerable disabilities – a powerful moral voice which is not too squeamish about frontiers and foreign suzerainty, but there may also be many, and of other denominations as well, who would not object if the Pope were to be even more forthright on some subjects and about some regimes. Some of the rulers, too, may welcome the intervention of the Pope when he cautions Catholic communities with prudent advice intended to discourage internal discord in the country concerned.

Nevertheless it is these, and other such, indications of Papal readiness to involve itself in the secular affairs of other powers, together with the long history of the Papacy as itself a considerable temporal power, that keep alive the bogy of Rome in the hearts and minds of Protestants, and cause Protestant states to be highly sensitive to any indications of seeming Catholic political aspirations.

These Protestant misgivings stem from the inherent nature of the Catholic Church as a world religion with a centralized structure of authority. It is that centre, the Vatican and the Holy See, which is foreign to all states other than itself. It is unique. No other great church has such widespread ramifications coupled with so much centralized authority. For that reason, no other church gives rise to – or itself has to face – comparable problems.

But do such technical – or even actual – Papal breaches of other nations
sovereignty matter any more? Is not Britain's precious Tudor insularity, and tha
of Ulster, already substantially breached by membership of NATO, the Common
Market and so on? Yes, but with a difference. There we are equal partners
We are privy to all secrets. We are there voluntarily. We have a full say both
behind closed doors and in open forum. But Ulster Protestants have no such
rights in Rome. The Vatican secretariat is secret. The Pope claims to be infallible
There is no arguing with his decrees. It is untrammelled power. England can now
ignore it, her Catholics having for centuries acted with absolute discretion. Bu
Ulster cannot ignore it. The forms of religious worship altogether apart, Catholic
power, and Papal influence, in the everyday affairs of life, are much too close
too real and too strong.

The Ulster Protestants are British, and, being British, are prepared to be governed
only by British parliamentary institutions, and are not prepared to render any
power over themselves into the hands of unelected priests. The priesthood is a
self-perpetuating hierarchy, and not responsible to the electorate which will no
suffer therefore to be in any sense ruled or governed by it.

In the context of religious considerations, it must be asked whether Catholicism
the Ulster Catholic minority apart, has for its part anything to fear from
Protestantism. The answer is that there is indeed a deep-seated, fundamental
Catholic concern about the menace of Protestantism to Catholicism. It hardly
concerns the Catholic laity, though it may affect them. It is a threat stemming
not from Protestants themselves, lay, priestly or episcopal – they pose no threat
– but of the possible attraction to Catholics of the concept of Protestantism, even
though there will always be those who prefer to have their religious life within a
more disciplined church.

The Reformation caused millions of Catholics to desert the Catholic Church
and to join the free and reformed churches. In some Catholic countries – France
notably – very large numbers of Catholics have recently been lapsing. If they have
not been joining the Protestant Churches, they have, like Protestants, been freeing
themselves from priestly tutelage.

The concept of freedom from every form of corporatism, including religious
corporatism, is an infection that might spread, and the Catholic hierarchy has
reason to be concerned about it.

CHAPTER 45

British Protestantism

IT MAY BE ASKED, is Britain really all that Protestant? And is religion, therefore, really a factor of importance in relation to the English–Irish problem?

In a letter to *The Times*, the Archdeacon of Westminster wrote some time ago of this being 'an age when to most people God is unreal and His worship meaningless'. He may have had Abbey tourists particularly in mind, but he did not exclude his fellow countrymen. The Religious Affairs Correspondent of *The Times*, also, drew attention to statistics suggesting that, by the time British school children leave school at the age of sixteen, they have largely rejected religion. A survey in Ulster revealed a similar trend in both Protestant and Catholic communities. Moreover, these authoritative statements must appear to be largely confirmed by the observation of many people of dwindling church congregations during the past sixty years.

It may, therefore, seem reasonable to question an assertion that Britain, including Ulster, is a very Protestant country, when there is now seemingly so large a number of people who are atheist, agnostic, humanist, unbelievers of one sort or another who don't care a fig for religion, or therefore for Protestantism, and who may, on that account, be supposed not to be much moved by the Catholic–Protestant question in Ireland. The answer lies in the nature and characteristics of British Protestantism.

British Protestants' view of their religious freedom goes much further than freedom to interpret holy writ for themselves, unbidden by their priests. Theirs, as they see it, is not to believe at all if they like, but nevertheless to remain members of their Church. They see no paradox in the concept of Anglican agnosticism. The priests, of course, could not, and would not wish to, condone such attitudes, but they are sensible enough for the most part to stomach them.

The Church remains for Protestant unbelievers a very pleasant, civilized, solid, durable and comfortable part of their background; a national institution to which they, as subjects of the Crown, feel themselves to have a prescriptive right to belong, and one which they share in a community spirit with their fellow citizens.

They see the Church also as an influence for good, and a comfort and help t
those who do believe, and deserving of their support on that account, and becaus
of its useful social activities.

There is also the fact that when the church was in former times the centre o
local social, as well as religious, life, it collared a lot of the fun – marriages
funerals, baptisms, glorious buildings, pageantry and peace. The doubters an
unbelievers see no reason why they should give up all that, and see no illogicalit
or inconsistency in going to church when they feel like it, and in particular t
enjoy the fun of the great festivals. The Church tries to pin them down witl
solemn oaths if they want to enjoy these things, leaving them no alternative bu
to engage in a little perjury, and thereby perhaps doing more harm than good.

Can the English, then, be called a very Protestant people when the churche
are largely empty – when even the believers seldom go to church? The answer i
that their very lack of diligence about attending church is itself a profound par
of their Protestantism. They can do as they like, go to church or not as the
please, and without fear of being disciplined by their priests.

And, moreover, they do now go to church, even though infrequently, in a wa
that they never could before. On great national occasions, a coronation, for instance
or a jubilee, the whole nation, through the medium of television, goes solidly t
church in Westminster Abbey or St Paul's Cathedral, and they share in a gloriou
service and in a royal occasion that in the past was the privilege only of the ver
few. And as the mighty organ swells to a thunder, and the state trumpets join thei
fanfare, and near two thousand voices tumultuously raise to heaven the grea
hymn, 'All people that on earth do dwell', to the tune of 'the Old Hundredth', th
heart of England is deeply moved, and its Protestantism is mightily reinforced an
reinvigorated. There is another and very delightful way in which very large number
now go to church. They regularly watch and listen to *Songs of Praise* on televisior
on Sunday evenings.

Protestant Britain remains tolerant of other faiths, but there is a cast-iror
underlying determination in the hearts of individual Englishmen and women t
keep their own free Protestant souls absolutely inviolate. Just as the Irishman
positive Catholicism is part of his Irishness, so, too, is the Briton's negativ
Protestantism part of his Britishness, and a part of what makes him so differer
from the Irish.

There is, also, another dimension to this paradox of church-going unbeliev
ers and church-abstaining believers. Even British Catholics, while acknowl
edging the technically schismatic nature of Protestantism, nevertheless, in
shadowy and non-religious sense, accept the Protestant Church as an elemen
in their civic patriotism. The local church, with St George's banner flying fror
the tower, might be even more lovable were it a Catholic church, but Englisl
Catholics would nevertheless feel a sense of national and patriotic loss were i
just to disappear.

British Protestantism is thus not solely a religion. The Protestant Church is not only the House of God. It is an ancient, much revered and venerated national temple to absolute personal and individual freedom of thought, and one in which believers, doubters and unbelievers alike, and Protestants and members of other denominations as well, can all find something for their comfort, their enjoyment, their satisfaction, their well-being, and their sense of community and national involvement in issues great and small – an essential part of the fabric of the character of Britain.

And that characteristic of English Protestantism, and in particular of the pre-eminent role of the Church of England within it, remains profoundly different from the place of the Catholic Church in Irish life, and thus contributes materially to distinguishing the two peoples from each other. English Protestantism is not only to do with religion; it is to do with England, and therefore with loyalty to the Crown, and is thus central to the question of the allegiance of the Ulster loyalist Protestant community.

CHAPTER 46

Britain's Relationship with Ulster

A CENTURY AGO when the first Home Rule bill wa tabled, England reserved the question of defence to herself. Nevertheless, th implication of the Home Rule provisions was that Britain saw no danger that a self-governing Ireland would ally herself to a hostile power. Has that view changed Does England now feel she must hold on to Ulster for strategic reasons?

Prima facie, she would seem to have more to gain strategically by being ou of Ulster. So long as Ireland remains partitioned, with Britain in a protective rol in Ulster, the Southern Irish are unlikely to feel able – or at any rate are not going to find it easy – to join a Western defence Alliance. But a united Ireland might do so, thus opening up the possibility of Irish facilities being placed at the disposal of the Alliance.

If that is the case, then the strategic argument still holds good for completing Gladstone's Home Rule intentions, and thus for letting Britain off the Irish hook. Yet more than a hundred years have gone by since then and Ulster, as in 1886, still hold up the realization of Gladstone's Scandinavian dream of an independent united Ireland

All that England has to do in order to disengage from Ulster is to withdraw her troops and her support, and to legislate certain constitutional instruments She has given categorical assurances to Ulster that she will not do so, unless a majority of the people of Northern Ireland wish it. But the people of Ulster regard those assurances with mistrust.

It is not that ordinary Ulstermen question the integrity of individual British ministers and senior officials. But they mistrust that abstract thing 'Whitehall'. They do not forget the three Home Rule bills. They do not forget that Whitehall wa on the brink of using the armed forces in 1914 to force them, as they saw it unwillingly into the arms of Rome. They do not forget that Britain abrogated the Act of Union in the South, and abandoned the Southern Protestants to wha they regard as the priest-ridden administration in the Republic. And they have seen the Protestant population there dwindle by more than a half during this century deliberate genocide, as they believe, through the instrument of the intransigen Catholic marriage rules.

Furthermore, the Ulster loyalists have watched 'Whitehall', as they see it, deserting Britain's friends all over the world. They do not forget that Britain withdrew from the south of Ireland leaving civil war behind her; and that she left India to a state of civil war; that she did the same to Palestine, and left incipient civil war conditions in Cyprus. They judge that Britain has shown a strong stomach when it comes to leaving her friends and loyal supporters in the lurch. Little wonder that there is an Ulster perception that 'Whitehall' is, in their colourful imagery, 'packed with Shinners' (Sinn Fein supporters), only too ready, given half a chance, to sell them down the river to Rome via Dublin.

The fact that the Northern Ireland economy has for a long time been in poor shape also tends to sap the morale of the Northern loyalists and to reinforce their feeling of a precarious dependence on Britain. Because Ulster is heavily subsidized by Britain, the loyalists have cause to wonder for how much longer mainland tax payers will remain content to continue paying the huge bill. This is an additional sombre thought for the embattled loyalists to add to their concern about Britain's possible intentions.

If Britain would give her eye teeth to be off the Irish hook, and if Ulster half expects it anyway, then why has she spent over a century shilly-shallying since 1886? Why doesn't she grasp this nettle and be done with it? If she was to do it now, she would not be faced with a mutiny of Irish officers in the armed forces as she was in 1914. There are not now enough of them to matter, nor would they, as in 1914, be asked to march against their fellow Irish Protestants in Ulster. They would simply be required to pull out. Indeed, it is to be supposed that the armed forces would be only too glad to be freed of the Ulster incubus.

De Gaulle did it within Algeria. He just pulled out, and in the teeth of very considerable opposition in his own armed forces. He just abandoned the same number of French *colons* – about a million – as there are Protestants in Ulster. He got away with it. The *colons* left Algiers and were re-settled and re-habilitated in France. But that was different. The *colons* could not have survived as an independent entity in Algiers. The Ulster Protestants believe they could survive, except in the unthinkable case of England blockading them into submission to Dublin. It is their expressed determination to fight it out if left alone to do so.

Is a blockade so unthinkable to the Northern Irish? White Rhodesia was British, Protestant and Loyalist, and the settlers had been encouraged by Whitehall to go there. They were blockaded. British policy there was governed by expediency, not sentiment; and Ulster believes that *au fond* expediency governs Whitehall thinking on Northern Ireland.

But, to answer the question, it must be supposed that the reason why Britain has not hitherto grasped the Ulster nettle by disengaging and pulling out is because of the dangerous uncertainty of what might happen were she to do so. To suppose that the Ulster loyalists would, like the French Algerian *colons*, pack up and withdraw; to suppose they could ever be coerced into an independent Catholic state; to suppose that they would not fight tooth and nail to preserve their integrity and their independence from the Irish Republic, would be perilously to ignore the signs and portents. They would have a population about the size of that of the Jews in Palestine when the British pulled out in May 1948, and would likely to be no less successful in defending themselves.

The I.R.A. groups, it must be supposed, believe that their campaign of terrorism will, if violent enough, and sustained long enough, cause England to tire of carrying the security burden and, as she seemingly did under similar pressure in other territories, to disengage, and wash her hands of Ulster. If that was to happen do the I.R.A. groups believe that it would lead to the submission of the Ulster loyalists? If they do, they have almost certainly misjudged their opponent. Let them read the story of the 36th (Ulster) Division at Thiepval Wood, in the Battle of the Somme, on 1 July 1916, and then think again.

British political judgement in such situations being essentially expedient, we must suppose that the decision would long ago have been to withdraw from Ulster and leave the loyalists to stew had not successive British governments judged that the almost inevitable result would be a civil war that would have even worse consequences for Britain than the security problems engendered by remaining in Ireland.

Might Britain change her mind? Could the British public so tire of the Ulster involvement, and seemingly futile loss of valuable British lives, and cost in British treasure, as to cause strong pressure to be brought upon the government to disengage?

Expediency, in this case, particularly with regard to the current nature of the I.R.A. groups, argues strongly against the likelihood that Britain would contemplate withdrawal. It would cause consternation in Dublin. The I.R.A. groups would not be likely to dissolve overnight, having achieved the goal of getting Britain out of Ireland. That is probably no longer their principal aim. On the contrary, they would be likely to turn all their efforts against the Southern government. The task of dealing both with the I.R.A. groups and a million hostile Protestants in the North would be beyond the capacity of the security forces of the South, leading to a state of insecurity there that would be intolerably dangerous not only to Britain, but also to the Atlantic Alliance as a whole.

There is, in addition, an overriding moral reason why Britain should not withdraw, leaving not only Ulster, but the whole of Ireland, to stew in the consequences.

History is not simply a dead record of the past to which are added the doings of today and tomorrow, of this week, and next week. At its most profound it is the long unfolding of great movements over centuries. Let us then beware of short-term petulance towards the slow, onward march of great events. We owe long-term debts to history, and England owes a long-term historical debt to Ireland. England spent three hundred years from the Reformation onward ınsettling' Ireland; indeed, a great deal longer if we trace the span of time back ɔ Norman days. That there was dire strategic need may excuse, but does not lter, the fact. 'Unsettled' Ireland was, and by England.

The re-settling is now in process. It may be long. It may be arduous. It may e painful. It may be costly. It may take three centuries in turn. Two centuries ave already been spent in the slow reversal of the 'unsettling'. It may take another hree centuries to complete. But in that process England has a solemn, historical, 10ral duty to assist. Let it never then come about that from impatience, or self-ıterest, she stomps off and leaves the people of Ireland to tear themselves apart.

CHAPTER 47

The Trend of Southern Irish Political Attitudes in the Context of Anglo-Irish Security

NOTABLE AMONG THE transformations that have bee
taking place in Irish life is the fact that the government of the Republic has bee
progressively shedding much of its former insularity. It has been finding itself a
increasing role in the councils of nations. The people of Ireland – a smal
chauvinistic, if vocal, minority apart – and, not least, many of the officials, wei
probably sincerely sorry to be out of the Commonwealth. The Irish are not ant
British, despite the anti-British teaching they have received in the schools. The
still have the right, if they wish to exercise it, to British citizenship. They misse
it when they suddenly found themselves – without consultation or referendum
no longer members of the Commonwealth club, many of whose other membe
have a much less close affinity to Britain.

Also, the Irish feel an almost proprietary interest in the Royal family, with who
they have organic links. English monarchs had been constitutionally kings an
queens of Ireland for four hundred years, and the Irish, with their Celtic tradition
enjoyed the institution of monarchy; and there were family connections between th
monarchy and the great Irish houses. In Tudor times, for instance, Garret More, th
great Earl of Kildare, married, as his second wife, a cousin of Henry VII, and his son
Garret Oge, married, as his second wife, Elizabeth, daughter of the Marquess c
Ormonde, a cousin of Henry VIII. And Anne Boleyn's grandfather was 7th Earl c
Ormonde, and head of the great Irish Butler family. And the late Princess of Wale
was one quarter Irish, her grandfather having been Lord Fermoy.

My maternal grandmother's aunt, Eliza Caroline Boothby, married the 1
Lord Fermoy who was the great, great, great, great grandfather of Diana Prince
of Wales who was thus my third cousin once removed, though I did not know he

But outside the Commonwealth, membership of the United Nations and th
European Union has given the Irish the opportunity to mingle with the natior
of the world on equal terms; and, in particular, Ireland's significant military ro
with the peace-keeping forces of the United Nations has been an enormous boo
to Irish self-confidence and self-assurance, as well as a valuable experience fc
her armed forces.

The Irish economy has advanced enormously during the past few decades. At times its growth-rate has been higher than elsewhere in Europe. Ireland is no longer a poor country, the people are well off, and they are benefiting from the fact that affluence breeds leisure, and that leisure breeds higher levels of civilized interests. Should oil be found in the Irish seas in significantly recoverable quantities, Ireland may become enormously wealthy on a per capita rating, because of her small population.

In Northern Ireland, the violence of the last thirty years has, in this age of mass communication, caused many in both communities to take an almost intellectual interest in the problem, and to ask themselves what there is that is so different about the other side as to cause this schism. This beneficial inquisitiveness, together – in a religious milieu – with an often genuine wish to show a Christian spirit, has led to deliberate, new and quite widespread inter-denominational contacts of one kind and another, particularly among the better educated. The all-Ireland leaders of the Catholic and Protestant churches meet monthly, a practice which, even at its least fruitful, must ensure that many misunderstandings are avoided.

There is in Dublin an ecumenical school of theology, founded in 1970 by a Jesuit. The staff are mixed Catholic and Protestant. During the time that the college has existed, the students have been both Catholic and Protestant of several denominations, mostly Irish from both sides of the border, but also from the British mainland, and from Europe, America, Asia and Africa.

In the secular field, too, useful initiatives have been taken, both at the political level, and by independent responsible bodies which believe that they have a contribution to make to better relationships and understandings. Ever since the 1921 treaty there have been close relationships at the official level between ministries in Dublin and London, and there have been recent substantial initiatives from both sides, including the terms of the Good Friday 1998 Agreement, to strengthen and extend these relationships, and there is an enormous commercial interdependence between the Republic and Britain.

With some aspects of sports there is a total unity. In Ireland rugby union, cricket, and other sports have all-Ireland teams. The British Lions are all-Ireland. And, of course, there is nothing new in the idea that the development of common services outside the political field – for instance a shared electricity grid – cannot but have beneficial political consequences, however slight.

The 1998 Good Friday Agreement has been a major step towards closer relationships between Britain, the Republic and Northern Ireland and will provide new means for close association and consultation between the governments, the communities, and the political parties involved, if it does not break down because of Sinn Fein/I.R.A.'s refusal to get rid of their arms. The problem of gunmen has hung over the Irish scene spasmodically throughout the long period since Irish independence in 1921.

The declared objective of the I.R.A. throughout that time has been to end pa tition by the use of force and violence. Nevertheless, it can be safely said that th great majority of the people of Southern Ireland are not interested in the borde question or in partition. The whole thing is a great bore. It does not directly affe their lives, except perhaps beneficially if they live near enough to the border t enjoy the vast smuggling possibilities it offers. They can travel to and fro with out let or hindrance, and they do so in their thousands between Dublin and Belfa and other centres every weekend for football matches and other sporting event There is also an enormous volume of daily traffic for business and private affair of all kinds. That the Ulster Catholics get a bit of a raw deal means about a much to the great mass of their Southern co-religionists as unemployment o Tyneside does to a person living in the West Country. But it is a useful point fo politicians. That the Ulster Presbyterian is a different sort of person, and to the not as Irish as themselves, the Southerners accept as a feature of Ulster, and no one worth squabbling about. It is certainly not one that is worth the price of th I.R.A. groupings, which they dislike and fear. They would like to see the map of Ireland solid green, but not at the cost of the serious disturbance of their ow lives – it can wait until the time comes, whenever that may be. In the meantim if the border can be treated for practical purposes more or less as an irrelevanc that suits everyone well enough. Everyone, that is to say, except the securit forces, for the I.R.A. has been able to exploit the border to its own advantage, pa ticularly in the extent to which it has been able to use the South as a base fo operations in Ulster and elsewhere, and as a refuge from the British and Ulster force of law and order.

Inevitably, the Catholic Church in Ireland is itself subject to nationalist infl ences. Its priests and bishops are drawn from 'the people' where nationalism ha its deepest roots. It is not a middle-class priesthood. Its ranks are solid gree patriotic Irishmen. But, being a self-perpetuating hierarchy, it does not have to loo over its shoulder for votes. It can therefore place the full weight of its authorit behind causes that are moral, theological and social. It has thus always bee strongly inclined to constitutional attitudes, even in the days of British rule, an disposed to urge the people to uphold the constitution and the law. In additio to a general concern to uphold standards of Christian morality, it is deepl concerned that Ireland shall not be a strife-torn land. It does not want regimes o violence. It does not want its sons in wickedness and trouble, and it does no want their families, or their victims, whether Catholic or Protestant, in sorrow an distress. At times an odd priest here and there has sided with the extremists, bu the Catholic Church holds no brief for the I.R.A., and its bishops condemn i lawlessness – though, in the past, not always without nationalistic equivocation For all that, the Irish gunmen ignored the Pope.

CHAPTER 48

The Gun and the Bomb

THERE IS IN THE REPUBLIC of Ireland, and among the Catholic community of Northern Ireland, a small body of extremist republicans who are determined to see Ireland united and wholly shamrock green in their own lifetime, and governed by themselves. They are Sinn Fein/I.R.A., a terrorist organization who have carried out many acts of violence.

In 1998–99 an attempt was made to set up a devolved government in Northern Ireland, consisting of an Assembly (House of Parliament) of 108 people, and an Executive (Cabinet) of twelve people, each of whom would have ministerial responsibility over a government department. Two seats on the Executive were to be reserved for Sinn Fein, the I.R.A. mouthpiece. The setting up of this Northern Ireland devolved government was to be dependent on the agreement of all parties to arrangements for Northern Ireland set out in a document known variously as the Belfast Agreement or the Good Friday (1998) Agreement, covering details known as the Peace Process. It had been drawn up after exhaustive discussion between all parties concerned, and was signed by the British and Irish Governments. One of the strands of the agreement was to advocate the decommissioning of the arms illegally held by paramilitary groups including the I.R.A.

During the discussion of this document, Sinn Fein/I.R.A. agreed to a ceasefire, and in return were granted a number of concessions. The chief of these was the withdrawal of some military forces from Northern Ireland; the early release of hundreds of I.R.A. terrorists serving long sentences in gaol; a commission to examine the Royal Ulster Constabulary (R.U.C.) with the hope that it will be emasculated. One of the Sinn Fein/I.R.A. demands is that the R.U.C. should in part be manned by the I.R.A. The Sinn Fein/I.R.A. spokesman, Martin McGuinness, went so far as to say that if the commission currently reviewing the R.U.C. does not recommend its disbandment there will be 'big trouble'. He was also said that 'there is no possibility of the surrender of I.R.A. arms'.

The Good Friday ceasefire did not mean the cessation of all illicit activity. The I.R.A. continued their large-scale beatings, mutilation, knee-capping, and shootings. In February 1999 the I.R.A. called off these activities. But they have still not called off all their illicit doings. As one member of the public put it, 'The have turned into a Mafia. They have called a ceasefire with the Army and th Police but not with their own community.' It is also said that in some Cathol housing estates they rule by fear, and the Police never visit such places on foo only in Land Rovers.

The I.R.A. has also followed a policy of sending large numbers of people int exile, either away from their own district or out of the Province altogether. 1998 some 440 people are said to have been exiled. In one area the I.R.A. a so dominant that only the Republican flag can be flown, and the street name have been changed from English to Irish. As one resident has said, 'The pea process has changed nothing'. The I.R.A. are still recruiting, training and addir to their weapons.

During the peace process there has been one major bomb outrage, at Omagl in which 29 people were killed, and there have been a number of smaller bombing The Omagh bomb was exploded by a splinter group of the I.R.A. callin themselves the Real I.R.A.

The I.R.A. are not the only illegal armed paramilitary groupings. There a also the so-called loyalist paramilitaries. They were set up initially as an illegal arme Protestant response to the I.R.A., but they have additionally become offensive. Lik the I.R.A. they have also been engaged in murders, beatings, mutilations and s on, and one of the groups has said that it will murder I.R.A. terrorists who hav been serving long sentences and have been prematurely released from gaol. The have also attacked many Catholic churches.

Lengthy discussion of the Good Friday Agreement and the peace process brok down when it became clear that the I.R.A. would not decommission its arm and the Protestant Unionist Party of Ulster refused to join the proposed Norther Ireland Cabinet – the Executive – if the Sinn Fein party, representing an illega armed terrorist organization, the I.R.A., was allowed to take their two seats.

The Ulster problem is at present insoluble. The I.R.A. will not give up their arm Arms are the reason for their existence. Equally the Ulster Unionists, the mo powerful party in Ulster, will never agree to sharing power with an armed terrori organization – Sinn Fein/I.R.A. Although the Belfast Good Friday Agreement a a whole has thus broken down, it is to be hoped that some of its provisions ca be rescued and enacted, because it contains some excellent and far-reachin beneficial proposals for much closer ties between Britain, Ireland and Ulster.

The I.R.A. seem now to be on a dangerous high, and it is to be feared tha when, under veiled threats, it can obtain no more concessions from the British c Irish Governments, it will return to violence. The I.R.A. and its group of splinte organizations appear to be an amalgam of three different types of people:

- Genuine, if misguided, patriots;
- Modern, ruthless, international-type terrorists;

- Boys who fall into the clutches of the I.R.A. at the dare-devil stage of life, and then cannot get out. They would be shot, or at least maimed, if they tried.

The genuine patriots in the I.R.A. groupings are misguided not only because they are breaking the law, and therefore acting contrary to the will of the great majority of their fellow citizens, but also because, in logic, the use of force can never succeed in bringing about what they claim to be their aim – a united Ireland. Violence serves only to postpone the day when that may come about. Moreover, growing repugnance at their increasing callousness and brutality has progressively weakened even such limited sympathy and support as their patriotic claims have in the past engendered in extreme nationalist circles both at home and abroad. Those members of the I.R.A. groupings who regard themselves primarily as patriots may argue that their grandfathers achieved the liberation of the twenty-six counties of the South by force of arms; and that what their grandfathers did in the South, they themselves can do in the North.

The Irish are addicted to mythology. It conforms to their romantic streak. Historical fact is, therefore, apt to reappear in mythological guise. Thus the mythology of what happened years ago in Ireland has come to differ from the facts, and in this instance is dangerous to the Republic of Ireland itself, and to others. The grandfathers of the present I.R.A. groupings did not set out to liberate the present Republic of Ireland. Their aim was an independent united Republic of all Ireland, which they determined to achieve by force and violence.

Politics being the art of the possible, every political realist was well aware that there was at that time no possibility that the Ulster loyalists would be prepared to accept a minority role in a united Ireland. But the leaders of the I.R.A. (originally I.R.B. – Irish Republican Brotherhood) were not political realists. They were romantic visionaries with an unfortunate and brutal disregard for human life and suffering. Their campaign of violence did not, in the event, lead to a glorious victory; it failed, as it was inevitably bound to do. And what the I.R.A. could not achieve eighty years ago, the gunmen of today cannot hope to achieve.

Nor is there any substance in the claim that the 1919–21 rebellion, even if it did not achieve a united Ireland, did nevertheless bring about the independence of the twenty-six counties of the Republic of Ireland. That would have come about in any case through political negotiation.

Relations between Britain and the people of Ireland had probably never been better than they were during the first eighteen months of the 1914–18 Great War. The Home Rule bill had reached the Statute Book; and the British and Irish were united in a common war effort. Then, during the Easter weekend of 1916, came the Sinn Fein rising. It was quickly crushed, but not before extensive damage had been done to the centre of Dublin city. Casualties, too, were high on both sides. The rising had no public support. It was seen at the time by the people of Ireland as a futile, but damaging, affair. The rebels were treated with contempt – indeed with vilification by the Irish people.

After their surrender, they were jeered as they were taken through the streets to gaol. And the British soldiers who suppressed the rising received unstinting support from the civil population. The husbands, brothers and sons of many of the people of Ireland were at the War risking their lives alongside the British. A distraction in Ireland could only increase the danger for those at the Front. So, 'down with the Sinn Feiners' was the overwhelming immediate reaction. It was not the Sinn Fein rebels who were then the heroes of Ireland. The heroes were men like Private Michael Cassidy V.C. His name rhymed with 'audacity', and his valour was the subject of a catchy ballad song that was on everyone's lips. And the most popular war song of all was 'It's a Long Way to Tipperary'.

But during the next two years the mood was to change, and native Ireland was to revert to its more customary feelings of antipathy to England. Support fell away from the constitutionally elected political leaders of Ireland in the Whitehall Parliament, and passed to the unconstitutional militant Sinn Fein leaders.

The execution, over a period of ten days, of some of the leaders of the 1916 Easter Rising caused disquiet. After the first few were shot, responsible Irish leaders warned the British government that to continue the executions would have an adverse effect on the mood of the people of Ireland. But the executions went on. Fifteen were shot, including an infantile paralysis cripple, and one so badly wounded in the rebellion that in order to be shot he had to be carried to the execution ground on a stretcher and sat in a chair. There was public concern, and sympathy for the rebels began to be aroused.

There were probably three other principal factors which affected the temper of the people towards Britain. Nearly a hundred rebels had been condemned to death. There was doubtless anxiety lest there be further executions. Then, a large number of the captured rebels were taken out of Ireland and imprisoned in Britain. Who knew what might happen to them once they were across the water? More disquiet. When, after a short incarceration, they were brought back to Ireland and released, they were greeted rapturously, and treated as heroes. The third factor was the threat of conscription and this was widely regarded as unacceptable in Ireland. Many Irishmen were prepared to join the British forces voluntarily – and many were not. None were prepared to be dragooned into them.

The upshot was that by 1919, when the war was over, Sinn Fein had acquired overwhelming public support among Irish Catholics. In January 1919 they opened, with the brutal murder of two policemen, the widespread and destructive – and altogether unnecessary – rebellion, known at the time, and ever since, as 'The Troubles', which was to last until mid-July 1921 when the I.R.A., having shot their bolt, were forced to come to the conference table.

Sinn Fein had had their opportunity to act constitutionally and with politica maturity and responsibility. Instead of refusing, they ought to have taken their seat at the 1917 Irish Convention. It had been called as a forum where Irishmen could negotiate between themselves the political future of Ireland. The nationalist Home Rule Party, the Ulster Unionists, and the Protestant Ascendancy were separately represented, but Sinn Fein stayed away. Had they attended, they would have had the full weight of the powerful Irish American lobby behind them. That being so, there can be no doubt that, however protracted and difficult the negotiations, or whatever subsequent form they might have taken, the outcome would have been independence for the predominantly Catholic and nationalist parts of Ireland, without ever a shot being fired.

For half a century Britain had been moving toward Home Rule for Ireland. The 1914 Home Rule bill was on the statute book. There can be no question that without the 1916 rebellion, and the subsequent 'Troubles', a degree of independence, probably well in excess of anything foreseen in the Home Rule bill, would have been granted to those parts of Ireland – the twenty-six counties of the South – where nationalist Catholics were in an enormous majority over loyalist Protestants.

It is no less inconceivable that nationalist Ireland could have failed to obtain a substantial measure of independence in consequence of the far-reaching discussions of the constitutional position of the White dominions during the 1920s which culminated in the Statute of Westminster. This, in effect, granted complete autonomy to the dominions in 1931.

Nor is it possible to suppose that, if never a shot had been fired, nationalist Ireland would have been any less independent today than she now is – any less independent, for instance, than many other imperial territories which received their freedom peaceably without ever a gun being drawn from the holster.

In three centuries, since the 1641 rebellion, the only two significant occasions on which force had been used – the 1798 rebellion, and the Fenian outbreak in the mid-nineteenth century – it had achieved nothing. All the achievements – the amelioration and abrogation of the Penal Laws, the enfranchisement of Catholics, Catholic Emancipation, the disestablishment of the Church of Ireland, the succession of land laws (whereby the lands of Ireland were being restored to the native Irish in an orderly and civilized manner) and finally the 1914 Home Rule bill – had been achieved by political processes, even though there had been occasional, sporadic, localized agrarian violence.

Although there could have been no possibility that Ulster would have joined a united Ireland, she would have been encouraged by Britain to develop such close relations with the South as might have seemed reasonable and possible. But the rebellion, followed by the civil war among the Catholic nationalists in the South, in which they tore their country apart, and showed themselves hardly less merciful to each other than Cromwell had been, was no encouragement to the Ulster loyalists, Protestant or Catholic, to bed down with them.

The Irish Free State government which had been formed after the signing of the treaty with Britain in 1921, admitted officially to the execution during the civil war of more than four times as many members of the I.R.A. as the British executions of 1916. But that is probably only a fraction of the true figure. The stories, heard by those of us living in Ireland at the time, of whole squads of I.R.A. men caught with arms being secretly and summarily executed by the Irish army cannot have been without some foundation in fact. No graves were marked. No relatives were told. Numerous men who had taken up arms against the new Free State Government just disappeared. Ulster's distaste for a union with the South is understandable.

The later mythology, which raises the rebellions to heroic proportions, is indeed dangerous to Ireland. It would not have been approved by Daniel O'Connell who would have no truck with violence. It endorses a precedent that threatens Ireland's own institutions. The rebellions of 1916, and 1919–21, did not usher in a glorious chapter of Irish history. They set the tone and the scene for a long period of lawlessness and violent crime which has done much material damage to Ireland, caused great suffering to innocent people, dragged Ireland's name in the mud, and faced her today with a dangerous internal security problem.

Those of us who are living now are not responsible for what happened centuries ago, but we are responsible for what happens today. Let us consider what judgement history will pass on us in our turn. Teach history with understanding and not with malice.

England unsettled Ireland; true. But the Romans, the Danes, the Anglo-Saxons the French all unsettled England; and much more recently Germany unsettled almost the whole of Europe. But sensible men all over Europe have been doing what they can to bury those old, and not so old, hatchets. The magnanimity of France, the Low Countries, Denmark and Norway towards Germany is an example worthy of study. Compare the E.U. with the state of Western Europe in 1916, and in 1940. Fruitful beneficial accommodation between old rivals is not impossible.

It will surely be accepted by the great majority of Southern Ireland nationalists and by the American Irish lobby, that there are much greater things at stake than nursing ancient grievances against England, and that it is not to the advantage of Ireland to allow – let alone to cause – history past to mar history present and history in the making.

But there is also the other side of the coin. Why, the English ask often and wearily, can the Irish not forget the Battle of the Boyne, the seventeenth century Plantation of Ulster and all of that? It all happened three hundred years ago and more, and surely could now be buried and forgotten?

The question can be answered by analogy. Would the English – we may ask – forget if Louis XIV of France had conquered south-east England three hundred years ago, turned most of the English out, settled it with French citizens – Catholic at that – and if the French were still there today, and south-east England still administered by France as a part of metropolitan France, with the inhabitants owing fierce allegiance to Paris? Would the English just accept it and forget it, even if the inhabitants of the French area had become somewhat Anglicized, and spoke English rather than French? The analogy – though inexact – is not over-distorted. Canterbury, for instance, would be in the French area, just as Armagh, an even older Christian foundation than Canterbury, and the seat of the Roman Catholic Primate of all Ireland, is in Ulster.

There is, too, another point. In asking why the Irish cannot forget, the English overlook the fact that Ireland is no more to them than an incidental part of their history. Indeed, some Irish believe that they have had to keep lighting bombs under the English to remind them of their existence and their grievances. To Ireland, England, looming large off her eastern shore, has dominated her history for many centuries past. Large in the mind of every Irishman is the Battle of the Boyne, but who in England has ever heard of the Battle of Stoke, when Ireland invaded England?

The proximity of England is a fact that Ireland has to live with. It is not comfortable for her to have to dwell cheek by jowl with a neighbour more than a dozen times her size in terms of population. She cannot but come under strong British influence, whether she likes it or not. It is an inescapable fact of her geographical situation. I think it was a former Canadian prime minister who said that for Canada the proximity of the United States is like being in bed with an elephant. Whenever it had nightmares it made things very uncomfortable. But there is nothing for it for Ireland but to lump it, and make the best of it.

Looking objectively, then, at the true history – as distinct from the mythology – of relations between England and Ireland, we cannot escape the conclusion that the gun did nothing to further Ireland's interests in the decades from 1916 onwards, and did much to damage her reputation and the fabric of her society. As a political weapon, it is uncivilized, and is bound to prove futile and unavailing. The I.R.A. could not in a hundred years use as many bombs in England as one night of German raids in the Second World War. Bombing Britain is only a pinprick to that nation. I must leave no-one in any doubt that I find equally abhorrent and barbarous the unlawful, violent Protestant response to the I.R.A., and I condemn it absolutely.

If Irishmen will not lay down the gun and allow conditions of peace to prevail, then the only unity will be a united determination of the rulers and authorities in Britain, Ulster and the Republic to be rid of this lawless, disruptive and dangerous element in their societies. If, then, genuine patriots within the I.R.A. groups will consider the logic of the situation, it is surely this. They cannot by force and violence coerce the more than a million loyalists in Ulster, including many Catholics, into a united Ireland under Catholic nationalist domination, and then hold them there by force for evermore. They are a numerically large community of gifted, tough and resolute people whom the I.R.A. have no hope whatsoever of defeating; and they are as much given naturally to action as the Southern Irish are to dreaming.

Nor will throwing bombs at the British achieve the aim of bringing the Ulster loyalists into a united Catholic-dominated Ireland. Partition was not created by, and is not sustained by, the British. Even if throwing bombs at the British was to cause them to pull out of Ireland, that would not end partition. That would not bring about a united Ireland. On the contrary, every shot that is fired, every bomb that is exploded, whether at the British, or at the Ulster loyalists, further hardens the determination of the Northern loyalists to have nothing whatsoever to do with a union with the South.

If, therefore, there is ever to be a marriage between North and South, it can come about only if the Northern loyalists are wooed, not raped, though it has to be admitted that there is not going to be a ready response to wooing either. And shooting and bombing her mother and father – England – will contribute nothing fruitful to the wooing. In other words, in logic there is absolutely no argument to support a campaign of violence, and no justification for it, as it can never achieve the end at which it is claimed to be aimed – a united Ireland. This, of course, is what the great body of people in the Dublin Government, and in the South generally, have seen all along, and it is the reason why they have rejected the use of force, and have been prepared to act with patience. They have no intention of being ruled by a left-wing, Soviet-style republican government.

It seems beyond question that the I.R.A. has been attracting to itself a callous type of person, not so much concerned to carry on a misguided and unlawful patriotic crusade to unite Ireland, as to destroy the settled order of society in Ireland as a whole, North and South, and to do so by whatever means, however inhuman and brutal.

All pity choked by custom of fell deeds.
SHAKESPEARE, *JULIUS CAESAR*

To use those terms is not to fall into the trap of simply calling the I.R.A. names. To simply say that its membership is mad, or bad or psychotic, is dangerous. It risks the probability of underestimating the adversary. The old I.R.A. of eighty years ago had formidable, if misguided, leaders. The Irish being a far from unintelligent people, it were better to suppose that the current I.R.A. groupings are significant and capable opponents who, moreover, have powerful external support.

There is no likelihood whatsoever that they could succeed in Ireland against the loyal, competent and resolute security authorities and forces of law and order, both in the South and the North. Indeed, the role of the terrorist in Ireland must seem bleak and daunting in the extreme. Nevertheless, international terrorism is a growing menace which warrants the greatest vigilance, not least in Ireland with its endemic traditions of violence.

CHAPTER 49

The Changing Irish Scene
Points the Way Ahead

THE ASPIRATIONS OF North and South seem irreconcilable. Indeed, the aspirations themselves seem confused. The South want, and at the same time shrink from, a united Ireland. In principle they would like jurisdiction over the whole island. In practice they know that they could not contain a million hostile Northern Protestants. The aspirations of the North are not so much to remain British – though they need the support of Britain – as to remain a Protestant state, and outside the jurisdiction, as they see it, of the Catholic Church. The resulting problem cannot in the short term be solved by any brilliant plan or contrivance. That is not to say that violence must inevitably be expected to continue.

There is, however, a different and relevant consideration. Can the irreconcilables themselves be changed, or is there any likelihood that evolutionary processes will change them? With that question we are on more hopeful ground. Ameliorating evolutionary processes are already on the way.

In the past, the nub of the problem has been – and still is – that the Ancient Irish culture of the nationalists is too different from the Anglo-Saxon culture of the Northern loyalists to allow a full meeting of hearts and minds between the two peoples, and superimposed upon those deep differences are the distinctions of church.

Until the nineteenth century, the Irish were seen by the English as being a different people. They were distinguished by their dress, their customs and their language. Since the mid-nineteenth century, the most readily discernible distinctions have disappeared. The Irish now speak English and dress in the same fashion. The English are therefore not so much inclined to look upon them as a separate people, as to see them as a contrary sort of English.

However, not only is it a fact that the Irish have changed in the past century, but they are still changing, and doing so rapidly, and the changes hold out the prospect that, in the longer term, future generations may find acceptable means for very much greater accommodation between North and South than is now the case.

Changes have taken place in recent years that would have astonished our grandfathers. We, in our turn, might be no less surprised by the unexpected changes that may be round the corner.

Almost the most pertinent change that our grandfathers would notice would be the metamorphosis that had taken place in the influential Protestant Ascendancy itself. Not only would they find it had totally lost its influence but, more surprisingly, that it had largely ceased to exist.

It might be supposed that by the exodus, Hibernicizing and waning of the Anglo-Irish, Ireland is being 'purified'. The English infection is at last being eradicated from the holy land of saints and scholars. Yet that is not what is happening. While the Anglo-Irish gentry have been moving in one direction – Out – English influence has been moving superabundantly in the other – In.

The old Irish Ireland is becoming rapidly more Anglicized. Three centuries ago Irish was the first language of the whole of Ireland. A century ago, it was still the language of the West Coast. But, despite frantic efforts by the government to save and revive it, it is now spoken as a first language only in the tiniest pockets on the West Coast and in a few of the far western islands on the Atlantic fringe. A very great pity. As Dr Johnson said, 'I am always sorry when a language is lost, because languages are the pedigrees of nations'.

Seventy years ago, too, characteristic Irish dress was worn widely by country women throughout Ireland – the enormously full black skirt, and sometimes the famous red petticoat, the black bodice, heir perhaps to the ancient jacket, and the usually black shawl sometimes knitted, sometimes of plaid, sometimes other colours, lineal descendant doubtless of the mantle. Now such clothing has almost totally disappeared. The girls of the remotest cliffs of Connaught dress no differently from those of Kent or Surrey.

Here then is a people who are for the most part ethnically pre-Celtic, whose ancient culture and tongue was overlaid by the Celts two thousand years ago, and whose adopted Celtic culture has in turn been progressively Anglicized since the seventeenth century, and whose Celtic language was likewise lost in the nineteenth and early twentieth centuries. The people of Ireland have lost all that beyond recovery, and are faced with the prospect that, if they want a full and fruitful share in the life of the Western world, they have no alternative other than to adapt Anglo-Saxon modes to their own needs and environment, while keeping the Celtic for fun, pageantry, scholarship and interest.

But there is a paradox in the current Anglicization of the people of Ireland. As they adopt more English cultural modes, so do they become more self-consciously Irish. That is a reaction to their submission to Anglo-Saxon influences, and an assertion of the fact that below the surface they still remain truly Irish. And those manifestations of self-conscious Irishness have an important part to play particularly in Irish relations with England. They serve to remind the English that the Irish are essentially different from themselves. Unless the English thoroughly comprehend, and are constantly reminded of that, there will be continuing likelihood of misunderstanding.

There are also other important influences at work upon the Irish scene. Responsible politicians strive for a better understanding and for more amicable and fruitful relationships with their counterparts. A variety of bodies, both lay and clerical, will also continue to do so in fields and areas that they can reach and influence. But, while those endeavours may achieve beneficial results, they will not carry the mass of the people further or faster than they are ready to go. Root and branch changes can take place only to the extent that the hearts and minds of the people may change. But indeed it seems inevitable that Irish society is destined to evolve in a direction which offers a promise of spontaneous, rather than contrived, development and growth of better relationships.

Ireland is a part of the so-called 'developed world' which has itself been changing in an important way. The rampant nationalism which was concomitant with the development of individual nation-states that grew up on a mainly linguistic basis in Europe between the fifteenth and the nineteenth centuries is becoming a thing of the past in Western Europe. The enormous increase in communications, multi-national interdependence in trade and commerce, and in defence, have given the up-and-coming generations in all lands within the developed world – and beyond it into the 'third world' – an innate sense of internationalism which has taken much of the old-fashioned chauvinism out of national patriotism. These sentiments, which are becoming part and parcel of the inheritance of the new generations, cannot but have a beneficial and ameliorating influence upon the Irish scene. It has to be admitted that this goes hand in hand with urges towards cultural separatism designed to safeguard existing cultures. But, nevertheless, overlaying everything is the spread of international uniculture.

Nor is that all. If prosperity continues to increase in Southern Ireland, particularly if oil wealth comes to her and raises still further the standard of living and education, there can hardly fail to be another change, and one that could have a very significant effect.

The change I have in mind is the probable increase in secularism, and a decline in the degree of political and social influence that the Churches will be able to exert on the people of the future. In the increasingly secular atmosphere of Western Europe today, it seems that the Irish Roman Catholic Church may already be losing some of its authority. If that is so, it will be followed by a reduction of Northern Protestant fear of it, and that in turn would decrease the justification for the anti-Catholic fervour of the Orange Order, whose influence would there-fore also progressively decline, the essence of its authority being its championship of the cause of 'No Popery!'

Furthermore, the Churches themselves, even if they do not reach fully their ecumenical goals, will doubtless continue to strive for a better mutual understanding, and closer relationships.

Also, future generations, increasingly involved internationally in fields of economics, trade, recreation and politics, are likely to have a diminishing regard for the authority of churches still inhibited by centuries-old entrenched differences about Elizabeth's 'trifles'.

There is fear that the younger generation in Ireland are being reared in habits of violence, and will continue them as a matter of course; also that their attitudes will be pre-conditioned to continue the provocative sectarian ceremonies, marches and so forth. Up to a point, this will be so, but the young, and particularly the emancipated young of today, are wont to look critically at the older generations, and are inclined to reject that which they find bad or wanting. It is likely that the well-informed younger people of today and tomorrow will be more concerned to eschew violence and provocation as outmoded in a world in which there is much greater cultural similarity between all. There may also be a growing demand – not least among the young themselves – for more inter-denominational education. If that cannot be easily and quickly contrived, the Province might at least adopt the cry, 'Let the children play together!', and promote extra-curricular games and sports for all. One of the healthy characteristics of youth is inquisitiveness. They want the experience of getting to know the other side.

Perhaps, it is not too imaginative to suppose that, by the time the next hundred years of the 're-settling' of Ireland has run its course – and possibly sooner, because time scales are much telescoped in our modern world – the Catholic Church might, under pressure of public opinion, have assumed an almost exclusively pastoral role, in which it might make little more attempt to influence politics, or to invigilate the secular lives of its members, than does the Church of England today. Any such diminution of the secular authority of the Catholic Church would result in a progressive falling off of the militant and defensive attitudes, and the authority over its members, of the Orange Order, whose sometimes provocative manifestations might then come to have no more significance than Guy Fawkes celebrations now have.

In short, what is holding the two parts of Ireland apart is culture, allegiance and religion. Culture is becoming more unified. Allegiance is being modified by a growing internationalism. Religion, in the increasingly secular state of educated Western European peoples, is a correspondingly decreasing cause of differences between them.

We do not know what constitutional or institutional arrangements will seem appropriate half-a-century, or a century, hence. Who, a century ago, could have forecast NATO, the E.U., the European Parliament, and so on? But we can, with some confidence, forecast accommodations between Northern and Southern Ireland, and with Britain, that will be a great deal better than today. The 1998 Good Friday Agreement was a move in this direction.

But such possibly better times will be slow to mature without sustained initiatives to remove the causes of fear, to alleviate poverty in ghetto areas, to provide fair treatment for minorities, and to cultivate all discernible areas of common ground; and unless militant gun-toting Irishmen abandon force and violence as the arbiter of political decision, and make a metaphorical pilgrimage to those old Atlantic cliffs, and there cast their guns into the abyss which was from antiquity the home of the spirits of the dead.

Might not 'No Guns!' serve as a motto to match Ireland's boast to be the 'land of saints and scholars'?

Index

Index

Index

Index

Marx, Karl, 192
Mason, A. E. W., 356
Mathew, Father Theobold, 253
Maudant-Richards, Major, 279
Maxwell's Irish Dragoons, 126
May Day, 30–1
Maynooth, 236–7, 238, 277
Maynooth Castle, 45, 52, 75
McAdam, John, 285
McGuiness, Martin, 401
Mears Court, 170
Mears, John, 170
Meath, 7, 16, 62, 76, 213, 260, 295, 328
Meath, Earls of, 212
Mediterranean, 6, 18, 23, 25, 50, 68, 99,
   100, 347, 376
Medelicote, 185
Medlicott, George, 186
Medlicott, Louisa, 186
Mel, Bishop, 283
Messiah, Handel's, 134
Michigan, 311
Midland Great Western Railway, 275
Mid-West, 310
Milesius (Mil of Spain, Mile-Spanaghe),
   9–10, 12, 14, 30, 102, 231
Miller, William, 310–11
Milltown, Lord *see* Leeson, Joseph
Milner, Lord, 372
Moate, 259, 282, 292, 301
Moira, Earl of, 175
Moloney, J. Chartres, 229–30
Moneyguyneen, 332, 336, 342, 360,
   363–2
Mongols, 360
Mons, Counts of, 128
Montagues and Capulets, 279
Montgomery, Lily, 211
Montreal, 264
Moony, George Enraght-, 296, 340
Moors, 230, 232
Morris, Colonel Herve de Montmorency,
   209–10, 371
Morton, H. V., 162
Moscow, 155
Mosstown, 210
Mostyn, Hon. George, 259
Mountains of Mourne', 336
Mountbolus, 298, 344
Mountjoy, General, 55
Moydrum Castle, 274

Moylurg, 3
Moylurg, Prince of, 3, 4, 19, 25, 35, 102,
   278
Muiredach, 20
Mullaghcloe, hill of, 79, 94
Mullaghmeehan, 62, 124
Mullingar, 79, 80, 108, 111, 259, 273, 274
Multifarnham Abbey, 79
Munster, 55
'Murtagh McCann', 168
Music, 86–7
Muslim, 235, 332, 336

Naas, 209–10
Napoleon, 155, 206, 302, 371
Napoleonic Wars, 51, 209
Nationalists, 217–19, 373, 379–8, 400,
   405, 406
Natural History Museum, 346, 348
Nebraska, 310
Nefertiti, 349
Nelson, Lord, 162, 163, 295, 347
Nesta, Princess, 33, 44, 45, 248
Netherville, Lord, 106
New York, 310
Nightingale, Florence, 290
ni Houlihan, Kathleen *see* Kathleen ni
   Houlihan
Nile, Battle of, 347
Nineveh, 15
Ninth Lancers, 258
Nolan, Biddy, 224
Normandy, 29
Normans, 27–34, 38, 40, 44, 46, 51, 54,
   72, 96, 97, 112, 134, 230, 245, 367,
   371, 375
Norsemen, 24, 28–9, 125
North Africa, 25
North Atlantic Treaty Organisation (NATO),
   390, 396
Northumberland Fusiliers ('Fighting Fifth'),
   343
Northumbria, 25
North Wall, 282
Norway, 405
Nugent, Sir Percy, 259

Oath of Supremacy, 167
O'Brien family, 12, 34
O'Connell, Daniel, 237, 406
O'Connor, Valentine, 247

O'Connor–Henchy, Ellen *see* Magan, Ellen
O'Connor–Henchy, Honoria, 247
O'Connor–Henchy, Mary, 254
O'Conor, King Roderic, 29, 30, 32
O'Conor, Kings, 3, 4, 11, 14–20, 246, 278
O'Conor Don, 4, 12, 165, 174
O'Conor family, 4, 10–12, 14–20, 23, 34,
    35, 61, 114, 139, 165, 188
O'Donnell, Earl of Tyroconnell, 64
Offaly (formerly King's County) 65, 183,
    240, 260, 273, 295, 298, 331, 332, 344
Offaly Historical Society, 258
Offenbach, 289
O'Flaherty, 20
O'Flannagan, 20
Ogham, 227
O'Higgins, Ambrosio, 149
Old Pretender, 167
Omagh, 402
O'Mallery, 20
Omar Khayyam, 247
O'Mulryan, The, Lord of Owney, 165, 208
O'Neill, Hugh, Earl of Tyrone, 64, 377
O'Neill, Shaen, 43, 69
O'Neill family, 34
Orange Society (Orange Order), 200, 201,
    202, 411, 412
O'Regan, Dr, 298
Ormonde, Marquis of, 398
Oudenard, Battle of, 153
Owen, Anne *see* Magan, Anne (wife of
    Humphry)
Owen, Sir Hugh, 67
Owen, Sir Richard, 61–2, 67
Owney, Lord of, *see* O'Mulryon
Oxford University, 338, 363

P–, Mr, 248, 252, 253
Pakistan, 222, 235
Pale, the, 34, 41, 52, 64, 93, 245, 376
Palestine, 395, 396
Pankhurst, Mrs Emmeline, 286
Papacy, 28, 33, 34, 53, 124, 380, 387–8
Papal State, 388
Paris, 214, 249
Parliament Act, 372
Parliament (British), 219
Parliament (Irish), 189, 194–9, 201, 204–5,
    207, 399
Parnell, Charles Stuart, 219
Partition, 374, 400, 408

Pavilion, the Brighton, 246
Peace Process, 401, 402
Peasantry, 219–29, 233, 234
Pedigrees, xiii, 3, 14, 15–17, 19, 61–4, 67
Peerage, 171–3, 205
Pembroke, Earl of *see* Strongbow
Penal Laws (Penal Code), 143–55, 165, 167
    170, 182, 194, 208, 210–11, 212, 213
    232, 239, 405
Pentateuch, 15
Percy, Henry, Earl of Northumberland, 67
Perkin Warbeck, 48–9
Persia, 7, 37, 66, 221, 234, 362
Peru, 149
Philipstown, *see* Daingean
Phillip II of Spain, 65
Photography, 344
Phytophthera infestans, 253, 263, 267
Pitt, William, 302
Plantagenets, 27
Plantation, the, 65–6, 101, 111, 171, 174
    195, 376, 377, 406
Plunket, Bishop Oliver, 80
Plunket, Rt Rev Dr, 213
Plunkett, the Hon Sir Horace, 290, 291, 295
    307
Pocahontas, Princess, 347
Poland, 235
Portarlington, 254–5
Portobello, 275
Post Office, the General (Dublin), 207
Potato, 82, 90, 91–2, 152, 262–4, 266–7
    312
Poteen, 90, 119
Pottery, 7
Poultry, 295
Presbyterians, 65, 103, 143, 147, 148, 174
    175, 178, 193, 194, 199, 200, 201, 203
    264, 400
Princes in the Tower, 36, 46, 48
Prosperous, 209–10
Protestants, 42, 65, 66, 101–14, 117
    120–31, 132, 137, 139, 143–8, 150, 151
    153, 154, 158, 161, 165, 167–9, 170
    171, 173, 176, 178–82, 184, 186, 189
    190–1, 193, 194, 196–8, 199, 200–20
    206, 218, 219, 235–6, 247, 265, 277
    291–2, 372, 373, 376–5, 380–83, 385
    390, 391–91, 395, 399, 405, 407, 40
    see also Ascendancy, Protestant
Protestant Clergy, 147, 253

Index